CHIEF JUSTICE CORNELIUS OF PAKISTAN

AN ANALYSIS WITH LETTERS AND SPEECHES

Chief Justice Cornelius

CHIEF JUSTICE CORNELIUS
OF PAKISTAN

AN ANALYSIS WITH LETTERS AND SPEECHES

Ralph Braibanti

Foreword by
Nasim Hasan Shah

OXFORD
UNIVERSITY PRESS

OXFORD
UNIVERSITY PRESS

Great Clarendon Street, Oxford OX2 6DP

Oxford University Press is a department of the University of Oxford.
It furthers the University's objective of excellence in research, scholarship,
and education by publishing worldwide in

Oxford New York

Athens Auckland Bangkok Bogotá Buenos Aires Calcutta
Cape Town Chennai Dar es Salaam Delhi Florence Hong Kong Istanbul
Karachi Kuala Lumpur Madrid Melbourne Mexico City Mumbai
Nairobi Paris São Paulo Singapore Taipei Tokyo Toronto Warsaw
with associated companies in Berlin Ibadan

Oxford is a registered trade mark of Oxford University Press
in the UK and in certain other countries

© Oxford University Press 1999

The moral rights of the author have been asserted

First published 1999

ISBN 0 19 579018 9

Printed in Pakistan at
Mas Printers, Karachi.
Published by
Ameena Saiyid, Oxford University Press
5-Bangalore Town, Sharae Faisal
PO Box 13033, Karachi-75350, Pakistan.

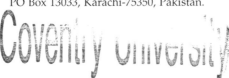

To

Lucy, Ralph L. and Claire
who shared the adventure of
our sojourn in Pakistan

CONTENTS

SELECTED SPEECHES OF A.R. CORNELIUS   199

THE CORNELIUS MEMORIAL LECTURES   332

TABLES

INDEX   377

FOREWORD

I feel greatly honoured to be asked to contribute the Foreword to this volume by Dr. Ralph Braibanti on the life and work of my benefactor, mentor, guide, and, above all, one of the greatest chief justices of Pakistan—Mr. Justice A. R. Cornelius.

I was privileged not only to have been a practitioner in his Court but also in having been nominated by him to act as editor of the official court journal—the *Pakistan Supreme Court Reports*. This series was published under his supervision and allowed me a unique opportunity to work under his personal guidance. On account of this rapport, a special bond developed between the Chief Justice and myself, a bond not dissimilar to the one which exists between a loving master and his devoted pupil.

Justice Cornelius possessed a complete command of the principles of law and jurisprudence and was a firm believer that in human affairs justice must be tempered with compassion and that laws were made for men and not otherwise. I am pleased that Professor Braibanti has included some analysis of the principle of compassion in the analytical part of this volume. Both Justice Cornelius and I have viewed this principle as central to any system of civilized jurisprudence. He found repugnant instances of inhuman and callous exercise of government power over the rights of citizens and sought to remedy such injustice whenever such cases came before him. He thought that an effective manner for ensuring control of this abuse of power was to introduce in Pakistan some system incorporating the principles of *Droit Administratif* in vogue in France. Knowing that I had studied in France for my *Doctorat*, he encouraged me to go to Paris for a closer study of this system and discussed my observations thereon at great length, on my return. The attention which is given to this institution in the first and third chapters of this volume is entirely justified. Chief Justice Cornelius mentions *droit administratif* in one of his letters published here for the first time and, of course, it is the subject of several of his speeches. As someone who has studied in France, I was amused at Chief Justice Cornelius' witty characterization of British revulsion of all things Napoleonic. This, too, is mentioned in one of his letters.

I should mention in passing the historical significance of the nine Cornelius letters published in this volume for the first time. We are fortunate that Professor Braibanti preserved them for some thirty years because they constitute an important documentary source for Pakistan's constitutional history.

The landmark judgments recorded by Chief Justice Cornelius in the field of human rights, personal liberty, and enforcement of the principles of natural law in the worst of times is an abiding testament to his great concern for the lonely individual pitted against the fury and might of the powerful state. Instances of these memorable judgments have been given by me in the First Cornelius Memorial Lecture I delivered on 24 December 1993—merely two years after he departed from our mortal world and which Dr. Braibanti has so graciously included in this work.

To me, Justice Cornelius was like a father and always came to my rescue whenever I was in any difficulty. I recall that when I was in despair about how to present my articles, speeches, and discourse on constitutional and other national issues in book form which, when collected together, ran into about four thousand typed pages, my great guide and benefactor stood by my side. With infinite patience and perseverance he waded through the entire material, advising me how to discard and weed out that which was repetitious and more ephemeral as opposed to that which was more relevant and enduring, so as to bring down the unwieldy bulk to more manageable proportions. It was only on account of Justice Cornelius' generosity and innate spirit of compassion for those he considered worthy of sympathy that my first book *Constitution, Law & Pakistan Affairs*, could see the light of day.

This kindness and generosity was not confined to me alone. Justice Cornelius performed an extraordinary act of grace toward his life-long associate on the bench, Justice S. A. Rahman, who was also an ICS/CSP officer. He makes casual mention of this gesture in one of his letters included in this volume. Professor Braibanti describes the incident further in his text. The off-hand manner in which Chief Justice Cornelius refers to that action should in no way belie its significance. Such a spirit of self-sacrifice can hardly be imagined amongst ordinary mortals and, indeed, in our judicial history. The letter in which he mentions this is an important document for the archives of our judiciary.

The life and work of this unique judge and great humanist has been felicitously portrayed with great feeling by Dr. Braibanti in this work. To supplement his conclusions, it may be appropriate if I might reproduce here a short extract from the tribute I paid him on his demise. I said 'The Supreme Court under the able stewardship of Justice Cornelius proved to be a mighty citadel from which however grave the night and however heavy the gloom, the bright light of law shone forth ushering and sustaining the rule of law and bringing solace and calm to agitated and troubled minds.' May his soul rest in peace.

Nasim Hasan Shah
Retired Chief Justice of Pakistan
22 December 1997

PREFACE

This study of Chief Justice Cornelius has its genesis in my first visit to Pakistan in December 1957. The occasion was the Thirteenth International Conference of the Institute of Pacific Relations at which I read a paper on the Southeast Asia Treaty Organization. Three of the Pakistani delegates—all advocates—attracted my attention:

The first one was Mian Mahmud Ali Qasuri, a brilliant trial lawyer who later became Minister of Law in the Zulfikar Ali Bhutto cabinet and subsequently resigned after sharp disagreements with Bhutto. He and his sons were victims of police brutality and harassment by both the police and the tax authorities. Mahmud Ali was born in Qasur (rendered as Kasur on official government maps) in 1910, the son of a well-known religious and political leader, Maulana Abdul Qadir Qasuri. He was educated at Bombay University and at King's College, London, and was called to the Bar from Gray's Inn. Qasuri was the first Asian to take first place in the Bar exams in England and was twice elected President of the West Pakistan High Court Bar Association. He was the only Asian member of the tribunal formed by Lord Bertrand Russell to investigate American war crimes in Vietnam. The Full High Court Reference (*1987 PLD*

Journal 127) made at his death in 1987, referred to the 'respectful, roaring voice of the legal lion.' His performances in court were operatic spectacles. In my opinion, he could easily have been a replacement for Luciano Pavarotti, both in appearance and in voice. Chief Justice M. R. Kayani of the Lahore High Court, once said that when Qasuri spoke in Lahore he could be heard in Kohat (some 250 miles away). We became warm friends and in later years he visited me at Duke with two of his sons, Omar and Danial.

The second friendship which evolved was with Rabia Sultana Qari, the first Muslim woman barrister-at-law in Pakistan, and probably in the entire subcontinent. Andrew Corey, the US Consul-General in Lahore, suggested that I meet her to get an understanding of the views of those in opposition to the government. Born in 1914, Miss Qari was a graduate of Kinnaird College, a Christian mission school in Lahore. She was an inspector of schools in the Punjab education department and after Partition was an official in the Ministry of Refugees and Rehabilitation. She was the first Pakistani to visit England as a guest of the British Council. After that visit, she returned to England where she joined Lincoln's Inn and was called to the Bar and certified as a barrister-at-law. Miss Qari was a political activist and a fierce defender of human rights and the rule of law. She knew no fear in her opposition to what she regarded as tyranny and was greatly admired by the legal community. She was elected President of the Lahore High Court Bar Association and worked closely with Qasuri in various freedom movements. It was in Miss Qari's flat at the top of a tortuous flight of steep, winding stairs in E-Plomer Building in Lahore, that my wife and I met dissidents out of favour with the government in office. The renowned poet, Faiz Ahmed Faiz, whom the Soviet Union decorated with the Lenin Peace Prize, was one of Miss Qari's guests. H. S. Suhrawardy, who had been prime minister for eleven months in 1956 and was later barred from holding public office under the Elective Bodies Disqualification Order 1960, was another. In later years, Suhrawardy and I were to share occupancy for a few days of the near-empty Shahbagh Hotel in Dacca. In 1975, Miss Qari was severely injured by police brutality. The Full High Court Reference made in memory of her death in 1977 was one of the warmest, most respectful tributes ever made in the High Court. (*1977 PLD Journal 155*). While I did not espouse many of the views of Miss Qari, or of the frequent guests at her gatherings, I found them intellectually stimulating. It was the only opportunity I had to meet political activists outside the circle of government.

These were fascinating excursions into the realm of political dissidence, but it was contact with a third friend which led me directly into study of the judiciary. This was Dr. Nasim Hasan Shah, later to become editor of the *Supreme Court Reports* and Chief Justice of Pakistan. In 1957, Dr. Nasim was a young barrister who had only recently returned from France. His early education was in the Christian Mission Cathedral School and in Government College in Lahore where he earned bachelor's and master's degrees in political science with highest honors. In 1952, he went to France where he earned the *Docteur en droit* degree (*très bien*) and a diploma (first position) from the Institute of Higher International Studies, both from the University of Paris. In 1954, he was awarded a diploma from The Hague Academy of International Law. Dr. Nasim was the only Pakistani advocate with such advanced training in France. He was intrigued by the French institution of the *Conseil d'Etat* as part of the *droit administratif* and wrote a series of articles in 1961 on this subject in the *Pakistan Times*. Along with his senior mentor, Chief Justice Cornelius, he advocated tirelessly for reform in Pakistan leading in that direction. Ultimately, he was partially successful: Article 212 of the 1973 Constitution now allows the establishment of administrative courts. Dr. Nasim was a junior advocate on the team representing the government in the renowned *Maulvi Tamizuddin Khan* case of 1955. He was appointed a judge in the West Pakistan High Court in 1968. Born in 1929, he was the youngest Supreme Court judge in the history of Pakistan when he was appointed to the Supreme Court in 1977, first as an *ad hoc* judge, and, in 1979, as a permanent judge. Dr. Nasim was appointed Chief Justice of Pakistan in 1993 and retired in 1994. During this period, he served as President of the South Asian Association for Regional Cooperation (SAARC) committee on law.

Towards the middle of his career, Dr. Nasim was one of the majority of four Supreme Court judges who upheld the Lahore High Court judgment which convicted former Prime Minister Zulfikar Ali Bhutto of conspiracy to commit murder and sentenced him to death. (*Zulfikar Ali Bhutto v. State, PLD 1979 SC 38*). As a Supreme Court justice, he wrote several opinions which were in the Cornelius tradition. Two of the most important ones were the *Nawaz Sharif* case (*PLD 1993 SC 473*) relating to the restoration of the National Assembly and the *Sharif Faridi* case (*PLD 1994 SC 105*) concerning separation of the executive and judicial branches. In two cases brought to the Supreme Court by former Prime Minister Benazir Bhutto (*PLD 1988 SC 416; PLD 1989 SC 66*) Dr. Nasim wrote separate concurring opinions guaranteeing the right of political parties to exist and function.

It can rightfully be said that Chief Justice Nasim Hasan Shah inherits the ideological mantle of Cornelius. Like Cornelius, he had an international perspective which enriched his analysis of the Pakistani condition.

These contacts in 1957 led to my return to Pakistan some twenty times, both as a researcher and in advisory capacities. During breaks in the Lahore conference, the long discussions I had with Dr. Nasim convinced me of the importance of the writ jurisdiction which at that time was the dominant theme in the juridical life of Pakistan. My early stays in Pakistan were mostly in the summer enduring the heat relieved only by the slowly whirling *punkas* in Faletti's hotel. It was here that I met Chief Justice Cornelius—first in Faletti's dining room, and, ultimately, in his office and residence—the famous Room 1 of Faletti's.

For two years starting in September 1960, (when I was chief advisor and professor at the Civil Service Academy on the Upper Mall) I lived with my family in the commodious bungalow known as Number 10-H in Gulberg, Lahore. Part of a team of the University of Southern California which had been contracted by the United States Agency for International Development, I was on leave from Duke and technically was on the USC faculty.

The Academy directors had been British officers in the ICS/CSP The last director who left in 1960 was Sir Geoffry Burgess. He was succeeded by the senior Muslim officer in the ICS/CSP, Mian Aminuddin, a former ambassador to Turkey and Iran, who was called out of retirement to preside over the transition from British to Pakistani leadership. This was a transition marked also by my presence to teach and, presumably, to advise. Mian Aminuddin was the ideal director for this period. Known by his colleagues as being more British than the British, his seniority, experience, and status in Punjabi society preserved the prestigious position of the Academy. After a successful one-year term he was succeeded by Agha Abdul Hamid, another senior ICS/CSP officer, who had been Joint Secretary in the Prime Minister's cabinet and more recently was Administrator of Karachi. I was privileged to have a warm and friendly relationship with both these distinguished officers and learned much from them.

My tenure at the Academy gave me ample time for research which was certainly needed as I read and briefed hundreds of High Court and Supreme Court cases. I attended as many sessions of both courts as I could, all of the High Court and Supreme Court hearings in the Snelson case, the infamous Gardezi case, and many others. There followed from this a series of interviews on the contempt power. The results of that study (the first to be undertaken) can be found in 'The Socio-Judicial Context of the Cornelius Era—1950–1970' in this volume. The contempt power was enormously important then as well as in 1972 during the martial law of Yahya Khan. Even in 1997, the contempt power retained its importance as the defining element in the conflict over the authority of the prime minister, the president and the Supreme Court.

A friendly relationship with Cornelius and Chief Justice Kayani slowly evolved. Both were guests in my home for dinner—a practice which they both said was without precedent. Following the judicial tradition, they eschewed social gatherings but since they were the only guests they agreed to come. The justifiable emphasis on the insulation and aloofness of judges (so well described by Justice Dorab Patel in his Third Cornelius Memorial Lecture (Appendix 20) was vividly brought home to me by their requests that no one else be present and that the house staff be instructed not to talk to them about court or other matters. This request was difficult to implement. In one instance, it was only partially observed, much to my initial embarrassment and to the subsequent amusement of us all. My wife became friendly with Mrs Cornelius and they often had tea together. We were both their occasional dinner guests at Faletti's. My contacts with Kayani were somewhat more formal. I attended many of his lectures—arriving early to get a seat in the auditorium where there was only standing room. Both Kayani and Cornelius were remarkably helpful in procuring documents, statistics, and in the time they spent discussing legal matters with me. I came to admire them as jurists and as men of virtue. They made an indelible impression on me, as did Mian Aminuddin, Agha Hamid, Nasim Hasan Shah, Mahmud Ali Qasuri and Rabia Sultana Qari, and convinced me on how a truly liberating Islamic perspective can mould personalities devoted to principle, compassion, freedom, and learning.

The Snelson case, especially, compelled my attention. In part, this was due to the fact that I knew the origins of the contempt citation which the High Court issued. For some weeks in Karachi, I studied at the Federal Secretariat Training Institute and became friendly with its director, Abdullah Jan. I used a desk in the Institute as a base from which I set forth for interviews and in search of documents for the Duke library. Abdullah arranged a meeting with President Iskander Mirza, the first of presidents and prime ministers I interviewed up to Nawaz Sharif. It was Abdullah who invited Sir Edward to give the talk in Rawalpindi which ignited the controversy. He claimed responsibility for sending a printed copy of the Snelson lecture to judges of the Lahore High Court. I was not aware of this until after it was done. This relationship with Abdullah Jan gave me a sense of intimacy with the Snelson case hearings. Abdullah subsequently visited me at Duke. We spoke little of the Snelson case but he was obviously proud of the stir he created. Abdullah was a very devout and stern Muslim who interpreted Islam in the strictest, most literal way. He appeared to have minimal appreciation of the intrusion of western values in his culture and even less for the legacy of British rule.

With our two children at the Woodstock School in Mussooree, India and a staff to take care of the household both my wife and I were free to pursue uninterrupted research. Together we read, classified and briefed more than a thousand court cases. *The All Pakistan Legal Decisions* became as familiar to us as an album of family records.

The research possibilities in Pakistan so impressed me that shortly after my return to Duke I convened (15 February 1964) a meeting of twenty-six scholars and government officials interested in Pakistan. Our purpose was to establish a research entity comparable to the American Institute of Indian Studies. This was followed by a visit to Pakistan in 1967 under joint auspices of the Department of State and the Committee on South Asia of the Association for Asian Studies. For reasons given elsewhere in the first chapter of this volume, no positive results came from this visit. It was not until 1973 that the American Institute of Pakistan Studies was established through the indefatigable efforts and diplomatic skill of Professor Hafeez Malik who was a personal friend of Prime Minister Zulfikar Ali Bhutto. Hafeez was Director of the Institute for more than ten years. I doubt if anyone in the United States has made a greater contribution to Pakistan studies. I was the Institute's first president and held that position for nine years. It has flourished under the leadership of Craig Baxter, Charles Kennedy, Afak Hayder, and Lawrence Ziring who have been its principal officers for several years. It has far exceeded the expectations I described in my inaugural address to Prime Minister Bhutto in 1973.

At Duke I was able to interest several of my graduate students in writing dissertations on Pakistan. Many more, however, wrote on India which seemed to have greater cultural fascination and easier access for field research. Gradually the activities of the Pakistan Institute changed that imbalance somewhat on many campuses. I convinced one of my students, S. M. Haider, an advocate from the Punjab with a law degree, that he should write his dissertation on the writ jurisdiction. He agreed and his dissertation was published in Pakistan. Before his death he was a researcher with the Law Reforms Commission with an office in the Supreme Court. He was able to collect several of Cornelius' speeches and edited them in the collection mentioned several times in this volume. Several other Pakistani students took their doctorates with me and are scattered in Pakistan, Bangladesh, Canada and in the United Nations Development Program. All have made distinctive contributions to a better understanding of Pakistan. Another student, Charles H. Kennedy, first went to Pakistan on a fellowship from the American Institute of Pakistan Studies in 1975 and the next year took my place at a conference in Pakistan which I could not attend. His interest in Pakistan was thus kindled and has not been extinguished. He is one of the most perceptive analysts of Pakistan government and has become the leading authority both on its bureaucratic development and the Islamization of its legal system. He is on the faculty of Wake Forest University and has been Director of the American Institute of Pakistan Studies for several years.

For years I reread the nine letters, now part of this volume, from Chief Justice Cornelius realizing they were important but not knowing quite what to do with them. Provoked by the rising sentiment in the United States that Islamic civilization must inevitably clash with the West, I tried to counter that argument by my essay *The Nature and Structure of the Islamic World* published in Chicago in 1995. I slowly came to the realization that the career of A. R. Cornelius was a living refutation of the civilizational clash hypothesis. Here was a real instance of a devout, practicing Christian who synthesized Islamic and Christian thought in a manner I have labelled in the first chapter as *Quintessentials*. I then read his letters in a new light. They now revealed that his thoughts conveyed privately to a friend were an even clearer exposition of his views than his public statements. The present volume is the result of that realization.

The polity of Pakistan is the most complex system I have ever studied. That is said after two years experience as a military government officer in Yamanashi, Japan (1945–47), three months in 1950 on Okinawa as an advisor to the Civil Administrator for the Ryukyu Islands and some time studying Saudi Arabia. It is a far more difficult system to understand than any of the other fifty-four states of Islamic dispensation. There are two reasons for this.

First, Pakistan has struggled for fifty years trying to graft an Islamic polity to a structure which has been deeply influenced by British law. This is sustained, indeed nurtured, by English as the language of law and government. Cornelius railed against this in favour of the native languages but to no avail. In court etiquette, it has taken nearly half a century to abandon the wig and 'Your Lordship' as a mode of address. Even now it is said only half in jest that if an advocate wants to win his case he'd better address the judge as 'My Lord'. The wig, now abandoned, and the mode of address are outward symbols of the inner epistemological conflict. No other Muslim nation has attempted to renovate the British-designed structure with a codified legal system (*Shar'ia*) evolved over fourteen hundred years. India inherited the same British structure but has not been faced with the transmutation of a sophisticated legal code renowned for its particularities and the elegance of its epistemology. The resulting efforts to reconcile the two systems has called for almost superhuman intellectual prowess and stamina on the part of the judiciary and the legal community. The challenge was met at least during the Cornelius era and, to a lesser extent, beyond.

The second reason is the fate of Pakistan in sustaining some fifteen major disarticulations in power, polity and structure and still preserving a national identity. One is tempted to explain this phenomenon only by recourse to celestial powers. Pakistan has been pummeled by such external events as three wars with India, the secession of Bangladesh and four periods of martial law—a total of twenty-seven years. These traumas of the Cornelius years are described in the first chapter of this volume. Much more has happened since then but that is beyond our scope here.

Overshadowing all these calamities was a series of demographic convulsions without parallel in modern history. The Partition of 1947 resulted in the migration of some eleven million and the massacre of half a million in Punjab alone; the Afghan war of the 1980s brought three and a half million refugees to Pakistan and the Bangladeshi secession moved another half a million. These were cataclysmic events. If the trauma of these demographic tragedies has been forgotten, one should re-read the descriptions by Collins and LaPierre in *Freedom at Midnight*, in the novel *Train to Pakistan* by Khushwant Singh, Bapsi Sidhwa's *Cracking India* or G. D. Khosla's *Stern Reckoning*. The largest initial migration of refugees wove a fabric of human misery worsened by a nearly paralyzed government. This compelled the judiciary to invoke the Muslim values of *adal* and *ehsan*, described in the first chapter, grafting them on the British structure of the writ jurisdiction. It is difficult to find a more creative, imaginative construction—a kind of reverse grafting—of two juridical traditions used to soften the edges of tragedy. Cornelius and M. R. Kayani were the leading architects of that edifice. The effects of all three migrations were not transitory. They have been at the heart of problems continuing to fester for half a century. The first migration included Urdu-speaking Indian Muslims who settled in Sindh. They gained political power by forming the *Muhajir Qaumi Mahaz* (MQM), a political party whose confrontations with native Sindhis are at the root of the near anarchy which prevails in Karachi in the 1990s. Lurking on the horizon is the dilemma of a potential migration of Biharis stranded in Bangladesh unable to settle in Pakistan because of Pakistan's fear of aggravating the refugee problem as well as its inability to cope financially with such an influx. The second migration of Afghans has continued to plague political stability. A million Afghans remain in Pakistan aggravating the problems of drug trafficking, smuggling and crime often by taking advantage of the instability of the Sindh.

This unique complexity of the legal system, as well as the seemingly endless traumas already described convinced me to include in this volume a reprinting of my earlier study on legal research. It appears in this volume under the new title 'The Socio-Judicial Context of the Cornelius Era—1950–1970'. It was written during those years and was concerned exclusively with them. No effort has been made in this book to go beyond the Cornelius period, hence that study is not out of date. It describes the configuration of legal research, as well as the ambience of the legal community during that period, and gives the background in considerable detail of the many issues which this Analysis has tried to simplify. The larger, global context into which Pakistan's legal system fits is dealt with in this volume by the companion study 'The Role of Law in the Political Development of Pakistan'. This projects Pakistan's political experience in the time of Cornelius against a backdrop of development theory. These two studies are reprinted exactly as they were originally published except that the titles have been modified and a headnote has been added to one of them. This has resulted in inconsistencies in the use of italics, capitalization, and the mode of citations. All of these are somewhat different than the style in the Analysis essay. This was essential to preserve the authenticity of the two reprints. The citation style in the Analysis uses English references rather than the Latin forms (such as *op. cit., ibid.*). This has been done deliberately to make the essay somewhat less formidable for the general reader who will find the other essays intimidating enough. In any event, these two studies, together with the Analysis, constitute a fairly complete description (with some overlap and duplication) of the historical and theoretical context of the political thought of Cornelius.

To maintain the authenticity of the Cornelius speeches and letters as historical documents, his transliteration of Urdu and Arabic terms has been preserved. Some awkward situations have resulted. Following are a few examples selected from several such instances. The Turkish compendium of Islamic law which he renders as *Mujallah* and *Majelle*, is more commonly transliterated as *Majallah* and *Medjelle*. His terms, *fikah* and *Shariah* are more universally rendered as *fiqh*, *fikh* and *Shar'ia*. These terms, used especially, though not exclusively, in Appendix 14, are at variance with transliterations used in other parts of the book.

There are other inconsistencies in transliteration: Punjab-Panjab, Kasuri-Qasuri, Zulfikar-Zulfikhar, Sind-Sindh. Readers familiar with transliteration of Arabic and Urdu will be at home with these variations. Others must not assume they are spelling or printing errors; they are normal variations which lend a degree of charm to research.

Much is owed to those mentioned earlier and to many others who have helped more immediately in the compilation of the present volume. Retired Chief Justice Dr. Nasim Hasan Shah, one of the legal trio whom I first met in 1957 has been of great help. He met with me in Durham, NC, on 1, 2, and 3 September 1997 and we exchanged fax messages since then aimed at improving the manuscript. Hamid Khan, Supreme Court advocate and partner in the law firm of Cornelius, Lane and Mufti, met with me in Washington, DC on 29 August 1997 to discuss a draft. This was followed by frequent and lengthy exchanges of fax correspondence. The efficiency, generosity, and legal acumen of Hamid reminded me of my legal friends of forty years ago. Certainly Hamid, already an author of two books on Pakistan's constitution, is a important figure in the contemporary development of law in Pakistan. Michael Cornelius, elder son of the Chief Justice, wrote a critique of the draft, provided genealogical data, and made other helpful suggestions. Although we have not yet met, telephone conversations and fax messages over a period of several months made me feel that he was truly the son of his father. Avinash Maheshwary, South Asian bibliographer at Duke University, helped to locate elusive documents. His patience, efficiency, and generosity have been extraordinary. Ameena Saiyid, managing director, Yasmin Qureshi, publishing manager, and Zohrain Zafar, Samina Choonara and Ghousia Ghofran Ali, assistant editors of the Oxford University Press (Karachi), and Aquila Ismail have been generous with their time and wise suggestions. Their editorial judgment as to the composition of the volume was critical in determining its final form. Debra Fields typed and retyped this manuscript. How she could put into shape successive revisions all hand-written and marked over with marginal notes is beyond belief. I am indebted to all those named above for their suggestions and help. I remain, of course, solely responsible for the contents of this volume.

Ralph Braibanti
Durham, North Carolina
1 May 1998

AN ANALYSIS OF THE THOUGHT OF CORNELIUS

It is virtue that moves Heaven; there is
no distance to which it does not reach.

The pre-Confucian *Book of History*

I

Prospectus

Of the fifty-five states which declare themselves to be constitutively Islamic, Pakistan alone has had a non-Muslim at the pinnacle of its judicial system. Other Muslim polities such as Egypt, Jordan, Lebanon, and Iraq have had non-Muslims in important ministerial posts although usually for short periods. Senegal's president for twenty years was Léopold Senghor, a Roman Catholic, but no other country has had a non-Muslim in the judiciary or in any important position over an unbroken tenure of two decades. A. R. Cornelius, a Roman Catholic, had a distinguished legal career from the establishment of Pakistan in 1947 to his resignation as law minister in the Yahya Khan cabinet in 1971. For seventeen years of this period, from 1960 until his retirement in 1968 he served on the Supreme Court as Chief Justice.[1] The only other instances of a non-Muslim on the Supreme Court of Pakistan was the five-year tenure of Dorab F. Patel, who served as a justice from 1976 to 1981 and Rustam S. Sidhwa, who retired in 1992 after serving for two years and eight months. Both were Parsis.

Pakistan has produced some remarkable jurists, each distinguished by different attributes. Sir Abdur Rashid and Sir Abdur Rahman were mentors of Cornelius. Muhammad Munir was a learned constitutionalist and prolific author; Malik Rustam Kayani was revered by the public and despite his witty, sardonic public criticism of martial law, won the admiration of Ayub Khan, its creator and administrator. Dr Nasim Hasan Shah, a superb legal editor and author of courageous court opinions, is the only Pakistani jurist educated in France and versed in the French legal system. S. A. Rahman and Muhammad Shahabuddin were respected for their learning and wisdom.

Cornelius belongs in this pantheon. Few jurists have been held in higher esteem by the legal community nor has anyone had greater influence on Pakistan's constitutional development. It is remarkable that in a country as self-consciously Muslim as Pakistan, the question of his religion was muted if not ignored. Except for one brief incident in 1970, it was never a serious political issue. In the many conversations this author had with him in Pakistan from 1960 to 1967, his religion was never mentioned. In subsequent letters through 1968, he alludes to the Catholic view of St. Thomas Aquinas, calling himself a 'neo-Thomist in attitude' and refers to himself as a non-Muslim[2] but these were personal letters, not public pronouncements.

In an account of a conference he attended in Sydney in 1965, he makes a rare reference in print to his religious affiliation. He does this obliquely in the third person:

> The opening ceremony at the Town Hall in Sydney was preceded by church services. Being a Catholic, the Chief Justice of Pakistan, Mr Justice A. R. Cornelius, attended the service at St. Mary's Cathedral, dressed in full robes with wig in company of some twenty other judges. The largest number of judges, however, attended the service at St. Andrews [Anglican] Cathedral.[3]

His name alone revealed his Christian identity, his Catholicism being only suggested by a picture of Pope Pius XII on a table in his sitting room at Faletti's hotel in Lahore, a picture that was sent from Rome with a papal blessing upon recommendation of the Bishop of Lahore. During the five days we spent together at the Villa Serbelloni, Lake Como, Italy, this question did not arise. I heard no mention of it in the legal community of Pakistan except for a comment made in admiration by the most senior member of the Civil Service of Pakistan (CSP) Mohammad Shahabuddin, a Supreme Court justice who served briefly in 1958 as acting chief justice. At a CSP reception in 1960, Justice Shahabuddin commented to me that A. R. Cornelius was 'more Muslim than the Muslims'. Cornelius referred to himself as a 'Constitutional Muslim'. Except for a lengthy adulatory account of Cornelius' death in Dawn, and passing mention in a Full Supreme Court Reference to his memory in 1992, other tributes do not mention his religion.[4]

One of his rare public mentions of Christianity without reference to himself was a brief homily he gave on 12 December 1962 in memory of M. R. Kayani, Chief Justice of the Lahore High Court, who died the previous month. Cornelius artfully pursued his theme of the complementarity of Muslim and non-Muslim values. The latter, he believed, are subsumed in the universality of Islam.

> A reading of the Christian scriptures leaves no room for doubt that precisely for the same reason, the late chief justice would certainly have gained an equal renown and position in a Christian community living according to the dictates of their religion. He...showed his independence by his predilection for natural justice as against the text of man-made statutes.[5]

Here Cornelius praised a fellow judge whose Shia Muslim values he deemed to be compatible with Christian virtues. In doing so, he invoked the doctrine of natural law (natural justice) which was the keystone of his jurisprudence. This reference to Christianity was a departure from the usual reticence which was reflected in his own sense of privacy and his respect for the privacy of others. It was his desire that his religion be subordinated to the facts that he was a Pakistani and a judge in an Islamic country. He neither concealed nor flaunted his religious affiliation but it was not a subject of discussion. The consignment of personal religion to the cloisters of silence and indifference can be explained by several factors. In the early years of Pakistan, the government legal establishment was not unaccustomed to having non-Muslims in its highest ranks. Sir Edward Snelson, KBE, was joint secretary of law from 1947 to 1951, when he became secretary. He remained in that position until his resignation in 1961, establishing the record for the longest continuous tenure held by a British official in Pakistan. During the first decade or so there were always some British officers serving in the courts as judge, registrar, or as legal remembrancer. The number of such judicial appointments was as high as nine in 1947 and dropped to two in 1961. Sir George B. Constantine, KBE, and J. Ortcheson, CBE, both judges in the Lahore High Court, retired in 1962 and 1965 respectively. Cornelius was Pakistani so the presence of other non-Muslim foreigners, all highly regarded, made his position less conspicuous.

Beyond the judiciary, the higher bureaucracy was comfortable with the presence of non-Muslims in important policy-making positions. At Partition in 1947, two Indian Christians, Cornelius and S. M. Burke, who was minister to Washington opted for service in Pakistan. Of the total of 158 officers of the Indian Civil Service (ICS) and the Indian Police Service (IPS) who opted for Pakistan thirty-six in the ICS and seventeen in the IPS were British. Thus one-third of the 158 were non-Muslim. As late as 1951, the CSP cadre of 202 officers included twenty-three British officers of whom five were in the judiciary.

It is important to name these officers, their positions, and the awards they received in order to recreate the ambience affecting non-Muslims at that time.[6] The awards suggest the high regard in which they were held both by Britain and by Pakistan.[7] The training of the highest level of civil servants was in the hands of non-Muslims for more than a decade: Geoffrey Burgess, CMG, CIE, OBE, was director of the Civil Service Academy and A. G.

Bunn, CBE, was director of the Finance Services Academy until 1960. The civil service structure was controlled from 1947 to 1961 by non-Muslim establishment secretaries: T. B. Creagh Coen, CIE, Eric Franklin, CBE, and J. D. Hardy, SPk., CBE. The Board of Revenue included S. B. Hatch-Barnwell, SPk., CBE, until 1966; R. D. Howe, SQA, MBE was census commissioner until 1962; R. A. F. Howroyd, OBE was chairman of the Lahore Improvement Trust until 1966. A powerful government corporation, the Water and Power Development Authority was headed until 1966 by David K. Power, SQA, OBE (who later converted to Islam). These non-Muslims and six others in somewhat less important positions, were gone by 1966 but clearly a non-Muslim in high government position during these two decades was not uncommon.

II

Non-Muslim Minorities—A Cursory Glance

Although Pakistan was created in the euphoria of Islamic triumphalism it did not neglect a concern for its minorities. In the design of its flag, Islam was represented by a green field with a star and crescent with a white stripe covering one-quarter of the area representing minorities. This was an accurate reflection of the reality of a minority population of nearly 24 per cent, almost all of whom were in East Pakistan. Communal harmony was uppermost in the minds of the founders. It was indelibly inscribed in the polity by the statement Jinnah made to the Constituent Assembly in 1947 that 'in the course of time, Hindus would cease to be Hindus and Muslims would cease to be Muslims, not in a religious sense, for that is the personal faith of every individual but in the political sense as citizens of the State.' That sentiment has been repeated by every leader and has been codified, indeed sanctified, ever since. The secession of East Pakistan in 1971, changed the numerical strength of minorities drastically, reducing them from 24 to 3 per cent of the population.

If a flag of the same plan were designed today, the white panel would be reduced to a barely visible thin stripe.

The uniqueness of Cornelius in Pakistan's polity can be better appreciated by a cursory review of the status of minority groups in Pakistan during the decade of 1960. The discussion is limited to Christians, Parsis, and Qadianis, since Jews, Buddhists and Sikhs (grouped, with Parsis, as 'others' in the census) are only minimumly involved in government or politics. They are small, inconspicuous communities with the Hindus mostly low-caste, or sub-caste farmers and small businessmen, numbering around one million. The Hindus live almost exclusively in Sindh and are a silent all but forgotten remnant of undivided India.

During the period of Cornelius' career, the ethos of Pakistan was not inconsistent with the Muslim tradition of respect for *ahl al-Kitab* (people of the Book), i.e., Jews and Christians. Non-Muslims known as *dhimmi* (or *zimmi*), are protected by elaborate and detailed provisions of Islamic law (*Shari'a*). These protections are subsumed in Article 20 of the 1973 constitution which grants the right to profess, practice, and propagate religions other than Islam and to establish, maintain, and manage religious institutions. Some form of this guarantee was specified in all five constitutions of Pakistan: the Indian Independence Act which served as Pakistan's constitution from 1947 to 1956, the constitutions of 1956, 1962, the interim constitution of 1972, and the 1973 constitution which is currently in force. While this special consideration has not extended to eligibility to be head of state[8], it was otherwise applied during the Cornelius era, although with occasional lapses, to Christians and other minorities. Article 106 of the 1973 Constitution reserves seats in the National Assembly (*Majlis-e-Shura*) according to which nine Christians, seven Hindus and Scheduled Castes, four Sikhs, Buddhists, Parsis, and others, and three Qadianis are to be included as members of parliament.

The data on minorities are approximate.[9] Non-Muslims are a small minority in Pakistan, between 2 and 3 per cent (about three million) of a total population in 1995 estimated at 128 million. The same proportions of minority size existed in the 1960s, though the absolute figures were somewhat (perhaps 4 per cent) lower. The distribution of government employment was probably (*mutatis mutandi*) also the same. The literacy rate for the whole of Pakistan, estimated at 37 per cent in 1995, was probably 35 per cent in the 1960s.

The Christian population is thought to be 1.3 million evenly divided between Roman Catholics and Protestants. About one million live in the Punjab with the second largest concentration being in Sindh, mostly in the city of Karachi which has a Catholic population of Portuguese-Goan ancestry. This is a diocesan seat headed by a Cardinal Joseph Cordeiro, till his death in 1994 and is the site of St. Patrick's Cathedral and School.[10] The Catholic Church has six dioceses, each ruled by a bishop. Christians are engaged in a variety of occupations mainly in menial labour but they do not hold high positions in government. Only 1.15 per cent of civil servants are Christian. In a classification system in which Grade 22 is the highest, only eleven Christians are employed in Grades 17–22. Some 6,000 of them work in low positions in government corporations or semi-autonomous bodies (para-statals) under federal control.

An apt description of the Christian community is found in the work of the Swiss Jesuit missionary, Robert A. Bütler, who worked in Lahore from 1961 to 1986. In addition to his theological studies in France and Lebanon, Father Bütler earned a doctorate in Islamic studies from the University of Basel, thus giving him special qualifications to interpret the conditions of the Christian community in Pakistan.

As a minority of about 1.5 per cent of the total population, they [Christians] do not seem to count for anything from the point of view of intellectual confrontation. Nine tenths or more of them indeed are a downtrodden class of sweepers, servants, farm or industrial workers, and what is more, are looked down upon with feelings of caste superiority. Un-Islamic as they may be, these feelings are a hard fact and, although not exactly structured as in Hinduism, are probably an inheritance from age-long intercourse with the

Hindus. As for the remaining middle-class Christians, they belong mostly to the community of Goans and Anglo-Indians with a sprinkling of Punjabis, often Protestants, in some cases pre-Partition converts from Islam. For the last few years they have shown a sharp trend towards emigration. Engaged as many of them are in business or social relations with the Muslims, they either are westernized and as such not considered different from the foreign Christians, or do not have a sufficient Pakistani cultural background to strike a Christian note of their own. This basic weakness of the local Christians thus results in their almost complete absence from a role of valid partnership in discussion with the Muslims at the intellectual level. In the latters' view Christianity is thus solely represented by the West.[11]

Cornelius did not fit Bütler's description of the Christian community. He was a third-generation Christian whose Hindu ancestors were land-holders, military men, and educators. He married a third-generation Catholic whose father and grandfather were medical officers in the Indian army and whose maternal grandfather was honoured by Pope Leo XIII. This genealogy alone set him apart from the Christian community. Of equal or greater importance was the fact that he opted for Pakistan in 1947 as an officer in the Indian Civil Service which, *ipso facto*, placed him at the pinnacle of Pakistani society and the political order.

The contribution of the Christian community to Pakistan's social milieu has been disproportionate to its size. Although they have not held high positions in government, they have had a significant influence in education and medicine. The Anglican church and other Protestant denominations are active in education and healthcare. There are at least five colleges founded under Protestant auspices. Forman Christian College and Kinnaird College for Women in Lahore have educated many of Pakistan's elite. It should be noted, for example, that Rabia Sultana Qari, Bapsi Sidhwa, Chief Justice Cornelius, Chief Justice Nasim Hasan Shah, and Justice Rustam S. Sidhwa, whose careers are described in this volume, all received part of their education in Christian mission schools. The Seventh Day Adventist hospital in Karachi is one of six other Christian (four are Protestant) hospitals in all parts of the country.

The Parsi community, another prominent minority group, of which Justices Patel and Sidhwa were members, is to be found mainly in Karachi and Lahore. Parsis are descendants of Zoroastrians who refused to convert to Islam after the Muslim conquest of Persia in AD 700. They are, as Delphine Menant has said, 'not only the remnants of one of the greatest nations in the East [Persia], but ... are the trustees of one of the loftiest creeds of antiquity.'[12] Zorastrianism was founded by Zoroaster (Zarathustra) probably in the first millenium BC although he is mentioned by Plato, Plutarch, and Pliny as existing before that period. Zoroastrianism is monotheistic, with Ahura Mazda as the Creator who speaks through his Prophet Zoroaster.

Fleeing Persia, Zoroastrians took refuge in AD 751 on the island of Hormuz in the Strait of Hormuz and shortly thereafter migrated to India, settling in Gujarat, mostly in Bombay. They became known as Parsis (Persians) and adopted Gujarati as their mother tongue. Some of them migrated in small groups to Karachi which was facilitated by the city's status as part of the Bombay Presidency. Throughout their long history, Parsis have maintained their ethnic identity and religious beliefs and have become perhaps the most literate, prosperous, and highly respected of the world's small religious minorities.

The population of Parsis is thought to be about 150 thousand, of whom about 120 thousand live in India, with 110 thousand settled in Bombay.[13] There are about two thousand Parsis in Pakistan, most of whom live in Karachi. These figures are fluctuating and approximate but it is generally agreed that the population of Parsis is declining—perhaps at an annual rate of 2 per cent. One reason for this is that migration to the United Kingdom, the United States, Australia, and Canada, is increasing. There is also a sharply declining birthrate amongst Parsis. It is estimated that nearly half the marriages of Parsis are now outside their community. Conversion to Zoroastrianism is not allowed thus the main factors in any religion's growth, fertility and conversion, have only a negative effect on the community's size. Many Parsi leaders fear the eventual disappearance of their ancient religion. However discouraging this prediction may be, the Parsi community in Pakistan continues to be highly influential and respected. Their relationship with Islam is one of mutual respect. Parsis, like Jews and Christians, are generally acknowledged to be People of the Book, i.e., *ahl al-kitab* (*dhimmi*), a relationship reinforced by the Prophet's (PBUH) harmonious relations with the Zoroastrians of Hajar (now Bahrain). The total acceptance of Parsis at the highest level of Hindu and Muslim social and political life is suggested by two events. Both illustrate entry by marriage into the ruling dynasties of early India and Pakistan. Indira, the daughter of Jawaharlal Nehru, who was the Kashmiri Hindu co-founder of modern India, married Feroze Gandhi, a Parsi active in the freedom movement as a close associate of Mahatma Gandhi (not related). Their marriage in 1942 ended in Feroze's death in 1960. Mohammed Ali Jinnah, founding father of independent Pakistan, married Ruttenbai Petit, daughter of the wealthy cotton merchant and shipping magnate of Bombay, Sir Dinshaw Petit. Ruttenbai converted to Islam when she married Jinnah in 1918 but they separated in 1928 and she died in 1929. Both these examples show a not uncommon disregard for Parsi strictures against marriage outside the community.

The literacy rate amongst Parsis is nearly 100 per cent. Most educated Parsis speak Gujarati, English, and one or more of the vernaculars such as Punjabi, Urdu, Sindhi or Baluchi. Although an affluent community, Parsis are known for their unostentatious lifestyle. Their generous philanthropic activities are renowned both within the community and in the larger context of Pakistani society. Indeed, their beneficence was known in the early days of British India when, in 1842, Jamsetjee Jejeebhoy was the first Indian to be made a Knight and in 1857 a Baronet, in recognition of his charitable works.

The influence of Parsis is greatest in Karachi. When that city was part of India it had, after World War I, a Parsi mayor,

Nuserwanji Mehta. Another leading philanthropist of this time, 'Khan Bahadur' Ardeshir Mama, founded the Mama Parsi Girl's High School which exists today as the leading girls' school in Karachi. Khan Bahadur was a title of distinction conferred upon him by the Government of British India. Ardeshir Mama was the maternal grandfather of Minoo P. Bhandara, owner of the Murree Brewery Co., Ltd. in Rawalpindi. Parsis are engaged in finance, real estate, shipping, and large-scale corporate activity, as well as in the professions of medicine and law. The 1983 census of Pakistan shows only nine Parsis in government service, but none of them above Grade 5. Government corporations employ sixty-seven Parsis, most of them in middle ranks, with fourteen in top, executive positions.

Parsis, wrote the Urdu poet Faiz Ahmed Faiz, 'have always been flamboyantly prominent in public life.' Their considerable influence has been not so much in political party activism as in a humanitarian and intellectual impetus in statecraft. Hence it is not surprising that despite their tiny numerical strength, they have held several important government posts. Minoo P. Bhandara was Minister of Minority Affairs, 1983–85. His intellectual proclivities are clearly indicated by his uncommonly perceptive essay 'Remembering Sir Isaiah Berlin' which appeared in *Dawn*, 4 December 1997. This tribute to the renowned Oxford political theorist on the occasion of his death analyzed the structure and the sources of Berlin's philosophy. Jamshed K. A. Marker, another prominent Parsi, was Pakistan's ambassador to Bucharest, Paris, Moscow, Washington, and the United Nations. He graduated from Cambridge University and during World War II served as an officer in the Royal Indian Navy. Marker became known throughout Pakistan as the leading commentator on cricket. His distinguished diplomatic career was recognized by the award of the *Sitar-i-Quaid-i-Azam* conferred upon him by President Yahya Khan in 1970. The eldest son of Kikobad Ardeshir Marker, one of the most distinguished and respected citizens of Quetta, Balochistan, Jamshed's grandfather, Ardeshir, arrived in Quetta in 1880 traveling by train from Bombay to Sibi and by camel to Quetta. He was successful in several business enterprises, especially in pharmaceuticals, which were further developed by his sons. The Marker family was renowned for its philanthropy and has been prominent in the public affairs of Quetta for more than half a century. Kikobad rebuilt his homes and businesses after the earthquake in Quetta in 1935. His two-volume autobiography, *A Petal from the Rose* (Karachi: Rosette, 1985) includes a fascinating account of the earthquake and its aftermath. It is especially noteworthy as a personal memoir of the growing affluence of a Parsi family in Pakistan and chronicles their constructive impetus in building a new nation.

Parsis have also been equally distinguished in journalism and in letters. Ardeshir Cowasjee, a wealthy shareholder in *Dawn*, Pakistan's pre-eminent newspaper published from Karachi, is a freelance writer whose frequent op-ed pieces in *Dawn* are courageous critiques of Pakistan's polity. Somewhat acerbic in tone, they are marked by an uncommon sophistication and insight. Minoo Bhandara, who does not agree with many of Cowasjee's views, has described him as a 'unique one-man institution...' who can be forgiven 'notwithstanding his wicked tongue, because he is brave. His heart is in the right place. Show me a person braver (and more honest) than Ardeshir Cowasjee.' (M. P. Bhandara, 'Give the Country a Chance' *Dawn*, 17 January 1998).

Bapsi Sidhwa, the sister of Minoo Bhandara, is the author of several novels published in England, the United States, and in Pakistan. One of her novels, *Cracking India* is a stunning analysis of the 1947 Partition of India seen through the eyes of a Parsi family living in Lahore.[14] This novel has been praised by Salman Rushdie as 'one of the finest responses made to the horrors of the division of the subcontinent' (*The New Yorker*, 23 and 30 June 1997, p. 60). It was listed by the *New York Times Book Review* as a Notable Book of the Year and received the American Library Association nomination for Notable Book. In 1991, it was awarded the *Liberaturpreis* at the Frankfurt book fair a prize given to women novelists from Asia, Africa, and Latin America. *Cracking India* has been made into a film in India.

A graduate of Kinnaird College in Lahore, Bapsi Sidhwa was a Bunting Fellow at Harvard in 1986–87, and a Visiting Fellow at the Rockefeller Foundation Study Center in Bellagio, Italy. She was awarded the Lila Wallace/Reader's Digest Writer's Award for 1993 and received a grant from the National Endowment for the Arts in 1987. In 1991, she was awarded the *Sitar-i-Imtiaz* by the Pakistan government. Her novels have been translated into German, French, and Russian. Now living in the United States, Bapsi Sidhwa has taught at Mt. Holyoke College, Brandeis, Columbia, and at Rice Universities and the University of Houston.

The sparse representation of Parsis in government administration makes the appointment of two Supreme Court judges from the community all the more significant. Rustam S Sidhwa was born in Surat (state of Bombay) in 1927. Educated at Cathedral High School and at St. Anthony's School in Lahore, he received bachelor's, master's, and law degrees from Punjab University. Following a career as an advocate, a government administrator, and as a faculty member of the law school of Panjab University, he was appointed to the Lahore High Court in 1978 and to the Supreme Court in 1989. After retiring from the Supreme Court in 1992, he was appointed to the International Criminal Tribunal for the former Yugoslavia in The Hague. The author of The *Lahore High Court and It's Principal Bar*, Justice Sidhwa is perhaps best known for his concurring opinion in a case which placed limits and conditions on the power of the executive to dissolve the national assembly. The Supreme Court's concurrence by Justice Nasim Hasan Shah included a long quotation from the Sidhwa opinion. (*Federation of Pakistan v. Haji Saifullah Khan, PLD 1989 SC 166*). Sidhwa died in 1997.

The second eminent Parsi on the Supreme Court, Dorab F Patel, was born in 1924, and belonged to a distinguished family which had settled in Quetta, Balochistan in the 1800s. The family was renowned for the development of the city of Quetta. After earning a master's degree and a law degree from Bombay University and a bachelor's degree from the London School of Economics and Political Science, Dorab F. Patel qualified as a barrister from the Inner Temple. Following an uncommonly successful career as an advocate in Karachi, he was appointed to the Karachi Bench of the West Pakistan High Court in 1967 and elevated to the Supreme Court in 1976. The Full Court Reference made by five judges honouring his appointment makes no mention of his religion.[15] A similar silence shrouded Cornelius' Christianity which was not so much calculated avoidance as indifference to a factor regarded as peripheral. Justice Patel was one of three dissenters in the Zulfikar Ali Bhutto case (*PLD 1979 SC 53*) in which the Lahore High Court found the former prime minister guilty of conspiracy to murder and condemned him to death.

As senior judge in 1981, Patel was in line to become Chief Justice. In that year, the controversial *Provisional Constitution Order—1981* was promulgated by the martial law government of General Ziaul Haq, imposing limits on the Supreme Court's jurisdiction and independence. Judges were required to take an oath of allegiance to that Order rather than to the Constitution itself. Justice Patel refused on grounds of conscience to take the oath. He relinquished his position on the Supreme Court and returned to private practice. This courageous assertion of independence was acclaimed by the legal community and society, in general, and his renown began to approach heroic stature. Patel died in 1997.

Patel was very much like Cornelius in ability and in perspective. He was selected to deliver the Third Cornelius Memorial Lecture in 1995, an honour he shared with Chief Justice Nasim Hasan Shah and Justice S. A. Salam who gave the first (1993) and second (1994) lectures respectively. In his lecture, Patel emphasized the importance of depoliticizing the appointment of judges—an issue which was central to the *Provisional Constitution Order—1981*. He gave much attention to the need for judges to insulate themselves from the maelstrom of politics and from society generally. The tradition of 'rigid aloofness of the judiciary from the executive', he said, and the 'duty to lead a secluded life' were absolutely essential to maintain the independence of the judiciary.[16] This behaviour was both prescribed and practiced by Cornelius.

The third important minority group in Pakistan is a religious community known as Ahmadiyya, named after their founder, Mirza Ghulam Ahmad (1835–1908) who came from the village of Qadian in Indian Punjab. The Ahmadiyya community is based in Lahore and is sometimes referred to as the Lahore Ahmadiyya. A group which broke away because of a crisis in the succession after Ghulam Ahmad's death was once known as *Qadiani*, a term that is now used to refer to both groups usually in a perjorative sense.

The separate identity of this group, which claims to be authentically Muslim, creates a sectarian split in the otherwise ethnically homogeneous community of Punjabis. According to their own views, they are Muslim although their interpretation of the Qur'anic *suras* relating to a prophet following Prophet Mohammed (PBUH) differs from that of other Muslims. While there is some ambiguity in their alleged claims of the 'prophethood' of their founder, other Muslims regard them as having defied the 'seal of the Prophet', the inviolable pillar of Islam, which proclaims that there can be no prophet after Prophet Mohammed (PBUH).[17] The first major protest against the Ahmadiyya community were riots in the Punjab in 1953 when Sir Zafrullah Khan, an Ahmadi, was appointed to the post of foreign minister. The commission to investigate the riots consisted of Cornelius' predecessor, Chief Justice Muhammed Munir and Lahore High Court Chief Justice Kayani.[18] In 1974, this resentment surfaced again at Rabwah, their religious headquarters which led to a constitutional amendment being passed which declared Ahmadiyya a non-Muslim minority. This step was taken despite the fact that five years earlier the Lahore High Court had held that the Ahmadiyya could not be declared non-Muslim and that they had the right to call themselves Muslim. (*Mobashir v. Bokhari PLD 1969 Lahore 113*).

Thereafter, the community was barred from the offices of president and prime minister since an oath swearing that Prophet Mohammed (PBUH) was the final prophet was required for those offices. In 1984, Ziaul Haq's government issued *Ordinance XX* which further restricted their activities. They were prohibited from employing a public call to prayer, etc. The Ahmadis challenged the constitutionality of the ordinance. In a lengthy decision analyzing the nature of Islam and the characteristics of Muslims, the Federal Shar'ia Court upheld the validity of the ordinance. (*Majibur Rehman v. Federal Government of Pakistan, PLD 1985 FSC 8*). More recently, the Supreme Court held that Ordinance XX was not in violation of Fundamental Rights and was therefore valid. (*Zaheer-ud-Din v. The State, 1993 SCMR 1718*). The courts have thus upheld the classification of Ahmadis as non-Muslims, much to the consternation of those seeking to expand human rights.

Ironically, Ahmadis have been stalwart missionaries of Islam particularly in Africa. Like the Parsis, they are an affluent, close-knit community, numbering (according to the 1983 census) about 110 thousand, half of whom live in the Punjab where they constitute a well-educated group. One of only two Muslims ever to be awarded the Nobel Prize was an Ahmadi, Dr Abdus Salam, who gained this distinction in Physics in 1979. (The other was Naguib Mafouz of Egypt, who was awarded the prize in literature in 1988). Born in Jhang, Punjab, in 1926, Salam was honorary science advisor to the President of Pakistan 1961–74. For several years before his death in 1996, he was with the International Center for Theoretical Physics in Trieste.

The size of the Ahmadi community is disproportionate to the seriousness of the challenge they have posed to the Islamic polity of Pakistan and to the definition of a Muslim. These questions were not resolved by the Munir Report of 1953 which, enshrouded these issues in further ambiguity. In the early years of Pakistan, Ahmadis held important administrative positions in government, even though they were excluded from the two highest political offices. Since the 1960s, however, they are rarely to be found in the top two grades of the civil service. The 1983 census shows a total of 604 Ahmadis (.39 per cent) in government service; ninety-four Ahmadis hold positions in Grades 16–20. The 1986 census shows 1,220 Ahmadis holding office in para-statal bodies controlled by the federal government. No Ahmadi has served on the High or the Supreme courts and such appointments are not likely to be made in future.

It is generally conceded that the formerly tolerant attitude toward religious minorities, codified in Article 20 of the Constitution which is in consonance with the Islamic injunctions on *ahl al-kitab*, has deteriorated since the time of Cornelius.[19] Official policies towards the Ahmadiyya are regarded as particularly grievous violations of the guarantees of religious freedom enshrined in the Constitution. They illustrate, however, that when the issue of the 'seal of the prophet' is involved, the parameters of tolerance have been crossed.

During the years that Cornelius was alive, a relatively benign attitude prevailed toward non-Muslim minorities, except for the Ahmadiyya community. The Parsis remained untouched, as they had always been, by any suggestion of discrimination. The attitude towards the Christians was not overtly unfavourable during the 1950–70 period. There was no serious inclination to expropriate their property although some restrictions were placed on their evangelizing with the aim of converting Muslims. The spirit of Article 20 was more or less dominant then but it gradually eroded and was compromised by Martial Law Regulation 118, issued by the martial law regime of Zulfikar Ali Bhutto in 1972.[20] That regulation ordered that all property of privately managed colleges shall 'vest' in either the central or in the provincial governments. MLR 118 was not enforced until 1979 when the martial law government of Ziaul Haq, urged on by militant Islamists, began to expropriate Christian church property. Building on the principles enunciated in Cornelius' decisions in the *Faridsons* and *Maudoodi* cases, the Supreme Court tempered the implementation of MLR 118. In *Board of Foreign Missions of the Presbyterian Church in the United States of America, through Lahore Church Council v. Government of the Punjab through Secretary, Education and Another (1987(1) PSCR 341)* Justice Nasim Hasan Shah ruled that government could not confiscate the property on which the private school was run. In 1988, the Court refused to review its earlier decision. (*Government of the Punjab through Secretary, Education Department and Another v. Board of Foreign Missions of the Presbyterian Church in the U.S.A., through Lahore Church Council [1988(1) PSCR, 187]*). In *Christian Educational Endowment Trust v. Deputy Commissioner and Others (1987(1) PSCR 357)*, the Court denied the right of the government to take over the property of Forman Christian College. It invoked the 'principles of natural justice' and of *audi alteram partem* which require that a hearing be held before such action is taken.

III

A Judicial Career—38 Years

The single episode touching the religious question in Cornelius' career which skirted the edge of political controversy occurred in September 1969. Cornelius had agreed to serve in Yahya Khan's government as minister of law. When the cabinet was dismissed in February 1971, Yahya asked Cornelius and G. W. Choudhry of East Pakistan to draft a new constitution. Zulfikar Ali Bhutto, then foreign minister, later to be president, objected to this assignment with the comment 'He is a *Dhimmi*. How can he make a constitution for a Muslim state?' Referring to that episode, *Dawn* praised Cornelius as the 'only non-Muslim technically in line for the highest job in the country, that of Head of State, constitutionally debarred from members of minority communities.'[21] This was an uncontroverted instance of the government's recognition of his religion. When President Zulfikar Bhutto asked Cornelius if he would seek support in Christian countries for the release of Pakistani prisoners of war in India. Cornelius declined the offer.

If such public indifference and personal reticence characterized the religious dimension of Cornelius' career, why should this essay direct attention to it? At the end of the twentieth century, the alleged antagonism of Islam and the West given impetus by Samuel Huntington's widely read theory of the 'clash of civilizations',[22] makes it important to study instances of compatibility, a theme that Cornelius symbolized. The case for the compatibility of Islam and the West (by which is meant Christendom), is stronger than the case for clash. It was perhaps less evident during Cornelius' life, partly because the notion of the 'clash' was not then popular. His devotion to the development of Pakistan, which he helped mould for nearly half a century, and his profound admiration for Islam were certainly factors which conditioned his visions. Drawing on a powerful intellect, he sought to validate the Islamic legal system and blend it with British legal norms. In some instances, his preference was for *Shari'a* rather than for western legal canons. The result of this intellectual *tour de force* was never collected in one volume but spread over hundreds of judicial opinions, speeches, and reports scattered in place and time. The cumulative effect of these efforts was the beginning of a synthesis suggestive in a rudimentary way of the dialectic of Thomas Aquinas. Rooted in theology, it emerges as philosophy but finds practical application in jurisprudence. Cornelius describes this diffusion of concepts:

> In the long years that I have passed as Judge in the High Court, the Federal Court and the Supreme Court, I could not fail to perceive that the judicial process at that level developed in me an understanding of the national ethos at a level approaching appreciation in terms of religion. The emphasis I have placed from time to time, within the limits lying upon me, to make the justice of our land a thing of the people, by infusion of concepts derived from Muslim law into the whole field of secular law, and by adoption of the people's language as the language of law and of justice, is a reflection of that obligation. The task is huge but it is also both essential and noble in the highest degree and I am confident that in time it will be undertaken and, with God's help, that it will be accomplished.[23]

The documentary record left by Cornelius, although physically scattered, is intellectually coherent. The exact number of public addresses he made is uncertain. The first mention of his speeches in any western source was in 1966 when six addresses on the theme of the role of the bureaucracy were published in the United States with commentary in an appendix to a single volume.[24] In 1981, S. M. Haider, who took his doctorate with me at Duke University in 1966, compiled, at my urging, forty different addresses on various themes.[25] Chief Justice Cornelius gave me typed copies of eleven addresses not included in either of these compilations. Some of these were published in issues of *All-Pakistan Legal Decisions (PLD) Journal* section. In some there are references to other speeches which have been published but are not presently available. Thus copies of fifty-seven addresses made between 1960 and 1977 are extant. Assuming that there were additional speeches, perhaps as many as twenty, for which no record exists, we can postulate that he gave about seventy-five major addresses. Most of the documented fifty-seven speeches are lengthy, scholarly efforts. My own published compilation and that of S. M. Haider total 417 printed pages. The eleven typed speeches in my possession would total about one hundred printed pages. By any standard, this publication record of more than five hundred pages is remarkable. It is astonishing that these efforts were extra-curricular while he served on the court, with virtually no research or editing assistance and only marginal clerical help. The institution of law clerks, so important in the American judiciary, did not exist in Pakistan.

In addition to public addresses and court work, Cornelius undertook the onerous responsibility of heading a commission caught in the maelstrom of politics. He was chairman of the Pay and Services Commission which took nearly three years to prepare its 300-page report submitted on 1 June 1962.[26] Much of the report was written by Cornelius himself, again with minimal and untrained staff assistance. Eight months after his retirement, he was appointed chairman of the Services Re-organization Committee.

In his seventeen years on the Federal/Supreme Court bench, Cornelius wrote 362 major opinions, concurrences, and dissents, as well as 416 briefer notes or *obiter dicta*, a total of 778 written works. All of these were published in one or more of the law report series (such as *PLD*). In addition, an untabulated number of unpublished decisions in typescript are filed in the office of the registrar of the Supreme Court. Most of these judgments, both published and unpublished, were written in longhand or typed by the hunt-and-peck system on an ancient Hermes portable typewriter. The typewriter has been kept by the law firm of Cornelius, Lane and Mufti as one of several Cornelius mementos. The notion of a 'paper trail' has been made important in the United States by the Senate confirmation hearings of the nominations of Robert H. Bork in 1989 and David H. Souter in 1990 to the Supreme Court. The former had a substantial trail and the latter a slender tendril. It is doubtful if any jurist in any country leaves a paper trail so rich in bulk and erudition as that of Cornelius.

Alvin Robert Cornelius was born in Agra, Uttar Pradesh (then the United Provinces) India, 1 May 1903. He was the eldest son of Professor Israel Jacob Cornelius who taught mathematics at Holkar College, a state institution in the princely state of Indore (now part of Madhya Pradesh), named after the dynasty of maharajas who ruled the state until independence in 1947. The Cornelius Prize in Mathematics is still awarded annually by the college to outstanding students.

He was descended from a family of Naikor landholders who rendered military service to the Madras East India Company. The family name was Kait Pillay. After the conquest of Burma (now Myanmar) in 1885, one member of the family, Perayya Kait Pillay (1837–1907) who had fought in Burma, settled in the Central Provinces. He became a schoolmaster and a Christian, adopting the name Cornelius, the name of a centurion in the *Acts of the Apostles* (who is characterized as 'a devout man who feared God with all his household, gave alms liberally to the people, and prayed constantly to God' (*RSV*, 10:1b2)). A. R. Cornelius' father was Perayya's son, Israel Jacob Cornelius (1878-1935). Israel Jacob was a deeply religious man fitting the biblical description of the centurion whose name Pillay adopted. A. R. Cornelius' mother was Tara D'Rozario (1879–1966). Tara's father, Michael (1845–1915) was Deputy Range Officer-Forests, Central India. The D'Rozario family were also Christian converts from Hinduism.

Cornelius was brought up a Presbyterian and converted to Roman Catholicism after his marriage in 1931 to Ione Francis, a devout Roman Catholic. She was the daughter of a Pathan, Khushhal Khan Safi (1875–1937), a convert who took the Christian name Leo Francis and the granddaughter of a Persian-Punjabi, Miran Baksh Utarid (1856–1939) whose Christian name was Marcus Benedict Utarid. Both her father and grandfather were civil surgeons in the Punjab Medical Service. After his retirement in 1915 Marcus Benedict Utarid translated the Douay (Douai) Catholic Bible into Urdu. It became the authoritative Urdu translation for which he was awarded the *Honoris Crux: Pro Ecclesia et Pontifice* by Pope Benedict XV. Her paternal grandfather, Said Shah Safi (1835–1904), was in the Foreign and Political Department of the Government of India. Said Shah, though a Christian convert, did not change his name.

A. R. Cornelius attended St. John's College, an Anglican institution, in Agra. He received the bachelor of science degree from Muir College, a constituent unit of the University of Allahabad, a distinguished residential institution founded in 1887. He ranked first in his class winning all available awards including the Homersham Cox Gold Medal for Mathematics. This early education was within the ambit of a Protestant Christian and British ethos. He describes his Islamic education in terms characteristic of his delicacy and sensitivity toward others:

My own education was in scientific subjects and what I learnt of Islam was a mere smattering of the Persian language for the purposes of passing the matriculation examination. Our teacher in the State High School at Indore was a member of the Jaora Nawab's family, a genial and courtly person whose knowledge of Persian was probably much wider than he cared to show. His inclination to impart the knowledge was at a somewhat lower level and the students learnt the prescribed material by heart, gaining the meanings of words and sentences much more from each other than from their teachers.[27]

In Letter 8 he mentions that he 'had fair Urdu and some Persian; I began to nose into Arabic a bit.'[28] These comments were self-effacing and excessively modest as befitted his personality. He did study some Persian, Arabic, and the vernaculars as part of his ICS probationer's training. His writings, judicial decisions, and speeches, as well as his letters published here, suggest not only his respect for but also his profound knowledge of Islam. Hamid Khan, an advocate of the Supreme Court, who knew him well as a senior partner in the law firm of Cornelius, Lane and Mufti, reports that 'he translated into English the Commentary of the Holy Qur'an by Maulana Shabbir Ahmad Usmani. Due to certain unfortunate circumstances, this endeavour did not go into print and is somehow untraceable.'[29] His abstruse commentary, 'Faith Vanishes into Sight', published in the 1979 (No. 3) issue of *Hamdard Islamicus* seeks to explicate the origins of the universe. In extensive quotations from the Qur'an he uses both Arabic and English.

After successfully passing the most competitive examination in India, he was sent as a probationer for two years study at Selwyn College, Cambridge University. In 1926, he entered the Indian Civil Service, regarded as the 'steel frame' and the 'corps d'elite' of India. Training in Britain was customary in the ICS and was continued in the Pakistani counterpart (CSP) of the ICS until 1959. Upon his return to India, he was posted to Ambala district in the Punjab. From 1926 until his death he lived and worked in the Punjab, mostly in Lahore. He had a fascination for the Punjab which he rightly regarded as the best administered province in the subcontinent. Cornelius considered Lahore 'his city'. One of the deputy commissioners under whom he trained and for whom he had high regard was Evan Meredith Jenkins, later Sir Evan, Governor of the Punjab. Cornelius felt much more temperamentally suited for the judicial aspect of his district duties and in 1930 was appointed to the judicial branch of the ICS. He served as a judge in various districts of the Punjab, including Amritsar and Lahore. At Partition ICS officers were given the choice of remaining in India or opting for Pakistan. Cornelius opted for the latter and joined his 157 fellow officers of the ICS and IPS who left for Pakistan. The remaining one thousand officers felt their destinies were in India. His first assignment in Pakistan was the drafting of laws governing the assets of evacuees and refugees victimized by Partition. He was appointed to the Lahore High Court in 1946. While still on the High Court, he was posted in April 1950 as Secretary of Law, a position he held until 31 May 1951 when he was elevated to the Federal/Supreme Court. He became chief justice of that court in 1960 and served as minister of law in the Yahya Khan cabinet from 1969 to the fall of Dacca, 16 December 1971. For nearly a year between his retirement on 29 February 1968 and his appointment as minister of law, he was uncertain about what he would do. In Letter 3 he writes that the consulting he was doing could be done as easily in Karachi as in Lahore. He consulted occasionally with the law firm of Lane and Mufti in Lahore from 1977 to 1980. Much to the firm's surprise and embarrassment, his fees were markedly lower than those charged by much less distinguished lawyers. In January 1980, after three years of persuasion by the firm and several polite but firm declinations by Cornelius, he signed an agreement with Lane, Mufti which made him the senior partner; the firm then became Cornelius, Lane and Mufti. Except for the fact that he was the firm's only senior partner, his work was somewhat like what in American legal practice would be called 'of counsel'. Zafar Samdani, a local journalist, writes that he worked six days a week from around ten in the morning till a little after mid-day 'but there were no strict hours. "It is a shop", would muse the judge who did not miss the fancy trappings of the past, smilingly adding, "I wait for a customer".[30] This comment should not be construed to suggest that he was not actively intellectually engaged in discussing cases and advising and sometimes drafting briefs (in longhand or on his ancient typewriter). Hamid Khan, who worked closely with him during this period, asserts that he was very active for about five years after which his memory faded periodically. From 1988 on, he was bedridden and thus ceased all legal activity.

Although Cornelius wrote about philosophical issues which were universal, he tended to see them through the prism of Islam and Pakistan, yet he did not lack perspective and was a well-travelled man. In 1955, Cornelius was appointed by the International Labour Office in Geneva to a three-man committee to inquire into labour conditions abroad. The committee was headed by Lord McNair, a Cambridge don of Gonville and Caius College, with whom Cornelius forged a friendship. He retained his seat on the court, however and accepted my invitation to lecture at Duke University with travel expenses paid by the Asia Foundation. As he states in Letter 2, he planned to add this to his trip to Singapore in August 1962. As he examined the travel schedule more carefully and considered the need to be on hand for the opening of the Supreme Court with time to prepare for that opening, he decided against the trip to North Carolina. Among his many overseas trips was his representation of Pakistan at the first Asian Judicial Conference in Baguio, the Philippines, in 1963. He also made frequent trips to England where his wife resided part of the year and where his sons were studying. He was especially pleased with an official visit to England in 1963 under the auspices of the British Council when he was received with full dignity and respect for his office instead of as merely a spectator in the courts. Cornelius was equally pleased by the visit in December 1963 of Lord Denning, Master of the Rolls, to Pakistan who made 'direct contact with our superior judges on a level of equality.' In 1965, he read a paper at the Third Commonwealth and Empire Law Conference in Sydney, discussed in greater detail later in this chapter. He was scheduled to attend the Second Conference on World Peace Through Law in Washington that same year but 'could not attend due to the events arising from the treacherous invasion of

Pakistan by the neo-expansionist India.'[31] He was able to attend that organization's conference in Geneva in 1967. He participated in a seminar at the University of Singapore in 1962 and in 1967 attended the Third Annual Asian Judicial Conference in Bangkok. In 1968, he was invited to a judicial seminar in Lagos, Nigeria but did not attend it. In 1970, he was unanimously elected (by thirty-three nations) chairman of the UN Commission on Minorities.

He enthusiastically accepted my invitation to be honorary chairman of an international conference on political and administrative development held at the Rockefeller Foundation's Villa Serbelloni, Lake Como, Italy, 16–22 July 1967. After pertinent introductory remarks, he presided over all the sessions with a *gravitas* and graciousness befitting the setting of a princely villa. His informal remarks throughout the meeting reflected his own long study and experience with administrative systems and gave the sessions a clear direction and cohesion. The conference papers were published in a 688-page volume.[32] He was favourably impressed with the Villa Serbelloni conference. In an address extolling the virtues of Muslim and Jewish classical learning and the importance of dedicated teachers, he described the conference in some detail, concluding with this observation: 'That is how responsible teachers in the West occupy their vacations; reviewing old knowledge, acquiring new knowledge, and returning to their academies refreshed and eager to disseminate among their pupils, the latest processes of thinking in their respective fields.'[33]

Neither a compulsive nor an inveterate globetrotter, Cornelius was cautious about the sponsorship of invitations to other countries. The US Department of State was interested in having him visit the United States and I made overtures on its behalf to invite him but he refused to be a guest under governmental auspices. This was not because of any animosity towards the United States; but his fear of entanglement in international politics and the delicacy of his position as chief justice of a nation deeply involved in a web of global affairs. He was also justifiably wary about the operations of foreign and domestic intelligence. At the request of an American foundation with which I had no connection, I presented its invitation for him to visit the United States. He politely declined. In December 1964, I had a long conversation with him on behalf of the Department of State discussing the establishment of an American Institute of Pakistan studies. He was suspicious that such an institute might be a cover for intelligence operations. A paperback, *The Invisible Government*[34] had just been distributed to ministers' and secretaries' offices. On that trip, I encountered the book on each visit to a dignitory, including an interview with President Ayub Khan. The Secretary of Education, S. M. Sharif, was especially suspicious. Even President Ayub held up the book and said he hoped 'this would not happen in my country'. Cornelius was not oblivious to this climate of suspicion. On one visit he looked at an attaché case I had placed next to my chair and said half jokingly that it could easily contain a recording device. I found an opportunity to open the case thus revealing its innocent contents of blank paper and airline tickets. (This was an important lesson: Never again did I visit an office with a case of any kind). Spy-craft was a regnant idiom of the times. It was only two years after the Soviets shot down Francis Gary Powers in a U-2 spy plane based at a secret installation in Peshawar. Moreover, the hotly contested election between Fatima Jinnah and Ayub Khan was scheduled for 2 January 1965. During the campaign, the suspicion of United States' intervention hung thickly in the air. It reached its climax in public accusations by Ghulam Nabi Memon, the West Pakistan provincial minister of information, that the United States was actively supporting the Combined Opposition Party against President Ayub. Commenting generally on this alleged interference, *Dawn* in its issue of 31 December 1964 stated, 'The latest disclosures have made many Pakistanis ask whether Pakistan has become the latest playground of America's 'Invisible Government'—the CIA.'

Although sensitive to spy-craft, he was more disturbed by the vulgar intrusion of foreigners who had no understanding of

Islam and the culture of Pakistan. In 1962, we attended a reception given by the US consul-general in Lahore. He looked around at the many Americans present, turned to me, and asked, 'What are all these people doing in my country? Do they understand our culture? They are destroying it.' After presenting his compliments to his hosts he left graciously and (insofar as it is possible for a chief justice) unobtrusively. I was secretly delighted by his reaction, for I shared the same view. He made his position clear when it came to admitting an American research student to the Supreme Court. Cornelius had accepted a doctoral student from the Asia-Africa programme of Syracuse University who began his assignment as a researcher in September 1964. Initially, the Court 'welcomed this initiative from abroad, which will help spread knowledge of the laws and justice of Pakistan in English-speaking countries all over the world.'[35] Within a few months, Cornelius had misgivings about his decision. He explains his reservations in Letter 3 of 3 July 1965 in response to my suggestion that he accept an American intern to work in the Supreme Court.[36] He re-asserted an argument which was the quintessence of his view of the relationship of a non-Muslim to an Islamic state. The argument went, that the constitution of Pakistan mandates a society compatible with Islamic values. It is the jurist's duty to enforce that mandate. Islamic values are so universal that a non-Muslim who is a God-fearing believer has no trouble living in an Islamic society. This is the 'thesis' of Pakistan, but a non-citizen of Pakistan who may not be a believer is not bound by this constitutional requirement. Such a person at work in the Supreme Court is unlikely to view Islam or Pakistani culture in any manner other than as an 'anti-thesis'.

Cornelius' lifestyle seemed anomalous in a culture which enjoyed the legacy of Mughal ostentation and splendour but it was consistent with his expressed views. 'For our people', he once said, 'affluence is poison'.[37] The Cornelius family lived in rented government-allocated houses until 1948 after which they moved to Nedou's Hotel. In 1949, they moved into

Mrs. Cornelius' mother's house at 13-A Warris Road, Lahore until it was sold in 1952 when they moved to 6 Egerton Road. From 1953 until his death on 21 December 1991, Cornelius and his wife lived in two rooms in Faletti's hotel in Lahore. After the death of his wife in November 1989, to whom he had been married for fifty-eight years, he moved into one room. It was customary for officials of his rank to have an official car and driver and to be accompanied by aides, retainers, and, sometimes, by official guards but this was not Cornelius' style. When he came to dinner at my home in Gulberg in 1961, he drove his own car, a 1953 Wolsely. (The car, still in running order, is maintained by Jawwad S. Khawaja, a partner in the Cornelius, Lane and Mufti law firm). He had requested in advance that no other guests be present at the dinner. On visits to his office and to Faletti's hotel, I noted the absence of *chaprassis*, *peons*, and other retainers who usually hover about a man of consequence like him. Having dinner with him and his wife at Faletti's, I detected an unusual show of genuine affection and respect accorded him by the staff which was of a different quality than the customary deference and obsequience shown to superiors in the highly status-conscious society of Pakistan. Samdani records that Cornelius was one of ten life-members of the hotel and that he was charged the same room rent that was in effect 'over three decades back'.[38]

Hamid Khan reports that he was a model judge, every advocate's ideal, a soft-spoken man who was the epitome of patience and tolerance.[39] Muhammad Ilyas, acting chief justice of the Lahore High Court in 1992, describes his 1952 *viva voce* examination for appointment as a civil judge in Punjab where Cornelius was the judicial examiner. Ilyas was frightened because he 'did not belong to an affluent family...and did not have...gaudy dress to wear' nor did he move in the same social circles as other more sophisticated candidates. Cornelius asked him if it was proper to have an Islamic constitution when the country had non-Muslim minorities. Ilyas replied that an Islamic state guaranteed equal social justice for all. He stood first in the total exam as well as in the *viva voce* and credited Cornelius for the outcome. But he dared not seek to confirm this 'from the illustrious Judge who was regarded as a true patriot and whose extraordinary legal acumen, even-handed justice, impeccable integrity, amiable disposition, and other sterling qualities of head and heart are widely acclaimed.'[40]

The sensitivity and magnanimity which Cornelius showed towards his colleagues is illustrated by his final official act before retiring as chief justice. His successor was to be the senior justice, S. A. Rahman, who would reach the mandatory retirement age of 65 on 4 June 1968. Had Cornelius invoked his normal retirement date of 1 May 1968, S. A. Rahman's term as chief justice would have been limited to thirty-five days. By voluntarily retiring 29 February, 1968 (as he explains in Letter 7), Cornelius made it possible for Justice Rahman to be chief justice for two additional months. This is the kind of unheralded gesture which won him the affection and esteem of his judicial colleagues and the entire legal community.

Cornelius was an ardent cricket player. He wrote the constitution of the Pakistan Cricket Board and was regarded as 'one of the architects of the sport in Pakistan'.[41] He organized a young team called the 'Eaglets' and arranged for it to participate in first class cricket matches in England. The Eaglets played many games in England from 1953 to 1965 and Cornelius was sometimes on hand for some of the more important ones. In recognition of his services to cricket, he was given a honour rarely bestowed on anyone, least of all on foreigners and was made an Honorary Life Member of the Marylebone Cricket Club (MCC) of London which, since 1788, is acknowledged throughout the world as the authoritative source of cricket rules.

Cornelius lived his last few years in quiet dignity and in privacy. In his last year, his medical condition was not generally known. The High Court of Lahore issued a writ ordering a medical examination and later cited the Punjab government for contempt for not obeying immediately. Nothing could have been more suitable to his final hours. The legal constructs of the writ petition and the contempt power which he so vigorously defended in the court (especially in the *Snelson* case) were now invoked to help him in his final days. No coda of any symphony could have greater symmetry and harmony. Two days later, in early November 1994, a physician assigned to him had him removed to the Services hospital where he died at 8:30 am, 21 December 1991 at age 88.[42] He is survived by two sons, Peter at Staplehurst, Kent, England and Michael at St. Louis, Missouri. A funeral mass was conducted in the Roman Catholic Cathedral of the Sacred Heart, Lawrence Road, Lahore. Cornelius was buried next to his wife in the Catholic cemetery on Jail Road.

IV

A Philosophy of Statecraft

The contribution of A. R. Cornelius to the jurisprudence of Pakistan has been examined by Nasim Hasan Shah, S. M. Haider, and Hamid Khan elsewhere.[43] Chief Justice Nasim, who worked closely with Cornelius as editor of the Supreme Court reports and later as an advocate and justice, regarded him as a mentor. His conclusion that Cornelius left the court 'a mighty citadel ... sustaining the rule of law'[44] resonates throughout Pakistan's legal, government, and business communities. Haider praises his courage in preserving judicial review in the face of executive efforts to oust it. Hamid characterizes his stewardship of the Court as the 'golden period' in the history of the judiciary.

It is the consensus of the legal community of Pakistan that between ten and twenty decisions made by the Cornelius court are defining events in the development of constitutionalism. I have selected eleven of these which I shall call the 'Eleven Cornelius Greats'. Nine of these decisions are summarized here. The remaining two (the *Snelson* and *Mehrajuddin* cases) are dealt with later in this chapter. The earliest of these ground-breaking judgments was a brilliant fifty-three-page dissent in *Federation of*

Pakistan and another v. Maulvi Tamizuddin Khan (PLD 1955 FC 240). He asserted that assent by the Governor-General was not necessary to validate laws passed by the Constituent Assembly. This dissent became a basis for subsequent decisions limiting executive power over the legislature. In a nineteen-page dissenting opinion in *The State v. Dosso (PLD 1958 SC 533)* he elevated the position of Fundamental Rights by declaring that 'as essential human rights ... inherently belonging to every citizen of a country governed in a civilized mode' they could not be invalidated by martial law. He reaffirmed his *Dosso* dissent with a vigorous dissent of twenty-five pages in *Province of East Pakistan v. Mehdi Ali Khan Panni (PLD 1959 SC 387)*. In this case, he maintained that the constitutional guarantee of religious rights for non-Muslims and Muslims cannot be abrogated by martial law. This view was elaborated in subsequent decisions reaching an epitome in *Mohammad Afzal v. Commissioner of Lahore Division (PLD 1963 SC 401)* which established that the 'lawgiver' (martial law administrator) was not above the law. Two related decisions restrained the state from curtailing fundamental rights. In *Abul A'la Maudoodi v. Government of West Pakistan (PLD 1964 SC 673)* the state could not outlaw an association merely based on its opinion of that organization. The grounds for such action had to be stated and had to be objective, not subjective. Nor could citizens be detained merely because the state was 'satisfied' that detention was expedient in the public interest. That satisfaction must be based on reasonable objective grounds clearly set forth *(Ghulam Jilani v. The Government of West Pakistan PLD 1967 SC 373)*. Both Indian and Pakistani courts had followed a contrary doctrine of the British House of Lords in *Liversidge v. Anderson (LR 1942, AC 206)*. Cornelius' reasoning in the *Ghulam Jilani* case was subsequently adopted by the courts of both Britain and India. In *Faridsons Ltd. v. Government of Pakistan (PLD 1961 SC 537)* Cornelius re-asserted the principles that no man can be condemned without being heard and that justice must not only be done but must be seen to be done. In a related case, *(Zafrullah Khan v. Custodian of Evacuee Property, PLD 1964 SC 865)*, in which government attempted to seize evacuee property, Cornelius held that due procedural process must be followed and that justice must be seen to be done. The most important decision of the Cornelius court *(Mr Fazlul Quader Chowdhury v. Mr Mohd. Abdul Haque, PLD 1963 SC 486)* is as much a landmark in Pakistan's constitutional development as *Marbury v. Madison* was in the United States. The court upheld a brilliant judgment of the Dacca High Court, blocking an effort to obscure the distinctions between parliamentary and presidential forms. In so doing, it unequivocally established the principle of the inherent power of the courts to interpret the constitution and to review legislation for its constitutionality.

The nine cases briefly dealt with above certainly justify Hamid Khan and Nasim Hasan Shah's description of the Cornelius court. That 'golden period' established precedents which give strength and independence to the judiciary as it stands today. They had stunning impact on the jurisprudence of their time as well as an immediate operative effect on the conduct of government. I have not dealt at length with the complex legal reasoning of these cases, some of which are dealt with in the memorial lectures in the appendices to this volume. Further analysis in this chapter focuses on the broader social and philosophical issues raised by Cornelius in speeches and articles as well as in court opinions. From these latter, I have extracted subsidiary issues, often *obiter dicta*, which reveal his attitude towards the diffuse cultural and religious issues into which he was thrust.

While acknowledging the contributions of British rule, Cornelius consistently maintained that the Islamic character of Pakistan must be maintained and its indigenous institutions treated with respect. This did not mean a rejection of non-Muslim influences or institutions. On the contrary, a careful synthesis of western ideas and the values of Pakistan was to be achieved in a reciprocal relationship. This should not be a unilinear transaction; Islamic principles should be applied to western structures as well as the reverse. Attention should also be paid to the experience of other Muslim states.

He was impressed with the *Mujallah*, a comprehensive code drawn up in Turkey in the late 1800s, translated into English in 1901, and reprinted in Pakistan in 1967. In its comprehensiveness, it has been compared to the Napoleonic Code. An Arabic copy had been given to him in 1963 by the Iraqi ambassador to Pakistan. He noted with approval the use of *Shar'ia* courts in the Turkish empire and urged their establishment in Pakistan. He urged that something similar be done in Pakistan. [*Shar'ia* courts were established during the *Nizam-i-Mustafa* regime of Ziaul Haq 1977–88.] This would require an analysis of *Shar'ia* and the adjustment of British law to conform with *Shar'ia*. Extensive research would be needed and doctoral programs should be established in Islamic jurisprudence. The *Shar'ia* should be the dominant motif. It was his belief that 'the religious way of life carries the highest measure of hope for the living of the perfect life... This belief can also be found in a well recognized philosophy in Christianity which commenced with the well known saint, St. Thomas Aquinas.'[45] The notion of infusing western structures with Pakistani, hence Islamic, norms was carried a step further when Cornelius advocated translating the Fundamental Rights into Arabic, the language of the Qur'an. They (Fundamental Rights) would thus be 'invested with overtones of undeniable obligation...and their assimilation into the public conscience...greatly enhanced.'[46]

His defense of another indigenous Pakistani institution was eclipsed by the dramatic impact of the regnant issue in the case, i.e., the validity of martial law. The *Dosso* case was perhaps the most significant decision made during the martial law period of Ayub Khan—1958–69.[47] The case arose from a challenge to the validity of the Frontier Crimes Regulation, deemed to be invalidated by martial law annulment of the 1956 constitution. The Supreme Court validated the new martial law regime but re-asserted the paramountcy of fundamental rights which the annulment did not vacate. It was this aspect of the decision which made the *Dosso* case a landmark in Pakistan's history. Cornelius agreed with the majority opinion written by Chief Justice Munir and in a concurring opinion, which he later called a dissent, defended and lauded the system of justice indigenous to the tribes of the North-West Frontier Province. This was an institution known as the *jirga* which tried criminal cases by tribal elders without recourse to British law which was applicable to the rest of Pakistan.[48] The 'punishments awarded in the Frontier Crimes Regulation', he wrote in the *Dosso* dissent, 'certainly make a greater concession to principles of humanity than those laid down by the Penal Code in operation all over Pakistan.'

He favoured extending the *jirga* system beyond the tribal areas as a means of curtailing crime which existing British law had failed to control. He expressed this view at an Asian Chief Justices' Conference in Manila in 1963,[49] summarizing a longer analysis made in Rawalpindi in July 1962. The extension of the *jirga* system would repair the 'damage done to the national character during the period of subjection.' Quoting extensively from Sir Olaf Caroe's classic book, *The Pathans*,[50] he emphasized the need for a system of justice compatible with indigenous culture. His praise for the *jirga* was fulsome: 'for a *jirga* acting honestly there is no duty except that of ascertaining the truth by whatever means may be available to them, and there can be no doubt that in the Frontier areas, those means can hardly be confined with any hope of success within the rigid requirement of the law of evidence and the Criminal Procedure Code.'[51]

He expanded his appeal for extension of the *jirga* in an address in 1965 which gained more notoriety than any of his other views. The occasion was an address in Sydney before the Third Commonwealth and Empire Conference on Law. After recounting the astonishing increase in the crime rate in Pakistan, he praised the *jirga* system as a means of reducing crime. He then commented on punishment, expressing doubts regarding the utility of imprisonment. Noting the low crime rate in Saudi Arabia, he suggested a modern variation of the amputation of limbs as a deterrent. Amputation, he said, is not necessary. Medical science makes it possible to 'deprive a criminal of the use of a hand, or a whole limb by a small piece of surgery.' Use might be restored on 'proof of true reformation'.[52]

I was privileged to have heard about this view before it was presented in Sydney. Early in 1965, Cornelius invited me to tea at Faletti's hotel. He read me that portion of his address which dealt with this new variation of punishment and asked my opinion. I praised the effort to utilize traditional forms of justice such as the *jirga* system. I wondered if neurosurgery had yet found ways of temporarily immobilizing limbs and then restoring their use on a predetermined schedule. He thought this could be done. New techniques in bionics developed in 1997 suggest that he was prescient, although the high cost of such electronic implants casts doubt on the feasibility of their application. This unconventional view of punishment caused a sensation in Sydney. 'It was taken up', writes Cornelius, 'by the Sydney Press who attended all Sessions, with great vigour, being thought to be a callous and inhuman device, and there were photographs and articles on the subject in all the newspapers the following day. Explanations were sought from the Chief Justice by reporters, and the subject was one of the major topics dealt with in the Sunday newspapers on 29 August. It appears the matter aroused widespread interest, and the culmination was a television interview on the evening of 31 August, in a live broadcast...'[53]

His advocacy of the creative use of indigenous norms and institutions was not limited to the *jirga* and criminal law. The Islamic obligatory tax known as *zakat*, one of the prescribed five pillars of Islam, also received his attention.[54] He regarded *zakat* as having 'enormous human potential for communal betterment'. His scheme sought to adjust the principle to a modern money economy. Five-year *zakat* bonds were to be issued and the distribution of funds to charity would have to be modified. He noted that the twelfth century philosopher, Al-Ghazzali, and others had proposed criteria for allocation of relief funds. Cornelius found these acceptable but in a modern society eligibility on a voluntary basis is impossible to determine fairly.

To solve this, he advocated factually determined criteria carried out by government, following the pattern of welfare and relief administration in the United Kingdom and in other western countries.

Another venerable Islamic institution, *wakf*, received his careful attention and vigorous defense in 1959. The *wakf* is an endowment used exclusively for charitable religious purposes such as the support of mosques and welfare activities. In the *Mehdi Ali Khan* case involving East Pakistan certain *wakf* properties were taken over by the provincial government. The High Court of Dacca dismissed the plea that *wakf* were protected from such acquisition by the fundamental right in Article 18(b) of the 1956 Constitution. Chief Justice Munir, writing the opinion for the Supreme Court, decided on the same constitutional grounds as the *Dosso* case, i.e., that the acquisitions were valid because fundamental rights had been invalidated by martial law. Cornelius dissented in a brilliant thirty-page opinion reiterating some of the arguments used in his concurring opinion in the *Dosso* case. Both of the cases are renowned because they gave status to fundamental rights which transcended martial law and hence preserved those rights during periods of martial law until the present. But here we are concerned with Cornelius' defense of indigenous Islamic institutions. An important facet of the *Mehdi Ali Khan* case is that Cornelius based his dissent on tracing the history and defining the meaning of *wakf*. He cites a statement from Sayyid Amir Ali's *The Spirit of Islam*: 'That *wakf* is [thus] interwoven with the entire religious life and social economy of the Mussalmans.' Cornelius concluded that 'the expropriation of property vested in the Almighty, by any authority...is inconsistent with the paramount duty of submission to the Divine Will' and that 'as high as may be the authority of eminent domain, it lacks power to subject that which vests directly in the Almighty to secular uses.'[55]

At first tentatively, but later enthusiastically, Cornelius endorsed a plan for local government which was a modern version of the ancient institutions of *panchayat* and union councils in pre-Partition India. The decade-old experiment of Basic Democracies (1958–69) was initiated during the regime of Ayub Khan. The plan was a brilliant effort to throw off colonial and post-colonial intervention and to establish an indigenous polity. It attracted favourable attention world–wide and, had it continued, might have been a model for other developing countries. The system's potential for peaceful resolution of village disputes appealed to Cornelius. It is probably for that reason that he mentioned it briefly in his 1963 address on returning judicial responsibility to the people.[56] He did not give it as much attention as the *jirga* in his 1962 speech probably because it was as yet untested. In 1967, he waxed eloquent about Basic Democracies. In an address in Dacca he said that the key to understanding the full ethos and impact of the new 1962 constitution was Basic Democracies and that the constitution, deriving its power from the people, 'rests solely upon the Basic Democracies Order, 1959.'[57] He praised 'men of the people' who would be elected under this system. This scheme would do away with the election of people based on ancestry, wealth, or class 'conditions left behind by over a century of foreign rule.' Since the basic democrats elect to all higher offices, they will reflect the judgment of the people unaffected by 'television appearances, whistle-stop tours, or propaganda.' This was populist sentiment of the purest kind, sincerely meant and based on democratic political theory. The fall of the governments of Ayub Khan and his successors Yahya Khan and Zulfikar Ali Bhutto, the distractions of the 1965 war with India, the increased politicization of the system, and finally the secession of East Pakistan, brought about a drastic re-organization of the system. Local government ordinances, promulgated in 1979, consolidated arrangements made under the Basic Democracies Order of 1959. The electoral base was broadened and officials were elected directly instead of indirectly. With these changes the euphoric spirit of the 1959 Basic Democracy system faded away.

Though wedded to the idea of basing change on modification of indigenous culture, he was not oblivious to experimenting with different institutions based culturally in the west. In the 1960s some members of the legal community were receptive to *droit administratif* with its *Conseil d'Etat*, a concept which is the cornerstone of the French administrative and judicial systems. Nasim Hasan Shah, who had a *doctorat en droit* from the University of Paris, was a leading advocate of this manner of dealing with administrative law.[58] Cornelius called for serious study of the French system as early as 1959 and reiterated his interest in it over the next half decade.[59] Noting the decision in the British *Liversidge* case of which he disapproved, his lengthiest analysis of the French system was his 1960 address to the All-Pakistan Lawyers Convention in Karachi. A year later, he gave judicial cognizance to the idea in an *obiter dictum* in which he expressed 'regret that there is no procedure similar to that of French Administrative Law...[or] to a system of Administrative Courts which prevails in the United States.'[60] His droll comment in Letter 5[61] blames the prejudice of the English-speaking world towards the Napoleonic regime for failure to appreciate the virtues of *droit administratif*. The depth of his interest in the French system is suggested by the fact that he devoted at least eleven documented major addresses to it. Except for Islam, this topic received more attention by him than any other. Perhaps this was related to the issue of the writ jurisdiction which burdened the high and supreme courts with dockets almost impossible to clear without unconscionable delay. An administrative court system, modified to suit Pakistan, seemed a solution. The long and persistent advocacy for administrative courts finally bore fruit. Article 212 of the 1973 Constitution permits the establishment of administrative courts. The Supreme Court has appellate jurisdiction in cases involving a 'substantial question of law of public importance.'

His choice of institutions which might be adapted to Pakistan was judiciously selective. For example, he firmly objected to a proposal made at the 1965 Third Commonwealth and Empire Law Conference in Sydney for the establishment of a Commonwealth court of appeal. It was more than a question of sovereignty. He re-asserted the primacy of understanding the culture of Pakistan. He noted that the English delegates assumed that because English was the court language of Pakistan, English judges would have competence to rule on appeal. 'They could not', said Cornelius, 'appreciate that the currents of thought and feeling which now inspire our laws...could not be sensed by any person who was not fully familiar with the ideological and cultural background of Pakistan...We might as well have accepted a computer as our final authority.'[62] The chief justices of India and Australia also disapproved of the idea and it was dropped.

V

Writs, the CSP, and Chief Justice Kayani

While in administrative law A. R. Cornelius would have borrowed from the French, he supported with uncommon vigour the British institution of the writ jurisdiction as a fundamental power of the High Court.[63] Granted, the use of the writ was overwhelming the judicial system and needed to be facilitated by a network of administrative courts but until such change occurred, the writ jurisdiction would remain the principal bulwark against bureaucratic tyranny and the citizens' most effective recourse for the redress of grievances.

The issue of writ jurisdiction at both the emotional level as a popular symbol of liberty and in its legal dimension as an assertion of judicial independence and the right of judicial oversight of administration reached climactic heights in 1961. This was the trial in the Lahore High Court and the appeal in the Supreme Court of charges against the secretary of the law ministry, Sir Edward Snelson.[64] The case arose because of comments made by Snelson regarding the high courts and the writs. In the mind of the literate citizenry who followed the case with avid interest, the issue between what they regarded as an arrogant bureaucracy dominated by martial law and a sympathetic judiciary which was seen as a defender of liberty, was combined. It was all the more dramatic because Snelson was one of two remaining British members of the ICS, now CSP, in the central government and hence had become a symbol in the popular mind of the colonial bureaucracy of the British Raj. A bit of notoriety was added to the case by the fact that Sir Edward's first wife was the movie actress Greer Garson whose starring roles in such films as *Mrs Miniver* (which won seven Academy Awards in 1942), *Random Harvest* (1942) and *Goodbye Mr Chips* (1939) were well known and widely acclaimed in Pakistan. That Snelson was a Roman Catholic was irrelevant to the case but the ironic twist to it was that the appeal came before Chief Justice Cornelius.

The focus of attention was not Cornelius but rather the Lahore High Court Chief Justice M. R. Kayani, one of the most distinguished judges in Pakistan whose reputation was even more widespread among the masses than that of Cornelius. The High Court was better known because it was an old institution dating back to 1866 in British India. The Federal/Supreme Court in Pakistan was established after Partition in 1947. For nearly fifty years after Partition, the Supreme Court had no building of its own. It was first housed in cramped quarters in the High Court, an impressive building of a blend of Saracenic and Indian architectural styles, built in the 1880s. For a few years it was housed in temporary quarters in Rawalpindi. In 1994 it moved into a splendid new Supreme Court building in Islamabad. Originally, the Punjab Chief Court, its name was changed to Lahore High Court in 1919. [It underwent further name changes as the territorial structure of Pakistan changed. In 1955, it became the West Pakistan High Court and in 1970 became again the Lahore High Court which is the name it bears today.] The High Court, whatever its designation, was the visible monument to justice in the popular mind. The bulk of the work on writs was in the High Court which had original jurisdiction; the Supreme Court was an appellate court. Chief Justice Kayani was a celebrity as a speaker. From his installation as Chief Justice in April 1958, until his death in November 1962, he gave no fewer than fifty public addresses which became far more important commentaries on Pakistan's affairs than ordinary speeches. They were reported verbatim in both Urdu and English language newspapers. His use of allegory and parable drawn from Qur'anic and vernacular as well as western literature was easily grasped by the larger public. His sardonic wit and satirical style camouflaged his stinging criticism of martial law. To prove that he was not offended by it President Ayub wrote the preface to the first volume in the four volume collection of Kayani's speeches.[65]

The writ jurisdiction refers to the orders of *mandamus, certiorari,* prohibition, *quo warranto,* and *habeas corpus,* long used in British law. With these writs the High Courts may compel the executive to act or may restrain the executive from acting injuriously to rights judged to be of superior concern. They became the principal means of seeking redress for administrative wrongs and were used in Pakistan for all manner of grievances from contesting university test scores to appealing promotion issues in the public service. From 1955 to August 1962, nearly fourteen thousand writ petitions were filed in the two High Courts and many appealed to the Supreme Court. Pakistan became one of the most litigious societies in the world. The administrative branch found writs annoying and various efforts were made to curb the courts' power to issue them.

Kayani's defense of the writ jurisdiction made in dramatic public statements and embellished court opinions was unequivocal. His address at his installation as Chief Justice of the High Court of Lahore in 1958 emphasized this issue. '*Mandamus* and *certiorari,*' he said, 'are flowers of paradise and the whole length and breadth of Pakistan is not wide enough to contain their perfume.'[66] Nor was this his only metaphorical reference to the divine. Even though the Governor-General's use of the ordinance power in 1935 'laid' the writ jurisdiction 'low in the dust', it made no difference to the High Court 'For we thought', he concluded, 'that God fulfills Himself in many ways and that we are the humble instruments of his fulfillment.'[67] Thus he confirmed an earlier remark that 'the writ jurisdiction is the modern manifestation of God's pleasure and that God's pleasure dwells in the High Court.'[68]

Notwithstanding the greater attention which writs focused on the High Court, Cornelius also figured as their champion. His defense was more moderate and lacked the theatrical flair of Kayani's many public performances. Although he recognized that the High Court occasionally interpreted its use of the writs too broadly, he did not waiver in his support of them. Article 98 of the 1962 constitution eliminated the Latin terms for the writs which had been adopted from British law but a description, amounting to a definition of each writ, remained. Cornelius felt that this change from one-word labels to a 'long form of words' would probably not effectively curtail the court's exercise of the same jurisdiction the writs allowed under their Latin names. The High and Supreme Courts, after all, had the power to interpret the Constitution and it would be unlikely that 'earlier precedents would lose their value as guidance.'[69]

The *Snelson* case arose on the issue of the court's power to punish for contempt but it involved writ jurisdiction. Sir Edward gave an address to section officers in Rawalpindi in February 1960 under auspices of the Secretariat Training Institute in Karachi. The talk was printed in an official government pamphlet and distributed to court and other officials. The topic was 'The Transitional Constitution of 1958'. In these remarks, Snelson commented that the High Courts claimed a 'jurisdiction to interfere with the government itself without reference to the strictly defined frontiers of the prerogative writs...' thus leading to 'chaos, duplication, fraction, usurpation of function, uncertainty, and public confusion.' The High Court of Lahore found these remarks contemptuous and the Supreme Court concurred. Sir Edward Snelson was fined and the governor of the Punjab suspended the sentence. Sir Edward resigned and left Pakistan. Although the case focused on the courts' contempt power, the decisions, particularly those of the High Court, were a vigorous defense of the writ jurisdiction as a protection against bureaucratic excess.

A member of the elite ICS who transferred to the CSP in Pakistan, Cornelius had no great love for that service as it then existed. While I was chief advisor (1960–62) at the Civil Service Academy in Lahore, I discussed several issues of training of senior officials with him. I taught, for the first time in the history of the Academy, a seminar in Pakistan case law. Probationers were required to read High Court and Supreme Court decisions and brief them in class. Many of them had Pakistani law degrees but they had never read court cases at this level. Cornelius was enthusiastic about this innovation and arranged to furnish the Academy with a set of *Pakistan Supreme Court Reports (PSCR)*.[70] I augmented this acquisition with sets of the unofficial, though more current *All-Pakistan Legal Decisions (PLD)*. Another curricular subject we discussed was the course in equestrianism directed by an able retired *subadar* from the Indian army. Attendance at riding classes early in the morning was more strictly enforced than attendance at academic classes. In one of our conversations on this subject Cornelius dismissed this vestigial remnant of the British Raj with the quip: 'If we had elephants, they'd be taught to ride elephants.'

It was not without satisfaction that he accepted the onerous position of chairman of the Second Pay and Services Commission which was convened from 31 August 1959 to 28 May 1962.[71] In doing so, he followed in the footsteps of his illustrious predecessor Chief Justice Muhammad Munir who headed the First Pay and Services Commission of 1949–50. Cornelius had already publicly expressed his view that the civil service structure should be articulated to the political philosophy of the state. An address he made in 1961 was the first comprehensive statement relating political theory to administration made by an eminent public figure in Pakistan.[72] In that address, he criticized the lack of opportunity for personal growth in a civil service which was compartmentalized and caste-structured. The static nature of the system prevented advancement beyond a pre-determined level. The system violated the principles of the Objectives Resolution incorporated in the preamble to the 1956 constitution. He asserted that the 'rational test of equality for the determination of the status of two persons engaged in work of the same or equivalent character would appear to turn on the possession of necessary qualifications coupled with the capacity to produce results.' Without mentioning it by name, he was referring to the character of the CSP whose elitism, derived directly from the ICS, was created originally by the British for British officers and only slowly Indianized.

Cornelius' disdain for the CSP was well known long before the report of the Pay and Services Commission was completed in 1962. The inclusion of two CSP officers on the commission mitigated against the secrecy of its infrequent deliberations. The CSP Association was in effect a senior executives' union—an old boys' club—a powerful interest group. Its members held all the key positions in central, provincial, and local government. In 1961, the CSP cadre had 366 officers including the cabinet secretary, secretaries of most ministries, five ambassadors, the foreign secretary, four British officers, and eight justices of the Supreme and High Courts (M. Shahabuddin, Sir George Constantine, A. R. Cornelius, S. A. Rahman, J. Ortcheson, M. B. Ahmad, A. R. Khan, M. R. Kayani, S. A. Haq). In 1961, the Association's president was Chief Justice Kayani of the Lahore High Court. He succeeded Justice S. A. Rahman of the Supreme Court and was followed by Justice M. Shahabuddin, also of the Supreme Court. Cornelius was never seriously considered for this position which had great prestige but, of course, no official status. He was not active in the Association although he usually attended its annual formal dinners held at the Civil Service Academy at which, by tradition, the President of Pakistan or the Governor of the Punjab, was guest of honour. The views of CSP members were in 1961 divided roughly between old-line conservatives, i.e., the 106 officers who were in the pre-Partition ICS and the 260 younger officers who entered the service after

Partition. Mian Riazuddin Ahmad, who had joined the ICS in 1944 and was Commissioner of Co-operative Societies in 1961, was a mediator between the two groups. Not that the groups were widely divergent in their outlooks—they were not. The ICS transfers, trained in Pakistan by British officers and at Oxford or Cambridge, regarded themselves as guardians of the ICS 'steel frame' tradition. Chief Justice Kayani, though a Shia Muslim Pathan of the Bangash tribe from the town of Kohat in the North-West Frontier Province, was an outspoken advocate of this tradition. His identification with British values is suggested by his election in 1962 for a third consecutive term as president of the Association of Alumni of British Universities. Cornelius' ties were much more with the Punjab and Pakistan than with England. His sentiment for England was vaguely cultural and intellectual. There was no ancestral bond, although his wife lived in England from 1954 to 1960 while their two sons were pursuing their studies there. Cornelius identified himself somewhat more with younger reform-minded members of the CSP All were united, for self-preservation if for no other reason, in their belief that the CSP was an elite group whose destiny, inherited from the ICS, was to govern Pakistan. Virtually all were opposed to radical reform.

A hint of the attitude of the older group towards Cornelius, one of their own, can be deduced from a comment by Iftikhar Ahmad Khan, SQA, who was an ICS transfer to the CSP and in 1961 was Joint Secretary of Commerce. A devoted admirer of Kayani, he edited and managed the publication of Kayani's speeches. In the introduction to the third volume of speeches, he writes:[73]

The other outstanding member of the Civil Service who rose to the highest judicial office of the country was Justice Cornelius. However, what brought him distinction was talent of a different kind. Perhaps an analyst can throw some light on the psychological motivation behind his achievements. Being a Christian extremely well versed in European concepts which had shaped the development of civil and criminal law in this subcontinent he became an ardent advocate of

Islamic jurisprudence, and having attained eminence as a member of the Civil Service he came to regard it as anathema and made no insignificant contribution to is dissolution. While one [Cornelius] was an anguished voice of protest against the erosion of values, the other [Kayani] was a herald of popular sentiment and demands. There was, therefore, little in common between them. Justice Kayani was unpopular with authorities but was well loved by his people. Justice Cornelius was, however, popular with the authorities—and also to a degree with certain sections of the people.

Iftikhar's implication that Cornelius' advocacy of Islamic jurisprudence may have been because of his minority status may have been a view held by others but it was rarely articulated. I never heard it expressed. It is true that Cornelius and Kayani appealed to different audiences. It is also true that on the question of the CSP they were not in agreement. In the early 1960s the intensity of feeling about CSP reform bordered on hysteria and the blame was directed to Cornelius, who did not respond in rebuttal.

The depth of feeling about the drastic reforms advocated by the Cornelius Report was revealed in an acerbic address by Kayani at a dinner in his honour given by the CSP Association 29 October 1962 upon his retirement.[74] Brilliantly using the rhetoric of innuendo, satire, and sarcasm, he attacked not only the report but Cornelius as well. He ridiculed the report's criticism of corruption in the CSP: 'One might as well ascribe our misfortunes in cricket to the circumstances that the team was led by an officer who belonged to the Civil Service of Pakistan.' [Cornelius was president of the Pakistan Cricket Board]. He ridiculed obliquely Cornelius' support of the *Conseil d'etat*, Islamic ideology as an integrating force, and the opening of positions to non-CSP officials. Since the occasion was his retirement from the High Court, he was not restrained in his criticism of his colleague and judicial superior. He could not resist ending his address with a *coup de grace*: 'I should explain that after this speech had been written and typed, Radio Pakistan informed the people that government had not found it convenient to accept the report. On hearing this, one of my old colleagues told me at a dinner the same evening that my speech had leaked out.'

In many lengthy conversations I had with Cornelius and Kayani from 1960 to 1962, I did not detect any sentiment except mutual admiration on legal matters. All the public tributes of Kayani made by Cornelius reflect this feeling. In a memoir written for the first anniversary of Kayani's death, Cornelius quoted extensively from my laudatory evaluation of Kayani's work, an advance copy of which I had sent him and which was published the next year. He wrote, 'The praise, as we all know, is fully deserved. It stands out that in the estimation of this foreign scholar, Mr Justice Kayani's speeches had "enhanced the esteem of the High Court".'[75] Cornelius praised Kayani as possessing the 'faculty of wisdom' which 'he laboured to outline...often by drawing perimeters around it in terms of absurdity.'

The two figures who emerged as national heroes during the decade of Ayub Khan's martial law (1958–69) were Cornelius and Kayani. Their careers intersected at many points although their paths veered on to slight detours. Kayani, born 18 October 1902 was six months older than Cornelius. Their terms as ICS probationers at Cambridge overlapped for a year (1926); Kayani was at Trinity College, Cornelius at Selwyn. There is no evidence of close friendship between them during this time. In letters to his brothers, Kayani mentions several of his Indian colleagues, especially S. A. Rahman who was his close friend and who later succeeded Cornelius as Chief Justice of the Supreme Court. Cornelius is mentioned only once along with several colleagues whose examination marks are listed. It is well known that Kayani suffered from asthma all his life and that his health was frail. His studies at Cambridge were interrupted by a stay at the King Edward VII Sanatorium in Midhurst from 23 November, 1926 until late April or early May 1927 (his letters are not clear about this latter date). He refers to his malady in his customary oblique manner: 'We are the elect of Heaven, or rather of tuberculosis, and appreciate each other better than people who have not suffered and therefore do not know how to sympathize.' He describes his condition more clearly in a subsequent letter: 'I should thank my stars for blessing me with tuberculosis which has been the indirect means of giving me an idea of Christmas.'[76] Cornelius is not known to have had any serious health problems.

Cornelius was in the judicial service longer than Kayani. Four years after his first posting in the ICS, he opted for the judiciary. Kayani waited eight years before transferring to the judiciary in 1938. Both served as district and sessions judges. Kayani also did a tour as legal remembrancer in the Punjab government. He was appointed to the High Court in 1949 and was its chief justice from 1958 until his retirement in 1962. (Mandatory retirement age for High Court judges was 60 years of age; for Supreme Court judges 65 years of age). Less than a month after his retirement, he died—at age 60—in Chittagong where he had gone to deliver an address. Although his experience on the High Court was limited to thirteen years, his impact on the judicial system was remarkable primarily because of his robust defense of the writ jurisdiction epitomized in his judgment in the *Snelson* case.

Kayani attained heroic stature less for his opinions than for his speeches which, while not openly defying martial law, gently ridiculed it by wit, satire, innuendo, and double entendre. His bachelor's degree in Persian and his master's degree in English from Government College seemed to resonate in his Persian, Urdu and English poetic and literary allusions. During this period, he was without question the most popular speaker in Pakistan often giving an address a week in places widely separated by more than a thousand miles.

Cornelius' career was almost entirely in the judicial service. He served a total of twenty-two years on the High and Supreme Courts. This tenure was interspersed by membership on commissions, frequent lectures abroad, and international assignments. In this respect, his career was less geographically circumscribed than Kayani's.

The style of these two jurists was markedly different. While Kayani was shy and self-effacing, these characteristics were offset by a powerful will, stubborn independence, and irrepressible wit. His speeches seemed to ramble from one digression to another, from parable to aphorism, from poetry to sacred scripture yet the final impact was stunning. His points were made while keeping the audience on the edge of their seats and quoting him for days afterward. Cornelius captured the essence of the Kayani style when he described it as wisdom within the perimeters of absurdity. Both jurists led simple, austere lives. Both were deeply religious, of impeccable character, untainted by the faintest hint of challenge to their probity.

Cornelius' style was one of *gravitas*. His decisions were long and erudite, rarely leavened by any trace of humour. Occasionally, a bit of dry wit would intrude—so dry as to escape the notice of all but the most discerning. Such was his sardonic comment that the British were reluctant to consider *droit administratif* because of their repugnance to anything Napoleonic. But the brilliance of his opinions—both dissenting and majority— is confirmed by their impact on Pakistan's constitutional history as the memorial lecture by Chief Justice Nasim in Appendix 18 in this volume makes clear. His public addresses made up in profundity what they lacked in theatricality. They were carefully written in advance, presented in perhaps too sober a style; the thesis flowed smoothly along a neatly crafted channel of reasoning. Just as the study of Persian and English may have influenced Kayani's eloquence, so science and mathematics, in which Cornelius excelled, may have affected the structure of his reasoning.

Although working separately with no interpersonal contact whatever, they made a remarkable team during the Ayub decade. In different ways, they softened the hard edges of martial law and preserved an ethos of judicial rationality which helped the nation through successive constitutional crises at least until 1973.

Certainly, on legal issues Kayani and Cornelius were very much in agreement, especially in cases involving the contempt power, the writ jurisdiction and natural law. Rarely did the Cornelius Supreme Court overturn judgments of the Kayani High

Court. In some instances, most notably in *Khwaja Ghulam Sarwar v. Pakistan (PLD 1962, SC 142)*, Kayani's dissent in the High Court was supported on appeal by the Cornelius Supreme Court. To be sure, the parameters of authority for issuance of writs by the High Court were redefined in the opinion Cornelius wrote in *State of Pakistan v. Mehrajuddin (1959, 1 PSCR 34)*. This limited the issuance of orders and directives to the five standard writs in English law. Not even Kayani, contentious though he was, was disturbed by this judgment. In his inimitable style he said: 'Sometimes we deliberately make mistakes in order that the Supreme Court may correct them and out of the hundreds of cases that we have disposed of, the number of lapses can be counted only on our fingers.'[77]

As old-line ICS/CSP officers retired from service, Cornelius' views on the CSP faded into the shadows. His reputation in the legal community for his acumen, fairness, erudition, and independence was scarcely affected by those views. While his report compounded the antagonism of the CSP, it increased his popularity among the much more numerous non-CSP government workers and in the legal and business communities. That he was highly regarded by educators is suggested by the fact that the University of the Panjab awarded him the honorary Doctor of Laws degree in 1956. The esteem with which the government of Ayub Khan held him is evidenced by his decoration in 1967 with the *Hilal-i-Pakistan*, the highest civil award given by Pakistan.

When combined with his repeated proposals for creation of administrative courts, the Cornelius Report's advocacy of internal democratization of the bureaucracy struck sharply at moral, philosophical, and legal premises on which the system was based. The report was classified as secret and was not released for discussion by the National Assembly. Its more drastic recommendations were not accepted by President Ayub who was against radical change in the existing system. Continuity should be preserved, he said, 'in the functions and organization of the public services, which have grown in time and become familiar to the people ... and nothing should be done which might involve the risk of disrupting the administrative fabric.'[78]

The Cornelius Report, somewhat less revolutionary than anticipated, was radical enough to compel the two CSP members out of a total of twelve, to issue a minute of dissent. The majority report, if implemented, would have broken the monopoly of the CSP. It also would have elevated the value of technical training and managerial experience, hence reducing the worth of the generalist administrator. The ethos of the whole bureaucratic system would, as Ayub Khan feared, have been completely changed. These changes were made ultimately during the more radical governments of Zulfikar Ali Bhutto and Benazir Bhutto when the People's Party of Pakistan was politically dominant. The classification system of the entire civil service was made less rigid. The designation CSP was abolished and replaced by District Management Group (DMG). The CSP Academy in Lahore became the DMG Campus. The entrance age was raised from the twenty-four years to admit older, more experienced candidates. As a result, many of the trainees already had technical education in engineering, medicine, accountancy, law, and business. Women were admitted to competitive examination. Equestrianism continues to be compulsory; even though the elephants facetiously referred to by Cornelius have not yet arrived.[79] Ironically, Cornelius' ideas were blocked by a president whom he greatly respected. They were put into effect, *mutatis mutandi*, by regimes much less favourable to him.

VI

Islamic Justice

Justice, like community, is one of the central tenets of Islam. Mona Abul-Fadl refers to it as the 'goal and propellor of Muslim consciousness'.[80] The pursuit of justice, she points out, is a duty incumbent on the community as a collectivity. If it is not discharged by the agents of the community, it then becomes a personal responsibility of every Muslim. The source of justice is transcendental, its details changing within differing spatial and temporal contexts but there are some constants, two of which are equality and compassion. One of the most systematic elaborations of Islamic justice by Cornelius is found in an address delivered in 1977. With extensive quotations from the Qur'an and scholars such as Shah Waliullah, he concludes that 'the people of Islam can take just pride in the thought that their judicial system was placed from the beginning on lines that in substance are no different from those of the best systems of today. Compared with other prevalent systems, it was distinguished by a higher degree of humanity towards criminals, even towards prisoners taken in religious wars, and a deeper understanding of the basic needs of human beings.'[81] The two constants which predominate, compassion and equality, should lead to an equilibrium in social relations and economic status. That is, compassion for all humans should tend towards greater equality in the distribution of societal goods. Equality also must prevail in the standing of all persons before the law. Cornelius linked the two characteristics which was in consonance with the canonical Islamic concepts of *adal* (Justice) and *ehsan* (compassion, kindness, forgiveness, mercy) and with the institution of *zakat* to which he attached importance as a wealth redistributive mechanism.[82]

The tempering of justice with compassion and equality is a dominant theme in Cornelius' way of thinking. While its derivation is unequivocally Islamic philosophy, it is coloured by the unique experience of Pakistan's creation *de novo* as a Muslim state. The quarter of a century during which Cornelius served in Pakistan's judiciary was a period of acute political disequilibrium and social trauma. No other new nation attaining post-colonial independence after 1947 suffered the institutional discontinuities or the shredding of the social fabric which Pakistan experienced. It took longer than any other new nation to approve a constitution in 1956—fully nine years after independence. During the time that Cornelius lived, the country had three different constitutions. Its territorial structure—the crucial relationship of space, power, and culture—was re-arranged three times: from five provinces to two, then again to five, and with the secession of East Pakistan, to four. Its political structure wavered from a parliamentary to a presidential system, then back to the parliamentary which is the form existing today. In between, there were futile attempts to combine the two systems. Simultaneously with these changes was an adjustment from a unicameral to a bicameral legislature. There was a long period in which both the legislative and political processes were suspended. These changes occurred in the context of more than a decade of martial law under Ayub Khan, Yayha Khan and, for a few months, under Zulfikar Ali Bhutto. During this period, there were three wars with India, including the only successful war of secession among new states in the post-colonial period. East Pakistan was lost but so was national confidence and faith in the capacity of Islam to sustain national cohesion. Further, few nations, with the possible exceptions of South Korea, Taiwan, and South Vietnam, experienced such a massive infusion of technological and economic aid from the United States or linked their foreign policy so closely with that country. Nor have many new nations been required to adjust their foreign policy to a multilateral set of relations coupled with a renaissance of Islamic connections once the futility of exclusivity with the United States was realized.

The transmigration of millions of evacuees—Hindus and Sikhs leaving for India and Muslims leaving India for Pakistan—created legal problems in property ownership. The absence of property records made for chaos. The absence of personnel records made it impossible to validate seniority and job assignment in the civil service which was the largest single employer. The determination of evacuee assets was Cornelius' first assignment in the new state of Pakistan. The human suffering resulting from such massive human displacement made an indelible impression on him. The newly formed bureaucracy was unable to cope with these crises. The judiciary was the most stable of all the institutions of government. By expanding the writ jurisdiction it sought to ameliorate the conditions consequent to Partition. Cornelius deplored the incapacity of the newly reconstructed Pakistani bureaucracy to deal with the human suffering consequent to the trauma of Partition. In the *Mehrajuddin* case, he could not refrain from observing that the government did not show proper regard for the needs of its employees. In the case of *Pakistan v. Abdul Hamid, (1961, 1, PSCR 1)* government refused to pay arrears in salary *ex gratia* to employees who had been re-instated by court order. In his majority opinion, Cornelius referred nostalgically to cases decided in British India by the Privy Council *(R. T. Rangachari v. Secretary of State, AIR 1937, Privy Council, 27; R. Venkata Rao v. Secretary of State, AIR 1937 Privy Council, 31)* in which it was affirmed that payment of arrears is the 'responsibility...and, their Lordships can only trust, will be the pleasure of the executive Government.' He summarized some twenty comparable judgments in which payment was urged *ex gratia*. He concluded with regret that conditions of bureaucratic responsibility and compassion alluded to by the Privy Council in 1936 did not prevail in the Pakistan of the 1960s. This required the judiciary to compensate by a sense of compassion and humaneness— attitudes set by Cornelius and resonating in both the Supreme Court and the High Court.

I made a major address on 9 May 1961 at the National Institute of Public Administration in Karachi,[83] in which I praised a recent speech by Cornelius in which he extolled the virtue of compassion. Referring to the difficulty of resolving claims of evacuee assets he said 'And where our hands have been tied by statute or we have otherwise acted in error, we can only hope that when we stand at the Bar ourselves, the same rule of forgiveness will apply to us as it is to the final saving of humanity.'[84]

Cornelius emphasized that the source of compassion as an element of justice was the Qur'an and sayings (*hadith*) of the Prophet (PBUH). He was impressed by the frequency with which *adal* and *ehsan* are mentioned in the Muslim scripture. There are two Qur'anic verses which clarify the meaning of *ehsan*. (Both are from the Yusuf Ali translation of the Qur'an). Perhaps the clearest is from the *Al Maidah Surah 5:45*: 'We ordained therein for them: life for life, eye for eye, nose for nose, ear for ear, tooth for tooth, and wounds equal for equal. But if anyone remits the retaliation by way of charity, it is an act of atonement for himself.' Again in the *Al Shura Surah 42:40*: 'The recompense for an injury is an injury equal thereto (in degree) but if a person forgives and makes reconciliation, his reward is due from Allah.' These principles, Cornelius said, 'rest on the rule of forgiveness as pervading the structure of Islam and of justice among the people as conceived from the outset....I can give you case after case in which our Courts have approximated to that degree of compassion which is held up as the sign of justice in Islam.' Later, describing his own education to a university audience, he said, 'If I were to find a single word to express in itself the governing spirit of the institutions in which I received my education, I would choose the word "compassion". We lived in a world of morals...governed by a sense of social justice...not a matter of law, but of behaviour growing out of actual relationships in the course of living, moving and breathing in a community guided and illuminated by mutual compassion.'[85] Earlier, in a case upholding a somewhat dubious High Court decision which bent the statute, Justice S. A. Rahman of the Supreme Court wrote 'we find it impossible to withhold our sympathy from the unfortunate subjects whose desperate condition very probably inspired the initiative taken by the High Court.' (*Government of West Pakistan v. Fazal-e-Haq Mussarrat, 1960 PSCR 124*).

Chief Justice Kayani, to whom I had sent an advance copy of my May 1961 speech in Karachi emphasizing compassion, sent me a letter calling attention to the fact that he had quoted part of my speech at length in one of his own addresses.[86] He pointed to the necessity of tempeiing justice with mercy: 'Sir, I ask you to allow compassion and humaneness to inspire your government conduct. The quality of mercy is not strained and it is mightiest in the mightiest. If this is pointed out to you occasionally by the High Court, do not say that the High Court is causing headache to you over the public servant or any other section of society for that matter.' Kayani was obviously fond of the celebrated quotation from Shakespeare's *The Merchant of Venice*. He used it in several speeches and as a twenty-four-year-old ICS probationer at Cambridge University in 1926 referred to it in letters to his brothers.[87] Kayani ended his career on this same note of compassion. At the High Court Reference made on his retirement, he admonished his fellow judges and advocates, 'If the legal sense is not blended with the moral sense you cannot expect compassion and humaneness in Judges and these are qualities without which we are not very different from animals.'[88] It is delightfully ironic that Kayani, a Shia Muslim, supported the concept of compassion with the speech of Portia to Shylock (a Jew) in *The Merchant of Venice*—a speech reflecting Judaeo-Christian beliefs. On the other hand, Cornelius, a Roman Catholic, who had available a treasure of supportive Judaeo-Christian scripture, relied exclusively on Muslim sources. This is an intriguing paradox which illuminates the relationship of these three Abrahamic faiths.

There is little doubt that, as the *Snelson* case suggested and as Kayani admitted, the High Court expansively interpreted statutory law through the mechanism of the writ petition. In so doing, the governing principle was the Islamic concept of justice. The tone, if not set, was certainly supported by the requirements of compassion and humaneness strongly advocated by the Cornelius court.

VII

Quintessentials

This analysis of the religious premises of Cornelius' judgments is not intended to diminish the enormous contribution he made to the constitutional history of Pakistan. He made possible judicial review of both executive and legislative acts, buttressed the writ jurisdiction as a means of redress of grievance, elevated Fundamental Rights to a position above man-made law, clarified the concept of separation of powers, and placed the constitution in a sanctified position. Moreover, he demonstrated the ultimate power of the well-reasoned judicial dissent of which he was a master.

Beyond these constitutional developments but tightly intertwined with them, his intellectual contribution in the larger sphere lies in the interplay and synthesis of Islamic and non-Islamic values. Here we have the drama of a Christian judge functioning with stunning success in a Muslim society and becoming, at least intellectually, a heroic figure. Here was a judge who led a life so devoid of materialism as to suggest overtones of a Punjabi version of Tagore's *Santiniketan* or Gandhi's *ashram*. But his venue was neither cloister nor *mimbar*. It was, instead, the court based on English traditions, on Blackstone and Privy Council decisions, replete with bewigged justices addressed as 'Your Lordship'. The instruments for conveying his ideas were two: erudite, lengthy legal decisions threading through the fabrics of English and Muslim law, and a blend of both woven into the law of Pakistan. These were intelligible to only a few people well-versed in the arcane language of cross-cultural jurisprudence cast in English. The second was the public address, some seventy-five of which were delivered to sophisticated audiences in a culture and at a time when this was the country's most influential means of communication. In these transactions, English was spoken and understood, even though Cornelius urged the use of the vernacular and of Arabic. The range of his intellectual interests seemed to have no boundaries. His decisions included the usual citations to the case law of Pakistan but also embraced British, American, and Commonwealth law as well as philosophical and religious works. His addresses, and less often his decisions, referred to Napoleon, Churchill, Iqbal, *Mujallah*, de Gaulle, Aquinas, Rousseau, Aristotle, Maritain, Machiavelli,

Hobbes, Hegel, Leo XIII, Pius XII, the Talmud, Al-Ghazzali, and Confucius, to name but a few. These were not peripheral references—a form of name-dropping to lend external validity or prestige to an argument. On the contrary, they were usually vital to the core of the thesis and often, as in the addresses on the Turkish *Mujallah*, Confucius, and Iqbal, comprised the whole of the argument. He had great respect for Jewish learning, especially because of its emphasis on the Torah, the Talmud, and Hebrew as a living as well as a canonical language. He admired also the Jewish passion for justice and the capacity for abstract thinking. These virtues he attributed to a traditional system of religious education which he hoped Pakistan would emulate.[89]

But his weightiest reliance was on the Qur'an, *Sunnah*, and *Shar'ia* as well as on Muslim theologians. References to Christianity were few and usually marginal. His intellectual efforts demonstrate the permeability of cultural boundaries and especially the non-linear diffusion of norms and institutions. Indigenous values interact inevitably with exogenous influences but primacy must rest with an evaluation of the indigenous values. That re-evaluation must presume their superior validity. Institutional and attitudinal change thus becomes a reformulation of thought, a reconstruction of institutions in terms of new perceptions of the present and the future, and a receptivity of externally introduced norms. These norms must not be blindly accepted merely because of their novelty or modernity.[90]

Cornelius' epistemology is that of natural law, although he does not deal with it in a thorough, systematic, or even an explicit way. Admittedly, natural law is a difficult concept to grapple with. Both its origins and its definition have been debated for centuries. The dialectic, begun with Aquinas, John Calvin, Hugo Grotius and others, continues in our time.[91] The question is whether natural law as a body of ethical imperatives is derived from a supernatural source or from common patterns of behaviour recognized experientially as imperative. If the latter is thought to be the source then such a body of law, or pattern of behaviour, is autonomous and does not derive its validity from a supernatural source.

Certain features of natural law as defined by Thomas Aquinas in *Summa Theologica* have been central to Roman Catholic thought. Giorgio del Vecchio, a leading Italian natural law philosopher, conceives of it as a system of highest truths based upon common elements in man's nature. Other advocates of natural law, especially Victor Cathrein, move away from the metaphysical to the theological origins of natural law.[92] Thus the primary source is God; human law must correspond to this God-given law but cannot transcend it. This is the theory which undergirds the concept of 'unalienable rights' in American political thought. The equivalent is the doctrine of 'Fundamental Rights' incorporated in the Pakistan constitution by way of the Objectives Resolution and the constitution's preamble.

It is at this point that Islam and natural law (conceived as derivative from a transcendent source) intersect. The Fundamental Rights of Pakistan are derived from Allah revealed to man by Prophet Mohammed (PBUH), his final messenger. The Qur'an is its revelation, the *Sunnah* is a subsidiary source and the *Shar'ia* is the corpus of Islamic jurisprudence (canon law) which has accreted.[93] Cornelius reiterated this formula in many contexts. The *Shar'ia* becomes incorporated in the constitution to which all citizens must pledge allegiance. Whenever alien norms are reconstructed for consideration they too must correspond with *Shar'ia*. These Islamic norms must permeate the interstices of society and the law aided by the use of the scriptural language—Arabic.

He deplored the fact that lawyers and judges who litigate on the Fundamental Rights of the constitution do not draw inspiration from the Qur'an. He urged them to study legal Arabic and to expound before the court relevant Qur'anic sources.[94] The *Shar'ia* as a 'ground norm' is not a retrograde step. This false idea, Cornelius believed, comes from the secularization of English law.[95] The most dramatic implementations of this doctrine are the polities of Iran and Saudi Arabia. The latter denies that it has a man-made constitution and claims that its constitution is the Qur'an. Most other Muslim states, while not going to that extreme, have mechanisms to assure that man-made law is not repugnant to *Shar'ia*.

The ideas of Cornelius are more relevant thirty years later than they were when he propounded them. The new millennium ushers in an era of great hope for a mutual understanding of Muslim and non-Muslim values. In the real world, this potential is contorted by a residue of animosity generated by the half-century-old Palestinian problem, and this affects the ideational realm as well. The Catholic attitude towards Islam has changed markedly. There is a new sentiment which provides a philosophical underpinning and emotional climate which is encouraging a new partnership between the West and Islam. Louis Massignon is credited with having had enormous influence in the new Christian understanding of Islam. Georges C. Anawati OP, writes that in celebrating the richness of Islam, Massignon rediscovered his own Catholicism.[96] This is once again, confirmation of the congruence of the Islamic and Christian epistemes. Massignon emphasizes Abraham and the Virgin Mary as critical points of confluence between Islam and the Judeo-Christian tradition. Henri Corbin, the French scholar, is convinced that mysticism is the most profound element in all religious thought and is hence the nexus between Islam and Christianity.[97] James Bill and John Williams in analyzing Shia Islam and Catholicism point to sainthood, martyrdom, the 'organic-statist model of government', [i.e., based on natural law] and the respect accorded Mary and Fatima as points of congruence.[98] These are but a few examples from a rich and fast growing literature illuminating the relationship of the two faiths. The papal encyclical, *Ecclesiam Suam* (1964), the Vatican II documents *Lumen Gentium* (1964), and *Nostra Aetate* (1965) clearly established this new Catholic respect for Islam. It was *Nostra Aetate* which set forth this relationship most clearly and fully:

The Church has also a high regard for the Muslims. They worship God, who is one, living and subsistent, merciful and almighty, the Creator of heaven and earth who also has spoken to men. They strive to submit themselves without reserve to the hidden decrees of God, just as Abraham submitted himself to God's plan, to whose faith Muslims eagerly link their own. Although not acknowledging him as God, they venerate Jesus as prophet, his Virgin Mother they also honour, and even at times devoutly invoke. Further they await the day of judgment and the reward of God following the resurrection of the dead. For this reason they highly esteem an upright life and worship God especially by way of prayer, alms-deeds and fasting. Over the centuries many quarrels and dissensions have arisen between Christians and Muslims. The Sacred Council now pleads with all to forget the past...

It defines the points of congruence and, in the last two sentences, sets the tone for the future. These views are buttressed by a new attitude towards missionary effort set forth in *Ad Gentes* (1965) and *Evangelii Nuntiandi* (1975). *Redemptoris Missio* (1990) calls for inter-religious dialogue and understanding of recipient cultures for which the term 'inculturation' is used. This new attitude has been elegantly summarized by Pope John Paul II in his book of essays *Crossing the Threshold of Hope*[99] and is reflected in the policies of mainline Protestantism in the United States. John Paul II's admiration for some aspects of Islam is not without reservations. He deplores the militancy and tendency to violence of fundamentalism and is reported to have said that Islam 'teaches aggression' and 'is a religion that attacks'.[100]

Quite apart from theological complementarities there is also an increasing awareness of compatibility of views of Islam and Catholicism on many social issues. In 1994, Catholics and Muslims united in blocking sex education policies in public schools of New York City. The Vatican attempted to forge a similar united front with Islam to defeat birth control provisions in the programme document adopted at the United Nations international conference on population and development held in Cairo in September 1994.[101] Although a remarkably vigorous campaign was launched, it was not a total success. The stumbling block was the issue of abortion. Ironically, the Vatican's nemesis was a Muslim woman, Dr Nafis Sadik from Pakistan. A gynecologist, she met with the pope in her capacity as undersecretary of the UN Beijing conference. On the issues of abortion and birth control, there was no meeting of the minds. Bernstein and Politi report that Dr Sadik left the audience feeling that the pontiff was 'hard-hearted...dogmatic, lacking in kindness.' While the pope had Islamic doctrine on his side, he was not able to convince the key conference organizer who represented western and perhaps even Muslim feminist views. Again, the Vatican sought a partnership with Islam seeking to influence the UN Conference on Women held in Beijing in 1995. While the collaboration was successful the end result was not. Despite these setbacks, Muslim and Catholic views on social issues are very much alike. In a meeting 7 October 1997 with Italians in Badova, Italy, the secretary-general of the Muslim World League stated that Muslims and Christians stand together against atheism, immorality, social corruption, injustice, and discrimination and that they should work in partnership to combat these and other social ills. Apart from clearly defined theological and ecclesial differences and strictures against capital punishment, devout Muslims would feel comfortable with the social doctrines of John Paul II's encyclicals, *Redemptor Hominis* (1979) and *Evangelium Vitae* (1995).

The opening in 1995 of the largest mosque in Europe in Rome in the shadow of the Vatican symbolizes this new relationship. Another event of enormous symbolic significance was the meeting in Rome 12 September 1997 of the Supreme Pontiff and the Second Deputy Prime Minister of Saudi Arabia, Prince Sultan. This was the first time that a senior member of the Saudi royal family met with the head of the Roman church. This reversal in the attitude of antagonism which existed from the time of the Crusades in the eleventh and twelfth centuries is truly epochal. Perhaps if Dante Aligheri were writing today, his view of Islam would be quite different.

A strong sense of fraternal bonding of all Muslims has been one of the quintessentials of Islam. It has been both a fantasy

and an ideal but seldom a reality in Muslim history following
the Prophet's (PBUH) death in AD 633. The quest for community
expressed in the concept of *ummah* (community of believers),
continues to be given rhetorical expression in contemporary
Muslim affairs. It's mention in the Qur'an several times gives it a
sacral, canonical status. It emphasizes putting the community
good above personal desire and in directing the community
towards virtue and away from evil. There are several levels of
community solidarity. *Ummah* is the architectonic idiom whose
purpose ultimately is to embrace all mankind. It is the external
structural manifestation of the tacit inner dimension—the soul—
of Islam. An inner circle is the commonwealth of Muslims
dispersed in a variety of territorial divisions: Islamic states (*dar-
al-Islam*), Muslim minorities in non-Muslim states (*dar-al-harb*),
Muslim refugees or stateless persons (*dar-al-muhajirin*). Circles
within these are tribal or clan groups, modalities (i.e., Sunni,
Shia) and populations in sub-national political units such as
provinces, cities, towns and villages. The sense of responsibility
to one or several of these circles of solidarity infuses the Muslim
psyche, even though it is imperfectly applied in real life.

   This primacy of community over individual rights is another
point of congruence particularly between Catholicism and Islam.
Bill and Williams point this out in their comparative study of
Shia Islam and Catholic thought, some of which is pertinent to
Pakistan as well. Pakistan is a predominantly (probably 70 per
cent) Sunni Muslim country. While not all features of *Shia* Islam
which are similar to Catholicism are characteristic of *Sunni* Islam
(e.g. clerical hierarchy, role of the *imam*, martyrdom of Hazrat
Ali (RA), devotion to saints) the concept of community is. Cornelius
acknowledged the special status of community unequivocally.
He credits the British introduction of common law for its
solidifying effect with other nations which came under British
rule and praises the Privy Council for the unifying influence it
had on the resolution of conflicting interpretations among those
countries. But that linkage was one of subordination to a foreign
imperial power. When colonial rule ended, the former colonies

were faced with the problem of injecting British jurisprudence with Islamic ideals of equality and social justice. It was necessary to transfer loyalty from the community of British law to a community of Islamic law. The solution lay in linkages with other states where *Shar'ia* governed.[102] At a national, rather than at an international level, 'importance is primarily given to human communities, their integrity, security, welfare and progress.' The rights of individual members must be consonant with the cohesion and health of the community, 'the individualistic colour is absent'. All humanity is composed of such communities. 'Without minimizing the importance of each community, paying attention to the welfare of individual members, the obligations of these members to the community must certainly rank higher.'[103]

While the polities of most Islamic states aspire to epistemological integrity, they are thwarted by several factors. The modern Islamic state with universal suffrage is twisted into a deformed caricature by non-Islamic and often anti-Islamic values from the West and from within. The cultural/commercial imperialism described earlier enmeshes Islamic polities in a web of dependency from which escape is almost impossible. This has occurred at the very moment in history when the system is trying to reshape its warped contours resulting from the imposition of colonial forms. The Islamic predicament is particularly poignant because it is governed to a large extent by the irrepressible effervescence of Islam. Reaction to these difficulties may be an internal secularizing revolution (as in Turkey) or an internal revolution in which militant iconoclastic Islamist forces deliberately seek confrontation with the West regarded as the great Satan. The result is sometimes a defense of indigenous Islamic culture by a retreat to a real or imagined idyllic past or it may be capitulation to the exogenous juggernaut, or a combination of both. Any one of these responses creates formidable obstacles to the refashioning of Muslim national identities.

VIII

Conspectus

The legacy of Cornelius is greater than his impact on the constitutional development of Pakistan. It is testament to the fact that recipient cultures are not necessarily simpler or more passive than those which radiate by means of colonialism, superior technology, or cybertronic competence. It is an example of interactions of norms and institutions among civilizations. These interactions cannot accurately be described by the geological metaphors of fault lines or plate tectonics. Such a metaphor connotes massive shifts in earth's mass which demetaphorizes into social cataclysm or civilizational clash.

Civilizations are delineated by permeable membranes which filter norms, institutions, and behaviour circularly rather than in a unilinear fashion. There is no unilinear progression which follows a route from West to East or from East to West. We must not think in terms of transfer of ideas and norms because transfer is a unidirectional term connoting movement from a radiant source to a recipient system. We must think, instead, in terms of global diffusion rather than transfer. The quality and rate of diffusion through the delineating membranes depending on the viscosity of the substance being filtered, the force of radiation, and the absorptive quality of the recipient culture.[104]

In the case of Pakistan, the radiating source for more than two centuries has been the British Raj. It had the authority of physical power and, despite the enormity of its positive influence on India, had a demeaning effect on the recipient culture. For the last half century, this political colonialism was replaced by a cultural imperialism. It was not deliberately imposed as such, but rather was the inevitable consequence of the dynamics of global commerce, cybertronic communication, and national (particularly American) hubris. These forces are accelerated by widening differences in the technological competence of recipient and radiating nations sustained by corresponding differences in national wealth. This circular relationship between cultures is also affected by the intellectual qualities of leadership in the recipient system. That intellectual quality must be capable of assessing the value of radiating ideas as well as determining the value of traditional, endogenous ideas. From such evaluation, constructive amalgam must emerge. Pakistan and Cornelius comfortably fit this construct. The intellectual leadership of such men as Cornelius and Nasim Hasan Shah was capable of blending the new (such as *droit administratif*) with the endogenous (such as *Shar'ia* and its related institutions such as *wakf* and *jirga*). This was a process which was intellectual within the ambit of jurisprudence, relatively insulated from politics. The process of transmission (radiation and receptivity) of ideas and norms can be understood only if we distinguish, as Oswald Spengler did, between culture and civilization.[105] Culture embraces the inward-dwelling, tacit dimension, the aesthetic continuum, the soul of a people. Civilization consists of artifacts, institutions, structures, technologies. The elements of culture and civilization are diffused at different rates of speed and with different force. Culture lags behind civilization in this process of diffusion. Thus television may be quickly introduced but the acceptance of the substance of its programme content may be delayed or even rejected. There are factors of impedance and facilitation in the acceptance of these radiating elements. Where there is a highly developed endogenous culture which is diffused throughout society and sustained by a coherent body of belief codified in scripture and interpreted by persons of learning and wisdom the intrusion of a radiating culture may be impeded. It may at least be delayed long enough for an integrated whole of the endogenous and the exogenous to be formed. This is the theoretical explanation of the plight of Pakistan and of other Muslim societies. The flow of technological innovation is facilitated by cultural exchange of intellectual leaders (Cornelius, Kayani, Qasuri, Qari, Patel in England; Salam in England and the United States; Nasim in France) and by cybertronics of communication but the culture of the radiating society meets resistance. Attempts to impede the diffusion of culture are often frantic and in vain for the values of culture cannot be completely separated from the artifacts or structures of civilization. They may flow through the membrane at different speeds and intensity or may blend together in mixtures indiscernible to the recipient system. Every institutional and technological item is encased in a penumbra of epistemological premises as well as attitudinal and behavioural postures from which it cannot be detached. The confrontation of an endogenous value system with new radiating sources may elicit submerged or depressed values equivalent to those which generated the new institutions in their original milieu. This is precisely what happened in Pakistan. The British institution of the writ gave new life to the scripturally validated endogenous Islamic concepts of *adal* and *ehsan*. The concepts merged with the structure. This occurred instinctively, without recourse to this rather abstruse theoretical construct. It was guided by the intellectual leadership of jurist-statesmen like Cornelius, Nasim Hasan Shah, Kayani, and others.

The problem of reconciling endogenous values with values emanating from radiating, external sources is epitomized in the issue of human rights. This problem was dealt with by Cornelius implicitly in almost all his speeches and explicitly in three speeches found in Appendices 15, 16 and 17 in this volume.[106] The relentless campaign by private interest groups to compel all nations to apply the Universal Declaration of Human Rights in the same manner is particularly vexatious to Muslim countries. That they derive from nature or God is axiomatic in Islam and in Christian interpretations of natural law. Their very transcendence over earthly law affirms their universality for humankind. Nevertheless, the specific application of such norms raises enormous philosophical and practical problems. Earlier in this study, the co-operation of Muslim and Roman Catholic states in resisting some terms of the final declarations made by the Cairo conference on population in 1994 and the Beijing conference on women in 1995 has been described.[107] It is of some heuristic utility here to use the eight-part value construct first devised by Harold

Lasswell in 1950 and explicated and applied by him in a variety of contexts in a wide array of publications.[108] The eight Lasswellian values are suggested by his acronym—PEWBSARD which refers to power, enlightenment, wealth, well-being, skill, affection, respect, and rectitude.[109] The advantage of this construct is its potential for universal application since these values will be agreed to by all societies. The problem lies in filling in their skeletal generality with the specificity of local application. This is made difficult by several constraints. Respect, affection, and justice have different meanings in such disparate cultures as Sweden and Pakistan. The public display of nakedness or sexual activity, allowed under the rubric of freedom of expression, is reprehensible in a Muslim society. Islamic justice, which Cornelius praised as being superior to western justice, is based on retribution, punishment, tempered by compassion and on repentance rather than on sociological premises of rehabilitation. Moreover, it considers the victim of crime sympathetically. Should an Islamic system of justice give way to the forms of the United States or of Sweden? Ironically, western forms are slowly moving towards some of the Islamic principles, notably punishment and victims' rights. Cornelius did not succumb to western blandishments on these matters. Thus he praised the *jirga* system and proposed modifications in punishment for *hudood* crimes. Each of the eight *PEWBSARD* values will be similarly transformed by such endogenous values.

The specific content of each value may also be in a different rank order in the sequence of historical development of a polity. The relationship between political stability and unrestricted freedom typically poses this problem. It emerges in Pakistan in conflict over the contempt power of the courts. That power was invoked for the slightest criticism of the courts on the assumption that stability depended on respect for the judiciary and that neither the mass media nor a largely illiterate public could understand the reasoning of the courts. The freedom to publicly criticize judges and court decisions which prevails in the United States is intolerable in Pakistan.

Regnant values are rarely valid in all of society. Variations exist among geographic areas, ethnic, and religious groups. Hence tribal areas in Pakistan are subject to a criminal law different from that of the rest of the country—a situation approved of by Cornelius. Variations in family law of different groups outside Islam and modalities within Islam (*Shia, Sunni*) are judicially recognized.

The difficulty faced by Islamic states in adjusting the specificities of a universal value system to their own values is compounded by another factor. Devout Muslims perceive their values to be increasingly dissonant from those of western liberalism which seems to have lost its moorings in piety, morality, and ethics. This is what Cornelius meant when he commented that Americans in Pakistan were destroying its culture.[110]

Every condition of human existence (codified in such a formula as PEWBSARD) has its own scriptural inspiration and internal consistency. Each is part of a total epistemology and must be judged in part by internally generated criteria. Yet this is not the whole answer. Unless a state chooses isolation as did Myanmar or Albania, it must admit, consider, and integrate exogenous norms of its choice. That which is native is not always best. The loftiest tradition of scriptural values become corrupted with time. Muslim states' greatest challenge is the alternately harmonious and abrasive confrontation with the non-Muslim world. This confrontation is exacerbated by the juggernaut of both Muslim and non-Muslim cultural interventions. The integration of these forces into a viable polity is a daunting task. It must be dealt with on two levels: the political and the intellectual. Ideally, the latter should precede the former but this rarely, if ever, happens. Typically, the intellectual and political forces function unsynchronized both in time and with respect to subject. Cornelius laid the intellectual groundwork for the achievement of an integrated polity. The polity follows suit asymmetrically with respect to subject and spasmodically with respect to time.

I first used a metaphor of Oswald Spengler in a paper written in 1977[111] which Cornelius kindly read and to which he refers in Letter 9 when he mentions the 'world cavern of Spengler's imagery'.[112] Spengler wrote that the Islamic community (*ummah*) 'embraces the *whole* of the world cavern, here and the beyond, the orthodox and the good angels and spirits, and within this community the State only formed a *smaller unit of the visible side*, a unit, therefore, of which the operations were governed by the major whole.'[113] This is the episteme of natural law, at least in its theological interpretation. The visible part of humankind is but a small part of the whole cavern which includes the invisible. In Islam, the invisible is the universe of Allah; the connection with the visible is the Qur'an, and the *Shar'ia*. In the case of Pakistan, Cornelius would assert the continuum is made intact by the constitution and by its faithful observance by the citizenry. Non-Muslims living within its sphere of validity do not break the continuum for their own beliefs are subsumed under the rubric of the universality of Islam.

Cornelius has shown both by the example of his career and by his jurisprudence and philosophy that it is possible to achieve reconciliation and harmony in a society which includes non-Muslims. His letters in Appendices 1–9 attest eloquently to this. The clash of Islam and the West is not inevitable. He called attention once again to the common origins of human freedom in an analysis of the philosophy of Sir Muhammad Iqbal: 'I refer only to the two famous encyclicals, the first by Pope Leo XIII ... *Rerum Novarum* and the second by Pope John XXIII, *Pacem in Terris*. The curious will find in these notable documents much in direct parallel with the fundamental rights with which they are familiar.'[114] Three problems remain: Muslim states must achieve internally a transcendence of Muslim values over obscurantism, iconoclasm, and terrorism. Externally, they must manifest enough pride and strength to thwart the incursion of destructive non-Islamic values and they must have the courage and wisdom to examine non-Islamic norms and adapt them when advantageous in accordance with the tradition of their civilization. Construction of an ideological framework has been helped materially by Cornelius' effort. Samdani astutely characterized Cornelius as 'a man always at peace with himself'. This was possible because he understood the relationship of the visible and invisible worlds as a believing Christian; he also accepted the episteme of Islam. Indeed, his son Michael reports that in his later years Cornelius developed an ever-deepening affinity for Islam as a religion and culture. It may well be that the Islamic component of his thinking was the structure to which the Christian elements were attached. In this respect, Chief Justice Shahabuddin was correct, Cornelius was more Muslim than the Muslims and he sought to make the new state of Pakistan resonate with that episteme. In so doing, he reached in his philosophy for a transcendence of ideas common to two religions. In his jurisprudence, he sought to give that transcendence meaning in the affairs of statecraft.

NOTES

1. From 1951 to 1956, the Supreme Court was called the Federal Court.
2. Letter 3, 3 July 1965.
3. 'An Account of the Third Commonwealth and Empire Law Conference' held in Sydney, Australia from 25 August to 1 September 1965. *All-Pakistan Legal Decisions* (Hereinafter cited as *PLD*) *PLD Journal*, pp. 172–78. No authorship is shown for this account. In a letter to the author dated 18 October 1965 Cornelius said that he wrote 'accounts [of the Sydney and Canberra meetings] mainly from the Pakistan point of view, which have been printed in the October number of PLD.'
4. No mention of religion is made in the editorial or the news account in the *Pakistan Times*, 23 December 1991 or in the brief account in the *Pakistan Times-Overseas Edition*, 27 December 1991. The Full Court Reference of the Supreme Court made in his memory 9 January 1992 refers to him as 'the first non-Muslim Pakistani appointed on this highest post'. *Pakistan Law Journal (PLJ) 1962 Magazine*, 33–34. The Full Court Reference by Chief Justice Mahboob Ahmed of the Lahore High Court is not available. It's author does not recall mentioning this issue. Other tributes referred to in notes 21, 25, 38, 39, 40 are similarly silent. The Lahore bureau report in *Dawn*, 22 December 1991 makes no reference although the editorial on p. 3 of the same issue does.

5. 'Most Just Judge', typescript, undated. This copy was given to me by Chief Justice Cornelius. It appeared in the *Pakistan Times*, 31 December 1962 with the attribution 'Contributed'.

6. These postings can be found in annual editions of the *Gradation List of the Civil Service of Pakistan* from 1951 to 1966 published by the establishment division of the President's secretariat. For more detailed analysis see Ralph Braibanti, 'Public Bureaucracy and Judiciary in Pakistan', in Joseph La Palombara ed., *Bureaucracy and Political Development* (Princeton, NJ, Princeton University Press, 1963) pp. 360–440.

7. The awards conferred by the Government of Pakistan were: *Sitar-i-Pakistan* (SPk) and *Sitar-i-Quaid-i-Azam* (SQA) The British awards were: Knight of the British Empire (KBE), Order of the British Empire (OBE), Commander of the British Empire (CBE), Member of the British Empire, (MBE), Companion of the Indian Empire (CIE), Companion of the Order of St. Michael and St. George (CMG).

8. The reference here is to Article 32 of the Constitution of Pakistan which restricts the office of president to Muslims. The oath of office for president and prime minister prescribed by the Constitution includes an affirmation that the swearer is a Muslim and that he believes that Mohammad (PBUH) was the final prophet of Allah. This belief, commonly referred to as 'The Seal of the Prophet' is one of the Five Pillars of Islam. As such it is beyond questioning by the faithful.

9. There are conflicting estimates of minority size—some as high as 5 per cent and six million. The demographic data in this section relating to Christians, Parsis, and the Ahmadiyya are derived from tables in Charles H. Kennedy's article cited below, n. 17. These tables are based on: Board of Investment, Prime Minister's Secretariat, Government of Pakistan, *Table: Basic Facts – 1995* (Islamabad, September, 1995); Government of Pakistan, Population Census Organization, Statistics Division, *1981 Census Reports of Provinces* (Islamabad, Census Organization, Printing Press, 1984); Government of Pakistan, Public Administration Research Centre, O/M Division, Cabinet Secretariat, *Federal Government Civil Service Census Report – January 1983* (Islamabad: Bergson's, 1984) and by the same organization and publisher, *First Census of Employees of Autonomous/Semi-Autonomous Corporations/Bodies Under the Federal Government* (1986).

10. See Joseph Cardinal Cordeiro, 'The Christian Minority in an Islamic State—The Case of Pakistan', in Kail C. Ellis, OSA ed., *The Vatican, Islam and the Middle East*, (Syracuse, NY, Syracuse University Press, 1987) pp. 279–95.

11. Dr Robert A. Bütler, SJ *Trying to Respond: Essays and Reviews on Islam, Pakistan and Christianity* (compiled and edited by M. Ikram Chaghatai) (Lahore, Pakistan Jesuit Society, 1994), p. 327. See also Rev. Dr Charles Amjad Ali, ed., *A Look Towards the Mountains: A Report on the Two Consultations on the Role and Future of the National Council of Churches in*

Pakistan...1993 (Rawalpindi, Christian Study Centre, 1993) and *Whither the Church in Pakistan?: A Report on the Consultation of the National Council of Churches in Pakistan...1994* (Rawalpindi, Christian Study Centre, 1994).

12. Mlle. Daphine Menant, *The Parsis*, being an enlarged and copiously annotated, up-to-date English translation of Mlle. Daphine Menant's *Les Parsis*, translated by M. M. Murzban (Bombay, Danai, 1944, 2 vols.). Quotation in Vol. I, 9. This valuable, encyclopedic work was first published in Paris in 1898. See also Piloo Nanavutti, *The Parsis* (New Delhi, The Delhi Parsi Anjuman, 1992).

13. Accurate demographic data on Parsis are complicated by several factors. The 1981 Pakistan census groups Parsis with Sikhs, Jews and Buddhists as 'Others'. Parsi marriage to non-Parsis, unless the father is a Parsi and the children have undergone ritualistic rites of passage, excommunicates the family. Yet the family may continue to call itself Parsi. See Dr Perin H. Cabinetmaker, *Parsis and Marriage* (Bombay, Samachar Press, 1991).

14. This novel was first published as *Ice-Candy-Man* (London, William Heinemann, Ltd., 1991), then as *Cracking India* (Minneapolis, MN, Milkweed Editions, 1991). Sidhwa's other novels are: *The Crow Eaters* (London, Jonathan Cape, Ltd., 1980 and New York, St. Martin's Press, 1981); *The Bride*, (London, Jonathan Cape, Ltd., 1983 and New York, St. Martin's Press, 1983); *An American Brat* (Minneapolis, MN, Milkweed Press, 1993).

15. Full Court Reference, *PLD 1976 Journal 40*.

16. Dorab F. Patel, *The Third Cornelius Memorial Lecture, 23 December 1995*. Appendix 20.

17. This problem is well described in Charles H. Kennedy, 'Towards the Definition of a Muslim in an Islamic State: The Case of the Ahmadiyya in Pakistan', in Dhirendra Vajpeyi and Yogendra Malik, eds., *Religious and Ethnic Minority Politics in South Asia* (Delhi, Manohar Press, 1989), pp. 71–108.

18. Government of the Punjab, *Report of the Court of Inquiry Constituted Under Punjab Act II of 1954 to Enquire Into the Punjab Disturbances of 1953*. (Lahore, Superintendent, Government Printing, 1954).

19. See Tayyab Mahmud, 'Protecting Religious Minorities: The Courts' Abdication', in Charles H. Kennedy and Rasul Baksh Rais, eds., *Pakistan 1995* (Boulder, CO, Westview Press, 1995).

20. Hamid Khan, *Eighth Amendment: Constitutional and Political Crisis in Pakistan* (Lahore, Rana Hameed Law Book House, 1995) pp. 110–12.

21. Zafar Samdani, 'Cornelius, a man always at peace with himself', *Dawn* (Karachi) December 22 1991.

22. Samuel P. Huntington, 'The Clash of Civilizations?', *Foreign Affairs* Vol. 72, No. 3 Summer 1993; pp. 22–49. This thesis appeared in expanded and slightly modified form in Huntington's, *The Clash of*

Civilizations and the Remaking of World Order (New York, N.Y., Simon and Schuster, 1996). For an extended analysis see Ralph Braibanti, *The Nature and Structure of the Islamic World* (Chicago, Ill., International Strategy and Policy Institute, 1995).

23. 'World Peace Through Law Movement', no date or venue of presentation given. (Haider, ed., cited below, n. 25; pp. 137–40).

24. These appeared as appendices in Ralph Braibanti, *Research on the Bureaucracy of Pakistan* (Durham, NC, Duke University Press, 1966) appendices 10–15, pp. 466–532.

25. S.M. Haider, ed., *Law and Judiciary in Pakistan by Mr Justice A. R. Cornelius*, (Lahore, Lahore Law Times Publications, 1981). This collection includes a forty-five page preface by Dr Haider which analyzes legal issues dealt with by Cornelius. It is a source for some of the texts of addresses cited in this essay. It is hereinafter identified as Haider, ed. Haider's doctoral dissertation was published as S.M. Haider, *Judicial Power and Administrative Discretion in Pakistan* (Lahore, All Pakistan Legal Decisions, 1967). Some of his analysis deals with decisions by Cornelius.

26. Government of Pakistan, *Report of the Pay and Services Commission* (Karachi, Manager of Publications, 1969) See also Masood Hasan and S. M. Haider, *A Review of the Cornelius Report* (Lahore, National Institute of Public Administration, 1970).

27. 'Justice of the People, By the People, For the People', *PLD 1963 Journal*, 39–43; quotation at 39.

28. Letter 8, 14 November, 1977. In this letter he refers to Max I. Dimont, *Jews, God and History* (New York, NY, Simon and Schuster, 1962).

29. Hamid Khan, 'In Memory of Justice (Retd) A. R. Cornelius—A Great Judge', *Pakistan Law Journal, (PLJ) 1992 Magazine Section 70–74*; quotation at 74.

30. Samdani, cited above n. 21.

31. 'An Account of the World Peace Through Law Conference held in Washington 12–18 September, 1965'. *PLD 1965, Journal, 179–184*. No authorship of this account is shown.

32. Ralph Braibanti and Associates, *Political and Administrative Development* (Durham, NC, Duke University Press, 1969). Cornelius' introductory remarks, 'Issues of Theory', were published in *PLD 1967 Journal, 105–113*.

33. 'Constitutional Conscience and System of Education', no date or venue of presentation shown. Probably given late 1967 or 1968. (Haider, ed., cited above n. 25; 152–60; quotation at pp. 154–5).

34. David Wise and Thomas B. Ross, *The Invisible Government* (New York, Random House, 1964). This book was an early exposé of CIA operations abroad. It was thought in Pakistan that it was distributed throughout the government by the Soviet embassy.

35. 'Working of the Supreme Court During the Year 1964 (an official report)' *PLD 1965 Journal, pp. 32–36.* No authorship given. Quotation at p. 36.

36. Letter 3, 3 July 1965.

37. 'Constitutional Conscience...', cited above, n. 33; p. 153.

38. Samdani, cited above n. 21.

39. Hamid Khan, cited above, n. 29.

40. Mr Justice Muhammad Ilyas, 'Foresight of Justice Cornelius', *PLD 1992 Journal, pp. 46–50.*

41. *Dawn,* editorial, 22 December 1991.

42. *Dawn,* Lahore Bureau report, 22 December 1991.

43. The Haider and Hamid comments are cited above, notes 25 and 29. Chief Justice Nasim's analysis is in *The First Cornelius Memorial Lecture December 24, 1993,* Appendix 18.

44. Dr Nasim Hasan Shah, 'A Salute to the Supreme Court (A Tribute to the Cornelius Court)' *PLD 1992 Journal,* 17–20. The Cornelius legacy lauded in this tribute is revealed further in Chief Justice Dr Nasim Hasan Shah, (edited by Professor Dr M. A. Mannan) *Judgments on the Constitution, Rule of Law and Martial Law in Pakistan* (Karachi, Oxford University Press, 1993).

45. 'Address to the Legal Aid Society, Dacca, March 12, 1964' *PLD 1964 Journal,* 125–132. This view was noted with approval in one of the few public references to Cornelius' religion. After observing that George Bernard Shaw called Islam the future religion of the world, Sh. Abdul Haque, a Lahore advocate, writes that 'we have now a clarion call from another Christian intellectual friend ... Cornelius (who) in spite of his obvious handicaps has called for the application of Islamic principles.' Sh. Abdul Haque, 'Plea for Practical Steps to Implement Qur'anic Laws' *PLD 1965 Journal, pp. 8–14.*

46. 'Leadership and Churchill: The Power of Language'. Address in Hyderabad, 13 February 1965. Appendix 11.

47. *The State v. Dosso and Another PLD 1958 SC, pp. 533–70.*

48. See Braibanti, *Research on the Bureaucracy of Pakistan* cited above, n. 24, esp. pp. 183–99 for a detailed analysis of the legal aspects of tribal governance.

49. 'Address at BNR Center, Asian Chief Justices' Conference, Manila, 25 June 1963'. *PLD 1963 Journal, pp. 58–66.*

50. Olaf Caroe, *The Pathans—550 B.C.—A.D. 1957* (New York, NY, St. Martin's Press, 1958).

51. 'The Legacy of Imperial Rule and the Restoration of National Character'. Address in Rawalpindi, 11 July 1962. Appendix 10;

52. 'Crime and Punishment of Crime'. A Paper Read at the Third Commonwealth and Empire Law Conference at Sydney, (Australia) 27 August 1965. Appendix 13.

53. 'An Account of the Third Commonwealth and Empire Law Conference held in Sydney, Australia from 25th August to 1st September 1965.'

PLD 1965 Journal, pp. 172–78; quotation at 174. No authorship is shown for this entry. In Letter 4, 18 October 1965 Cornelius said that he wrote 'accounts [of the Sydney and Canberra meetings] mainly from the Pakistan point of view, which have been printed in the October number of PLD.'

54. 'A Plea to Introduce *Zakat'*. Address in Peshawar, 2 May 1969. (Haider, ed., pp. 360–71).

55. *Province of East Pakistan v. Md. Mehdi Ali Khan PLD 1959 SC, 387*; quotation at 429. In this judgment, Cornelius aptly quotes from the illustrious Indian Muslim scholar, Sayyid Amir Ali (1849–1928) whose monumental study, first published in 1873, appeared in a revised and expanded 515-page edition under a new title, *The Spirit of Islam: A History of the Evolution and Ideals of Islam, with a Life of the Prophet* (London, Christophers, 1922). This was an enormously influential work, revised posthumously in 1935 and reprinted several times since.

56. 'The Legacy of Imperial Rule...' Cited above, n. 51. Appendix 10.

57. 'Constitution of Pakistan', address at the Pakistan Council for National Integration, Dacca, 15 June 1967, *PLD 1967 Journal, 78–90*.

58. Dr Nasim Hasan Shah, 'The Concept of Administrative Law' *Pakistan Times*, Part I, 18 January 1961; Part II, 19 January 1961. See also his 'Droit Administratif—A Study' *PLD 1964 Journal, pp. 45–54*. See also Hafizullah Khan, 'Administrative Law for Pakistan' *PLJ 1961, pp. 24–62*; Mushtaq Ahmad Khan, 'Administrative Tribunals and their Durability in the Legal System of Pakistan', *PLJ, 1961, pp. 116–25*.

59. The following addresses deal with administrative law and the writ jurisdiction. (H indicates they can be found in S. M. Haider *Law and Judiciary in Pakistan*, cited above, n. 25): Punjab University Law College, 1959 (H., pp. 111–20); Rotary Club, Lahore 1961 (typescript); All-Pakistan Lawyers Association, Karachi, 1960 (H., pp. 248–60); High Court Bar Association, Karachi, 1960 (H., pp. 261–65); Rotary Club, Karachi, 1960, (typescript); Civil Service Academy, Lahore, 1964 (*PLD 1964 Journal, pp. 73–80*); Administrative Staff College, Lahore, 1966 (H., pp. 96–103); Sind Muslim Law College, Hyderabad, 1967, (H., pp. 104–10); Rotary Club, Karachi, 1968 (H., pp. 235–40).

60. *Faridson's Ltd. v. Government of Pakistan PLD SC pp. 537–73*; quotation at 547.

61. Letter 5, 21 September 1961. The references in this letter are: Sir William Reynell Anson, *The Law and Custom of the Constitution* (Oxford, Clarendon Press, 2 vols. 1922, 5th edition); Brian Chapman, *The Profession of Government: The Public Service in Europe* (New York, NY, Macmillan, 1956).

62. 'The Judicial System of Pakistan', address at National Institute of Public Administration, Lahore, 12 May 1969. (Haider, ed., pp. 266–78).

63. For a cogent summary of the development of writs see the Cornelius judgment in *State of Pakistan v. Mehrajuddin, (1959) Pakistan Supreme Court Reports (PSCR), 34*. See also Ralph Braibanti's chapter in La

Palombara, ed. *Bureaucracy and Political Development*, cited above n. 6; pp. 418–40.

64. *The State v. Sir Edward Snelson* PLD 1961 Lahore 78; *Sir Edward Snelson v. Judges of the High Court of West Pakistan*, PLD 1961 SC 237.

65. Fifty of Kayani's speeches have been compiled in four volumes by Iftikhar Ahmad Khan, a CSP officer. They are published by the Pakistan Writers' Cooperative Society of Lahore: *Not the Whole Truth* (1963); *A Judge May Laugh* (1970); *Some More Truth* (1977); *Half-Truths* (n.d.).

66. 'Address to the Karachi Bar Association' 11 December 1958, Kayani, *A Judge May Laugh* cited above, n. 65; p. 105.

67. 'Installation Address of M.R. Kayani', *Pakistan Times*, 3 April 1958.

68. 'On the Writ Jurisdiction in Pakistan', Kayani, *Not the Whole Truth*, cited above, n. 65; p. 44.

69. 'Writ Jurisdiction of Superior Courts', Civil Service Academy, 25 April 1964, *PLD 1964 Journal, pp. 73–80.*

70. Letter 1, 21 September 1961.

71. The commission's report is cited above, n. 26.

72. 'Equality of Opportunity in Public Service' an address before the Rotary Club of Lahore, 1 September 1961', (Braibanti, *Research on the Bureaucracy of Pakistan)*, cited above, n. 24; pp. 489–500.

73. 'Background', *Some More Truth*, cited above, n. 65; xi.

74. M. R. Kayani, *Half Truths*, cited above, n. 65, pp. 99–100, 102.

75. 'Late Justice Kayani—A Memoir', *PLD 1963 Journal*, 109–116. The excerpts quoted by Cornelius are from Ralph Braibanti's chapter in La Palombara, ed., cited above in n. 6, quotation at pp. 417–18. Three additional tributes by Cornelius, typescript copies of which he gave me, are equally adulatory of Kayani. One was a Reference made at the opening of the Supreme Court, 16 November 1962. Another, 'Most Just Judge' is cited above, n. 5. The third was a Remembrance, undated, but probably made in the Supreme Court in November 1963.

76. Dr M. Bashir Husain, ed., *Letters by Justice Kayani* (Lahore, Aziz Publishers, 1974) pp. 145–47.

77. 'Address to the Karachi Bar Association', 11 December 1958. (Kayani, *A Judge May Laugh*), cited above, n. 65; 105. About twelve High Court cases involving the writ were overturned by the Supreme Court. Cornelius wrote six of these decisions. See the 'Socio-Judicial Context of the Cornelius Era 1950–70' in this volume, pp. 125, 129–33, 173.

78. Government of Pakistan, *Speeches and Statements, Field Marshal Mohammad Ayub Khan* (Karachi, 1965) VI; p. 188.

79. Pakistan is not alone in continuing the equestrian tradition. The Lal Bahadur Shastri Academy of Administration in Mussooree, India's training center for the Indian Administrative Service (IAS) descendant of the pre-independence ICS, has the same course. In both countries, the justification has shifted from the requirements of travel in the field to the need for physical exercise.

80. Mona Abu-Fadl, 'Community, Justice, and Jihad: Elements of the Muslim Historical Consciousness', *American Journal of Islamic Social Sciences*, Vol. 4, No. 1, (1987) pp. 13–30.

81. 'Concept of Islamic Justice'. Address at the Pakistan Academy for Rural Development, 8 November 1997. Appendix 16.

82. The concepts of *Adal* and *Ehsan* are explained further with quotations in Arabic and English from the Qur'an in the judgment of Chief Justice Nasim Hasan Shah in *Qazalbash Wakf and others v. Chief Land Commissioner, Punjab and others. PLD 1990 SC 99*. Further elaboration can be found in an address by one of Cornelius' successors an admirer and close friend, Retired Chief Justice of Pakistan Hamoodur Rahman. See 'Administration of Justice in Islam' *1997 PLD Journal 273*.

83. This address was later published. See Ralph Braibanti, 'The Philosophical Foundations of Bureaucratic Change', Inayatullah, ed., *Bureaucracy and Development in Pakistan* (Peshawar, Academy for Rural Development, 1963) pp. 79–89.

84. 'Justice of the People, For the People, By the People', cited above, n. 27; quotation at 43.

85. Address delivered at the Annual Convocation of Government College, Lahore, 15 May 1965, *PLD 1965 Journal, 71–78*, quotation at p. 74.

86. 'Address at the Annual Dinner of the British Universities Alumni Association', M. R. Kayani, *Some More Truth* cited above n. 65; pp. 125–45. Also published in *Pakistan Times*, 12 December 1961.

87. Husain, ed., Letters by Justice Kayani, cited above n. 76; p. 108.

88. *Civil Military Gazette* (Lahore) 19 October 1962.

89. 'Constitutional Conscience and System of Education', cited above, n. 33.

90. See Ralph Braibanti, 'Political Development: Contextual, Non-Linear Perspectives' Politikon No. 3, October 1976, pp. 6–18.

91. Charles Grove Haines, *The Revival of Natural Law Concepts* (Cambridge, MA, Harvard University Press, 1930) See esp. pp. 278–306. See also Carl F. H. Henry, 'Natural Law and a Nihilistic Culture', *First Things*, January 1995, Number 49, pp. 54–60. See also A.P. d'Entrèves, *Natural Law: An Introduction to Legal Philosophy* (New Brunswick, NJ, Transaction Publishers, 1994). Nobel Laureate F. A. Hayek attributes the rise of the Nazi, fascist and communist systems to the paramountcy of man-made law and the rejection of its natural law premises. F. A. Hayek, *The Rule of Law* (Menlo Park, CA, Institute for Humane Studies, 1975) pp. 22–29. There is a contemporary resurgence of interest in the origins of natural law stimulated by Edward O. Wilson's *Consilience: The Unity of Knowledge* (New York, NY, Alfred A. Knopf, 1998). Wilson's argument denies the transcendental origin of a code of morality (natural law) and suggests instead that it emerges from an evolving system of ethics based on biology and genetics.

92. Haines, cited above n. 91; esp. pp. 280–88.

93. 'Development of Islamic Jurisprudence Through Sharia'. National Institute of Public Administration, Karachi, 23 January 1965. (Haider, ed., pp. 125–32, quotation at p. 130).

94. 'Law, Fundamental Rights and Religious Conscience'. Second Law Conference at Sind Muslim Law College, 11 March 1965. (Haider, ed., pp. 63–68, esp. pp. 66–67).

95. 'The Legal System as Transnational Unifying Force'. Pakistan Institute of International Affairs, Karachi, 4 June 1964. Appendix 12,

96. Anawati's chapter in Ellis, ed., cited above in n. 10; pp. 53–54.

97. Henri Corbin, *En Islam Iranien*, (Paris, Gallimard, 1978).

98. James A. Bill and John Alden Williams, 'Shia Islam and Roman Catholicism: An Ecclesial and Political Analysis' in Kail Ellis, ed., cited above in n. 10; pp. 69–105.

99. His Holiness, John Paul II, *Crossing the Threshold of Hope* (New York, NY, Alfred A. Knopf, 1994).

100. Carl Bernstein and Marco Politi. *His Holiness, John Paul II and the History of Our Times*, (New York, Penguin Books, 1997) 441.

101. For an account of the Vatican's new attitude towards Islam and its efforts to join with Muslim organizations to influence the Cairo and Beijing conferences, see Bernstein and Politi, cited above, n. 100; 517–530. See also George Hunston Williams, *The Mind of John Paul II: Origins of His Thought and Actions*, (New York, NY, The Seabury Press, 1981) 328f. Tad Szulc, *Pope John Paul II* (New York, NY, Scribner, 1995) 425, 431. See also George Weigel, 'What Happened at Cairo', *First Things*, February, 1995, No. 50; pp. 24–32.

102. 'The Legal System as a Transnational Unifying Force'. Cited above, n. 95; Appendix 19.

103. 'Islam and Human Rights'. Pakistan Academy for Rural Development, Peshawar, 8 November 1977, Appendix 15.

104. A lengthier analysis of this point to view is found in Ralph Braibanti, 'The Relevance of Political Science to the Study of Underdeveloped Areas' in Ralph Braibanti and Joseph J. Spengler eds., *Tradition, Values and Socio-Economic Development* (Durham, NC, Duke University, 1961) 139–81. See especially the schematic diagram at 154. See also his 'Context, Cause and Change' in John H. Hallowell, ed., *Prospects for Constitutional Democracy* (Durham, NC, Duke University Press, 1976) pp. 165–83.

105. Oswald Spengler, *Decline of the West*, (New York, NY, Alfred A. Knopf, 1939) Vol. I, pp. 31–33.

106. 'Islam and Human Rights', cited above, n. 103 and 'the Concept of Islamic Justice', date and venue of presentation unknown, Appendix 16. See also 'Morals: The Islamic Approach', Appendix 17.

107. See text above, pp. 62–63.

108. The rudimentary beginnings of this value construct can be found in Harold D. Lasswell, 'Afterthoughts: Thirty Years Later' in *Pyschopathology and Politics* (New York, Viking Press edition, 1960)

pp. 269–319. The acronym appears in later writings a list of which can be found in Ralph Braibanti 'Values in Institutional Processes', Harold D. Lasswell, Daniel Lerner, John D. Montgomery, eds., *Values and Development: Appraising Asian Experience*, (Cambridge, MA, The MIT Press, 1976) pp. 133–52, especially p. 149. A recent effort to apply the PEWSBARD formulary to non-Islamic Asian cultures can be found in: John D. Montgomery, ed., *Values in Education: Social Capital Formation in Asia and the Pacific* (Hollis, NH, Hollis Publishing Company, 1997).

109. To construct this acronym Lasswell used the B in well-Being and the D in rectituDe in place of the first letters.

110. See text above, 28.

111. Ralph Braibanti, 'Saudi Arabia in the Context of Political Development Theory' in Willard A. Beling, ed., *King Faisal and the Modernization of Saudi Arabia* (London, Croom Helm, Ltd., 1980) pp. 35–37.

112. Letter 9, 1 March 1978. The term *Wahdat* which he uses several times is a concept highly developed in Sufi Islam and associated with Ibn-al-Arabi. It is more than *tawhid* (the unity of God); it is the personal experience of that unity.

113. Oswald Spengler, *The Decline of the West*, cited above, n. 105, Vol. II; p. 243.

114. 'Iqbal's Political Message', University of the Punjab, Lahore, 21 April 1964. (Haider, ed., pp. 371–78, 377).

THE ROLE OF LAW IN THE POLITICAL DEVELOPMENT OF PAKISTAN*

*Men should not think it slavery to live according
to the rule of the constitution; for it is their salvation.*
Aristotle's *Politics*

The principal contention of this brief essay is that the study of legal institutions and the legal community has been neglected in analyses of the political development of new states. Yet not only is the strengthening of legal institutions crucial to the viability of new political systems, it is equally true that law also has a role as an agent of social change, as a source for the diffusion of attitudes, ideas, and norms which may have a modernizing and innovative impact on the social order.

A point of departure are two references separated in time by about two centuries and in space by more than ten thousand miles—two kinds of separation which have some bearing on what I propose to discuss. My purpose in using these two references is a simple one, namely, to suggest that conditions and attitudes regarding legal institutions in the new states and in analyses of political development are somewhat different from those which prevailed in the early days of American nationhood. We shall start with Edmund Burke's comment on the American colonies that 'in no country, perhaps in the world, is the law so

---

* Reprinted from the author's chapter in Robert R. Wilson, ed., *International and Comparative Law of the Commonwealth* (Durham, N.C., Duke University Press, 1968). The title has been modified.

general a study. The profession itself is numerous and powerful, and in most provinces it takes the lead...I hear that they have sold nearly as many of Blackstone's Commentaries in America as in England.'[1] Burke's description is enriched by figures which are well known in American history, namely, that twenty-five of the fifty-two signatories to the Declaration of Independence were lawyers, as were thirty-one of the fifty-five members of the Continental Congress.[2] Lawyers were indeed the high priests of early American political development, a development dominated by what to Tocqueville appeared to be an aristocracy of the robe.[3] To be sure, a century later, the priests may have become deacons or even acolytes to party politicians as Bryce writes in 1888 of lawyer's waning influence, but even in that observation he contrasts this with the 'first and second generations of the Republic'[4] when legal influences dominated the evolution of our political system. When we turn to the corpus of analytics relating to our own emerging nationhood we find hundreds of studies, like A. Lawrence Lowell's *Essays on Government*, replete with references to the dominance of lawyers and, more important for our purposes now, to the significant confluence of legal and political norms in the evolution of a viable state system.

Our second reference is taken from the contemporary political thought of one of many states newly sovereign after World War II. Again, we shall use this reference as an indicator suggestive of a larger complex of dispositions. Addressing lawyers in 1960, President Mohammad Ayub Khan suggested that they often 'fabricated evidence in the support of their clients, that the legal profession was overstaffed and that this, 'apart from locking useful manpower unnecessarily, created cut-throat competition in the profession, ushering in all sorts of abuses.'[5] This, of course, was not a new view of lawyers on the Indo-Pakistan subcontinent; on the contrary, it was consistent with the views of many British officers during imperial rule, including Sir Malcolm Darling, F. L. Brayne, and Philip (Mason) Woodruff.[6] President Ayub's view of the situation in Pakistan is similar to the attitude of at least one of the Indian law commission's analyses of the same condition in contemporary India. Thus the Setalvad Commission could say in its fourteenth report that law schools were 'attracting, by and large, students of mediocre ability and indifferent merit,' and that 'the lawyer has lost his leadership in public life.'[7] It quoted with approval the statement of an Indian lawyer that the time has arrived when 'we must make up our minds whether we think that democracy means that anybody should become a lawyer and engage in cut-throat competition or whether it means that anyone who has talent can join an honourable profession.'[8] The Law Reform Commission in Pakistan expressed similar apprehension regarding legal training, although it was much more moderate in tone.[9] This attitude toward not only lawyers but the legal profession is common to developing states. Thus Guyot, writing on Burma, characterizes 'law as a "contentious" profession and medicine as a "constructive" one, which seems roughly to have been their roles in Burma.'[10] The 'overbalance' of lawyers, assuming the validity of this judgment of law and medicine, represents according to this political scientist, 'a misallocation of educational resources.' Such views are commonly held. They may be summarized in this way: in developing states, there are too many lawyers and, therefore, a consequent disproportionate emphasis on legal modes of thought (or legalistic formalism) that are antithetical to the needs of political and economic development. Presumably, legal modes of thought are conducive to maintaining the status quo and not to attitudes of or innovation commonly associated with a 'development orientation.' In the rapidly developing corpus of analysis of political development by western scholars, we find the same lack of emphasis on the critical importance of juridical activity. This is very different from what we found in an earlier period in American political development. This significant contrast in attitudes can be studied in the series of six volumes on political development published under the aegis of the Committee on Comparative Politics of the Social Science Research Council by Princeton University Press.[11] All six deal with critical influences on political growth: communication, education, political parties, and bureaucracy; while the last two volumes deal generally with modernization in Japan and Turkey and with the construction of a general theory of political development. One is struck by the fact that no study has been made of the legal institution and its link to political development. Similarly, we search in vain for an analysis of this subject in Public Policy, the yearbook of the Kennedy School of Government of Harvard University where interest in political development is keen. While the 1966 study had more than half its bulk devoted to 'Problems of Development', no article treated the subject of law and development.[12] One would have thought that law was the cradle of political development. The centrality of law to development may be suggested to us if we consider political development for a moment in somewhat literary, perhaps even romantic terms. Subsequently, we shall approach this problem in more scientific terms but, for the moment, informally we may say that political development is the ordering of the affairs of men into a polity at once commonly agreed upon, clearly known, and capable of rational adjustment, the whole being infused with qualities of freedom ennobling the lives of those who form the state. Let us put it in another way. Political development is essentially a series of progressions, with periodic regressions and even oscillations, from ascription to personal achievement, from ambiguity to certainty in the use of public power, from alienation and withdrawal to enlightening participation in collective social life, from coarseness and coercion to refinement and sensitivity in public action, from contraction to expansion of free choice. These are the attributes of collective earthly existence which in the past have come to us largely by encompassing them within a context of law and its consequent institutions. To be sure, law has often been an impediment to these progressions yet however imperfect legal institutions may be, we cannot conceive of such political development outside the ambit of law.

Growth of Institutions

It behooves us now to inquire into what happened between 1789 and 1967 to mute this emphasis both in the reality of political life and in the sometimes unreality of political analysis. In the realm of political analysis, has the once crucial role of legal institutions been eclipsed by other segments of the political system? Does law have any relevance to political growth and, if so, what is that relevance? Merely to raise these questions is to suggest the impossibility of answering them within the brief compass of this essay. We can only suggest a few reasons for the lesser attention given to law and political development, and we make these suggestions with considerable humility, aware of the fact that we raise profound and controversial issues and then quickly leave them. First, social science insight applicable to political growth has, in recent years, emphasized functionalism rather than institutions and, in so far as law has been studied as an institution, it has shared the decline of institutionalism generally. To be sure, there is a vigorous functional or behavioural school of jurisprudence, but social science analysis has not conjoined with that approach within law. Rather, it seems to skirt about the edges of legal scholarship and in so doing encounters its institutional rather than its functional manifestations. It may well be that this is a consequence of or at least related to the condition so well described by Cowan, 'It is an astonishing fact of American intellectual life that both law and social science have been able to expand so enormously in the present century without significantly affecting each other.'[13] Be that as it may, the dichotomy between institutions and functions is, in my view, a false one. Institutions perform functions, mould behaviour and modify themselves. Indeed, the tracing of function as institutions adjust to new demands can best be done by institutional analysis. Political behaviour flows imperceptibly into the interstices created by institutions, and its flow is regulated and conditioned by the locus and effectiveness of institutional power. Although institutionalism as a mode of analysis has been eclipsed by functionalism, this eclipse, is coming rather quickly to an end. The cruciality of institutions in political development has been brought to our attention by Huntington in the context of the need for balance between the demands or crises of the social order and the capability of institutions to convert these demands into policy or action.[14] Bertrand de Jouvenel reminds us that the political scientist is an expert on institutions and behaviour who must 'foretell the adjustments suitable to improve the adequacy of the institutional system to cope with changing circumstances.'[15] Pennock neatly stated the case:

> First, whether political and governmental structures are formal or informal, incorporated in the legal structure or not, it is of great importance that they be institutionalized and the process of institutionalization is as surely a part of development as is the specialization of function and the differentiation of structure. It is when certain forms and procedures become the accepted ways of doing things that they become effective instruments of stability and of legitimation.[16]

Second, the most spectacular and pervasive motif in political development has been rapid expansion of political participation—a consequence of popular sovereignty. Such power diffusion has been accomplished largely through political parties or community development structures, both rooted in an ethos of spontaneity and extra-legal norms. Third, legal institutions in most new states spring essentially from norms, attitudes, and structures of mature constitutional systems in the West. Since power diffusion derives from indigenous sources, legal institutions come to be regarded not only as alien but even as impediments to the rapid diffusion of public power. Fourth, we are obsessed in the social sciences by the micro-recording of actual behaviour. As a consequence, normative concerns have been replaced too often by adulation of what we think we see in man's behaviour. When we observe incongruence between law and behaviour, we judge law to be the contaminant despoiling behaviour which we judge to be ideal. This relationship overlooks a classic problem in the history of political and legal thought, namely that there has always been imperfect articulation between law and behaviour. This is certainly nothing new nor is it becoming of political anthropology to suggest that lawyers and political scientists have been unaware of this condition. Aristotle set forth the problem and we have pondered it since. In Aristotelian terms, 'political society exists for the sake of noble actions, and not of mere companionship.' The purpose of statecraft is constantly to adjust behaviour of men to legal norms which reflect the state's noble ends. Such adjustment is reciprocal; that is, legal norms and their consequent sanctions modify and direct human behaviour which influences norms and sanctions. If law merely certified man's conduct, some of which derives from his baser nature, then it would have no function except as an instrument to record what we do. This is neither the ideal nor the actual function of law. Law derives its augustness and its power from its perennial struggle to lift man to his own nobility, while at the same time it compassionately reflects man's own ignoble state. If the term 'majesty of the law' has any significance, it is that.

There is a fifth reason closely related to the fourth, namely the preoccupation of growing numbers of both legal scholars and political scientists with activist movements, involving physical agitation for immediate change in society. This has commonly been called 'confrontation politics'. Here we wish to distinguish this phenomenon, which I shall call physical agitation, from two related behaviours: intellectual provocation and legal realism. The former involves influencing the will and searing the conscience so that it compels behavioural change through educative means within the established order in the direction of peaceful innovation. The seared conscience stops and totters precariously on the brink of physical agitation. Legal realism is the intellectual apprehension of actual behaviour, the use of empirical evidence, and the awareness of the reciprocal (as against the uni-directional) relationship between law and behaviour. Both intellectual provocation and legal realism operate within, indeed are nourished by, the values and the ethos of erudition: caution, prudence, detachment, reflection, and total immersion in a refined and rational thought process tempered by intuition. But physical agitation breaks through the perimeter of the ethos of erudition. We witness on all sides the immoral provocation of eighteen-year-old students to foresake the 'sterility and irrelevance' of systematic learning in favour of decision-making beyond their competence or maturity. We witness involvement in party politics and a preoccupation with curbside judicare—a lawyer's secularization of the preacher's social gospel. By serving a master of agitation rather than being mastered by the rigour, order, and beauty of detached analytical scholarship or, what is worse, by attempting to serve both masters, we engender an ethos which distorts the significance of anything which does not appear to be agitation-oriented. Agitation minimizes and eventually corrodes the vitality of law and of institutions. The above are merely five of many reasons which might be related to the prevalent relationship of law to political development.

Legal Studies

We propose now to discuss a set of characteristics of political development and to suggest how legal studies may enrich the subsequent construction of a model of political development. In so doing we shall examine five attributes of political growth and within the context of these attributes we shall propose a strategy for legal research. The relevance of legal studies to some of these attributes shall be immediately evident and these we shall pass over quickly. Others which may not be so obvious, we shall develop at somewhat greater length. The attributes which we have isolated here are not necessarily the same as those singled out by other students of political development. Among such students some of the concepts are the same although the terminology is different. The study of political development is too primitive to allow for common definitions and nomenclature. Huntington has succinctly analyzed the varying lists of criteria as used by Ward and Rustow, Emerson, Pye, and Eisenstadt.[17] He identifies four sets of categories which recur continuously: rationalization, national integration, democratization, and participation. He notes that the last-mentioned characteristic is given greatest emphasis and deplores the failure of most definitions to emphasize or even mention political institutions essential for converting demands produced by accelerated participation. Drawing on the works of about thirty writers (reaching Wilson, Burgess, and Weber), Packenham[18] lists five conditions commonly stressed: a constitution, economic base, administrative capacity, participation, and civic attitudes. Lasswell,[19] reviewing the first three volumes of the Social Science Research Council-Princeton series alluded to earlier in this chapter,[20] folds them into the context of his own brilliantly conceived six-part model: self-sustaining power accumulation, power-sharing, national independence, a responsible role in world politics, an internal decision-making process conducing to wider participation in all values, and timing of elements in the sequence of development.

Space requires us to eschew the temptation to correlate these summaries or to analyze them in greater depth. For immediate expository convenience, we shall give our list of five attributes of political development and relate certain research possibilities to each.

1. The first attribute is agreement on a fundamental polity of the state, an over-arching purpose which gives form, cohesion, and direction to all public action within a sensed community. This is typically embodied in a constitution and, in some cases, such as in India and in Pakistan, in segments of the constitution such as the non-justiciable but ideologically crucial directive principles of state policy. The relevance of law to this attribute is obvious. The drafting of constitutions and their subsequent interpretation through judicial case law are classic legal activities to which a moderate amount of research attention has been given

but the research done is excessively exegetical or focuses on textual criticism reminiscent of research in constitutional law done in the United States two or more generations ago. What is sorely needed is legal analysis of the permeative effect of constitutional law as it confronts antagonistic indigenous norms with its own juridical norms derived from western systems. The nature of this confrontation and the degree to which it is a factor in maintaining national integration in the face of often overwhelming centrifugal forces is of crucial significance and is almost totally neglected. Another important but critical subject for analysis is the changing pattern of dependence upon indigenous American, British, and other foreign precedents. For example, in Pakistan, the change to a presidential system and a division of powers into enumerated central and reserved provincial requires, and in fact, has resulted in a shift away from British to analogous American precedent.[21]

Finally, a whole new area of legal research has been dramatically opened by Sec. 201(b) (7) of the Foreign Assistance Act of 1966.[22] Inserted by the Senate Committee on Foreign Relations,[23] this amendment adds a significant criterion which must be taken into account in making development loans. That criterion is the 'degree to which the recipient country is making progress toward respect for the rule of law, freedom of expression, and of the press, and recognition of the importance of individual freedom, initiative and private enterprise.' The construction of criteria for measuring these qualities, and the question of balance between freedom and order so critical in new states, call for the most sophisticated comparative analysis of jurisprudence and the contextual relevance of an ethos of law.

2. A second attribute is the establishment of an institutional apparatus which has the potential to convert valid expressions of popular will into actions fairly predictable and consistent with the fundamental polity of the state. Here the role of administrative law is crucial. The problem is that of infusing administrative action with the spirit and substance of the basic polity. This involves two kinds of compatibility: compatibility of

administrative process with the polity—usually a variation of due process of law—and compatibility with the spirit of the statute. This relationship, always difficult to achieve in even mature systems, is much more difficult to attain in new, highly unbalanced systems. Here we find that the bureaucracy, long accustomed to near-paramountcy under imperial rule, relies less on statutory sources for its actions and more on its internal resources and on synaptic relations with extra-statutory sources. Such systems may be tottering on the threshold of administrative lawlessness. Ambiguity of function in the whole system, inadequacy of legislative oversight, and other weaknesses allow administrative discretion to flow with minimal reference to the channels—a predicament of which we were well warned in the West as early as 1929 by Lord Hewart of Bury's *The New Despotism*.[24] This kind of despotism is the more dangerous in immature systems. We need research in administrative law to measure the gap between fundamental polity and administrative discretion and to ascertain how law can reduce the gap and render bureaucracy effectively accountable to polity. One is impressed by what a judiciary which is powerful, erudite, and independent can do to regulate this articulation. One of the most influential decisions in Pakistan law was that written by Chief Justice S. M. Murshed in the 'Pan case' of 1964. In this historic judgment, Murshed, relying heavily on the Schecter Poultry Company and Panama Refining Company cases, infused into Pakistan law the established doctrines of administrative law essential to curb bureaucratic lawlessness. Commenting on the untrammeled power given to bureaucracy by an unsophisticated legislature, he said:

What policy has it laid down? What standard has it formulated? What yardstick has it given? What principles has it formulated? What limitations has it imposed? What guidance has it given? None whatsoever...An effective and efficient legislation could easily be passed to meet the exigencies of the situation within the framework of the Constitution. The Constitution is not unworkable in this behalf. If a valid law had been passed, it could have started functioning from the date on which such law had come into existence. We should not be understood to hold that we do not consider such a legislation to be desirable or expedient, but the essential condition of a valid law is that it must be confined within the limits set by the Constitution. It should not be allowed to 'burst the banks' and the protective barrage set up by our Fundamental Law, namely, the Constitution. There can be selection of commodities for regulation of transport. There may be a specification of means of transport sought to be regulated. Frontiers of regulation may be defined. Standards and norms can be laid down for such regulation of movement. The objects and purposes of regulation can be set out. It would be a salutary provision to require orders in this behalf to be made under public notification. The Constitution requires, and it is possible to do so, that reasonable direction and guidance should be given in various ways under which the Executive may be vested with substantial disrectionary powers to work out the details of legislative policies and norms.[25]

While we know much about administrative law in Pakistan, we know very little of it in India and even less in the other developing states. Moreover, we know nothing of the comparative effectiveness of this mode of control of bureaucracy in the former imperial states of France and Britain.

3. The third attribute of political development is the capability of maintaining national integration through orderly and just accommodation of cultural, religious, and similar divisive forces. Here the importance of legal arrangements has not been recognized in research even though in reality legal means are heavily relied upon to bring about this integration. But the adequacy of differing modes of sanctions and the articulation of sanctions to social stress need to be re-examined in the context of political development. Arens and Lasswell's early study on sanction law[26] needs to be reconsidered in terms of our experience since 1947. Finally, the role of legal sanctions in integration in the British and French imperial traditions should be compared. Within such a comparative context, we may get some glimmer of the differing social effects of codification, non-codification, and blends of both.

4. Fourth, a transitional state must have the capacity to blend elements of the popular will in markedly disparate stages of development into an aggregate—an aggregate which must be normatively consistent with the basic polity of the state. Herein lies perhaps the most challenging of research problems for law. The basic polity typically derives from western sources but the popular will derives from indigenous sources. The ideological cohesion of the social order may be, and usually is, badly disturbed. Politicization may proceed on the basis of western constitutional norms often divorced—even in language—from the mainstream of the social order, and within that order even minimal popular comprehension of polity may not exist. In this connection, legal research must re-examine the dynamics of adjustment between indigenous norms and state polity. It may not be possible for the polity to draw into its ambit by osmosis the body of indigenous thought. It may be that legal research will have to find a reconstructed indigenous tradition in which strands of thought equivalent to assumptions underlying western constitutional systems have been identified, elucidated, and woven into a cohesive doctrine. Or it may be that the role of courts and of administrative law as diffusers and mediators of conflicting norms will have to be strengthened to deal with the gap between behaviour and norms which, as stated earlier, always exists everywhere, but which is far more crucial in the bifurcated social orders of emerging states.

Closely related to this question of blending elite and popular wills is the issue of adjustment of spheres of juridical norms. The relationship between tribal, religious, and other indigenous juridical systems and systems of law derived from the West needs further study. Here the work of such pioneers as J. N. D. Anderson, L. C. Green, and S. A. de Smith must be singled out for attention but there is altogether too little work of this kind. The interaction of spheres of validity bears crucially on the problem of national integration as well as on the problem of blending of wills. A case in point is what has happened in West Pakistan with respect to the effort to extend the *jirga* system of tribal elders in certain criminal cases under the Frontier Crimes Regulation of 1901. What started as an effort to 'return' to simple tribal justice ended as an institutional and normative adjustment of two legal systems—tribal law and British criminal law but what is especially instructive is that the adjustment was far more complex than mere contraction or expansion of spheres. What we find is that the spatial validity of a blend of western and tribal norms has expanded, but the normative content of that blend has become somewhat more western than tribal. Thus, it may be that spatial expansion combined with subtle normative modification can serve as a legal mechanism which can be deliberately contrived and effectively used as a means of blending two or more legal systems.

5. Let us now consider the fifth and final (in this tentative listing) attribute of political development. This is the involvement of the entire population in political life—the diffusion of power to the periphery of the social order. Ideologically, this derives from concern for enhancement of human dignity, reflected juridically in the concept of popular sovereignty. We may variously call this power-sharing, power diffusion, politicization, mobilization, or even the participation explosion. Of all five attributes here discussed, this one, at least in its quantitative dimension, has been given the most attention. Virtually no concern has been shown for the quality of such participation, that is, for such factors as literacy, responsibility, understanding of issues, to the quality of civic culture generally.[27] The emphasis has been on the acceleration of involvement—almost for its own sake. This emphasis is understandable especially because in the past determinations as to the quality of public participation have been used as justification for continued imperial rule, and even now as excuses for authoritarianism. Lest we be misunderstood here, let it be said immediately that it is abundantly clear to us that the rapid involvement of large numbers of people—that is to say, the quantitative aspect of power diffusion—is a necessary aspect of development. Only such diffusion can bring about that degree of meaningful participation which enlarges choice and

experience, develops responsibility, and enhances human dignity. Moreover, efforts to sedate, repress, or delay such diffusion should be regarded with some wariness since they may be guises for authoritarianism. Nevertheless, we cannot overlook the stress and the crises caused by accelerated power-sharing. The problem can be simply put. New states often simply do not have the institutional strength necessary to convert demands into action. More importantly, they do not have a sufficiently even diffusion of juridical norms to infuse the whole political system with the strength of the basic polity. This is primarily why new systems collapse, not because of corruption, not because of infiltration, not because of institutional weakness, but because of uneven diffusion of norms, and because of the unnatural straining of stronger institutions, such as the judiciary, to take up the slack of the weaker institutions. Let me put the problem in a somewhat more abstract way. The importance of this fifth attribute of power diffusion lies in the fact that rapid diffusion to the perimeters of the social order changes the nature and quantum of political demands, thus increasing the strain on the capability of institutions to convert such demands into effective governmental action.

This condition is aggravated when demands are escalated by the intervention and massive uncontrolled infusion of foreign norms through technical assistance and international entities bent on dissemination of idiosyncrasies without regard to institutional capacity to handle such demands. The possibility of this demand-conversion crisis's being pushed to the brink of political disintegration by foreign ideological inducement makes us wary of the possible effects in developing states of Title IX of the Foreign Assistance Act of 1966.[28] Title IX states that in carrying out programs of development assistance, specifically those financed by the Development Loan Fund, and those involving technical co-operation, development grants, the Alliance for Progress, and Southeast Asia multilateral and regional programs, 'emphasis shall be placed on assuring maximum participation in the task of economic development on the part of the people of the developing countries, through the encouragement of democratic private and local government institutions.' It is clear that the House of Representatives Committee on Foreign Affairs which inserted Title IX in the act feels that 'there is a close relationship between popular participation in the process of development, and the effectiveness of this process.'[29] The degree of jeopardy in which the demand-conversion dilemma will be placed by Title IX remains to be seen. Much will depend on the means of implementation used by the United States Agency for International Development and on the criteria for and definitions of participation. It is clear that the House Committee on Foreign Affairs 'plans to keep close check on the manner in which the intent [of Title IX] is carried out' and that it expects USAID 'to develop and use in its next presentation to the Congress, meaningful criteria for judging the results of this effort.'[30]

Imbalance between demands and capability is one of the primary causes of the collapse of new political systems. For simplicity's sake, let us call this the demand-conversion crisis. Public bureaucracy is the principal institution for the conversion of such demands. Imbalance can be moderated either by reducing demand incidence, modifying demand content, or by increasing bureaucratic capability to handle the demand-conversion crisis. Where bureaucratic strengthening occurs, it must be done within the general restraints imposed by the polity and without total retraction of power diffusion if, in fact, diffusion is part of that polity. This delicate balance, extraordinarily difficult to achieve, is crucial to the maturation of political systems. In developing systems, spontaneous adjustment to acute imbalance has assumed various forms. In India, we find containment, diversion, and sedation of demands by the spatially diffuse and substantively competent single mass party. In Pakistan, similar consequences are achieved by indirect elections and by near-paramountcy of juridico-administrative norms. Elsewhere, we witness total or partial suspension of participative behaviours and dominance of authoritarian oligarchies, usually military. The elaboration of the process of such adjustment, its contextual relevance, and its ultimate political consequences are crucial research objectives for which the disciplines of political science and law are now ready.

What is the relevance of this demand-conversion crisis to law and to legal institutions? The relevance lies in the adjustment which the system must make to the crisis. Such adjustment may be spontaneous or contrived. We have already mentioned some of the forms which such adjustment may assume. Virtually no systematic studies of the adjustment mechanisms have been made. Many of these adjustments are in the realm of law. One such adjustment which has almost unlimited explanatory power is the construct of ambiguity. Ambiguity is a powerful force. It can be used positively as a device of control and is commonly used in all administration as a means of power. Uncertainty, unease, ambivalence, diffusion of responsibility through alternate invocation of committee jurisdiction and single officer jurisdiction: these and other variations are common even though unhealthy devices of power in church, business, university, and public administration. Ambiguity of polity and structure is and can be used effectively in regulating the demand-conversion crisis. Consider the case of Pakistan. The new political system is suspended between a parliamentary and a presidential system and is based on an ambiguous distribution of legislative powers between the central and provincial governments. Such ambiguity is neatly illustrated by the 1964 preventive detention cases in Pakistan involving Maulana Maudoudi and the ultra-orthodox Muslim group, the Jamaat-e-Islami. Preventive detention is the concern of two levels of government. The Jamaat-e-Islami was disbanded and certain leaders arrested in two provinces under different laws, both central and provincial. Moreover, the ambiguous powers of the governors acting as agents of the president confused the situation. The mixture of actions made it impossible to focus accountability. It demolished the possibility of legislative oversight, since each legislature ruled out discussion of crucial aspects of the case, aspects which it was impossible to separate. It took a woman member of the National Assembly,

Begum Shamsun Nahar Mahmood, to identify aptly this confusion of responsibility when she said, 'if some question about preventive detention is asked...the Central Government refer it to the provincial government...If provincial authorities are approached they in turn refer it to the Central Government.'[31] In the context of such ambiguity, the role of the judiciary is critical simply because it is the only agency in the whole political system capable of dealing with the totality of such actions and thus spreading an umbrella of normative uniformity over an assortment of actions not otherwise amenable to control and crucially at variance with the basic polity of the state. We have suggested that such structured ambiguity may be beneficial in that it regulates demands by putting them through baffles but this is probably a short-run benefit. In the long run, excessive ambiguity damages any social system. After all, a mature political system must be characterized by focused accountability, clarity of policy, courageous acceptance of decision-making by officials, and a high degree of rationality. The dangers of spontaneous, whimsical, or capricious action must be balanced not by structured ambiguity but rather by countervailing loci of power, each with enough autonomy to be resilient and gently resistant, and each maintaining boundaries of insulation rather than merging ignominiously into a haze of interlocking structures. The effects of ambiguity may appear as a syndrome: frustration, alienation, withdrawal from political life, violence. The quantum of alienation resulting from ambiguity needs to be measured. It is probably a significant source of counter-productivity in the whole political process. The ultimate danger of structured ambiguity as a regulating device lies in the frustration such ambiguity engenders. Frustration leads to repressed and often simmering animosity against power and eventually to violent action, which may then bring crisis to the political system. The evidence for this in political systems is overwhelming. The role of ambiguity both as a regulator and as an agitator of crisis has not been studied. Theoretically, there may be an articulated progression—a gradual decrease of ambiguity as a system matures. Perhaps this is what is occurring in Pakistan. We would need to know why such ambiguity decreases. Do law and the judiciary conduce to its decrease, as we suspect they do, or to its increase? This calls for careful microanalysis of legal and administrative structure and of the substance of all public decisions. It calls for measurement of how much and what kind of ambiguity is desirable and at what point it ceases to be an effective regulator of crisis and become instead an agitator of crisis. This kind of study transcends law itself, but it must be rooted in legal analysis if it is to have significance.

There is still another means by which such adjustment can occur. The kind of adjustment we now have in mind is not so much adjustment of the demand-conversion crisis, but rather the infusion of the whole unbalanced political process with juridically impelled values basic to the polity. Imagine for a moment the whole political system as a twelve-cylinder engine, with noisy tappets, gummed-up cylinders, the timing off, and the points and spark plugs inefficient. The engine makes horrible noises and the car bucks like a bronco. Imagine somehow spraying the engine with a penetrating yet thick plastic foam which muffles the noises and somehow evens out the car's motion. Such can be the effect in a new political system. Such has been the effect of the formulary of natural justice embodied in the maxim *audi alteram partem* as interpreted in Pakistan. What we find is a highly uneven diffusion of a standard derived from western jurisprudence. The judiciary enters a vacuum created by absence or erosion of this norm. It applies the doctrine—spraying it about like foam. It has some good short-term effect—perhaps even good long-term effect. We need to know more about expansive interpretations of such a doctrine of natural justice—how it is related to natural law and to due process of law. Most importantly, how does it relate to judicial self-restraint or non-restraint and how does such application sedate the whole political process—quieting the noises and smoothing the ride. Again, virtually no analysis of this important role of law and political development has been made.

The Legal Community

So much for a research agenda in the context of five characteristics of political growth. There is one final item of research which we cannot fit neatly into any of the five categories already discussed; hence we shall deal with it now separately. This is the question of the total impact of the legal community in maintaining some semblance of a constitutional system. We are convinced by our experience in Pakistan that size may be an important positive force. Certainly, in Pakistan, the size of the legal community has partly made it the most powerful countervailing elite in the system. We estimate the number of legally trained persons at 18000. From 1954 on, 17 per cent of the total university degrees conferred have been law degrees, the average output of law degrees being 1000 a year. The ratio of legally trained persons to population would be about one lawyer to 5,500 people; in the United States this ratio in 1960 was one lawyer to 630 people.[32] This comparison will be surprising to many who have assumed that the ratio of lawyers in new states is higher than in old states. Beyond that, we are not certain what these figures mean but of this we are convinced, we need statistics and ratios on the total number of legally trained persons, not only practicing lawyers, in all systems. If we had that information we could work out some fascinating hypotheses on the relationship of size to influence on political development but we have these figures only for Pakistan and only scanty, eccentric data for other states. Of another thing we are certain for Pakistan. The sheer size of the legal community, strongly organized into bar associations and closely allied with equally strong courts, has not only been a major source for the diffusion and regeneration of norms generally but by weight of numbers has enabled the courts to remain strong and has prevented the rise of administrative lawlessness. There is a curious anomaly here. The legal community, while often antagonistic to government and constraining executive action, is nevertheless closely identified normatively and culturally with the bureaucratic elite. This identification, coupled with healthy antagonism, actually enhances the strength of the legal community. It derives popular support from its ostensible opposition to government and at the same time elicits bureaucratic support from its command of western-oriented norms and techniques. Yet it also commands the fearful attention of bureaucracy because of its support in the community at large. It has a network of relationships in rural areas and the cities. A coterie of retainers and para-lawyers such as *munshis, dalal, mukhtars,* clerks and scribes are dependent on British legal proceedings for a livelihood and serve as linguistic and cultural mediators between lawyers and the vernacularized community at large. Curiously, Tocqueville's description of this phenomenon in early America neatly fits the situation in Pakistan. 'Lawyers belong to the people by birth and interest and to the aristocracy by habit and taste; they may be looked upon as the connecting link between the two great classes of society.'[33] In short, the legal community is a force to be reckoned with. It has challenged the executive during and after martial law, defined efforts to restrict court jurisdiction, it has compelled justiciability of fundamental rights, and forced the abrogation of several restrictive enactments. Is this law as an impediment to political development? Is this misallocation of scarce resources in the system? Is this unproductive use of non-productive manpower? On the contrary, it seems to us that this is the very genius of political development.

Is the experience of Pakistan unique? We do not know. We need careful studies of the impact of the total legal community on development in French-derived and British-derived new states. There may be counter-productivity in some systems. Studies of this kind appear to be the most crucial and the most relevant in establishing a nexus between law and political development.

Conclusion

In conclusion, we have tried to suggest only a few of many legal problems for research on political development. In this we have been guilty of at least two distortions. We have deliberately idealized the law and legal institutions. We have also not treated law in the context of economic growth and as a potential generant of social innovation. This is an artificial and risky separation of law from its contextual tissue. Several papers could be written on the impact of law—especially corporation or company law— on the development of entrepreneurship, on the formation of capital, and on the consequent effect of a competing commercial elite balancing the power of government. Further, we have not drawn attention to certain salutary developments in legal research. A few of these might be mentioned. First, the phenomenal rise in interest in the sociology and anthropology of law. Second, a vigorous behaviouralism has influenced legal studies in political science and is bound to have the effect of rediffusing juridical studies through the discipline. Third, publication of the *Law and Society Review*, the first issue of which appeared in November, 1966, will provide a publishing focus for this rediffusion in the social sciences generally. Fourth, a series of two summer conferences on South Asian law under auspices of the University of Chicago Law School in 1963 and 1967 has accelerated the transfer of juridical research to certain Asian states, especially India. Fifth, the small Conference on Law and Developing Countries sponsored by the Board of Review and Development of the American Society of International Law in Washington, 16 and 17 July, 1965, may ultimately generate research interest within the international law fraternity. Sixth, the keen interest of the Rule of Law Research Center of Duke University and of its director, Arthur Larson, in the operational relevance of law as a source of social change (in problems of population control, for example) may lead ultimately to a significant use of legal means in American foreign assistance efforts to induce change. Finally, the continuous emphasis on legal research and on the centrality of institutions which, under the leadership of Robert R. Wilson at Duke University and others, has resulted in a significant corpus of research and in the training of a large number of scholars, is very significant. This conference is one manifestation of such emphasis which has not diminished for more than thirty years.

We are heartened by such indicators as these of a renewed appreciation of law. Unless we re-establish the centrality of legal studies in analysis of political growth, the most important dimension of that process will be lost. Political development is a struggle to achieve human dignity and a finer aesthetic quality of life. Pope Paul VI in his encyclical of March 1967, *Populorum Progressio*, put it simply and profoundly in his statement that the basic aspiration of man is 'to do more, know more and have more in order to be more.'[34] That law can contribute to so majestic and noble an aspiration we must accept as a given. The challenge is that we must reconsider its importance and infuse much of our research with its implications.

NOTES

1. See 'Speech on Conciliation with America' (1775), Burke's Works (Boston, 1865), II, pp. 124–25.
2. Heinz Eulau and John D. Sprague, *Lawyers in Politics: A Study in Professional Convergence* (New York, 1965), p. 11.
3. Alexis de Tocqueville, *Democracy in America*, Henry Reeve text, ed. Phillips Bradley (New York, 1945). Tocqueville's classic analysis of the legal aristocracy can be found in Vol. I, pp. 272–80 of this edition. See also a critique of the views of Tocqueville and Bryce on this matter in Eulau and Sprague, *Lawyers in Politics*, esp. pp. 32–39.
4. James Bryce, *The American Commonwealth* (New York, 1908), II, p. 570.
5. Full text accessible in Government of Pakistan, *Speeches and Statements of Field Marshal Mohammad Ayub Khan* (Karachi, 1961), III, p. 27. This point of view is reiterated somewhat more strongly in Ayub's autobiography, *Friends Not Masters* (Karachi, 1967), pp. 102–7.
6. See, for example, Darling's striking description and analysis of what he regards as the evil economic consequences of excessive litigation in the Punjab in his *The Punjab Peasant in Prosperity and Debt* (4th ed.; London, 1947), pp. 67–69. Brayne's Socratic dialogue attacking the 'curse and

the futility' of litigation is both amusing and uncommonly perceptive: F. L. Brayne, *Socrates in an Indian Village* (8th ed.; London, 1946), pp. 108–13. A delightful fictional account of the same phenomenon is Philip Woodruff's *Call the Next Witness* (London, 1945).

7. Government of India, Ministry of Law, Law Commission of India, *Fourteenth Report: Reform of Judicial Administration* (New Delhi, 1960), I, p. 556.

8. Ibid, pp. 556–57.

9. Government of Pakistan, Ministry of Law, *Report of the Law Reform Commission*, 1958–59 (Karachi, 1959), pp. 115–16.

10. James F. Guyot, 'Bureaucratic Transformation in Burma', in Ralph Braibanti and Associates, *Asian Bureaucratic Systems Emergent from the British Imperial Tradition* (Durham, NC, 1966), p. 361, n. 12.

11. These volumes are: Lucian W. Pye, ed., *Communications and Political Development* (1963); Joseph LaPalombara, ed., *Bureaucracy and Political Development* (1963); Robert E. Ward and Dankwart A. Rustow, eds., *Political Modernization in Japan and Turkey* (1964); James S. Coleman, ed., *Education and Political Development* (1965); Joseph LaPalombara and Myron Weiner, eds., *Political Parties and Political Development* (1966); Leonard Binder, James Coleman, and others, *Crises in Political Development* (1967).

12. *Public Policy* (Cambridge, Mass., 1966), XV (1966), ed. John D. Montgomery and Arthur Smithies.

13. Thomas A. Cowan, 'What Law Can Do for Social Science,' in William M. Evan, ed., *Law and Sociology: Introductory Essays* (New York, 1962), p. 91.

14. Samuel P. Huntington, 'Political Development and Political Decay', *World Politics*, XVII (1965), pp. 386–430.

15. 'Political Science and Prevision', *American Political Science Review*, LIX (March 1965), pp. 29, 32.

16. J. Roland Pennock, 'Political Development, Political Systems, and Political Goods', *World Politics*, XVIII (1966), p. 418.

17. Huntington, 'Political Development and Political Decay', p. 387.

18. Robert A. Packenham, 'Political Development Doctrines in the American Foreign Aid Program', *World Politics*, XVIII (1966), pp. 194–235.

19. Harold D. Lasswell, 'The Policy Sciences of Development', *World Politics*, XVII (1965), pp. 286–310.

20. This series is cited in n. 11 above.

21. This phenomenon is developed further in Ralph Braibanti, Research on the Bureaucracy of Pakistan (Durham, NC, 1966), pp. 280–89; Ralph Braibanti, 'The Higher Bureaucracy of Pakistan', in Braibanti and Associates, *Asian Bureaucratic Systems Emergent from the British Imperial Tradition*, pp. 209–42, 312–27.

22. Public Law 89–583 (80 Stat. 795).

23. United States Congress, Senate, *Foreign Economic Assistance, Report of the Committee on Foreign Relations...on S. 3584*, 89th Conq., 2d Sess., Report No. 1359 (Washington, DC, 1966), pp. 7–8.

24. (London, 1929.)

25. *Ghulam Zamin v. A. B. Khondkhar* 16 D.L.R. (1964), 486, quotation at pp. 502, 514.

26. Richard Arens and Harold D. Lasswell, *In Defense of Public Order: The Emerging Field of Sanction Law* (New York, 1961).

27. An exception is the analysis of J. Roland Pennock, cited above in n. 16, who in the context of 'political goods', which he holds to be security, welfare, justice, and liberty, suggests that the substantial universality of these 'goods' is tempered by contextual relativity of their implementation. '[H]uman interests are subject to certain natural orderings,' he maintains, and the persistence of the political system must take priority over other 'goods' (p. 426). A significant effort to relate varying qualities of civic culture to the effectiveness of political systems is Gabriel A. Almond and Sidney Verba, *The Civic Culture* (Princeton, NJ, 1963).

28. Cited in n. 22 above. The background and theoretical implications of Title IX are explored in greater detail in Ralph Braibanti, 'External Inducement of Political Administrative Development: An Institutional Strategy', in Braibanti and Associates, *Political and Administrative Development* (Durham, NC, forthcoming).

29. House of Representatives, *Foreign Assistance Act of 1966. Report of the Committee on Foreign Affairs on H.R. 15150*, 89th Cong., 2d Sess., Report No. 1651 (Washington, DC, 1966), p. 27.

30. Ibid, p. 28.

31. Pakistan National Assembly, *Debates*, 5 July 1962, p. 1066.

32. This phenomenon is further examined in Braibanti, *Research on the Bureaucracy of Pakistan*, pp. 246–61.

33. Tocqueville, *Democracy in America*, I, p. 276.

34. *Encyclical Letter of His Holiness, Paul VI, Pope. On the Development of Peoples [Populorum Progressio]*, 26 March 1967 (official translation into English distributed by the United States Catholic Conference, Washington, DC), Part I, par. 6, p. 9. There is some controversy as to accuracy of the meaning conveyed in various translations of this encyclical. See New York *Times*, 29 March 1967, p. 1, and *National Observer*, 3 April 1967, p. 5. Apparently, there can be little argument that the English version has correctly transferred the meaning of this particular section. In the official Latin version issued by the Vatican, this expression appears as '*hoc est, ut magis operentur, discant, possideant, ut ideo pluris valeant,*' *Sanctissimi Domini Nostri Pauli Divina Providentia Papae VI, Litterae Encyclicae...De Populorum Progressione Promovenda* (Typis Polyglottis Vaticanis, 1967), Part I, par. 6, p. 7. In the official Italian version, the expression appears as '... in una parola, fare,

conoscere, e avere di piu, per esser di piu...,' *Populorum progressio, Lettera Enciclica di S. S. Paolo VI sulla sviluppo dei popoli* published in a special issue of *Quaderni di Ekklesia,* I (1967), 127–72, quotation at p. 131.

THE SOCIO-JUDICIAL CONTEXT OF THE CORNELIUS ERA—1950-70*

Six hours in sleep, in law's grave study six.
Four spend in prayer, the rest on nature fix.

Sir Edward Coke, *Pandects*

Legal research is of particular importance to study the bureaucracy, not only for the usual reasons of the relationship of administrative law to bureaucratic action, but also because of characteristics of government especially prominent in Pakistan. The legal community takes pride in the fact that Article 2 of the 1962 Constitution declares that it is the inalienable right of every citizen to be treated in accordance with law. This provision is in addition to justiciable fundamental rights which are specified in detail by the first amendment. The constitutional eminence thus given law is symbolic of the eminence and pervasiveness of legal influence in total society.

First, there is a confluence of administrative and judicial power in local government where division commissioners and district officers are responsible for courts in their respective areas. There is no separation of executive and judicial functions in Pakistan despite the continuing demands of bar associations for such separation. For this reason, a significant part of the training and

---

* Reprinted from the author's *Research on the Bureaucracy of Pakistan* (Durham, NC, Duke University Press, 1966). Footnotes refer to the text and appendices of that book, not to this study of Cornelius. The title has been modified, the headnote added, and the three tables have been renumbered.

behaviour of the elite cadre focuses on law. Second, a portion of the Civil Service of Pakistan is posted to the 'judicial side' of the service. Transfer to judicial work is normally made early in the fifth year of a CSP officer's service, although such transfers may be made later in a career as well. In 1964, 6 per cent of the CSP cadre served in full-time, permanent judicial posts. Third, members of the judiciary have played a major in role in administrative reform. Chief Justice M. Munir headed the first Pay and Services Commission, 1949–50; Chief Justice A. R. Cornelius was chairman of the Second Pay and Service Commission of 1962. The interest of Cornelius in bureaucracy extends beyond the work of that commission, as is indicated by his important statements on the functioning of the bureaucracy, some of which are included in the appendices to this essay. Fourth, the judiciary has been actively involved through the medium of the writ in dealing with internal problems of bureaucracy relating to civil service matters and in external problems relating to achieving due process in the exercise of administrative discretion. The extent of this involvement, probably greater in Pakistan than in any other developing state, is suggested in subsequent analysis and elsewhere.[1] Lastly, court judgments are indispensable case studies of administrative situations, rich in detail and illuminating in analysis. In the absence of other case materials they constitute the sole source of empirically derived descriptions of bureaucratic behaviour.

Some of the impediments to research efficiency discussed elsewhere in this essay are absent in the pursuit of legal studies. The century-old tradition of justice pursued in full public view has resulted in an efficient, reliable system of public reporting of court decisions in constitutional, statutory, and administrative law. So far as published judgments are concerned, classification is no barrier to accessibility. A commendable degree of competition between commercial and official systems of reporting has resulted in a condition of speed and accuracy in publishing and efficiency in distribution which surpasses many other categories of public record issuance.

Nevertheless, there are difficulties. Research on the administration of justice is hampered by the absence of statistics on categories of cases for the entire judicial system. Copies of dockets and data showing time lags in decisions are difficult to obtain. There is some improvement in this matter as a consequence of the new practice of the Supreme Court and the high courts of releasing for publication in the journal section of *All-Pakistan Legal Decisions*, a report on the disposition of cases, listed by category, after each session of the court. Uniform rosters and lists of judges and their qualifications are not available except in the provincial civil lists. Presumably, the registrar of each court keeps such data but their availability for research not officially connected with the work of the court is necessarily limited to whatever arrangements can be made *ex gratia*. Research is also limited to published cases. Unpublished cases are usually available in typed or mimeographed form but usually in only one copy. Copies, however, can be made from the record on court premises. Lawyer's briefs, or 'paperbooks', used in the course of trial are difficult to obtain, although they are now being printed and may be more easily accessible. Below the Supreme Court and High Courts, judgments are not published. Sometimes they are typed or mimeographed but they cannot be easily obtained. The research apparatus of citator systems or a *corpus juris* have not been well developed. Reliance must be placed exclusively on an official decennial digest of Supreme Court decisions, two unofficial decennial and quinquennial digests, and the annual index of *All-Pakistan Legal Decisions* which is indispensable.

Another possible impediment is the state of legal scholarship within the legal profession and within the academic community. Closely related to this is the stringency of the contempt law that may possibly affect scholarly work which states or implies criticism of courts and their judgments. In a sense, each of these impediments may be viewed as an advantage rather than a disadvantage, at least for the foreign researcher. As a consequence of the first, the entire research field is open to original inquiry. The second possible impediment challenges the researcher to observe that due caution, moderation, and a sense of suspended judgment, which should be hallmarks of scholarship in any case but which the contempt law may make somewhat more urgent in Pakistan.

The Environment of Legal Scholarship

There are six law colleges in Pakistan, each affiliated with a major university. Of these, the law colleges of the University of the Punjab in Lahore and Dacca University in East Pakistan (now Bangladesh) are probably the most highly developed. The work of none of the colleges compares favourably with adequate legal education in advanced western nations. There are also some private, commercial colleges which conduct evening courses and whose standards are generally lower than those of the six university law colleges.

Law colleges are handicapped by the quality of students who seek law degrees and by the lack of professional interest of many of them. Typically, the best students attempt to enter one of the central superior civil services and those in law college are often marking time between civil service examinations. Others enter law college because there is no alternative means of employment or activity. Since there are few full-time professors of law on the law faculties, the standard of instruction lacks the tone of professional scholarship. Those who teach law tend to be young lawyers without established practices who need the slight extra income earned by lecturing. Lectures tend to be anecdotal and are often based on chatting about cases the lawyer has in progress. There is little use of the case method in Pakistan's law schools and the typical graduate will not have read judgments of the Supreme Court or the High Courts of his own country.

This condition of legal education was recognized by the Law Reform Commission which made several remedial proposals. It suggested uniform degree requirements in all law colleges and a three-year course beyond the AB for a limited number of students whose admission into law schools would be restricted. It proposed the abolition of evening classes, revision of the examination system, and the appointment of at least three full-time teachers in each law college. Chief Justice Cornelius, alluding to the need for research and for legal journals, had proposed the establishment of honours schools of law and of Islamic jurisprudence to stimulate legal research.[2] Plans have already been made to establish a Law Research Institute in Karachi, financed in part by private funds.

There is virtually no published research on Pakistani legal problems in Pakistan. *The Law Journal*, published as a quarterly at the University of the Punjab Law College, consists largely of anecdotal speeches and brief essays describing tours to the United States or similar matters. Occasionally, a research article will appear but it seldom relates to Pakistani law. Several years ago, considerable interest was shown in the establishment of a legal research center in Lahore under an independent board of trustees. The Asia Foundation provided funds for a library and the Pakistan Legal Centre was established. Its principal activity is publication of the *Pakistan Bar Journal* which has appeared since 1955 jointly under its auspices and those of the Pakistan Bar Association. The administrator of the centre, Miss Rabia Sultana Qari, a barrister, maintains its headquarters in her home across the Mall from the High Court in Lahore. The Journal often publishes short articles of good quality but they are almost invariably topics in international, British, or American law written by Pakistani lawyers who studied abroad.

The *All-Pakistan Legal Decisions* (PLD), primarily a commercial service, follows the established custom of the *All-India Report*, of which it is a descendant, in having a journal section for comments and research. The journal section had thirty-one pages in 1960, thirteen pages in 1961, fourteen pages in 1962, 116 pages in 1963, and 144 pages in 1964. The increase in 1963 and 1964 was due largely to the printing of several addresses by Chief Justice Cornelius. None of the articles in the journal can be characterized as a research piece in the tradition of American legal journals. The typical article on Pakistan law in the *PLD* and other journals consists almost entirely of extensive quotations from judgments and has little or no analysis or evaluation of issues.

There are several hopeful signs suggestive of improvement in research conditions. First, there is general recognition by the legal profession of the problem of legal education and research. The law colleges, especially those of the Punjab and Peshawar universities, are making strong efforts to raise their standards and to stimulate research. Libraries are slowly improving, and certainly publications are better now than a decade ago but conditions remain unconducive to written legal analysis by professional scholars.

In Pakistan, the legal community is probably the most powerful elite group, outside government service. The total strength of legal practitioners and legally trained persons in the country, from which much of this elite's prestige is derived, is almost impossible to calculate from available data. Since the annual output of persons with law degrees can more easily be determined, it would appear convenient to begin an estimate of the size of the legal profession with a statement of this output of newly trained law graduates. Table 1 shows that the six university law colleges have awarded about 8,820 law degrees in the decade from 1954 to 1964. During the eight-year period, 1954 through 1961, (the only years for which data on all university degrees are available), these six universities conferred a total of 30,356 degrees of all kinds.[3] During the same eight years, the same universities conferred 5,346 law degrees and 3,710 medical degrees. Hence law degrees constituted 17 per cent and medical degrees 12 per cent of the total number of degrees conferred from 1954 to 1961. The ratio of law degrees to total number of degrees has remained at about 17 per cent during this eight-year period. The average output of law degrees from 1961 on (as shown by Table 1) approximates one thousand each year but since the total number of university degrees conferred for those years is not known, the ratio of law degrees to all degrees conferred cannot be determined. It is likely that the ratio has hovered around 17 per cent. To put these data in some perspective, it might be noted that in the United States of a total of 490,628 degrees of all kinds conferred in 1961, 9,514, or approximately 2 per cent were law degrees and 6,986, or approximately 1.5 per cent, were medical (M.D.) degrees.[4]

Table 1. Bachelor of Laws Degrees Granted 1954–1964

University	1954	1955	1956	1957	1958	1959	1960	1961	1962	1963	1964[a]	Total
Punjab	163	331	282	259	291	304	212	339	303	458	309	3,251
Karachi	105	193	148	187	153	175	160	250	412	399	280	2,462
Dacca	26	109	93	95	76	133	141	124	192	355	145	1,489
Peshawar	50	53	45	73	64	54	63	140	62	66	45	715
Sind	15	19	31	19	24	76	53	82	104	112	100	635
Rajshahi	—	—	34	23	21	31	14	37	53	61	18	268
Total	359	705	633	656	629	749	643	972	1,126	1,451	897	8,820[b]

Sources: For 1954–1961: Inter-University Board of Pakistan, Letter, 15 January 1964. For 1961–1964: Correspondence with principals of law colleges, September and October 1965.

a. Does not include results of supplementary examinations held in May 1964, not yet announced in December, 1964. Results of this examination will probably make 1964 total similar to that of 1963.

b. This total would approximate 9,500 if an estimate of results of the May, 1964 examination (see note a) were added.

Statistics showing the numbers of legally trained persons employed in legal work have a reliability roughly comparable to the hierarchy of the profession, the least accuracy being found in the bottom ranks. Any estimate of the size of the legal community, therefore, should include a brief description of the organization of the profession. Graduates in law first become pleaders with the right to practice before district and sessions courts but not before the high courts or Supreme Court. In East Pakistan, *munsifs* who have the equivalent of a high school education, practice criminal law below the sessions court level. Advocates, the rank above that of pleader, practice before district and sessions courts and may be enrolled for practice before the High Courts only after several years of practice and after being approved by a panel of High Court judges. Advocates may also appear before the Supreme Court after five years of practice and certification by the judges and chief justice of the High Court. The chief justice and judges of the Supreme Court may select from the roll of advocates 'persons who are judged, by their knowledge, ability and experience, to be worthy' to be senior advocates.[5] At the pinnacle of prestige are the barristers who studied in England at one of the Inns-of-Court. Barristers were distinguished from other legal practitioners by the privilege of practice before the High Court immediately upon completion of their training. Attorneys were not allowed to plead at trials before the Supreme Court and generally functioned as process servers and as residents at court for litigants. Some revisions of this organization were made in 1962, the principal one being that senior advocates of the Supreme Court are appointed not on the basis of seniority but for a distinguished legal record. The Supreme Court now designates some attorneys as senior attorneys with the privilege of pleading before the Supreme Court if they are associated with a legal firm. Legal firms have been allowed only since 1962. Senior attorneys must have at least seven years' practice and generally serve as assistants to senior advocates. At the top of the official hierarchy are members of the bench.

It is probable that there are approximately 18,000 persons trained in law in Pakistan. This figure is so tentative, however that an explanation of how it was determined is in order. As Table 2 (items 9, 10) shows, beginning at the bottom of the hierarchy there are about 12,599 legal practitioners of all categories practicing in subordinate and high courts in Pakistan; 7,289 are in West Pakistan and 5,310 are in East Pakistan. Of these, 649 are enrolled for practice before the East Pakistan High Court and 3,132 before the West Pakistan High Court.[6] The total number enrolled for practice before the Supreme Court is only 702[7], or about 18 per cent of those enrolled before the High

Table 2. Estimated Number of Legally Trained Persons in Pakistan, 1965

Classification	West Pakistan	East Pakistan	Total
1. Supreme Court judges	3	2	5
2. High court judges	29	15	46[a]
3. District and sessions judges	64	43	107
4. Subordinate court judges and *Munsifs*	153	66	319
5. Law officers[b]	76	50	126
6. Executive officers (provincial service) with judicial powers	643	738	1,381
7. Executive officers (CSP) with judicial powers	114	65	179
8. Legal practitoners enrolled in Supreme Court[c]	533	169	702
9. Legal practitioners enrolled in high courts	3,132	649	3,781
10. Legal practitoners enrolled in subordinate courts	4,157	4,661	8,818
11. Legally trained persons not performing functions related to their training	711	1,000	2,311[d]
Totals	9,615	7,558	17,775[e]

a. Includes two *ad hoc* judges not tabulated in provincial columns.
b. Registrars, government prosecutors, pleaders, legal remembrancers.
c. These figures can be further classified into 425 advocates and 108 attorneys for West Pakistan; 129 advocates and 40 attorneys for East Pakistan; total of 554 advocates and 148 attorneys.
d. Estimated from *Census of East Pakistan Government Employees* (Lahore: Government of West Pakistan, 1963) which shows (pp. 34–35) 711 of 8,814 gazetted officers with law degress in 1962. Assuming this proportion to be somewhat higher in the central government and in East Pakistan, I have estimated three hundred for the former and one thousand for the latter and have added three hundred for those outside government service. Six hundred in central government and outside government are not included in provincial columns.
e. This figure is 602 more than the sum of provincial totals for reasons given in notes a and d.
The figure has been rounded off to 18,000 in the text.

Sources: Correspondence and civil lists. Final results (except for item 11) prepared with help of Office of the Supreme Court of Pakistan, May 1965, and the chief justice, East Pakistan High Court, June 1965. Item 11 is an arbitrary estimate by the present author. Estimates of item 11 have ranged as high as ten thousand. My estimate of 2,311 is undoubtedly less than the real figure.

Courts, and about 5 per cent of the total enrolled for practice before any court. The sharply diminishing number at the top of the pyramid is an index of a marked difference in competence and skill between subordinate court practitioners and those in the superior courts. It is somewhat difficult also to estimate the number of officers involved in judicial work because of the variety of officers holding judicial powers. There are five judges on the Supreme Court, fifteen on the East Pakistan High Court, twenty-nine on the West Pakistan High Court, approximately one hundred district and sessions judges and approximately three hundred lower judges and *munsifs* in the two provinces. In addition, each of the sixteen division commissioners and seventy-four district officers and their assistants have judicial powers in certain categories of cases. Probably between fifteen hundred and two thousand persons are part of the judicial system. Using the figure 2,000 in Table 2 being 2,037) and the figure 13,427 for legal practitioners who are not judges, the ratio of judges of legal practitioners is in the order of 1:7.

Outside the formal structure of legal practice are an unknown number of law graduates who have never practiced law Although most of them are in government service, the civil lists do not always indicate the fact of legal training hence the number in this group is a cruder estimate than those given above. I estimate this group at 2,311. This is based on the fact that 711 gazetted employees of the West Pakistan provincial government are known to have law degrees (note d, Table 2). It is assumed that a somewhat higher proportion will be found in the central government and in East Pakistan. Estimating one thousand with law degrees in the East Pakistan government and three hundred in the central government, we have a sub-total of 17,475. I have added to this total an additional three hundred for an estimate of those with law degrees, outside government employ. This makes a total of 17,775, which is rounded off to eighteen thousand. Since several sources in Pakistan insist that my estimate of 2,311 persons in item 11 of Table 2 is much too low, it is probable that the total of 18,000 is an underestimate. I am reluctant to increase it, however, without further clues as to limits. In any case, eighteen thousand is a base figure which can be improved by subsequent research.

Using 18,000 as the figure for persons with legal training, some suggestive tentative ratios can be constructed which might ultimately be compared with analogous ratios for Burma, Ceylon, Malaya, and India, all of which shared the common experience of British imperial rule. For example, assuming total public employment in Pakistan to be 995,000 the ratio of legally trained persons in all pursuits to the total number of government servants would be 1:55. Or, given (in 1965) a population of 99 million, the ratio of legally trained persons to population would be 1:5500. These ratios can be compared to similar data for the United States which indicate 285,933 lawyers (both practicing and non-practicing) registered in 1960.[8] Using the official population estimate of 180 million for that year, the ratio of licensed practicing and non-practicing lawyers to total population in 1960 is thus about 1:630 for the United States. This comparison will be surprising to many who assumed that the ratio of 'lawyers' to population is higher in many new states than in old states. In any case, these comparative data really have very little meaning and must be interpreted with the utmost caution. They clearly suggest that the per capita ratio of legally trained persons in Pakistan is much less than in the United States. On the other hand, it was shown earlier that the proportion of law degrees to total degrees is markedly higher in Pakistan than in the United States. The significance of these comparisons is not clear. The vast difference between the legal needs of an industrial society and those of an agrarian economy, as well as the high status of alternative professions in the United States, should be considered in interpreting the data.

It is common to assume that developing states in the British imperial tradition have too many lawyers and that the consequent disproportionate emphasis on legal modes of thought is antithetical to the needs of development. This has been the view of President Ayub in Pakistan, although no measures have been taken to curtail the output of lawyers which, it has been shown, remains fairly constant. Ayub's view was summed up in an address before the Pakistan Lawyers Convention in Karachi on 30 September 1960, when he suggested that lawyers often gave assistance 'in the fabrication of false evidence to support the case of their client.' He added that the legal profession appeared to be overstaffed and that this, 'apart from locking useful manpower unnecessarily, creates cut-throat competition in the profession ushering in all sorts of abuses.'[9] This condition is probably aggravated by the large number of lawyers. On the other hand, it can be argued that in Pakistan the very size of the legal group, strongly organized into bar associations and closely allied with equally strong courts, has not only been a major source for the diffusion and regeneration of western norms generally but by sheer weight of numbers has enabled the courts to remain strong and has impeded what some would regard as administrative lawlessness. It is not here suggested that size alone has made possible the power of the legal community in Pakistan. There are other factors contributing to this condition. An important one is the absence of effective competing elites such as business, artistic, professional, trade-union, ecclesiastical, political, agricultural, or educational interest groups. Some of these groups, such as the business community are localized in Karachi and are not well organized. Others are rising in importance but none can rival the elites of the civil and military bureaucracies and the legal community in prestige, effective power, and close identification with the ideology and techniques of modernization.

The legal community, while often antagonistic to government and constraining governmental behaviour, is nevertheless closely identified normatively and culturally with the bureaucratic power elite. It is, in fact, this identification curiously coupled with antagonism, which enhances the strength of the legal community. It derives popular support from its ostensible opposition to government and at the same time elicits bureaucratic support from its command of western-oriented norms and techniques and commands the rather fearful attention of bureaucracy because of its support in the community at large. In the absence of other competing elites, it holds the field. Yet important though these factors are it is doubtful if the legal community could be such an effective political force without the large number of persons within its ambit of influence.

The influence of legal practitioners is further strengthened by a network of relationships in rural areas and cities. A coterie of retainers such as *munshis, dalals, muktars,* clerks, and scribes are dependent on British legal proceedings for a livelihood and serve as linguistic and cultural mediators between lawyers and the vernacularized community at large.

Students in law colleges who, at any given time approximate fifteen thousand in number, must also be included as a source of strength for the legal community as an interest group. They are often as vocal and effective as agents of western legal norms as law graduates. Indeed, considering the freedom as students to participate in anomic actions they can and do fill an agitational role unavailable to their established colleagues.

Adding law students and retainers to the figure 18,000 we can estimate the larger community of law-oriented persons at roughly 33,000. It is true that those at the fringe of this larger community have only partial comprehension of the legal norms of western jurisprudence. But at the core of the group stand persons of power and intellectual mastery of those norms who determine the style of the larger group. To society at large, the internal stratifications of understanding are not visible; it regards the entire law-oriented group, core and fringe alike, as the vanguard of modernization. The persistent challenging of governmental policy during and after martial law was successful primarily because of the size of the legal community and its consequent network of influence throughout the country. In short, the legal community is of some magnitude and is a power to be reckoned with. It has, *inter alia,* compelled the justiciability of fundamental rights, forced modification of the extension of the Frontier Crimes Regulation, and successfully agitated for amendment or abrogation of other restrictive enactments.

By and large, the judiciary, especially the Supreme Court and high courts, are highly respected and several important and influential judges such as Md. Munir, M. R. Kayani, Shabir Ahmed, M. Shahabuddin, S. A. Rahman, S. M. Murshed and A. R. Cornelius, have contributed not only to legal thought but to other aspects of the country's development. Legal erudition diminishes usually as the rank of the court becomes lower but this is true of most judicial systems. Only one instance of a senior judge being debenched because of improbity has been noted since partition. This was the case of Syed Akhlaque Husain of the West Pakistan High Court, an able jurist who was debenched for income tax evasion and falsification of expense accounts (*The State v. Mr Justice Akhlaque Husain* [1957] 1 PSCR 231) and later suspended from practicing law as well (*In the matter of Akhlaque Husain* [1959] 2 PSCR 146). Although the bench is highly respected, some lawyers of considerable ability are reputed to have refused appointment to the bench because of what they regard as relatively low salary, early retirement age, inadequate retirement pension, and prohibition against legal practice after retirement. The salary of a Supreme Court judge is 5,100 rupees a month and mandatory retirement is at the age of 65; a High Court judge receives 4,000 rupees a month and must retire at 60 years of age. These salaries compare favourably with civil service executive salaries (a full secretary receives 4,000 rupees a month) but are lower than the income of a few very successful lawyers. Salaries are fixed by the Second Schedule of the 1962 Constitution but the disqualification provision is found in Legal Practices (Disqualifications) Ordinance, 1964, published in the *Gazette of Pakistan, Extraordinary*, 30 January 1964. The Law Reform Commission recommended improving the pension scheme rather than changing the retirement age or the provision concerning disqualification from practice.

The legal profession in Pakistan is an influential, articulate group and is probably the most important group in national politics. Many active political leaders such as Khan Abdul Qayyum Khan of the Northwest Frontier, H. S. Suhrawardy Mahmud Ali Qasuri, and Mian Mumtaz Daultana were lawyers. Highly organized through regional bar associations and associations of members practicing before various courts, lawyers have in the past exerted substantial pressure on the government on behalf of such issues as fundamental rights, constitutional reform, and against extension of the frontier Crimes Regulation. If, perhaps, they have a tendency to assume that the country is in a more advanced state of political development than is actually the case, they are not unlike the intelligentsia in other developing countries who are suspended between the vision of a society based on the norms in which they are immersed and the realities of the social order. Be that as it may, the more distinguished lawyers are held in remarkably high regard by the public and by government. The legal profession as a group was opposed to the Constitution of 1962 and when Manzur Qadir was appointed chief justice of the West Pakistan High Court, several bar associations passed resolutions condemning the appointment, largely on grounds that he was the author of that Constitution.[10] Their earlier opposition to martial law and opposition to the 1962 Constitution and the form of government which evolved from it makes them the most powerful educated group in Pakistan. It is significant to note that many of the political leaders arrested in the sixties were lawyers. The arrest of Mahmud Ali Qasuri, who with others attempted to organize the National Freedom Party as a coalition of several defunct groups, also revealed the interest of such distinguished lawyers as A. K. Brohi and Z. H. Lari as well as H. S. Suhrawardy, all of whom came to his support. Bar associations have been uncommonly vigorous in taking stands on political issues. The cohesion of the legal profession with its several thousand practicing members and the sense of identity of some 31,000 persons trained in law or being trained have made the associations powerful institutions in articulating sentiments of the country. The network of followers of each legally trained person enhances the power of the legal community in villages as well as urban centers. Virtually all of the bar associations, including the two most important ones, the Lahore District Bar Association, and the West Pakistan High Court Bar Association, supported the Combined Opposition party's presidential candidate against President Ayub in the election of 2 January 1965.[11] The West Pakistan High Court Bar Association's support was virtually unanimous; there were only two dissenting votes of several thousand cast. Some of the most distinguished lawyers such as A. K. Brohi, Z. H. Lari, and Mahmud Ali Qasuri were active organizers of the Combined Opposition party. It is not surprising that the emphasis of the COP's manifesto[12] was on details of the concept of rule of law, such as the right of superior courts to review and revise administrative decisions and to issue writs to all citizens, and the separation of executive and judicial functions. The COP also stood for repeal of eight specific statutes, such as the Press and Publications Ordinance, Universities Ordinance, and Criminal Law (Amendment) Act which it deemed violated due process of law. So vociferous have bar associations been in their extra-courtroom political advocacy that they have been warned by otherwise sympathetic legal practitioners that they were assuming a role unbecoming their position. Thus, Khurshid Ahmed, Minister of Law in the central government, warned the associations during the election campaign that they were not political parties and could not organize like political parties.[13] Chief Justice Cornelius of the Supreme Court regards as inappropriate the public criticism through formal statements of laws which may ultimately be the subject of judicial scrutiny. In an address before the Karachi High Court Bar Association on 5 June 1964,[14] he said that he felt 'some anxiety regarding the exact demarcation of the duties of lawyers in a political-legal complex such as that under which we live,' and that he often felt regret when lawyers or bar associations openly criticized actions under statute law. 'Even the private citizen,' he continued, 'hesitates to offer such criticism in fear of an action in contempt where on the face of the matter recourse to the courts seems plainly probable.'

He deplored the tendency of bar associations to pass resolutions disapproving laws which are likely to be brought before the courts. 'In fact said Cornelius I often suffer the apprehension that should a bar association pass a resolution condemning a political-legal action in such circumstances, the association and each of its members would find it difficult to discover a defence against a writ of contempt which an affected party might choose to take out. The predominant ethos of the legal profession appears to be that of political activity, concern for national political development, and preoccupation with trial advocacy rather than with theoretical legal research. Members of the legal fraternity feel keenly that the future of constitutional government in the nation rests with the legal profession. In this respect, they share with the civil and military bureaucracies the sense that they are the guardians of the polity of the state.

The judiciary—powerful, respected, sometimes feared—has preserved its integrity throughout martial law and has been perhaps the most stabilizing institution in the development of Pakistan. One of the outstanding characteristics of the whole legal-judicial system in Pakistan is the strong sense of corporate unity and *elan* between the courts and legal practitioners and between levels of courts. To some extent, this unity was enhanced by martial law and what was regarded as an executive effort to curtail judicial power and to limit fundamental freedoms. The very fact that lawyers and judges could not be divided against each other was important in the re-emergence of judicial review, justiciability of fundamental rights, and the writ jurisdiction. The high courts and the Supreme Court have been a cohesive group viewing major problems of doctrine in a similar way. The few classic instances of disagreement involved somewhat peripheral rather than fundamental questions. For example, in the Gurmani defamation case (*M. A. Gurmani v. Suleri et. al., PLD 1958 Lah.* 747) Justice Shabir Ahmed made adverse remarks against Prime Minister Malik Feroze Khan Noon which were later ordered expunged from the record by the Supreme Court. Similarly, in the Snelson Case (*The State v. Sir Edward Snelson, PLD 1961*

Lah. 78), Shabir Ahmed imputed certain motives in the action of the attorney-general and this imputation was rejected by the Supreme Court (*Sir Edward Snelson v. Judges of High Court of Pakistan, PLD 1961 SC 237*). In the recent case of the arrest of Mahmud Ali Qasuri, the chief justice of the High Court, Manzur Qadir attached a political condition to the granting of bail which was stuck down by the Supreme Court (*Mian Mahmud Ali Kasuri and others v. The State, PLD 1963 SC 478*). This intellectual compatibility is sometimes given more specific institutional form. For example, the Supreme Court co-opted three judges of the high courts, thus making a special bench of seven judges to decide a major case affecting contract employees of government (*Khwaja Ghulam Sarwar v. Pakistan, PLD 1962 SC 142*). In such a major issue as the ruling of the East Pakistan High Court that cabinet ministers could not also serve as members of the legislature, the Supreme Court not only concurred but elaborated the doctrines of presidential government and judicial review in a significant way (*Fazlul Quader Chowdhry v. Md. Abdul Haque, PLD 1963 SC 486*). Even in such matters as overruling the High Court on the issuance of writs, twelve instances of which are discussed below, the courts did not disagree as to the authority to use writs but merely on interpretation of a particular set of circumstances surrounding each instance of writ issuance. The absence of serious division on crucial juridical concepts accounts in large measure for the success of the courts in maintaining a rule of law against, at some periods, very great odds.

Contempt of Courts Power

Ironically, the very power and prestige of the judiciary, essential as it is in a new state, might be regarded as a source of discouragement in the pursuit of legal research. The power and prestige of the judiciary derives in part from the stringent law of contempt and its equally stringent interpretation and enforcement by the courts. Many able lawyers in Pakistan state that they are reluctant to comment analytically on judicial decisions for fear of being found in contempt of court. They assert that this is the reason for research being focused on foreign law, which is 'safer', and for the few studies of Pakistan law being limited to extensive quotation from decisions with no commentary. To some extent this may be merely a rationalization for the absence of scholarly analysis of law in Pakistan. It is also probably true that the concept of 'critical research' does not have the same connotation of meticulous, balanced, impersonal, and, above all, responsible research as can be found in American law Passions run high in verbal altercations in Pakistan, and it might be felt not inappropriate to use intemperate, irresponsible language or to venture to make patently subjective judgments on a judge's erudition or ability. In any case, the power of each of the courts to determine if contempt has been committed and the correlative power to debar a lawyer from practicing before it is not taken lightly by some legal practitioners of Pakistan.

The basic law on contempt, the Contempt of Courts Act (XII of 1926) now incorporated in the 1962 Constitution as Article 123, has been interpreted by the courts in several important judgments. One of the earliest contempt cases decided after independence was *Haq v. The Honourable Judges of the High Court of Judicature at Lahore* (1953) FCR 206, in which a lawyer in addressing to the Supreme Court an appeal from a High Court decision, stated as a ground for appeal that the remarks of the Honourable Judges betray a lack of the knowledge of elementary principles bearing on the administration of criminal justice. The Federal (Supreme) Court felt that the range of accepted legal expression was sufficient without belittling judges and that while it is one thing to point out an error in a judgment, it is quite another 'to apply a damaging label to the Judge or Judges whose error is the sole matter requiring attention.' The federal court, noting that the criticism made by the advocate was necessary in this instance, did not uphold the High Court's suspension. The publisher of a newspaper, which allegedly made a 'technical error' of reporting that certain contempt proceedings 'had been dropped in view of the qualified apology tendered by the contemner, while in fact the court had reserved orders,' was found guilty of falsely guiding the public mind as to results of a case so as to embarrass the judge in his function. It was further held that intention or malice were not necessary attributes of contempt (*Abdus Salam v. The State* [1958] 1 PSCR 427). That allegations against a judge may be true or that they may be made in a legal application for transfer of a case are not sufficient reasons to justify scandalizing the judiciary (*Israr Hussain v. The Crown* [1951] 2 FCR 7). The court trying contempt charges against itself may 'follow the procedure it consider[s]...suitable,' since the Criminal Procedure Code is not applicable to contempt proceedings (*Abdur Rashid v. The Crown* [1954] 2 FCR 177).

The celebrated Snelson case dealt with the problem of contempt of court in High Court and Supreme Court judgments totaling some 140 pages (*State v. Sir Edward Snelson, PLD 1961 Lah. 78; Sir Edward Snelson v. Judges of the High Court of West Pakistan, PLD 1961 SC 237*). Sir Edward, secretary of the Ministry of Law, and the most senior pre-independence British ICS officer remaining in Pakistan, talked informally to government officials participating in an administrative training programme in Rawalpindi. His talk, dealing with the transitional Constitution of 1958, was published by the Secretariat Training Institute and circulated to government officers including High Court judges. By 'transitional constitution,' Sir Edward meant a series of instruments under which the nation was governed under martial law. They included the Proclamation of Martial Law, the Laws (Continuance in Force) Order, 1958, and four other instruments. The judges took the view that certain remarks made in the talk appeared to be contemptuous and charged Sir Edward with violation of the Contempt of Courts Act. These remarks dealt with the issue of the writ petition. Sir Edward said, in part:

> 9. Between 1956 and 1958, the High Courts had used the language of the 1956 Constitution, with its reference to orders and directions in the nature of writs—to claim a jurisdiction to interfere with the Government itself without reference to the strictly defined frontiers

of the prerogative writs...the Law Ministry has had to appeal a large number of times to the Supreme Court to have the position properly established and has succeeded in every appeal but one. All this has cost a great deal of money, and to try to put the situation right without having to spend more money on more appeals a clause was inserted in the Order we are discussing giving the High Courts the power to issue the named 'writs' (not 'orders or directions' and so on, but writs) of *mandamus* and the rest. This was to indicate as politely as possible, that a writ was a writ, confined to known limits, and the limits could not be exceeded. I must confess that, even with this civility, we have not entirely succeeded even yet, but this clause on the one side, and some very severe observations by the Supreme Court on the other, have at least had the effect of indicating that after all there are limits and that the limits must be observed. The great thing, in any orderly system of government (and without orderliness there is chaos) is that every organ of the government should be best adapted to the work it has to do and should know what the work is and what its own frontiers are. This avoids duplication. It avoids friction. It prevents usurpation of function and consequent uncertainty, with all the public confusion and private misery that it can lead to...

10....Perhaps you would have wished me to say something about the services, seeing that what was originally a single paragraph, Article 6, has now been increased to a further six paragraphs, some modifying the terms and conditions of service already guaranteed— but not all: one of the additions establishes the power to grant extensions of service, a power which was denied by the High Court. We have never been able to understand the judgment: We would, of course, have appealed against it, and I have no doubt we should have succeeded, but there was no time—a certain loan from abroad was made conditional upon the continued retention of certain people, and since the High Court had denied the power to retain, and we could not wait for the months an appeal would take, the existence of the power was formally asserted in an explanation...

In pretrial questioning by some of the High Court judges, Snelson asserted that he 'had written the Talk in the midst of pressing official preoccupations and that if he had had more time he might have used different language' but that 'nothing in the language he has used was meant in any way to ridicule or be derogatory to the High Courts' (*State v. Sir Edward Snelson, PLD 1961 Lah. at 98 and 99*). In this conversation Snelson 'admitted that in paragraph 9 of the Talk he had intended to say that writs could not issue to Government. The High Court unanimously found Snelson guilty of contempt on the basis of the remarks in paragraphs 9 and 10. The court maintained (a) that Snelson indicated that it did not have the power to issue writs which, in fact, it had, (b) that Snelson impugned the court by suggesting a usurpation of executive functions, (c) that the tone of the talk was offensive, particularly in the comment that government could not understand' a High Court decision. The Supreme Court unanimously upheld the decision. Chief Justice Cornelius made this comment:

> [The] words 'as politely as possible' are used ironically, and...they carry the implication of the use of courtesy where none was justified.... At the same time, a hope of greater success is expressed which is based upon the wording of the amended clause and 'some very severe observations by the Supreme Court' which it is said have had 'the effect of indicating that after all there are limits and that the limits must be observed. The existence of limits is very often anathema to a judicial body charged with the function of interpreting written words conveying powers to itself. The reminder of actual corrections by a superior appellate authority adds a string which could not have been lost upon the audience of section officers.

At the time of Snelson's talk, the Supreme Court had overruled the High Court of West Pakistan in at least twelve judgments involving the use of writs. The Supreme Court's view of the use of the writ appeared to be somewhat more restrained than that of the High Court. Snelson did not mention these judgments nor did he quote the language of the Supreme Court in disagreeing with the High Court. The language of the Supreme Court in these twelve cases may illustrate the range of permissible expression not involving contempt. It should be made clear, however, that this language is that of the Supreme Court commenting on the High Court's judgments. The moderate tone suggests the need for even greater moderation on the part of a researcher not a member of the bench. Cornelius, who was later to become chief justice, wrote six of the twelve judgments. The

first of these deals with an issue which had been raised by
Snelson in his talk, namely, the construction by the High Court
of the term 'directions, orders or writs' to mean more than writs.
Under this construction, the High Court had ordered payment
of salary. Cornelius overruled the High Court on the ground
that the power to issue directions and orders did not exceed the
confines of the power to issue writs. Since writs could not be
used to enforce payment of salary, neither could directions or
orders. 'It represents,' said the chief justice, 'a diversion of the
due and orderly administration of the law into a new and (we
say so with proper respect) and improper course, which cannot
be supported, and must not be allowed to become a precedent
for the future' (*State of Pakistan v. Mehrajuddin* [1959] 1 PSCR 34).
This is the very issue to which Snelson referred. Although he
had rather loosely summarized the view of the Supreme Court,
his mode of expression lacked scholarly precision and
circumspection. In the earliest relevant case, Amiruddin Ahmad
said that the High Court made an order 'without taking into
consideration all the factors relevant to the case...[and it] had no
jurisdiction to interfere by means of writ' (*Central Board of Revenue
v. Asad Ahmad Khan* [1959] 2 PSCR 215). In another case, he stated
that 'the learned Judges considered that the first decision was
taken properly and in the light of the facts; it would appear that
this decision is plainly incorrect' (*Province of West Pakistan v
Akram Wasti* [1959] 2 PSCR 285). In a significant case overruling
a High Court verdict that prospects of promotion were a
'condition of service' which cannot be changed by the
government, Cornelius held that 'it seems to us impossible in
the face of the wording of this proviso to support the conclusion
reached by the learned judges, which has the effect of overriding
a power necessarily invested in the government' (*Government of
West Pakistan v. Fateh Ullah Khan* [1959] 2 PSCR 215). On at least
two occasions the Supreme Court disagreed with a value
judgment of the High Court which had ruled that a certain officer
was entitled to promotion. Cornelius wrote, 'consequently the
order issued by the learned Judges was, speaking with respect,

wholly inappropriate to a man of his type' (*Government of West Pakistan v. Fida Muhammad Khan* [1959] 2 PSCR 187).

Similarly, Cornelius later said 'in our opinion, the learned Judges of the High Court, in issuing the writ here under appeal did not place the correct interpretation upon the order' (*Province of East Pakistan v. Md. Abdu Miah* [1959] 1 PSCR 259). On another occasion, the Supreme Court did not sustain a High Court order of writ because of inordinate delay in the applicant's prayer and because of other special circumstances (*Lahore Central Cooperative Bank Ltd. v. Saif Ullah Shah* [1959] 1 PSCR 164). Justice S. A. Rahman, writing two of the twelve opinions used such language as 'the High Court seems to have erroneously assumed' (*Pakistan v. Hasan Ali Jafari and another* [1960] 1 PSCR 26), and 'the direction to order payment of arrears of salary was misconceived and must be set aside' (*Government of West Pakistan v. Fazal-e-Haq Mussarrat* [1960] 1 PSCR 124). In another case, Chief Justice Md. Munir wrote that the view taken by the High Court was 'wholly unsustainable' and that the High Court was 'plainly wrong in the view...' (*Pakistan v. Hikmat Hussain* [1958] 2 PSCR 257). Munir, noting that the relief granted by the High Court was different from the one requested, referred to the 'error in proceedings' of the High Court as being fundamental (*Pakistan v. Ali Afzal* [1959] 2 PSCR 160). Finally, former Chief Justice Md. Shahabuddin stated, 'one would have expected a fuller consideration of the language of the rule in question in the judgment of the High Court.... They have, however, relied on observations in two cases which no doubt appear to support their conclusion but are clearly in the nature of *obiter dicta*' (*Pakistan v. Liaquat Ali Khan* [1958] 2 PSCR 234).

Perhaps Snelson intended to say no more than the Supreme Court said in these twelve judgments. Clearly, he erred in suggesting that the courts could not issue writs against the government for this has never been the law nor has the Supreme Court ever denied the authority of the high courts to issue writs. It has, however, differed with the high courts in specific circumstances surrounding the issue of writs and on at least these twelve occasions has reversed the lower court's verdict.

In the view of the judiciary then, it was not the mere reference to the Supreme Court's overruling of several High Court decisions but imprecision of language, tone, incorrect facts, and suggestion of judicial usurpation, which led to Snelson's conviction. This observation appears to be supported by the late Chief Justice M. R. Kayani's comments in correspondence with the present author[15] in which he stated, 'To say that the High Court had a different view of the writ jurisdiction from the Supreme Court would not scandalize or ridicule either court. There would be no contempt in saying the High Court or the Supreme Court view was more reasoned, etc. It should be treated as legal criticism.' It appears to have been corroborated more recently by remarks of Chief Justice Cornelius made in the course of a lecture at the Civil Service Academy, Lahore, 25 April 1964:

> What provided some light basis for the view expressed in the [Snelson] lecture was that a number of Writs issued by the High Courts had been recalled on re-examination of the matter in the Supreme Court but it was clear that the criticism was misguided and misdirected and that the language employed was of a lowering type which the High Court could not be expected to tolerate, if it was to retain its position in the organization and functioning of the State.[16]

It is noteworthy that both courts were unanimous in the Snelson decision, that distinguished lawyers such as Mahmud Ali Qasuri who appeared in the case as *amicus curiae*, supported the decision, and that it was praised in the press. The *Pakistan Times*, for example, stating that 'fresh lustre' had been imparted to the judiciary and the 'country's prestige in the outside world has been enhanced.'[17] The case suggests quite clearly the consummate delicacy and caution which might be required in legal research. To the American scholar, this might present a challenge because the tradition of legal scholarship is more openly critical in the United States and the law of contempt of courts, as Justice Shabir Ahmed noted in the High Court judgment in the Snelson case, is also less stringent in the United States.

The seriousness of contempt is further indicated by the fact that the High Court judge, Shabir Ahmed, who found Sir Edward Snelson guilty of contempt of court in 1960, was found guilty of contempt of the very High Court of which he had been a judge after retirement while practising as an advocate. Shabir Ahmed had issued a statement supporting the validity of a ruling by the chief justice of the High Court attaching a condition to the bail bond of a defendant. The statement was published in the *Pakistan Times* and both the newspaper and the retired justice were found in contempt on the ground that the matter commented on was still under consideration by the court. Strict interpretation of the usual status of legal practitioners who are certified to practice before the courts as being officers of the court with the responsibility of assisting the court in obtaining justice may also affect research by Pakistani scholars. Just how far an officer of the court may go in criticizing or disagreeing with decisions of that court or with the line of reasoning even in activities outside the courtroom may not be clear or legal scholarship.

To determine attitudes toward scholarly legal criticism, the present author discussed this issue extensively with the late Chief Justice M. R. Kayani of the West Pakistan High Court, and present Chief Justice A. R. Cornelius of the Supreme Court of Pakistan. In an effort to elicit guidelines for acceptable scholarly criticism, the author submitted to each judge extracts or reprints of representative legal scholarship in the United States. One of these was a long quotation from the annual review of legal developments in the United States published in the *American Political Science Review*.[18] Fellman in this review used such expressions as 'Considering...the expansivenes of his colleagues, Justice Black's opinion for the Court was unusually brief, and on the crucial constitutional issue almost peremptory...The Chief Justice reviewed rather discursively and uncritically...The Court has at long last come to grips...Justice Jackson's dissenting opinion sounded more like a concurring opinion.' The second sample was an article on the relations of lower courts to the United States Supreme Court.[19] The third was the text of a theoretical essay on the nature of the judicial decision[20] in which the author called for a re-appraisal of the judicial process which he regarded as essentially a trial by combat between counsel for opposing interests.

The specific reactions of Chief Justice Kayani to these samples are noteworthy.[21] With respect to Fellman's review, Kayani said:

> The words 'expansiveness of his colleagues,' 'usually brief,' 'peremptory,' 'rather discursively and uncritically' used in relation to the Judge in the first passage are the only words which will attract attention. In Pakistan, phrases and words less blunt would be used but no action [for contempt] would be suggested even against the use of these words. In the second passage, the words 'at long last came to grips' and 'sounded more like a concurring opinion' would be of the same class, but would not be actionable.

Regarding Murphy's analysis of the capacity of lower courts to check Supreme Court power, Kayani asserted that this substantive analysis would not be made since lower courts in Pakistan could not evade an order of the Supreme Court or High Court. Of Swisher's article, Kayani said, 'This is a criticism of the method of working in a Court, and would be most welcome in Pakistan. The only objectionable passage occurs in part IV, where a judge is described as possibly "getting illumination "from conversation with his law clerk or gossip with his secretary".' In a general statement, the High Court chief justice said:

> The law of contempt applies if the manner of criticism is contemptuous, that is to say, it lowers the Court in the eyes of others. So far as the criticism of judgments goes the law is now stated in Article 123(2) (b) of the new [1962] Constitution. A person commits contempt if he scandalizes the Court or otherwise does anything which tends to bring the Court or a Judge of the Court into hatred, ridicule, or contempt. This is an easily understandable definition, and if a legal critic merely states that an argument used by a judge is wrong and gives reason for it, good or bad, I do not see how he can use the law of contempt as a pretext for the lack of a critical faculty.

Of course, I can understand that, since there has been no legal criticism in Pakistan so far, judges will for some time be sensitive to an adverse discussion of their judgments but whatever be the private feelings of a judge on such occasions, they will never have the temerity of taking action in a body unless the criticism is scandalizing.

But it must be made clear that the law of contempt in Pakistan is based on the English law and that it is more rigid than the American law. This, in my opinion, is wholesome, because criticism in Pakistan is not so advanced as to steer clear of lapses into the personality of a judge.

In dealing with this issue, Chief Justice A. R. Cornelius did not comment for publication on the specific examples discussed. He summarized his view in the following statement authorized for publication:

I have never entertained the apprehension that the Superior Courts in Pakistan were intolerant of reasoned analysis and criticism of their judgments. The field for academic examination and exposition of the principles underlying these judgments and for critical appraisement of the decisions reached in relation to earlier cases in Pakistan or elsewhere, is entirely open. Judges and lawyers alike would indeed welcome review of the development of law through the Courts, by detached and well-informed observers.

Thus, in legal research, the scholar must function within the conditions of responsibility, temperateness, and maturity prevailing in society, in general. The extensive quotations in the foregoing analysis suggest the channels for criticism which might not be contemptuous. It is not yet clear if an independent scholar would be allowed to say of the High Court what the Supreme Court said in the twelve cases cited, that is, it was 'plainly incorrect,' had 'no jurisdiction to interfere,' its direction was 'misconceived,' its view 'wholly unsustainable,' and that it had 'error in proceedings.' It is clear that the utmost tact, precision of language, and discretion are essential. Sir Edward Snelson was neither clear nor accurate in his review of the writ petition and the combination of absence of clarity, indiscreet language, and a tone of facetiousness led to his conviction. The challenge thus presented to research is immense. For whatever reasons, it has not yet been taken up by Pakistani legal scholarship. The standards of research and the limits of legal criticism will be determined by the milieu of Pakistan and especially by the courts' assessment of the conflicting demands of order and freedom. The political context is one of unstable equilibrium, the tradition of disciplined, responsible criticism is weak, the sensitivities consequent to imperial rule are acute. Transcending all of these is a strong and proud judiciary which regards its integrity as a mainstay of order and is intent on preserving that integrity. Perhaps the dictum quoted by the Supreme Court as a guide for comment on the judiciary is equally relevant to legal research: 'If there must be an excess, let it be an excess of gentleness.'[22]

Documentary Sources

During the period of martial law from 7 October 1958 to 8 June 1962, all legislative bodies were suspended hence there was no daily record of proceedings of the National Assembly and the two Provincial Assemblies. Publication resumed on 8 June 1962, when the legislatures reconvened. The proceedings of the new national assembly are now known as *National Assembly Debates, Official Report*. A separate issue appears for each day of the session. The *Debates* are well edited, competently printed, and fairly well indexed on the front cover. One difficulty, however, is the fact that only 350 copies are printed. Since there are at least twenty libraries in Pakistan and thirty libraries in foreign countries which should get copies, as well as 156 legislators and one hundred government officials who need them in their work, this stock may not be adequate. The time lapse between date of the session and date of printing is about ten months which makes contemporary research difficult. The same comments are pertinent to the debates of the two provincial assemblies, except that the debates of the Provincial Assembly of East Pakistan are not printed in separate pamphlets for each session. Instead, the proceedings of several sessions are combined in one publication usually about five hundred pages in length. In an effort to reduce the gap between the session and publication of proceedings, the secretary of the West Pakistan Assembly is having the printing done by several commercial publishers instead of exclusively by the West Pakistan Government Press. This will speed publication considerably.

One of the problems consequent to partition and re-organization is that of knowing what laws are currently valid. While the Ministry of Law publication, *Unrepealed Acts and Ordinances of the Central Government*, has been published through Volume XII to include 1954, there is a time lag in publication. Of particular utility is the Central Laws (Statute Reform) Ordinance, 1960, which lists in appended schedules the current legal status of laws of the central government and of West Pakistan from 1834 to 1949. This is published in the official reporting service, *Pakistan Law Reports* West Pakistan, September, 1960.

The Ministry of Law of the central government publishes annual compilations of laws, the latest being *A Collection of Central Acts and Ordinances* for the year 1954, but there is a time lag of several years. The Law Ministry has also published a twelve-volume compilation, *Unrepealed Central Acts*, 1844 to 1954. The most convenient and useful sources of new laws are the leading commercial reporting systems for court decisions, the *All-Pakistan Legal Decisions*, and the analogous commercial and official government reporting systems for the two provinces. These are described below. Laws, ordinances, and rules are published in the central and provincial gazettes, and separate copies of such enactments are available within a few days of issuance at the government presses and such commercial agencies as *All-Pakistan Legal Decisions* in Lahore, Pakistan Law House in Karachi, and Obaidullah, of *Dacca Law Reports* in Dacca. Especially useful are 'Bare Acts,' separate acts published in pamphlet form by PLD and available almost immediately after enactment. Although all government publications list an extensive network of authorized sales agents which are book stores scattered throughout the nation, these agents rarely have government publications available and are not inclined to attempt to procure them energetically.

Statutory law passed by the national assembly and the two provincial assemblies, ordinances and laws issued by the president and governors, both before and after martial law, can be found in several sources. Copies of many of these are available from the central and provincial government presses. Since each law is listed separately, the catalogues of the three government presses are themselves a fairly complex index of statutory law. The primary official source for acts of the national assembly, as specified by Rule 80 of the *Rules of Procedure and Conduct of Business in the National Assembly of Pakistan*, is the *Gazette of Pakistan*, which has already been described as an important source of notification of assignments of officials, appointments of officials, and texts of laws and reports.[23] It serves as an organ of both the executive departments and the legislature and as the legal instrument which actuates operation of ordinances, laws, rules, and all other legislative actions published in it. All three gazettes are used in the same manner, hence all are indispensable sources of legislative and executive matters. A dramatic instance of the importance of the *Gazette* fulfilling the function of statutory activation is found in an important judgment of the High Court of West Pakistan (*Abdul A'la Maudoodi v. Government of West Pakistan, PLD 1965 Kar. 478*) involving dissolution of the influential orthodox Muslim group, Jamaat-e-Islami. The Governor of West Pakistan had extended the application of the Criminal Law (Amendment) Act to the whole of the province and under authority of this law he immediately declared the Jamaat to be an unlawful association. Notice of extension of the law and of declaring the Jamaat unlawful appeared in the same issue of the *Gazette* on the same day that the government sealed the Jamaat's headquarters. One of the issues in the case was whether the two actions were properly publicized. The court upheld earlier judgments that an act becomes operative when published in the *Gazette*, a requirement specified in the West Pakistan General Clauses Act (VI of 1956), although it differed with earlier judgments which had specified that a reasonable opportunity to see the *Gazette* be given the affected party. The court held the actions to be operative instantly upon publication of the *Gazette* and relied on a definition from Webster stating 'publish' to mean causing to print or issue from a press. In the court's view no element of distribution, dissemination, or reading of the material was involved. The works manager of the West Pakistan Government Press testified that the two notices were published within an hour after the press opened at 7.30 am. The court accordingly ruled that extension of the act became operative at 8.30 am, and declaration of the Jamaat as unlawful became operative at the same time since it followed the extension notice both in numbering and in location in the *Gazette*. The precise time of printing was at issue because the Jamaat's offices were sealed at 4.00 am, four-and-a-half hours before publication of the notices. The High Court, upholding the government's action, dismissed this fact as a mere 'irregularity.' The judgment was upheld by the Supreme Court of Pakistan (*Criminal Appeal No. 43 of 1964 and Civil Appeal No. 19-D of 1964*, decided on 25 September 1964). It is the first case in which the act of printing a notice in the *Gazette* figures so prominently, and it is the most recent reaffirmation of the *Gazette* as a crucial legal instrument.

The official government series reporting Supreme Court and High Court cases consists of three separate publications. The *Pakistan Supreme Court Reports* which, prior to 23 March 1956, was called *Federal Court Reports*, is the official reporting medium for the Supreme Court. These reports are carefully printed and are distinguished by meticulously edited headnotes which are invariably checked by the judge writing the judgment and often prepared by the editor of the reports. The time lag between date of judgment and publication has been reduced to somewhat less than two months. Only a small proportion of cases decided by the courts are published in the reports. A careful survey of previous unpublished decisions was made to determine if important constitutional principles were involved. Such decisions, together with those already published, are included in a new decennial digest, the first issue of which, covering the 1950–1959 period, appeared in October, 1961: Dr Nasim Hasan Shah (ed.), *The Pakistan Supreme Court Digest, Decennial Digest, 1950–1959* Karachi, Government of Pakistan Press, 1961. This 383-page digest is of considerable research utility. It follows the same headnote system used in the Supreme Court reports and is a well-edited summary of about seven hundred cases. The work of reporting and research in the Supreme Court has been accelerated by the personal interest of Chief Justice A. R. Cornelius and the registrar, A. A. Mirza. The survey of unpublished decisions is continuing, and it is possible that the publication of additional digests will result. In the meantime, a commercially published digest of Supreme Court decisions is of considerable utility: Sheikh Shaukat Mahmood (ed.), *The Supreme Court Digest* 1950–June 1964, Lahore: Pakistan Law Times Publication, 1964. Mahmood's digest is carefully written and is highly regarded by judges of the Supreme Court.

Each province publishes a reporter series corresponding to the *Supreme Court Reports*, but there is not, as yet, an official digest for the high courts. The provincial series are called, respectively, *Pakistan Law Reports—West Pakistan and Pakistan Law Reports—Dacca Series*. These are somewhat more comprehensive than the national series, since they include many Supreme Court as well as High Court decisions and often print the texts of central and provincial statutes and administrative rules in a second part to each monthly volume. While these publications are the official government sources on case law and statutes and are accurately and well printed there is a time lag of a year or more between the judgment and publication. Both of the official provincial series have adequate annual indexes and digests of cases.

Because of the delay in printing the official series, lawyers rely more on several equivalent commercial reporting systems. The most useful of these is the series known as *All-Pakistan Legal*

Decisions, published in Lahore by a corporation of the same name at the Punjab Educational Press. The PLD, as they are cited, appear monthly and include judgments of both high courts, the Supreme Court, and the Board of Revenue. The reporting is relatively current; judgments rendered as recently as a month before often appear in the printed monthly volume. PLD publishes nearly twice the number of cases as do the three official series. An incidental advantage of PLD is the advertisements which inform the reader of the most recent law publications. PLD also publishes a *Quinquennial Digest* of civil, criminal, and revenue cases, the latest issue being for the 1957–1961 period, and a *Decennial Digest,* the last issue of which covered 1947–1956. Two specialized reporting systems, both published by *All-Pakistan Legal Decisions,* are *All-Pakistan Tax Decisions* (PTD) and *Pakistan Labour Cases* (PLC), both of which publish ordinances, rules, and notifications relating, respectively, to tax and labour law. All of these reporting systems publish the texts of statutes and ordinances. PLD does not publish all materials on East Pakistan although some items appear intermittently. The publishing work of *All-Pakistan Legal Decisions* is a noteworthy episode in the history of Pakistan. Without the speedy, efficient, and imaginative work of this concern, research would be far more difficult. PLD was founded by Malik Mir Muhammad who served as an apprentice in the Punjab Government Press before partition and later established a private printing firm. At partition, he founded PLD as an equivalent to the *All-India Reporter* (AIR). The work is carried on by his son, Malik Mohd. Saeed. The counterpart of PLD in East Pakistan is the commercial publishers, Obaidul Huq Chowdhury in Dhaka, who publishes the *Dacca Law Reports* which promptly reports criminal and civil judgments of the High Court of East Pakistan and most of the judgments of the Supreme Court and the West Pakistan High Court. Obaidul Huq Chowdhury also edits and publishes the *Up-To-Date Civil Reference* (1st ed; Dacca: Dacca Law Reports Office, 1960), which is useful because it covers the period 1947–1960 and is arranged by statute as well as by the usual civil law headings. Another valuable compilation is Kazi Muhammad Ashraf, *Legal Topics* (Lahore: Mahmood and Co., 1961), a digest of cases decided by the privy council, supreme courts, and high courts of Pakistan and India from 1798 to 1961. The Pakistan Law House in Karachi publishes annual compilations of laws, the latest being *Collection of 1960 Central Acts and Ordinances*. Since much of the work of the district officer has been judicial, knowledge of criminal and civil procedure is necessary for an understanding of district administration. The leading compilations, published by All-Pakistan Legal Decisions, are *Code of Civil Procedure*, 1961; *Code of Criminal Procedure*, 1960; and *Pakistan Penal Code*, 1960, all three of which are edited by M. M. Hasan Nizami and C. Fazal-i-Haq.

The authorized mode of citing these reporting systems is as follows:

I. Official Government Reporting Series

  A. *Federal Courts Reports* and its successor (starting on 23 March 1956), *Pakistan Supreme Court Reports*: (Year of judgment), volume number (if any) in arabic numbers, abbreviation of series, first page of judgment.
  Example: (1954) 2 FCR 105
  (1958) 1 PSCR 432

  B. *Pakistan Law Reports* (West Pakistan Series): Abbreviation of series (year of judgment), volume number, bench abbreviation, first page of judgment.
  Example: PLR (1957) 2 Lah. 635

  C. *Pakistan Law Reports* (Dacca Series): Abbreviation of series (year of judgment), volume number (if any; Dacca series seldom has multiple volumes), bench abbreviation, first page of judgment.
  Example: PLR (1964) 1 Dacca 302

II. Commercial Reporting Series
  A. *All-Pakistan Legal Decisions* (authorized by government):
      Abbreviation of series, year of judgment, name of court or
      bench abbreviation for one of six benches of West Pakistan
      High Court or Board of Revenue, first page of judgment.
      Example: PLD 1964 SC 537
      PLD 1964 Lah. 77

Tax Decisions and Labour Cases series are cited as follows:
    1963 PTD 1
    1963 PTD (Trib) 1
    1963 PLC 1
  B. Dacca Law Reports:
      Volume number, abbreviation of series (year of judgment),
      first page of judgment.
      Example: 2 DLR (1964) 190

III.   Authorized abbreviations for courts and benches:
SC   Supreme Court of Pakistan
Dacca   East Pakistan High Court of Judicature
          (also called High Court of East Pakistan)
Lah. or WP   High Court of West Pakistan
Azad J & K   High Court of Azad Jammu and Kashmir
Kar.   Karachi bench of High Court of West Pakistan
Pesh.   Peshawar bench of High Court of West Pakistan

BJ   Bahawalpur circuit of High Court of West Pakistan
     (Baghdad-ul-Jadid is the capital of Bahawalpur, which
     before 1947 was a princely state.)
Quetta   Quetta circuit of High Court of West Pakistan (Quetta
           is principal city in former Baluchistan States Union.)
WP (Rev.)   Board of Revenue, West Pakistan
   In Pakistani constitutional law, there are no case books as are
known in other countries. Four of the most important cases,
however, have been analyzed by Sir Ivor Jennings in the seventy-
five-page introduction to his *Constitutional Problems in Pakistan*

(Cambridge, 1957). The remainder of the book consists of the text of the judgments in these cases which relate to the governor-general's power of assent and its bearing on the constitutionality of government in Pakistan. A standard commentary on the 1956 Constitution is Volume VIII by Alan Gledhill in the series edited by George W. Keeton, *The British Commonwealth: The Development of Its Laws and Constitution* (London, 1957). A. K. Brohi's *Fundamental Law of Pakistan* (Karachi, Din Muhammadi Press, 1958) is the longest and perhaps the best printed book published in Pakistan. It is both an analysis of the 1956 Constitution and a prodigious effort to integrate much comparative jurisprudence and political theory with Pakistan's constitutional development. It contains a valuable appendix of documents such as the Constitution and the Indian Independence Act. A revised edition of Brohi's book, based on the 1962 Constitution, appeared in 1964. Like the first edition, it is more than a commentary on constitutional law and is essentially a study in comparative political theory and jurisprudence. Another authoritative, critical commentary on the 1962 Constitution is *Constitutional and Organic Law of Pakistan* (Lahore, All-Pakistan Legal Decisions, 1965), written by former Chief Justice M. Munir. The author also served as minister of law and parliamentary affairs and is highly regarded by the legal profession for his critical scholarship. Copies of the 1962 Constitution are available in pamphlet form at the sales depot of the manager of Central Government Publications in Karachi.

Legal Issues Relevant to Bureaucracy

a. The 1956 Constitution and martial law

The proclamation of martial law on 7 October 1958, abrogated the 1956 Constitution, dismissed the central and provincial cabinets and assemblies, and abolished political parties. Although the *tabula rasa* thus created made possible a totally new juridical and administrative system, this did not eventuate. Three days after proclamation of martial law, the President issued the Laws (Continuance in Force) Order, 1958, which declared that the nation was to be governed 'as nearly as may be in accordance with the late Constitution.' In effect, all laws were to continue in force unless specifically abrogated.

After the assumption of the presidency by General Mohammad Ayub Khan, the position of chief martial law administrator converged with that of president. The country was divided into three zones, each commanded by a military officer designated as zonal martial law administrator. In each zone, the chief secretary was designated as deputy martial law administrator and zones were subdivided into sectors commanded by subordinate officers. The legal instrument for the assumption of martial law was the proclamation, subsidiary to which were three categories of instruments: regulations, orders, and ordinances. The distinction between these categories is significant and figured prominently in at least three cases: *Khuhro v. Pakistan, PLD 1960 SC 237; Iftikhar-ud-Din v. Muhammad Sarfraz, PLD 1961 SC 585;* and *Mohammad Afzal v. Commissioner, Lahore Division, PLD 1963 SC 401.* Since no definitions of these categories are to be found anywhere in martial law enactments the distinctions must be derived by inference from previous practice and by judicial construction in these three decisions. It is clear that the proclamation of 7 October 1958, is the paramount instrument whose legitimacy was validated by the Supreme Court in several decisions starting with the Dosso case, discussed later in this section. Martial law authority assumed both legislative and executive powers and established a hierarchy of instruments analogous to the two hierarchies which had previously existed. Immediately below the paramount instrument (proclamation) were regulations which the Supreme Court in the Afzal case said were meant to describe laws of a general nature made by martial law authorities. Nearly one hundred regulations were issued during the martial law period. Martial law orders determined the manner in which the principles and policies of the regulations were to be carried out. Fewer than fifty such orders were issued by President Ayub as chief martial law administrator, and about one hundred were issued by the zonal administrators. The *Iftikharuddin* judgment held that in promulgating regulations and orders, the President exercised his 'super-constitutional' powers assumed by the *coup d'etat*. On the other hand, the issuance of ordinances promulgated by the President was in the exercise of his constitutional powers derived from the ordinance-making power of the 1956 Constitution, by which the nation was to be governed as nearly as possible. President's Order (Post-Proclamation) No. 1 of 1958 (Laws [Continuance in Force] Order) clearly removed from judicial scrutiny the proclamation, orders made in pursuance of the proclamation, martial law orders, martial law regulations, and orders of military courts.

An occasion for the courts to comment on martial law arose only six days after the proclamation of 7 October 1958, in *The State v. Dosso and another* (1958) 2 PSCR 180, in which four criminal appeals were grouped together for judgment. Under the Frontier Crimes Regulation, the deputy commissioner of Sibi referred a case of murder to a special *jirga* (council of elders) who found the respondents guilty. The respondents then applied for writs contending that the relevant provisions of the Frontier Crimes Regulation were void since they were repugnant to Article 5 (equal protection of the laws) of the 1956 Constitution. The High Court found the Frontier Crimes Regulation repugnant to Article 5, and the state appealed to the Supreme Court. The Supreme Court overruled the High Court, Chief Justice Munir reasoning that the Constitution itself, of which Article 5 was a part, had been abrogated, hence the Frontier Crimes Regulation could not be repugnant to an abrogated norm. Further, he maintained, the Frontier Crimes Regulation was revalidated by Article 1 of the Laws (Continuance in Force) Order. In arriving at this judgment, Munir found it necessary to 'appraise the existing constitutional position in the light of the juristic principles which determine the validity or otherwise of law-creating organs in modern states.' Relying largely on Hans Kelsen's *General Theory of Law and State* (Anders Wedberg, trans., Cambridge, Mass., 1945), he concluded that 'victorious revolution or a successful *coup d'etat* is an internationally recognized legal method of changing a Constitution,' and that such a revolution becomes a new law-creating organ. This view of the legitimacy of the 1958 *coup d'etat* has not been departed from by the judiciary. In a later celebrated case in which an Indian army officer was convicted of espionage, the legitimacy of martial law was upheld by Justice Murshed and the judgment was later sustained by the Supreme Court (*Bhattacharya v. the State, PLD 1963 Dacca 422*). There remained the further obstacle of dealing with fundamental rights, which as part of the Constitution were presumably abrogated. Do fundamental rights transcend national law-making authority? Munir reasoned that such rights are so fundamental that they cannot be taken away by law. Since under martial law there is no restriction on the president's law-making power, then there is no such thing as a fundamental right. As to the provision of the Laws (Continuance in Force) Order that Pakistan shall be governed as nearly as may be in accordance with the late Constitution, he reasoned that this applied to structure and form and not to laws which had been abrogated. This unanimous judgment was concurred in by Justices Shahabuddin, Amiruddin Ahmad, and Cornelius, but the latter— dissenting from the line of reasoning—wrote a separate opinion in which he was less certain than Munir that fundamental rights derive their validity solely from the Constitution. He then implied that certain rights are derived *de natura*. 'A number of these rights,' he reasoned, 'are essential human rights which inherently belong to every citizen of a country governed in a civilized mode, and speaking with great respect, it seems to me that the view pressed before us by the learned Attorney General involves a danger of denial of these elementary rights, at a time when they were expressly assured by writing in the fundamental law of the country merely because that writing is no longer in force.'

Cornelius developed further this line of reasoning as to the origin of fundamental rights in *Province of East Pakistan v. Md. Mehdi Ali Khan* (1959) 2 PSCR 1. Munir, affirming that the decision in the Dosso case was a right one, added that since 'the present legal system derives its authority from the success of the October Revolution and if the authority in whom, under the new regime, unfettered legislative powers vest, annuls or, alters the law declared by the Supreme Court, the superseding law has supremacy over and prevails against the original law as declared by the Supreme Court.' While Munir thus reinforced the view he advanced in Dosso's case, Cornelius appeared more certain of the validity of his Dosso 'dissent'. He attached greater significance to the words 'shall be governed,' which he described as mandatory in tone and effect. He asserted that martial law may be necessary in a peaceful country to reconstitute, in the light of past experience and future needs, the mode of exercising power in the state. In such a case, there is no need for alteration of the processes of government except the machinery of popular representation. Yet to establish a new sovereignty it is necessary to demolish the foundation of the old. Hence, the Constitution is abrogated but this does not mean that it ceases to operate as a source of positive law. Cornelius then advanced a new theory of the meaning of Article 2(1) ('shall be governed in accordance...'), a theory which is probably the most significant piece of legal reasoning resulting from the martial law cases. Article 2(1) is merely an assurance carrying no legal sanctions; it is not an obligation assumed as a matter of law. It is as immune from the legal process as martial law itself but this immunity is possible only because Article 2(1) has been subsumed into the martial law. Fundamental rights have a force not related to the Constitution but derived from martial law. Thus, Cornelius did not push further the natural law origins of rights which he seemed to invoke by implication in the Dosso 'dissent.' Instead, he cloaked the words 'shall be governed' with the highest importance and gave them immunity because they were subsumed in martial law. Since he included fundamental rights as part of the provisions of the Constitution according to whose provisions the country shall be governed, these rights 'have lost the operation which was conferred upon them' by the Constitution, and are 'valid to the extent assured by Article 2(1).'

b. The 1962 Constitution

The Constitution of 1962, the promulgation of which ended martial law, presents several challenges to subsequent research which can only be alluded to here. Continuity of polity is provided by Article 225 which continues in force all martial law orders except four which are specified and which repeals all martial law regulations except five which are listed. The major change affecting administration lies in the devolution of powers to the provincial governments in a pattern which departs significantly from earlier structural arrangements. The central, concurrent, and provincial lists of powers which the 1956 Constitution inherited from the Government of India Act are replaced by a list of forty-nine central government powers. These powers include defense, foreign affairs, inter-provincial and foreign trade and commerce, insurance, posts, telecommunications, and tourism. All other powers are presumed to be reserved to the provinces, except when the central government under Article 131 declares a subject as requiring central government legislation. Thus, the allocation of powers is somewhat like that found in the United States, although the terms 'enumerated' and 'reserved' are not specifically mentioned. Judicial construction has begun to resolve some of the ambiguities in the new structure but it is likely that much more clarification will be required before a firm pattern emerges. A leading case, *Manzoor Ahmad v. Commissioner, Lahore Division, PLD 1964 Lah. 194*, declares unequivocally that the distribution of powers rests on a basis totally different from the 1956 Constitution and the antecedent Government of India Act. The authority given by Article 131 to the central government specifies that it has power to enact legislation when the national interest requires it in relation to security, economic and financial stability, planning, co-ordination, or achievement of uniformity in different parts of the nation. In the Manzoor Ahmad decision, the court implied that this central power to legislate for uniformity must be declared in advance. Since the central government did not declare criminal law to be of such interest, criminal law was held to be a provincial power. This doctrine of prior declaration of interest or pre-emption has great potential for modifying the pattern of central and provincial powers. The provinces, by virtue of the residual doctrine, have powers over such matters as agriculture, education, commerce, industry, land and inland water transportation, law and order, and water and power development.

When the central government has declared a subject to be within the national interest, as it did with respect to industrial disputes on the ground of uniformity of law, there is apparently no question as to the supremacy of the central legislation. Such, at least, was the ruling in *Chittagong Mercantile Employees' Association v. Chairman, Industrial Court of East Pakistan, PLD 1963 Dacca 856*. It remains to be seen what will happen if the central government declares within the ambit of 'national interest' a residual subject already legislated on by the province. A progressively more comprehensive view of what is in the 'national interest' may produce the same effect as judicial construction of the commerce clause did in American constitutional development. There are, of course, other modes by which the central government can assert its authority, but the political realities of the two disparate provinces and the prevailing temper of the nation seem to indicate a significant devolution of power to the provinces as is reflected in the Manzoor Ahmad decision. In accordance with the new pattern of distribution of powers, several central government corporations have been reorganized into two provincial corporations and there has been a quickening of the administrative impulse in provincial governments.

A second major departure from the 1956 Constitution lies in the fact that the apparatus of government is now presidential rather than parliamentary. This was not clear from the 1962 Constitution itself, for although the president is ultimately responsible for executing state policy, the delicately balanced allocation of power among three branches of government was lacking and the legislatures have been organized on the pattern of parliamentary systems. Ministers, for example, usually attended sessions and answered questions during the question period. The use of parliamentary secretaries and the absence of strong legislative committees with substantive expertness and staff capable of focusing on relevant legislation contributed further to the ambivalence. It was, however, the relationship of cabinet ministers to the national assembly which precipitated what may be characterized as the most momentous court decision in the history of the law of Pakistan, a decision which halted the progression toward greater ambiguity and established the structure of government as being clearly presidential. The 1962 Constitution unambiguously provided in Article 104 that a legislator who might be appointed a minister, or to any other 'office of profit in the service of Pakistan,' could no longer be a member of the assembly. This provision suggested a presidential system. Article 224 of the Constitution permitted the President to make adaptations 'for the purpose of removing difficulties' impeding the implementation of the Constitution. He was granted this power for three months. Pursuant to this authority, President Ayub issued an order (Removal of Difficulties [Appointments of Ministers] Order, 1962) allowing ministers appointed from the assembly to retain their seats as legislators. According to a statement in the National Assembly by A. K. M. Fazlul Quader Chowdhury (who was subsequently elected speaker), the president issued this order because East Pakistan members of the National Assembly refused to accept appointments as ministers unless they could also retain their seats in the assembly (National Assembly of Pakistan, *Debates*, 19 June 1962, p. 145). An appeal was made to the High Court of

East Pakistan challenging the validity of the President's order. The result was a momentous decision by Justice Murshed, upheld by a unanimous judgment of the Supreme Court (*Mohd. Abdul Haque v. Fazlul Quader Chowdhury*, PLD 1963 Dacca 669; *Fazlul Quader Chowdhury v. Mohd. Abdul Haque*, PLD 1963 SC 486). The courts reasoned that to allow ministers to serve in the assembly was to alter the nature of the Constitution itself. The Constitution was intended to bring into operation a presidential system of government in which the executive was to be completely separated from the legislature. But the President's amendment would have changed that system to 'an anomalous Parliamentary form.' This would not have been mere 'adaptation' of a technical nature, which was the intent of the Removal of Difficulties Article but a major change which could be made only by the normal amending process. In declaring the President's order null and void, the Supreme Court decision unequivocally established the principle of the inherent prerogative of the courts to interpret the Constitution and to review legislation for its constitutionality. This power of judicial review had been in doubt because Article 133 specified that only the legislature could decide if it had the power to make a law under the Constitution. After a comprehensive examination of this provision, Justice Murshed concluded that this article was intended to apply only to that section of the Constitution dealing with the distribution of powers between the center and the provinces. This view was concurred in by the Supreme Court, and a somewhat different ground justifying judicial review was suggested by Justice Rahman in his assertion that the power of judicial review must exist and that there can be no absolute prohibition against judicial scrutiny of legislation. *Marbury v. Madison* was cited by Justice Fazle-Akbar, and indeed the Fazlul Quader Chowdhry case is already as much a landmark in constitutional development as the equivalent American decision which preceded it 160 years earlier. The doctrine of judicial review was expanded further in the public liberties case involving government's action prohibiting the Jamaat-e-Islami, an orthodox Muslim organization, from functioning (Supreme Court of Pakistan, *Criminal Appeal No. 43 of 1964 and Civil Appeal No. 19-D of 1964, decided on 25 September 1964*). Considering the constitutionality of the 1908 law under which the Jamaat was banned, Chief Justice Cornelius re-affirmed the right of judicial review of legislative acts and set forth principles guiding judicial review of executive action.

The 1962 Constitution included a chapter called 'Principles of Law Making and of Policy' in which sixteen principles of law making, including the usual freedoms (for example, speech, association, religion) were listed. Unlike the 1956 Constitution, they were not called 'fundamental rights' and they were not justiciable. Since the non-justifciability of these freedoms was perhaps the most unpopular provision of the Constitution, it was not surprising that the first amendment passed by the National Assembly restored the earlier term 'fundamental rights' and provided for their enforcement by the courts (Constitution [First Amendment] Act, 1963, published in *Gazette of Pakistan, Extraordinary*, 16 January 1964). Certain freedoms were added to the new list. The right which has direct bearing on the administrative system is No. VII, 'Discrimination in Services.' This prohibits discrimination based on race, caste, religion, sex, residence, or place of birth in making appointments to the public service. To permit the attainment of parity, particularly with reference to Bengali representation, posts may be reserved for a fifteen-year period to secure adequate representation of 'persons belonging to any class or area.' Thus, the question of parity in the services with regard to status and justiciability has been restored to the position it had in the 1956 Constitution.

Principles of policy in the 1962 Constitution have not been amended. They remain as directive canons but are not enforceable in the courts. Only three of these principles are relevant to administration: that administrative offices be provided in places convenient to the public, that disparity in remuneration in the public services be reduced, and that parity between the provinces in all spheres of central government power be achieved.

The most important constitutional provision directly relevant to the public service is Part VIII, Articles 174 to 190, on the services of Pakistan. Chapter 1 of Part VIII consists of five articles relating to terms and conditions of service which are much more specifically described than they were in the Constitution of 1956. The effect may be to take away some of the jurisdiction of the high courts through the writ petition in matters regarding internal bureaucratic grievances. Although this limitation is not specifically mentioned in Part VIII dealing with service matters, it is implied when this part, particularly Articles 174–179, is read with Article 98(3) (a) (b), relating to the jurisdiction of the high courts. Thus, a civil servant who has a grievance regarding a service matter cannot appeal to the court for redress unless that matter is based on a term or condition of service specified in the Constitution. The terms and conditions of service are clearly specified, but there is no mention of such issues as seniority and other matters, which in the past have been the source of most of the litigation. It would appear, therefore, that most of the issues about which civil servants went to court in the past cannot now be appealed to the courts. It is possible, however, that subsequent judicial construction may modify this situation. One of the conditions of service is remuneration. It is conceivable that the word 'remuneration' might be construed to include such matters as seniority and tenure simply because remuneration is contingent in part on seniority. Such a construction might serve to restore the position of seeking redress of grievance from the judiciary but this is speculation. No decisions have yet been made by the courts on such service matters under the 1962 Constitution.

c. Corruption

The problem of corruption in government has not been systematically studied, nor have government reports been issued on the subject. That it was fairly widespread in the administrative system has been generally acknowledged. Chief Justice Cornelius' address on this subject[24] and a talk by Chaudhury Mohamad Ali, given at the University of the Punjab, 8 March 1963, are general analyses. Mohamad Ali, secretary-general immediately after partition, helped establish the central government and is one of the most distinguished of Pakistan's civil servants. His talk, 'Corruption as an Impediment to Economic Development,' was given at the department of public administration at the university. Ralph Braibanti's 'Reflections on Bureaucratic Corruption,' published in the British journal, *Public Administration*, XL (1962), pp. 357–72, is based largely on experience in Pakistan. Few cases on corruption have reached the judiciary, hence the details of corrupt government operations are not as readily available as, let us say, disarticulation in the administrative system. Of the few relevant cases, the most revealing is *Bashir Saigol v. The State, PLD 1964 Lah. 148*. This judgment establishes the principle that a police officer serving the Anti-Corruption Establishment retains powers of an officer serving in the regular police force. More important for present purposes is the illuminating description of alleged collusion between a major textile industrialist and government officials in income tax matters. Another highly instructive decision which might serve as a case study is *Saeed Ahmed v. The State, PLD 1964 SC 266*, in which an attempt to bribe an inspector investigating alleged corruption is described in detail.

The bureaucracy of Pakistan inherited the mantle of protection which was given the Indian Civil Service under British rule While this protection was necessary to preserve the independence of the civil service and to shield it from extreme political pressures and the web of reciprocal obligations which characterized Indian life, it made removal from service a difficult, though by no means unheard of, feat. The controlling principles were laid down in case decided by the Privy Council in 1948, *High Commissioner for India and High Commissioner for Pakistan v. I. M. Lall, 75 I A 225* (1948). These principles held that termination of services at the pleasure of the government was limited by certain conditions. These conditions, elaborated by substantial procedural safeguards against capricious removal, were embodied in section 96-B of the Government of India Act, 1919, in sections 240–243 and 276 of the Government of India Act 1935, and were revalidated by Article 181 of the 1956 Constitution of Pakistan. The procedures for removal were detailed in Civil Services (Classification, Control and Appeal) Rules (CCA Rules) which had been enacted by the Government of India in 1930 and which were controlling in Pakistan until 1959. Under the CCA Rules, an elaborate process for removal was prescribed. This process was further amplified by a substantial body of case law. The procedural niceties included the requirement of two stages of inquiry. The first was to determine the nature of the punishment to be proposed and the defendant was informed in writing of the grounds on which action was to be taken. He was afforded adequate opportunity to defend himself in writing and an oral inquiry could be held at his request. After the provisional determination as to punishment, the defendant was once again asked to show cause as to why it should not be taken. He could then appeal at various levels to the secretary of state in council or, after 1947, to the president of Pakistan. Charges of corruption were to be tried in the regular civil courts. Charges of inefficiency could not be upheld unless supported by entries in the defendant's performance record. Only commission of a corrupt act was actionable; there was no such ground as 'reputation for corruption.' Article 188(2) of the Constitution of 1956, read with Article 22 which guaranteed the use of writs as a fundamental right, was the principal means of obtaining judicial review.

This pattern was changed in 1959. Faced with the problem of quickly and vigorously screening out corrupt officials without vitiating the effectiveness of remedial action by attenuated litigation, the martial law government thought it essential to change the means of removing officials without doing gross violence to accepted notions of due process of law. The result was a change in removal procedures which came to be labeled 'screening.' Since it involved officers of high rank and of the CSP cadre, the screening of central government officials, attracted the greatest attention. This was temporary, emergency, martial law screening carried out under the Public Scrutiny Ordinance and Public Conduct (Scrutiny) Rules, both newly enacted in 1959.[25] The emergency screening under the Public Scrutiny Ordinance seemed to remove any disciplinary action taken thereunder from judicial review. It was assumed at the time that litigation resulting from appeals in the writ jurisdiction would be eliminated, although this authority to oust the jurisdiction of the courts was later questioned by the judiciary. Another change from the CCA Rules of 1930 was the introduction of 'reputation of being corrupt' as ground for action. The new Public Scrutiny Ordinance did not explicitly guarantee to the defendant the right to confront and cross-examine witnesses, and it specified that the accused appear before a scrutinizing committee alone, 'with no friend, adviser, or legal practitioner' with him. Screening was done by some forty-nine committee whose findings were recommended to the President or other appointing authority for action. Membership of committees was announced in *Gazette of Pakistan, Extraordinary*, 28 January 1959, pp. 125–59. These committees were, for the most part, made up of respected members of the civil service many of them were known especially for their judicious temperament, although there is a touch of irony in the fact that two members of departmental committees were themselves later screened out.

The President announced the results of screening in a Nathiagali message on 27 June 1959, and the names of those screened were published the same day (*Gazette of Pakistan, Extraordinary*, 27 June 1959, pp. 1117–20). While the announcement was received with some shock by the higher bureaucracy whose security of position had been undisturbed since partition, the effects upon analysis do not appear either harsh or drastic. A total of 1662 employees of the central government were penalized by screening procedures. Press headlines and coffeehouse gossip notwithstanding, this does not mean that 1662 civil servants were actually separated from the service. On the contrary, only a relatively small number of officials were released. Table 3 below summarizes the screening of both central and provincial government employees. Only 49 per cent of the central government employees and 69 per cent of central and provincial civil servants penalized were separated from the service. Of the central government officers screened, only seventy-five were class I officers but it is difficult to determine how many of these were policy-making executives. Although the CSP cadre was deeply affected emotionally by the screening, statistically they were not badly scathed.

Table 3. Results of Initial Screening in 1959 and 1960 of Central and Provincial Government Servants

| Penalty[a] | Central Government | | | | West Pakistan all classes | East Pakistan all classes | Grand total all classes |
	Class 1	Class 2	Class 3	Total			
Dismissal	4	14	110	128	214	254	596
Removal	0	0	0	0	242	60	302
Compulsory retirement	71	68	547	686	0	877	1,563
Reduction in rank	8	31	163	202	202		
Special report	25	88	362	475	475		
Reduction in increment	2	5	0	7	88 [b]	152 [b]	247
Warning	27	14	121	162	162		
Displeasure	1	1	0	2	2		
Total	138	221	1303	1662	544	1,343	3,549

[a] Eight penalties listed here are those defined by the central government. See note b below.

[b] Provincial governments did not use central government penalties 4 through 8, hence one figure is reported for all categories of penalties numbered 4 through 8.

Sources: Compiled from Government of Pakistan, Press Information Department, Handout E, No. 3012, 2 July 1952; *Gazette of Pakistan, Extraordinary*, 27 June 1959, pp. 1117–1120; interviews with officials of the Home Department of the Government of West Pakistan and of the Services and General Administration Department of the Government of East Pakistan in 1959, 1960, and 1961.

Out of a total strength of 323 officers in 1959, only twelve (or 3.7 per cent) were screened. All of these were ordered into compulsory retirement, a penalty which permitted retention of full pension benefits. Ten of the twelve CSP officers had been members of the Indian Civil Service who opted for Pakistan. The most senior had nineteen years' service and the most junior three years' service at the time of partition.

Nevertheless, few bothered to analyze the statistics carefully and the shock effect on the government service generally was marked. Security of position had traditionally been one of the advantages of government service and there were few alternate employment openings in the essentially agrarian economy of the nation. These social conditions coupled with sensational rather than sober, analytical reporting, account for the unnerving effect of the martial law screening of 1958 and early 1959 on the bureaucracy.

What little articulate criticism there was of the screening procedures was directed principally against (1) the use of 'reputation for corruption' as a ground for penalty, and (2) the removal of review of the penalty from jurisdiction of the courts. Those who defended the former provision asserted that the Public Conduct Scrutiny Rules provided some guidance for an empirical determination of such 'reputation', principally analysis of income sources. The use of this ground was further defended by the government on the basis that guilty action would have been impossible to determine in an administrative climate which, prior to 1958, was highly unstable and characterized by an impenetrable network of intrigue and vindictiveness. Moreover, it was asserted that the judicial temperament of the screening committees mitigated against arbitrary action. Finally, it was noted that 'reputation for corruption' was used as a ground for action in only eleven cases of eighty-two class I officers penalized and was used scarcely at all in the cases of lower-ranking officers. The first open expression of criticism came from Z. H. Lari, president of the Karachi Bar Association, who deplore the absence of judicial review.[26] The response of the government was expressed by the foreign minister, Manzur Qadir, a distinguished lawyer who said, in part:

With reference to the screening process, you have advocated an appeal to a tribunal presided over by a High Court Judge. As a permanent measure, the setting up of an administrative tribunal of the kind envisaged by you is a step which has a great deal to recommend it. The need of the moment, however, is to ensure as quickly as possible that the work of the Government is not only done honestly and efficiently but also that it is done in such a way as to inspire the confidence of the people and to rehabilitate genuine respect for the functionaries.

All possible care consistent with bringing this process to a speedy end is being taken. In the matter of dealing with those not to be retained in the service, humanitarian considerations are being allowed to prevail. A process of check and recheck of these cases has been undertaken. To err is human. The best one can do is eliminate as far as possible, dishonest and interested judgment. The procedure adopted, it is hoped, will achieve this to an appreciable degree. No doubt the step recommended by you would ensure it to a great degree. It is felt, however, that the delay involved in a further appeal will more than offset the advantage gained.[27]

There is no way of determining in a scientific manner the nature of the screening process employed since records of the screening hearings have not been released. Shortly after the screening was completed, the case of Zafrul Ahsan, who protested his screening,[28] was decided by the High Court of West Pakistan and reviewed by the Supreme Court. The Supreme Court judgment is especially important because it describes the mode by which the defendant was notified and the procedure of his hearing. This description remains the only available published means of ascertaining the details of the hearing process. Beyond this item of ancillary interest, however, the Zafrul Ahsan case is of immense legal significance because the judiciary therein renders opinion on the martial law provision which ousted its jurisdiction in screening cases. Zafrul Ahsan, a former ICS officer of twenty-two years' service at the time he was screened out, was general manger of Pakistan International Airlines. He petitioned the High Court for a writ nullifying his retirement order. The petition was rejected on the ground that a remedy might have been sought administratively rather than a

law (*Zafar-ul-Ahsan v. Republic of Pakistan, PLD 1959 Lah. 879*).
The Supreme Court upheld the finding of the High Court that
the action of the screening committee was immune from judicial
review (*Zafar Ahsan v. Republic of Pakistan [1960] 1 PSCR 41*). The
Supreme Court, however, did not agree that its jurisdiction was
ousted in all instances even when the law so specified. Only
when certain conditions were met would its ouster be complete.
The court listed five such conditions: (1) the authority should
have been constituted as required by the statute, (2) the person
proceeded against should be subject to the jurisdiction of the
authority, (3) the ground on which action is taken should be
within the grounds stated by the statute, (4) the order made
should be such as could have been made under the statute, and
(5) the proceedings should not be in *mala fide* and the statute not
be used as a cloak to cover an act which in fact was not taken
though it purports to have been taken under the statute. In the
Zafrul Ahsan case, the Supreme Court found that all five
requirements were met and hence it had no jurisdiction to
question the order. In several subsequent cases, the reasoning of
the Zafrul Ahsan case was upheld. In the Muhammad Zaman
Khan case (*Muhammad Zaman Khan v. M. B. Nishat and others,
PLD 1962 SC 22*; see also *Muhammad Ali v. Commissioner, Lahore
Division, PLD 1960 Lah. 641*), the Supreme court upheld a High
Court judgment which invalidated an action of a screening
committee of the Rawalpindi Cantonment Board. This committee
had recommended the removal of four schoolteachers for
inefficiency and misconduct and the teachers were dismissed the
day after they submitted their show-cause explanations. The
High Court noted that this interval did not meet the requirement
of the Public Conduct Scrutiny Rules that fifteen days be allowed
between the show-cause notice and final action by the appointing
authority. The court held that the scrutiny rules were an essential
part of the ordinance, hence the fifteen-day interval provided by
Rules 6 and 7 had the same force as the ordinance. The court
found that the fourth requirement was not met, that is, that an
essential part of the procedure envisaged by the ordinance was

not complied with and that therefore its jurisdiction was not ousted. Accordingly, it dismissed the appeal of the government, thus overturning the screening action. In a subsequent case which attracted wide attention, the High Court of West Pakistan accepted a writ petition, thus declaring illegal the action of a screening committee on the ground that the Transport Board acted *ultra vires* in both convening the screening committee and hearing the appeal from its decision (*Syed Anwar Ali Shah and another v. West Pakistan Road Transport Board* [Writ No. 305, 1960, Hearing, 13 November 1961]). This violated the first of the five conditions specified in the Zafrul Ahsan case. In both of these cases, it is clear that the High Court and the Supreme Court refused to accept the ousting of their jurisdiction except under judicially defined circumstances and in 'accordance with a long line of decisions in England' (*Zafrul Ahsan v. Republic of Pakistan* [1960] 1 PSCR 41, at 51). This reasoning was subsequently upheld in *Pahlomal-Motiram v. Chief Land Commissioner, PLD 1961 Kar. 384*, in *Gulab Din v. A. T. Shaukat, PLD 1961 Lah. 952*, and in *Muhammad Zaman Khan v. M. B. Nishat and others, PLD 1962 SC 22*.

The martial law screening procedures did not escape the attention of the Law Reform Commission of 1959, although its comments were limited to the tentative proposal of substituting for the screening system the Board of Inquiry system used in Ceylon (now Sri Lanka). It is noteworthy that while the Law Reform Commission report and its dissenting minutes spoke out unequivocally on certain issues (notably separation of executive and judicial functions), they did not condemn the emergency screening procedures.[29]

Emergency screening under the Public Scrutiny Ordinance and Public Conduct (Scrutiny) Rules was replaced on 19 January 1960, by the Government Servants (Efficiency and Discipline) Rules 1960. They superseded Part XII of the Civil Services (Classification, Control and Appeal) Rules, 1930, which were in effect until 24 January 1959. These establish one procedure for cases of subversion and another for cases of inefficiency, misconduct, and corruption. In subversion cases, the inquiry committee consists of three secretaries to government and no consultation with the Central Public Service Commission is required. In other cases, initial inquiry may be made by a single officer who must follow procedural safeguards similar to those of the CCA Rules of 1930. Appeal to the appointing authority is allowed and the advice of the Central Public Service Commission must be considered before final action is taken. The new rules do not have the category 'reputation for corruption' as grounds for penalty. A new ground, however, is that an official 'may reasonably be considered corrupt' because he has resources disproportionate to his known income or lives beyond his ostensible means.

Concern for integrity in administration is also manifested in the work of anti-corruption agencies found in the central and provincial governments. In the central government, the Anti-Corruption Agency has existed since 1941 but was reorganized as part of the Special Police Establishment in 1948. The activities of these agencies differ from the screening processes described above in that they deal largely with crimes cognizable in the criminal code such as embezzlement, bribery, black marketing, and misappropriation of funds, and not with questions of inefficiency, misconduct, or suspicion of corruption. The Anti-Corruption Agency has special investigative powers and may initiate investigations or be invited by departments to conduct investigations. The central government agency concerns itself primarily with central government employees and the two provincial agencies with provincial civil servants. The Special Police Establishment of the central government is an organization of more than 450 employees with branches in each provincial capital, in the state bank, in the national capital, and in Peshawar, Quetta, and Chittagong. Its annual reports, submitted to the Ministry of the Interior are not in printed form. In 1959 and 1960, the Special Police Establishment investigated 1277 and 1557 cases, respectively. In 1960, 723 cases were sent to the courts and 68 per cent of the cases resulted in conviction. In the same year, the SPE estimated that it saved the government some 2.25 million rupees in recoveries, fines, forfeitures, and money which would have been lost without timely action.

The provinces have given increased emphasis to anti-corruption activities and increased the authority of their anti-corruption departments by giving the director the powers of an inspector general of police.[30]

It is of significance to subsequent research that the government maintains an attitude of candour and open publicity concerning matters of corruption. Statistics of the anti-corruption units are published in the press, public seminars on corruption are sponsored by the Bureau of National Reconstruction, and a serious effort is made to enlist the aid of the public in identifying and reducing corruption in public service. None of the reports of any of these agencies is published except in press release form. A convenient compilation of relevant ordinances and rules was published in 1962 by the Pakistan Publishing House in Karachi under the title, *Manual of Anti-Corruption Laws In Pakistan*, edited by Zafar Yusuf.

d. The writ and judicial review of administrative action

All significant legal issues relating to administration are closely related to the instrumentality known as the writ, the use of which is by far the most compelling intellectual problem in the law of Pakistan. In this book, the writ jurisdiction has been discussed in context of education[31] and in analysis of the case of Sir Edward Snelson as it dealt peripherally with the Official Secrets Act[32] and, more fundamentally, with the Contempt of Courts Act.[33] Since the writ jurisdiction has been analyzed elsewhere in considerable detail,[34] only a brief survey is needed here. The writs referred to are the five well-known extraordinary remedies for redress of grievance against a governmental action: *mandamus, quo warranto, prohibition, certiorari,* and *habeas corpus.* In the relations between administration and the courts, only the first four of these writs are commonly used. A convenient survey of the concept and development of writs can be found in the judgment of Chief Justice Cornelius in *The State of Pakistan v. Mehrajuddin* (1959) 1 PSCR 34; a less technical analysis is found in Cornelius' address, 'Writ Jurisdiction of Superior Courts.'[35]

In undivided India writs were regarded as one of the principal means of expanding and preserving Indian liberties. In 1954, the Constituent Assembly of Pakistan passed an amendment to the Government of India Act, 1935, enacting section 223-A of that act which gave to all high courts the power to issue 'writs including writs in the nature of' the named writs to any person or authority (Constituent Assembly, *Debates*, 6 July 1954, p. 189). The scope of the writ jurisdiction, implied by the words, 'in the nature of,' was perhaps not fully appreciated by the High Court until 1955 (Syed Akhlaque Husain, 'Writ Jurisdiction of Superior Courts in Pakistan,' PLD 1958, Journal, 3). In any event, reliance on that expression was not necessary, for the 1956 Constitution expanded the writ jurisdiction more explicitly. Article 22 guaranteed the right to petition the Supreme Court for enforcement of fundamental rights conferred by the Constitution and gave the Supreme Court the power to issue directions, orders, or writs for enforcing fundamental rights. Article 163 further empowered the Supreme Court to issue directions, orders, decrees, or writs as necessary to do complete justice in any cause or matter pending before it. But the widest jurisdiction was given to the high courts which were empowered by Article 170 to issue directions, orders, or writs not only for the enforcement of fundamental rights but for any other purpose. The limitation imposed by Article 163 on the Supreme Court, that the order relate to a cause or matter before it, was not placed on the High Court jurisdiction. It is probably for this reason that the term 'writ jurisdiction' is commonly thought of as applying primarily to High Court jurisdiction. What might have been an expansive interpretation of the terms 'directions and orders' was contained by the judgment in the Mehrajuddin case, which maintained that the power to issue directions and orders was not in excess of or beyond the confines of the power to issue the five specified writs. Even earlier, the Supreme Court had ruled that the words 'directions and orders' did not confer power to issue orders except with respect to those aspects of executive acts which are clearly judicial in nature.[36] Thus use of the writ to seek action against government became one of the most conspicuous features of Pakistani government. Under martial law, it was thought that the jurisdiction of the courts might be curtailed by three different means. First, the writ jurisdiction of the courts was thought to have been curtailed by omission of the power to issue 'orders and directions' and of the words 'to any government.' Secondly, many acts which were martial law instruments included provisions prohibiting the issuance of writs to certain martial law authorities. The courts interpreted this prohibition as being applicable only to the chief martial law administrator (President Ayub) and not to his subordinates (*Gulab Din v. A. T. Shaukat, PLD 1961 Lah. 952*), and only to 'Orders' spelled with a capital O, not to lesser instruments (*Khuhro v. Pakistan, PLD 1960 SC 237; Iftikhar-ud-Din v. Muhammad Sarfraz, PLD 1961 SC 585*). Further, the courts refused to accept the ousting of their jurisdiction except under judicially defined circumstances and 'in accordance with a long line of decisions in England' (*Zafrul Ahsan v. Republic of Pakistan* [1960] 1 PSCR 41). Thirdly, when writs were sought in behalf of fundamental rights in matters not related to specific martial law legislation, their validity seemed in the same doubt as the existence of fundamental law. These have been declared abrogated by martial law (*The State v. Dosso and another [1958] 2 PSCR 180; Province of East Pakistan v. Md. Mehdi Ali Khan [1959] 2 PSCR 1; Iftikhar-ud-Din v. Muhammad Sarfraz, PLD 1961 SC 585*).

The Constitution of 1962 and subsequent judicial construction of its provisions placed the writ jurisdiction in a somewhat stronger position in most respects. Article 98 defines the substance of writs without using the Latin designations. Any doubt that the powers granted by Article 98 were not intended to be equivalent to the writ jurisdiction appeared to be dispelled by Chief Justice Cornelius, who in discussing the status of writs under the 1962 Constitution stated that 'it is difficult to suppose that earlier precedents will lose their value as guidance.'[37] Less than a year after the new Constitution was made effective, a full bench of five judges of the West Pakistan High Court handed down the first major interpretation of the new writ power (*Mehboob Ali Malik v. Province of West Pakistan, PLD 1963, Lah. 575*). That power is strengthened by the fact that it is now Article 2 of the Constitution proper which can be invoked when a grievance by government is alleged. This article declares that it is an inalienable right to enjoy the protection of law and to be treated in accordance with law. Further, no action detrimental to 'life, liberty, body, reputation, or property' of any person can be taken except in accordance with law. The significance of Article 2 lies in the fact that it is part of the Constitution proper, rather than part of the ten fundamental rights enumerated in the first amendment. It was thereby possible to seek redress of grievance from the day the Constitution went into effect. Without this transcendent, all-embracing provision, the right to seek redress would have depended on the existence of enumerated fundamental rights in the first amendment which was passed by the National Assembly in December 1963, and made effective by presidential assent on 10 January 1964.

In the Mehboob Ali decision, Chief Justice Manzur Qadir clearly set forth guidelines for the judiciary in utilizing the remedy of the writ. The judgment stated that the use of *certiorari* has been enlarged because it is now available as a remedy for 'all orders passed in excess of lawful authority, whether by judicial, quasi-judicial or non-judicial functionaries.' Under the former Constitution, it was available only in relation to judicial and quasi-judicial actions. On the other hand, Manzur Qadir interprets the new writ jurisdiction as being somewhat curtailed by the constitutional requirement that it can be used only if there is no other adequate remedy. Setting forth a series of propositions by which such adequacy can be determined, he concluded that adequate relief must be requisite to the need created by the grievance. This interpretation of the writ jurisdiction was subsequently concurred in by the East Pakistan High Court in *Chittagong Engineering and Electrical Supply Co. Ltd. v. Income Tax Officer, Companies Circle IV, PLD 1965 Dacca (Dhaka) 11.* A different line of reasoning in a subsequent decision appears to have linked up the defined rights of Article 98 of the 1962 Constitution with the writs of the 1956 Constitution. In *Maulvi Farid Ahmad v. Government of West Pakistan, PLD 1965 Lah. 135,* Justice Sardar Muhammad Iqbal referred to habeas corpus as a 'high prerogative right' and as 'one of the most fundamental rights known to the Constitution,' in the exercise of which there is no limitation. The implication of this statement may be to cloak at least one writ with the same juridical eminence attained under the 1956 Constitution by transfer of the term 'prerogative' from 'writs' to analogous 'rights' under the 1962 Constitution.

The range of substantive issues arising through the medium of the writ is wide; only a few of the more important issues are outlined below.

The first issue for research is the problem of judicial scrutiny of administrative actions affecting the public outside the sphere of bureaucracy. This is the same problem which has faced older western constitutional systems and has been dealt with in the United States by the Federal Administrative Procedure Act of 1946 and related statutes. Several judgments suggest the range of legal-bureaucratic issues involved. It is clear that a consistent effort has been made to evolve a formula of judicial review presumably by restricting the court to defined channels of restraint. One of the earliest major decisions (*Muhammad Saeed v. Election Petitions Tribunal, PLD 1957 SC 91*) included a ruling by Chief Justice Munir that the court would not review a finding of fact, even when erroneous, unless the mode of ascertaining fact is outside the spirit and intent of the statute. This doctrine established a relatively expansionist interpretation of the court's role which has been a characteristic of the doctrine of judicial review of administrative action in Pakistan. The most important decision is that of the *Tariq Transport Company v. Sargodha Bhera Bus Service (1958) 2 PSCR 71.* An application for certiorari was made to review a decision of the Regional Transport Authority (RTA) which granted a route to a bus company without adequate announcement or proper hearing of the affected parties. The High Court had granted the writ which nullified the RTA's action. An appeal was made to the Supreme Court which resulted in a classic decision by Chief Justice Munir, which placed the standards of administrative law, in one respect at least, within the ambit of British and American practice. The Tariq Transport Company case clearly establishes that all administrative remedies must first be exhausted before appeal to the courts and that even then appeal must be against an action which is clearly judicial and not executive in nature. Whether the action is judicial is to be ascertained only by the nature of the process by which the executive is empowered to arrive at the decision. The important doctrine of judicial self-restraint is laid down in Munir's statement that expertise in modern states is such that the court cannot substitute its judgment for that of the administration.

In *Messrs. Faridsons Ltd. and another v. Government of Pakistan (1962) 1 PSCR 1*, it was held that the court had the power to insure that good procedure, such as a hearing, should precede withdrawal of a license even when the statute did not prescribe such procedure. The court's jurisdiction in such a case was determined by the fact that administrative action was quasi-judicial in function. This judgment suggests that the role of the judiciary in Pakistan is somewhat different than in other commonwealth states in Asia. The Pakistan ruling departs, for example, from the regnant doctrine in Ceylon (Sri Lanka), which is that the court will not compel an administrator to act judicially unless the statute so specifies (*Nakkuda Ali v. M. F. de S. Jayaratne [1950] Privy Council 102*). The Faridsons judgment declared that the Nakkuda Ali doctrine 'goes too far in restricting the power of the superior courts to control actions of the executive under statutes which plainly import the performance of a quasi-judicial act.' Further definition of the limits of administrative discretion was given in the judgment of *Ikram Bus Service v. Board of Revenue, PLD 1963 SC 564*, in which it was held that administrative agencies in deciding on applications for permits could not introduce considerations or criteria extraneous to the intent of the statute under which they functioned.

In some of these judgments, the classic issue of fact versus law or the impact of procedural niceties on substantive value determination is dealt with. Much litigation involving administrative decisions as to evacuee property, land reforms, fixing of rents and granting of licenses emerges within this ambit. An illustration of the difficulty in applying the fact-value dichotomy is in the case of *Ata Ullah Malik v. Custodian, Evacuee Property, PLD 1964 SC 236*, in which three judges agreed that the court could not substitute its judgment for that of the administrator since it was convinced that he had functioned within the spirit and intention of the Evacuee Property Law. The remaining two judges, after a detailed description of the process by which the decision was reached, concluded that the spirit and provisions of the law were not followed in several respects. Even if there had been agreement as to unjust process, it is likely that the case would have been returned to the administrative agency for a new decision in accordance with law, since this principle was established in *Azmat Ali v. Chief Settlement and Rehabilitation Commissioner, PLD 1964 SC 260*. One of the most important decisions relating to administrative discretion is the case of *Ghulam Zamin v. A. B. Khondkar 16 DLR (1964) 486*, decided by the East Pakistan High Court. Citing largely American precedent, Chief Justice S. M. Murshed ruled that the power to regulate by license is a legislative power which can be delegated to the executive branch only when the legislature has set policy guideline within which executive discretion must flow. The extension of this doctrine of legislative definition and guidance of executive implementation will do much to move the operation of governmental power more clearly into the limits of a presidential system in which the areas of executive and legislative responsibilities are more clearly defined.

While the foregoing survey deals with the external actions of bureaucracy, that is the actions of government over citizens, there is a second dimension which deals with redress of grievances within the bureaucracy. This involves 'service matters', complaints of civil servants regarding promotion, discipline, severance from service, and related matters. In these issues the courts, in the absence of Whitley councils, employee unions, effective public service commissions, and an effective internal mechanism, have played a major role. The conditions under which the courts review administrative action in these issues have been somewhat different than in 'external' matters. There has been disagreement not on principle but on the evaluation of circumstances surrounding the decision as the twelve cases analyzed earlier in the Snelson matter demonstrates. Both the high courts and the Supreme Court have been reluctant to act in many instances involving internal grievance but have felt compelled to in the interests of 'natural justice.' In a sense, the courts have actively infused the bureaucracy with their own norms of due process.

Since many of the principal cases dealing with internal service matters have already been mentioned in relation to the Snelson contempt case, only a few outstanding judgments will be analyzed here. A major case involved twenty police officers who held temporary posts and were dismissed without the procedural requirements of the civil service rules: *Noorul Hassan v. Federation of Pakistan (1956) PSCR 128.* Chief Justice Munir held that a temporary incumbent could be dismissed without a hearing but a majority of the court held that a hearing was required even for temporary employees. Subsequently, this protection was extended to employees engaged on contract for specified terms (*Khwaja Ghulam Sarwar v. Pakistan, PLD 1962 SC 142*). The determination of seniority and promotion has sometimes led the court to analyze the administrative structure of operating departments as it did in *Mohammad Ali Akhtar v. Pakistan, PLD 1963 Kar. 381.* Closely allied with the issue of preventing removal from service except in accordance with due process of law is the problem of payment of arrears of salary to an official, who, having been removed illegally, was reinstated by court order.

Until 1964, the courts held that the executive could not be ordered to pay such arrears. Payment of salary was regarded as the 'bounty of the crown,' and the court could only hope that the executive would pay such arrears ex gratia. But the executive defaulted in many instances and the courts deplored this condition of inhumaneness and irresponsibility (*State of Pakistan v. Mehrajuddin [1959] 1 PSCR 34; Government of West Pakistan v. Fazal-e-Haq Mussarat [1960] 1 PSCR 124*). The situation went to the extreme of a government department disobeying an order of the governor to pay arrears. Without departing from the principle that the court could not order payment, the court in this instance ordered compliance with the governor's order (*Rehmatullah v. Province of West Pakistan, PLD 1963 Baghdad-ul-Jadid 19*). Earlier Chief Justice Kayani held that the Supreme Court had already suggested a departure from the 'bounty of the crown' doctrine in *Pakistan v. Muhammad Hayat, PLD 1962 SC 28,* by ruling that it could compel government to pay salary at a certain rate. Kayani's interpretation was never brought to the Supreme Court. Ultimately, the question was resolved for litigation involving arrears averaging no more than 200 rupees a month simply by construing the terms of the Payment of Wages Act, 1936, to cover government employment. Thus, government can be compelled to pay arrears averaging no more than 200 rupees a month under terms of this act. This decision, *Divisional Superintendent, Northwest Railroad v. Muhammad Sharif, PLD 1963 SC 340,* does not reverse the 'bounty of the crown' principle, nor does it even mention it. It remains to be seen if the principle will be extended to arrears in greater amounts.

The burden which the judiciary has assumed in internal and external issues relating to the bureaucracy has led to proposals of other modes of judicial control over administration. The principal mode suggested has been the establishment of a system of administrative tribunals patterned after the French structure. Chief Justice Cornelius has been the major proponent of this scheme, which he first suggested in an address at the 1959 convocation of the Lahore College of Law. He expanded his views in a subsequent address before the Rotary Club in Lahore in 1960, in which he related bureaucratic probity to the existence of administrative tribunals.[38] His fullest analysis of the problem was in another address to the All-Pakistan Lawyers Association in 1960[39] and in an *obiter dictum* in *Faridsons Ltd. and Friederike Ltd. v. Government of Pakistan (1962) 1 PSCR 1*. Chaudhury Mohamad Ali, distinguished former prime minister, supported the proposal for administrative tribunals in his answers to Question No. 27 of the questionnaire of the Constitution Commission.[40] Apart from this, the proposal has not received widespread support. It was rejected by the Law Reform Commission which favoured instead modifications of procedure and of statutory law which would make redress of administrative grievance easier to achieve within the traditional bounds of the writ jurisdiction.

Readiness to involve the judiciary in administrative matters by appealing for review of administrative action is indicated by the extent of litigation relating to Basic Democracies. The Basic Democracies Scheme became effective 27 October 1959, yet through June 1964, twenty-four High Court decisions and four Supreme Court judgments were published. It may be assumed that a much larger number of appeals to these courts were rejected and that a greater volume of such cases reached district and sessions courts. A formula limiting the contours of judicial review of such administrative action is slowly evolving. No clear limitations such as those set by Munir in the Tariq Transport and Mohammad Saeed judgments are yet in evidence nor has there been a transfer of the Munir formularies from the review of administrative discretion to the realm of Basic Democracies. The character of action is not quite analogous, for Basic Democracies involves both political and formal bureaucratic participation. Hence, the formulary deemed suitable for review of exclusively bureaucratic action may not be found suitable to the mixed character of Basic Democracies. In any event, the conceptual aspects of the role of the judiciary in this matter have not yet been dealt with. The jurisdiction of the courts, except in removal of elected councilors, is clearly established by Article 86 of the Basic Democracies Order and is not challenged in any of the cases. Because of this exception, the determination of who is 'elected' and who is 'official' is crucial. This was the issue in *Manzur-ul-Haq v. Controlling Authority, PLD 1963 SC 652*, in which it was also held that a show-cause process preceding removal of councilors was discretionary. Most of the cases involve definition of terms rather than procedural questions. In *Mahmudal Haque v. Controlling Authority, S.D.O. (North) Chittagong, PLD 1963 SC 233*, the most important of these cases, Cornelius ruled that the court could not compel an elected councilor to be restored to his position when he had been disqualified because he was a government official. Subsequently, the Supreme Court ruled that the term 'business' in the Basic Democracies Order included election of the chairman (*Mohd. Nawaz Khan v. Ghulam Farid, PLD 1963 SC 623*). The contours of judicial review of administrative action within the ambit of Basic Democracies are only beginning to evolve into a definitive form.

NOTES

1. See the author's 'Public Bureaucracy and Judiciary in Pakistan,' in Joseph La Palombara (ed.), *Bureaucracy and Political Development* (Princeton, 1963), pp. 360–441.
2. A. R. Cornelius, 'Role of Law in Present Challenging Times,' PLD 1964 Journal, 9–13. In the same address Cornelius noted that 'we have not in our country as yet reached the stage of producing learned legal journals to explain and project the justice of our Courts before the academic minds of our own and other countries as well ...'
3. Data on total number of degrees are derived from correspondence with the Education Division, Pakistan Mission of the United States Agency for International Development, June 1964.
4. For the United States, data are taken from the United States Bureau of the Census, *Statistical Abstract of the United States for 1963*, 84th annual edition (Washington, 1963), p. 141.
5. Supreme Court of Pakistan, *The Pakistan Supreme Court Rules*, 1956 (Karachi, 1963), p. 5. These rules are amended up to June, 1963.
6. Limitations of data are described in notes to Table 7.

7. In 1962, the figure, taken from an untitled, unsigned article in PLD 1963 Journal, 104, which is based on data supplied by the Registrar of the Supreme Court, was 618. Thus, in two years, the number enrolled in the Supreme Court bar increased by eighty-four.

8. US Bureau of the Census, *Statistical Abstract...for 1963*, p. 162.

9. Full text in Government of Pakistan, *Speeches and Statements of Field Marshal Mohammad Ayub Khan* (Karachi, 1961), III, p. 27.

10. *Pakistan Times*, 4 August 1962, p. 1; 7 August, 1962, p. 7; 9 August 1962, p. 5.

11. For accounts of resolutions passed, see Dawn, 5 October 1964, p. 4; ibid., 15 October 1964, p. 5.

12. *Nine-Point Manifesto and Joint Declaration of the Combined Opposition Party* (Dacca, 14 July 1964).

13. *Dawn*, 8 October 1964, p. 7.

14. A. R. Cornelius, 'Speech at Annual Dinner of High Court Bar Association,' PLD, 1964 Journal, 107–112. Quotation at p. 110.

15. Cited in n. 21 below.

16. Full text is accessible in Appendix 14.

17. *Pakistan Times*, 7 May 1961, p. 6.

18. David Fellman, 'Constitutional Law in 1951–1952,' *American Political Science Review*, XLVII (1953), pp. 126–71.

19. Walter F. Murphy, 'Lower Court Checks on Supreme Court Power,' ibid., LIII (1959), 1017–1032. Carl B. Swisher, 'The Supreme Court and the Moment of Truth,' ibid., LIV (1960), pp. 879–87.

20. Carl B. Swisher, 'The Supreme Court and the Moment of Truth, ibid., LIV (1960), pp. 879–87.

21. Comments of Chief Justices M. R. Kayani and A. R. Cornelius discussed, quoted, and reproduced here are published with their permission and were written on 21 June 1962, with their understanding that they would be published. It is not unexpected that the possible effect of the contempt of court law would be viewed somewhat differently from the perspectives of the bench and of the researcher. Obviously, my own analysis is from the point of view of the latter. Chief Justice Cornelius after reading this chapter commented in a letter of 12 December 1964, 'We do not understand it [the contempt jurisdiction] as operating *in terrorem* quite to the extent that your text might suggest.'

22. *Haq v. The Honourable Judges of the High Court of Judicature at Lahore* (1953) FCR 206.

23. See above, pp. 143–44 ff.

24. See Appendix 10.

25. Text in *Gazette of Pakistan, Extraordinary*, 24 January 1959, pp. 109–16. The ordinance and rules were enacted under section 6 (3) of President's Order (Post Proclamation) No. 1 of 1958 (Laws [Continuance in Force] Order). A source of confusion and serious error in analyzing the emergency martial law screening lies in the fact that the same issue of the *Gazette* includes the Government Servants (Discipline and

Efficiency) Rules, 1959, which were originally intended to supplement the Public Scrutiny Ordinance and Public Conduct (Scrutiny) Rules. In fact, the 1959 rules were amended to come into force on such day as the President might appoint (see Cabinet Division Notification No. SRO 88, 2 February 1959, *Gazette* of Pakistan, 2 March 1959, p. 283). Since the President did not put these rules in force, the Public Scrutiny Ordinance and Public Conduct (Scrutinty) Rules governed the screening of civil servants from 24 January 1959, to 19 January 1960. (The writer is indebted to the President's Office for clarification of this point.)

26. Reported first in *The Statesman* (New Delhi), 4 May 1959, p. 5, and later in *Dawn* (Karachi), 6 May 1959, p. 4.

27. Text of address by Manzur Qadir to Karachi Bar Association as reported in *Dawn*, 3 May, 1959, p. 1.

28. The jurisdiction of the courts to call in question the actions of a screening committee was barred by Section 10 of the Public Conduct (Scrutiny) Ordinance. To eliminate conflict between this ordinance and section 6 of President's Order (Post-Proclamation) No. 1 of 1958, Laws (Continuance in Force) Order, 1958, which provided for continuance of civil servants in office, the substance of the Public (Scrutiny) Ordinance was incorporated into President's Order No. 1 by Laws (Continuance in Force) (Amendment) Order, 1958 (*Gazette of Pakistan*, Extraordinary, 10 March 1959, pp. 327–28).

29. Government of Pakistan, *Report of the Law Reform Commission*, 1958–59 (Karachi, Government of Pakistan Press, 1959), pp. 57–59.

30. West Pakistan Anti-Corruption Establishment Ordinance, 1961, 8 September 1961; East Pakistan Anti-Corruption Establishment Ordinance, 1961.

31. See.above, p. 35 ff.

32. See above, p. 58 ff.

33. See above, p. 236 ff.

34. See the author's, 'Public Bureaucracy and Judiciary in Pakistan,' in La Palombara, (ed.), *Bureaucracy and Political Development*. The text above is a synopsis of pp. 418–40 with added analysis of developments from 1962 through 1965.

35. See Appendix 14.

36. *Tariq Transport Company v. Sargodha Bhera Bus Service* (1958) 2 PSCR 71.

37. A. R. Cornelius, 'The Writ Jurisdiction of Superior Courts,' full text in Appendix 14.

38. Text in Appendix 10.

39. Text in Appendix 11.

40. Text of Mohamad Ali's answers in *Pakistan Times*, 13 June 1960, p. 8.

APPENDICES

APPENDICES

Appendix 1

LETTER 1
[Professionally typed on airmail stationery]
[See text pp. 39, 50]

Karachi,
21st September 1961

Dear Dr. Braibanti,

I thank you for your letter of the 15th September, which reached me yesterday. I have sent on your request concerning writ actions to the Registrar. They should be able to get out the information you need in the office without great difficulty.

I seem to remember that the passage you have quoted occurs in an earlier speech to the Rotary Club which I delivered in the summer of 1960 (probably August). It was printed in full in the 'Pakistan Times' the next day, but if you cannot get it out of your file of that paper, I think I would be able to get a copy for you.

The subject of control of public servants is one which the English-speaking world has grossly neglected. The reason, if it can be called that, is based on the perverse view that anything which Napoleon introduced must necessarily be bad and rightly to be consigned to oblivion. Something of dishonour to the victory at Waterloo would be involved in granting any merit even to so excellent a scheme of public law as the *droit administratif*, and so Anson buried it alive. I recommend to you the chapters on Control of Public Servants in Professor Brian Chapman's book "The Profession of Government". They would be of assistance in the preparation of your paper.

I am taking the liberty of sending you a copy of a speech I made the other day, at the presentation of certain law books to the Ambassador for Iraq. Some of the points made may be of interest in your work. Incidentally, I hope the Academy has sets of the official Reports of the Federal and the Supreme Courts. If not, I suggest you make a reference to the Supreme Court office. A set for the first ten years with a Digest, is in course of completion. It should be most valuable to the officers under training.

Yours sincerely,

/s/
(A. R. Cornelius)

Dr. Ralph Braibanti,
Chief Advisor and Professor,
Civil Service Academy,
LAHORE

Appendix 2

LETTER 2
[*Professionally typed*]
[See text p. 25]

Mr. Justice A. R. Cornelius,   LAHORE,
     Chief Justice.   30th June, 1962.

Dear Dr. Braibanti,

I find I have left your letter of the 9th June, conveying an invitation from your University, supported by the Asia Foundation to visit the States, unanswered all this time. Although the matter has been fully discussed between us, face to face, I recognise that I ought to have sent an affirmative reply earlier, and I do apologise.

It will be possible for me to make the journey in August-September of this year, probably in continuation of a short visit to Singapore where I have been invited by the University to attend a Seminar, commencing on the 27th August. I could go on from Singapore to the U.S., reaching there in the first few days of September, and I gather that by then you will yourself be back at Duke University. I would like to take aid and advice from you for the first week or ten days of my stay in giving final shape to my lectures, which could be delivered in the third week of September, shortly after the re-opening of the University.

When they are over, I shall have to return to Pakistan with all speed, to be here for the reopening of the Supreme Court on the 1st October.

You were good enough to undertake to get some literature from abroad which you thought might be useful material, for preparation of my lectures. I shall be glad to have it when it arrives. With grateful thanks for the assistance, and also for your kindness in procuring the invitation,

I am,
Yours Sincerely,

/s/
A. R. Cornelius

Dr. Ralph Braibanti,
Professor of
Comparative Government,
and Chairman, Committee on
South Asian Studies,
Duke University,
at LAHORE

Appendix 3

LETTER 3
[*Professionally typed on airmail stationery*]
[See text p. 28]

LAHORE,
3rd July, 1965

Dear Dr. Braibanti,

I am much grieved to be so late in acknowledging your letters of the 17th May and the 14th June. I had to go out on tour on the 15th May to Karachi for 3 weeks and on to Dacca for a fortnight, returning here on the 19th June, and from the 21st June until yesterday, the Court was hearing an intricate Constitutional case, in a Special Vacation Session. This continuous high pressure of work is my excuse.

I am glad the figures I was able to send will be useful.

Your suggestion of sending an intern to work for a doctoral thesis in Pakistan is naturally most attractive. It has aspects and implications which I have been turning over in my mind. One is that the end of the enquiry could be determined by the deep religious persuasion of the student. Another is the factor of political sympathy. As an instance of the latter, I have an American student attached to the Court under a similar U.S. University project with Ford Foundation aid. I put him on to study the introduction and the operation of the Martial Law in Pakistan, through the instruments and the judgements of the High Courts and the Supreme Court. I find his attitude is governed very largely by the day-to-day developments in the political relationship between Pakistan and the United States. It is not for me to guide him as to his conclusions; what he finally produces will be something which will place him most favourably in relation to public opinion in his own country. But I have little hope of his seeing the events of the years 1958–62 and later in the light of a great experiment in ameliora ion and re-sanification (if I might coin a word) of the politico-administrative complex which carries the responsibility for the continued integration and welfare of the 100-million population of Pakistan.

The element of religious obligation can produce an even more pronounced slant. There is, for instance, the theory that the Thomist philosophy owes a great deal to Avicenna (Ibn Sina), which the Muslim thinkers are willing to sustain by chapter and verse. In the Catholic view, St. Thomas Aquinas built directly on Aristotle, and writings to that effect are plentiful. In humility, I must decline the suggestion that any new juridical theory has come from me. I am a neo-Thomist in attitude, and am slowly beginning to understand what is built into the Constitution of Pakistan, in the way of political obligation, and what I can see distinctly, I try to project, as a matter of constitutional duty. In so doing, I have learnt that a non-Muslim can only be a full citizen of Pakistan if, *on the secular side*, he conforms to the requirements of the Objectives Resolution, read with the first 8 Articles, that is Parts I (the Republic of Pakistan) and II (Fundamental Rights and Principles of Policy). So far as I can see, at present, this is entirely possible, and would be easy, if there were some formulation of the basic principles contained in the Scriptures of Islam, in regard to equality, tolerance, social justice etc.

Could one, a non-Muslim, not bound in constitutional conscience, be trusted to see the matter in a balanced light? And if such a one were to undertake an intellectual investigation of the whole position, is it not clearly possible that he may produce, from honest conviction, and in the language of learning, an anti-thesis?

I would, therefore, while commending your initiative, rather not have the intern working in association with the Supreme Court. I would rather he worked entirely freely, on a basis of individual responsibility, being wholly unobligated to produce an apology on one side or the other. The conflict is very marked, and in my opinion, it has a powerful bearing on the development and practical application of political thought, in the ultimate reaches of moral obligation, even in the international arena. I would not wish to put your protegé in the position of having to choose between his deepest religious convictions and his Western political beliefs on the one side, and the integrated religio-political, essentially Islamic, structure, which I see in the Pakistan Constitution, on the other. As an unattached student, he could form and express his opinions in total freedom.

Rather a long letter, but I hope not too long to clarify this important aspect of the matter. I hope too you will believe me when I say that I appreciate it very greatly that you should have thought of me in this connection.

With the kindest regards to Mrs. Braibanti & yourself.

Yours Sincerely,

/s/
A. R. Cornelius

Dr. Ralph Braibanti
Duke University
Durham,
North Carolina 27706

Appendix 4

LETTER 4
[*Professionally typed on airmail stationery*]
[See text pp. 25, 26]

LAHORE,
18th October, 1965.

Dear Dr. Braibanti,

Thank you very much for your letter of the 15th September, addressed to Washington D.C. which reached me here today. As you may have heard, I did not go to Europe and the United States after all. I was at Karachi on the 6th September, having returned from Australia the evening before, and was preparing to start the onward journey to London the following morning, when the news of the Indian attack on Lahore came through. Further travel was put out of the question.

It was a fine opportunity to meet a great many distinguished men of law that I missed, and I much regret it. Nothing about the Washington Conference has appeared in any newspaper that I have seen here. I am wondering if the success of the Conference was in proportion to the hard work put in by the organisers. Some material which has reached the USIS has been promised to be sent to me, but I suppose the fullest accounts will come from the main office in due course.

The conferences which I attended at Sydney and Canberra, Australia, were very successful indeed. I have written accounts, mainly from the Pakistan point of view, which have been printed in the October number of P.L.D. If there is delay in this number reaching you, do let me know, and I shall send you copies by post.

Except for the embers of the late hostilities and a great anxiety in Pakistan about the fate of the Kashmiri people, all is proceeding peacefully. Lahore is exactly as you knew it except for some buildings that have been completed after you left!

I do hope you will get an opportunity of visiting Pakistan again. As for me, I despair of seeing the States, after so many disappointments.

With my kind regards to Mrs. Braibanti and yourself,

Yours sincerely,

/s/
A. R. Cornèlius

Dr. Ralph Braibanti,
Duke University,
Durham, North Carolina 27706

Appendix 5

LETTER 5
[*Professionally typed on airmail stationery*]
[See text p. 26]

LAHORE,
4th July, 1966.

Dear Dr. Braibanti,

I have to apologise for the delay in acknowledging your letters of the 18th May and the 11th June. Today, it has been intimated on the telephone that the President has approved of my accepting Chairmanship of the Como Conference next July. I am very glad of that, and more so that you can now go ahead with your plans. I have cabled the news to you today.

Your great book was delivered to me through the Foreign Office of Pakistan in the first half of June. Please accept my grateful thanks for so much that appears in the book, and what you have said in the inscription. I cannot think I have deserved such appreciation. But all of us in Pakistan owe you a great debt of thankfulness and praise for producing what is practically an encyclopaedia of marshalled information regarding our administration. Your devotion and scholarship, your understanding of the moulding of Pakistan's outlook and methods out of and away from the inherited system, your appreciation of the special influence of religion and tradition, call for the highest admiration. It is very pleasing to hear from you that the book has been favourably received in the States. It is certain to help spreading a truer appreciation there of what Pakistan is, what it stands for and why, and that there are basic imperatives, some of a non-material nature, which guide its destiny. When it is put on sale here, it will surely have a big reception.

I have a request to make, and I hope, if you find it burdensome, that you will not hesitate to refuse it. I have a son in Bolivia, working with the Mineral Bank, under US AID, as a nominee of M/S Price Waterhouse Peat & Co., the Chartered Accountants, by whom he is employed. He would very much appreciate a copy of this book, and both he and I would be most grateful if a copy could be sent to him. The convenient address will be:-

Mr. Michael Cornelius,
c/o U.S.A.I.D./Bolivia
(I M D)
U.S. Embassy, La Paz (Bolivia)

With my kind regards to Mrs. Braibanti and yourself,

Yours Sincerely,

/s/
(A.R. Cornelius)

Dr. Ralph Braibanti,
Duke University,
Durham, North Carolina.

[The book referred to in this letter is Ralph Braibanti, *Research on the Bureaucracy of Pakistan* (Durham, N.C., Duke University Press, 1966)]

Appendix 6

LETTER 6
[*Handwritten on aerogram*]
[See text p. 26]

Lahore
16th December [1966]

Dear Dr. Braibanti,

A brief line to send you & Mrs. Braibanti my best wishes for a happy Christmas and in the New Year good fortune and success in all your efforts. I am appalled at the amount of intellectual work you are capable of. You must be a truly exceptional person. Today the book from McGraw-Hill arrived "Approaches to Development" with the other two books I have had from you "Bureaucracy and Political Development" and "Tradition, Values, and Socio-Economic Development", this will make excellent preparatory reading for the conference.

I hope you are very well and send both of you my kindest regards. (My wife is away in England, but would surely join in the good wishes if she were here.)

Yours sincerely,

/s/
A. R. Cornelius

[The books referred to in this letter are: John D. Montgomery and William J. Siffin, eds., *Approaches to Development* (New York, NY, McGraw-Hill, 1966; Joseph J. LaPalombara, ed., *Bureaucracy and Political Development* (Princeton, NJ, Princeton University Press, 1963); Ralph Braibanti and Joseph J. Spengler, eds., *Tradition, Values and Socio-Economic Development* (Durham, NC, Duke University Press, 1961)]

Appendix 7

LETTER 7
[*Handwritten on Aerogram*]
[See Foreword p. xi and see text p. 30]

Faletti's Hotel, Lahore
3rd May [1968]

Dear Dr. Braibanti,

I write to acknowledge receipt of two reprints Nos. 20 (3 copies!) and 21 from the Centre for Commonwealth Studies— for which many thanks, to say how-d'ye-do and to let you know that I retired from the post of Chief Justice on the 29th February, two months before reaching the terminal age of 65. This was to give my successor two months and five days of his own: a very worthy person and an excellent judge, Mr. Justice S. A. Rahman whom you probably know. How are you? Very busy as usual, I suppose. It completely baffles me how you find the time for all the work you turn out.

I am proposing to stay on in Lahore for the present at this hotel, but it is out-of-date and uneconomic, in the face of competition from three newer hotels, and could be closed down within the year. I shall be sorry indeed, for in 15 years, I have enjoyed much comfort and freedom from care, and much loving service from the faithful old staff in Faletti's. Would probably find some other place to stay in Lahore. I am doing some legal consultation work which I could do just as well in Karachi but my wife likes Lahore better. We propose to go to England in June; I have an invitation to join in a Constitutional Seminar in Lagos, Nigeria in August for 10 days. Otherwise, till about the first of October, I shall be in England—address—c/o Mr. P. Cornelius "Mariabad". High Street, Smarden, Mr. Ashford, Kent. Would be glad to hear from you.

Kindest regards to Mrs. Braibanti and yourself from us both.

Yours sincerely,

/s/
A. R. Cornelius

Appendix 8

LETTER 8
[*Typed by A.R. Cornelius on Aerogram.*
Last 8 lines handwritten]
[See text p. 23 and n. 28]

Faletti's Hotel, Lahore
14th, November 1977

Dear Dr. Braibanti,

My warm thanks for your letter of the 13th October and for the considerable trouble you been at, on account of the young man Bashir Ahmed. I sent him a copy of the paragraphs of your letter relating to him, and was waiting for his reply before writing to you. No word from him so far. Your idea of the best line for him being to approach the Washington State University may have sunk in. I shall write again when I hear from him. I have had nothing from either of the State Universities of North Carolina and Virginia.

Your visits to Muslim countries interest me greatly, because my own search since relinquishing office in 1968 has been among the things of Islam. Under the British it was important to remain aloof from involvement in religion, as a condition of service, for which one was well conditioned by early immunization against anything non-Christian, and quick growth of disinterest in the established routines of Christian worship. At first, the over-charged religious atmosphere in Pakistan, permeating economic and material and political affairs was repellant, but hints of genuineness crept steadily in, particularly the existence of a vast Islamic literature, covering all of their 13 centuries, and every phase of human activity, began hazily to appear. I had fair Urdu, and some Persian; I began to nose into Arabic a bit, and by a fortunate chance, a book by Max Dimont, 'Jews God and History' came into my hands. The parallel with Islam, in the development of Scripture, covering under the single title of doctrine, everything pertaining to humanity was striking. The Torah and Talmud for the Jews; the Qu'ran and Sunnah for the Muslims. The spiritual and mental development of both communities had centred round these scriptures, their study and extension into the secular sphere. Muslims had the advantage, lost by the Jews in 70 A.D. of always having vast territories in which to make their experiments in political and administrative matters; with this went the risks inherent in the 'mutability of human affairs'; against the onset of the European peoples, greatly invigorated by the achievements of the Renaissance period, the heady wine of 'humanism' and the discovery of identity in democracy, the Muslims had nothing but the valour of the Sultans and nobles, leading armies drawn from 'client' countries—their experiments were frozen where they stood, power slipped from nerveless hands, their languages were declassed and became a barrier against new and necessary ideas, and only their religion, in its inwardness, remained as a refuge and consolation. There was in that single factor a strength which has kept every country Muslim, that once was Muslim, and today as they slowly move into modern ways of thought, practice and technique, Islam is coming into the ambience everywhere in these countries. If you have looked at the basic doctrine of Islam, its truth and strength-in-simplicity, the potencies for growth, spiritual integrity for the individual, outward and visible power through unity for the community, that are built into its rituals of *namaz*, the fast and the pilgrimage, which are still being extensively practised, the reason for the current of Islamicization in Muslim countries, that have re-sensed their identity and place in the World, will become apparent. I have been exceeding limits, first those of your patience, and then of this paper! Space for a sizeable speech was needed, but of your indulgence I can be sure, knowing the depth of your interest in the currents below the surface of affairs. I have always lacked the words to convey to you, my deep admiration and gratitude for the guidance in thought that meeting you and exchanging views with you, have brought to me. Perhaps one day I may be able to send you a collection of my speeches, Latterly in number, on Islamic subjects. Our very best wishes to you both.

Yours sincerely,

/s/
A. R. Cornelius

Appendix 9

LETTER 9
[*Handwritten on 4 pages of airmail stationery*]
[See text p. 71 and n. 12)

#1 Faletti's Hotel, Lahore
1st March 1978

Dear Dr. Braibanti,

Your letter is dated the 2nd December and has been with me, pricking my conscience for an answer, for over ten weeks! A scandal to one like yourself accustomed to immediate application to every matter arising out of your numerous functions but natural to a lazy and unpressured existence like mine. I see your very active university has added another school to its already extensive range of studies—this time reminiscent of the mediaeval Pope who made the study of Arabic and Islam compulsory in the schools of Europe. That was short-lived, but the Duke initiative holds out a high promise that methodical and well-compassed minds will now, at long last, be brought to bear on a study of sociological-religious importance that through centuries of dormancy has yet maintained its pressure on the intellectual conscience. Strength to your arm!

Thanks to your kind assistance, the two agricultural schools you mentioned have responded to the request for a place for my young protegé, Bashir Ahmed, and he is now in touch with the Virginia University. His means are slender and I doubt if he will get there. However, he has a job here.

The extracts from your paper that you have kindly enclosed with you letter show your customary wide and detailed grasp of the elements of the new phenomenon of Islamic identity, now sharply rising in the Muslim countries of Asia and North Africa where education in the European mode and the adoption of European techniques in political, judicial and administrative activities have created a dichotomy, against the basic Muslim beliefs of the people, held also, under the veneer, by the educated classes, which can only be resolved in one way—return to WAHDAT, the principle of integral unity, based on surrender of the will to Allah, appearing clearly in the agencies and instrumentalities of the state. Nothing less will be peacefully accepted by the Muslim people—witness the upsurge in Turkey, after half a century of de-culturization, and this, although their image of a 'golden age' is so much more diffuse and recent than that of the Arabs. Your paper stresses the sense of community in Islam. From the outset, the formation was of internationally independent communities, so that to live as communities in a non-Muslim state is not part of the original ethic, and an interesting forecast might be that the subordinate Muslim populations in Soviet Russia will, sometime, make a bid for freedom. It is part of the reason for the successful formation of Pakistan, though now in two separate parts. How the ferment might work in the very large Muslim minority in India is another question. It will never lose its identity, in the way that the Greeks in the Selucid empire who had ruled Iran 300 years, converting all the processes into the Greek language, appear to have lost theirs in the further centuries of Sassanian rule.

The organisation of government is a critical matter, in the Islamic context, and the question is a live one in nearly every Muslim state, outside the "homeland" Arabia, where monarchical rulers, now reduced to benevolence, seems to continue its success. Democracy, with its pretense of subsumation of the individual will to the formation of a General Will, through the starkly divisive processes of elections, must fight a stern and losing battle against WAHDAT, that obliges obedience to Allah and His Prophet (PBUH), to the Quran and the Sunnah. In Pakistan, a considerable section among thinking citizens inclines to the view that all policies, administrative, economic, etc. should not only be in line with those master guide lines, but should also be seen to be so. Isms, per se, will not do. It is part of the reason for the ouster of Mr. Bhutto. Another reason is that an election among people suffering from ideological frustration, whatever the declared issues on which it is being fought, has the virus of revolution just below the surface: we saw it in March 1977 in many city seats. One notable leader, Air Marshal (ret'd.) Asghar Khan declared in advance that if his party (PNA) lost the election, they would not accept the result—and so it proved.

I incline to the view that benevolent or constitutional monarchy is most in line with WAHDAT. In Saudi Arabia, the succession is not by birth alone, but by election from among the members of the royal house—and the people find that acceptable. The techniques of government in most Muslim countries outside the 'homelands' have attained such complexity that to fit such a cap of ultimate authority will require expert consideration—and good luck as well; a very modern instance is that of Spain, which Muslim countries under elected governments should watch with care. It is perhaps too early to give thought to the provision of an overall symbolic Head of Islam, the ultimate proof of the true WAHDAT of the Muslim "world cavern" of Spengler's imagery, whose absence through renunciation at the time of the Turkish Revolution has left a gap that aches in many minds. In a recent speech on the concept of state in Islam. I ventured to say that under present conditions, restoration of the Caliphate might be difficult, but perhaps a not less effective image of the unity and ethos of Islam might be provided by a United Muslim Nations Organisation, taking over among Muslim states, many or all of the major functions of the U.N. The money and the personnel are available.

I have probably tired you out, reading this long amateurish dissertation on a seemingly intractable theme! But I was impressed by the depth of inquiry that your paper clearly shows that you have applied to the subject, and this 'paper' has been taking shape in my mind for some time.

I hope you and Mrs. Braibanti are very well. My wife and I send you our best wishes.

Yours sincerely,

/s/

A. R. Cornelius

APPENDICES

SELECTED SPEECHES OF A. R. CORNELIUS

Six of the eight speeches selected for this volume have in common an emphasis on the need to recover and vigorously assert an Islamic polity. They make only peripheral mention of the congruence of that polity with Christian doctrine. The seventh address on the leadership model of Winston Churchill dwells on aspects of character which are widely, if not universally, respected. But even that address ends on a religious note which asserts that true leadership is possible only when anchored in religious principles. The eighth entry, *Morals—The Islamic Approach* is grouped with his speeches although there is no record of the time or place of its delivery. It is his most severe criticism of western moral values and his most fulsome praise of Islamic moral doctrine. There is a remarkable degree of consistency (and some repetition) in all these addresses: the re-assertion of indigenous culture; the unifying force of religious principles; the power of language especially scriptural language; the superiority of Islamic justice; the fallacy of the alleged universality of human rights, especially when those rights arise from secular rather than religious premises. Taken together, these eight addresses represent the quintessentials of Cornelius' philosophy of statecraft, jurisprudence, and the moral life.

The original typescript copies of these addresses which were given to me by Chief Justice Cornelius had no titles or sub-titles. Some of them were published elsewhere (in the Haider compilation, in *Pakistan Legal Decisions* or, in the case of the eighth, entry in a Hamdard Foundation publication) with titles and sub-titles added. In this collection I have adhered to the original as far as feasible. I have added my own titles, usually different from those already used. Sub-titles have not been used but, for convenience' sake, the texts have been divided by Roman numerals.

Cross references to parts of the Analysis chapter of this volume which deal with issues raised in the speech are given in parentheses at the end of each Explanatory Note in italics at the beginning of each speech.

Appendix 10

THE LEGACY OF IMPERIAL RULE AND THE RESTORATION OF NATIONAL CHARACTER

[One of the legacies of more than two centuries of British rule of the subcontinent has been the British legal system. While this has been an advantage, it has sedated the natural evolution of an indigenous system. In Muslim countries it is often regarded as a distinct disadvantage. Islam had a comprehensive body of law—Shar'ia—already highly developed before British rule. In this address of 11 July 1962 to officers of the Pakistan army at General Headquarters in Rawalpindi, Cornelius pursues this theme. The nation must now seek its true cultural roots and articulate its judicial system to them. To him while some British concepts of justice have validity, the Islamic concept of justice is superior in many respects. There must be a recovery of national identity by elucidating Islamic concepts of political responsibility and justice. Almost as afterthoughts, he advances two rather unpopular ideas. He praises Basic Democracies (as he does in other speeches) as the mechanism which can produce new leadership and once again urges the use of Arabic as the language truly reflecting the essence of Islam. (See text pp. 37, 38; notes 51, 56)]

I would like to assure you that it is with genuine pleasure that I accepted the invitation to appear before this group today. To any one who has a serious matter to present or expound, it is always a satisfaction to know that he is doing it before persons who are taking a real and responsible interest in what he is saying. I do not mean that any of you is in any way responsible to me in my office. The responsibility I speak of is the wide general responsibility of the citizenry of a country the maintenance of whose integrity and existence is the source of constant and pressing activity. The recent history of Pakistan shows that among the responsible sections of the community in Pakistan, the Armed Forces are entitled to a very distinguished position.

The subject which I have chosen for this address is one belonging to the large field of political responsibility or political obligation within an independent country, in aspects which are of direct interest to members of the Armed Forces. The Forces have their own system of domestic justice under Courts Martial. The system is operated with full formality whenever possible, that is to say everywhere outside the field of actual operations, and is highly regarded in all legal circles as a mode of securing right and proper justice according to the requirements of the occasion. By "occasion" I do not mean only the particular offence according to the formulated definition. I take it to include the surrounding circumstances, such as the welfare of the unit concerned, as well as the Armed Forces generally. If therefore, I invite you to apply your minds to the matter, as one of national concern, I do so in the confident belief that all of you already possess a fairly clear idea of the requirements of justice in a limited sphere.

I

I am proposing to speak of the importance to the national character of leaving the function of justice in its right and proper place. It has a strong bearing upon the capacity of a nation to stand independently on its own feet against all the perils of its international situation. Every human being is born with a well-developed sense of what is right and what is wrong. Unless blinded by personal considerations, hardly a man is found to be incapable of giving a clear opinion as to what is the requirement of justice in a particular case. In the ancient communities, the judicial function was always reserved to the community, that is to the heads of the various sections into which the community was divided. Through the ages, there had developed a sense of due process in these matters, namely, that a chance should be given to the person alleged to be in the wrong to explain his position, apart from which there were settled notions of the methods by which rights and the consequent liabilities were to be ascertained, and what was to be deemed to be a wrong. Different communities had also fairly clear ideas of the appropriate modes of correction in each case, supported by communal and religious sanctions.

It is in this respect that a firm foundation in one's religion and the principles which it inculcates is of the utmost importance to the establishment of uniform standards of justice among people. Where the religion preaches and practices equality, this is all the more prominent, and it is only when abuses have developed through use of power and other forms of tyranny that the population is faced with the calamity of having to accept any degree of inequality in rights. To take a small example, in the period of British rule down to very recent times, the Codes of Criminal Justice carried provisions which gave unequal privileges to European British subjects as against the people of the country. Those privileges were laid upon the law from the very earliest days of British rule, and were a source of constant irritation until they were finally removed some 35 years ago. The State religion of Pakistan, namely, Islam is strictly equalitarian, and provides a fully developed system of laws and procedures. Both the first as well as the present Constitution provide in detail for the assertion of equality over the whole range of State activity. There are people in all sections of the community in Pakistan, who wonder why there is so much outcry for introduction and application of Islamic principles in all the laws in force. They criticize the outcry on two main grounds, viz. firstly, that since the laws left behind by the British have been in existence for a great many years, and by legislative processes have been largely moulded to suit the requirements of the people, it will be dangerous to interfere with them, and secondly, they say that the British system of justice is applauded all over the world as one of the best and is by now well understood by the people. They therefore ask—why make a change?

II

These are superficial answers to the problem at the best. They often come from persons who are beneficiaries of the system, namely, the Judges and lawyers who can be relied upon to make something of a fight to maintain their livelihood. The mere fact that cases are decided does not necessarily mean that the system followed is fully adapted to the understanding and sentiment of the people. We all know of civil cases where after getting a decision from the final Court, the parties have to go home and make a compromise so as to produce a practical result more in consonance with what they know to be the natural justice of the matter. As for criminal cases it is probably correct to say that under the present system every decision has the quality of breeding more cases of the same kind. The Courts now rely upon evidence given in open Court under an oath whose value is precisely nil, and they follow a strict technique of exclusion of evidence, some of which would be most valuable for the ascertainment of the truth. The result is that cases in which guilty persons are acquitted probably form the majority. On the other hand, there are a number of cases in which innocent persons are convicted on the basis of oral evidence and even suffer death. In both these eventualities, the seeds of revenge have been well sown.

One feature of our country, under the British system of justice, which I always found to be remarkable was that the conviction of an innocent person, even when the fact of innocence was established was generally accepted so quietly by the public. Quite frequently in England, discoveries of this kind are made and usually create a public sensation. A more familiar feature is, of course, the general attitude towards the acquittal of persons who, to all appearances, were guilty of the most violent crimes. Presumably, this is tolerated on the theory, underlying the British system, that the benefit of all presumptions should go to an accused person and the whole burden of proof by evidence, which is received under high technical rules, is upon the prosecution. Cases are common enough where 10 or 15 persons have jointly slaughtered 3 or 4 of their enemies, and carried their heads in triumph aloft on spears through the village. One supposes that when they are acquitted, as they often are, the village lives in a state of terror from these persons when they return and the whole balance of life is upset once again, as it was when the murder took place and during the ensuing police investigation. By the inscrutable workings of the judicial system, a situation has been created, to which under the necessities of life the people have to adapt themselves and, at the cost of a part of their true character, they do so. Unfortunately, what is damaged in this process is that part of their character, which is the distinguishing feature of the strong and noble human being. Belief in truth diminishes. Denial of the strength of evil becomes impossible. So also when an innocent person has been hanged on the basis of evidence which the village knows to be false, I imagine that the relatives accept it as a stroke of fate and the rest of the village, as an incident of the judicial system from which at least one party has gained some advantage. But in this case as well, there is definitely a diminution in the public character in those respects which make for strength and stability.

III

One is tempted to ask—would not such results be avoided, if the function of doing justice were placed in the hands of the people themselves? How far can justice be allowed to travel away from the truth? Can such a state of affairs be allowed to continue indefinitely, without basically endangering the body politic? How does it happen that this condition has been developed in so many countries? It derives from the system and cannot be attributed solely to the character of the people. For there are no men on earth, who, if involved in a Court case, would not use all means in their power to manipulate it to their advantage.

The development is a matter of history. It is clearly an artificial condition, and it is worthwhile enquiring how it came into existence. Our legal system is a legacy left behind by the British. The British system of law first began to take shape under the Normans who conquered England in the year 1066. They found a local system of justice operated by communal and local courts, as well as by certain "franchise" courts, namely, the courts of landowners who had judicial powers by right of possession of certain land. The communal courts are still referred to in the books of English legal history as the "national courts". Much study has gone into the subject of how step by step the Normans and in particular, their great King, namely, Henry II (1154-1189) introduced a series of variations by which all jurisdictions were finally brought under the control of the King's Court. It is true that previously there was great diversity in the laws that were being applied. There were also abuses, so that the action of Norman kings could be applauded for bringing uniformity to the processes of justice. Moreover, the pre-Norman methods of settling disputes were mostly primitive. There was trial by battle as a test of the rightness of a man's cause, and this was also tested by ordeal namely, such as by being thrown into water or putting one's hand into live coals, etc. Another primitive method was by "compurgation", a relic of which lingers on even in our Courts. Under compurgation, a litigant was required to support his case by the oaths of a number of respectable persons usually his kinsmen, swearing that his case was true. The test of truth was that the witness was word-perfect. In our Courts too, each party produces a number of relatives as witnesses, and the effort to be word-perfect is only too plain, but unhappily, for them, such witnesses are usually ignored.

However, to go back to British legal history, it is clear that the Norman kings and particularly Henry II, attracted the people to the royal courts by a system of justice which excluded battle, the ordeal and compurgation, and instead put the decision upon evidence, and the opinion of a jury of their fellow-citizens. They had other and more subtle methods as well. For instance, the king with the aid of the ablest lawyers in the kingdom invented forms of writ which had the effect of withdrawing cases from the jurisdiction of all the local courts. Thus for instance, in a criminal case, the lawyers invented a form of words amounting to this that the offence constituted an infraction of the King's *peace*, and whether this was truthfully said or not, the case at once came before the King's Court. Another device of this kind was utilized in civil cases. In the plaint, a clause would be inserted to the effect that the Lord who had jurisdiction had remitted the case to the King's Court, and whether this was true or not, it was sufficient to give the King's Court jurisdiction to the exclusion of the local courts. A precept could be issued to the local court to report a case to the King's Court, and this effectively withdrew the case from the local Court. Great increase of work—and of legal revenue to the King and the lawyers of his Court—resulted and so a further reform was introduced. The King established the system of itinerant justices. You can see at once how the new law began to feed its own creators. The King gained revenue, but more important still, he gained a direct control over the people, in their everyday lives, brushing aside all intermediate feudal and communal authority and jurisdiction. The best lawyers of the period remained in the vicinity of the King's Court and all the additional work which their formulae effectively brought to the King's Court was for them meat and drink in one form or another. Professional judges became the fount of justice, and the dispensation of justice in communal form came to an end. The presence of a jury was, of course, a safeguard against arbitrary justice, in the interests of statecraft. But that was only a small part of the matter, in the view-point of the total assumption of the function of justice by an establishment of professional judges, aided by professional lawyers, operating a highly formalized system in a foreign language (first Latin and later Norman French) among a subject people. The birth of the system, moreover, lay in a deliberate plan to withdraw the agencies of justice from the people, and to replace them by instruments of Royal creation.

The further development of the English legal system is a long process to which I need not refer here, beyond saying that as time has gone on, it has not become any simpler, nor has the subject been afforded any relief against continuous intensification of formalism in all laws and procedures. It is a matter of history that by about 1200 A.D. in about a century and a half the plan behind the laws and administrative orders of King Henry II had been fully achieved. A direct result was that, except where the Royal interest was specially concerned, the courts begin to treat cases in a narrow fashion, that is, as if nothing mattered except that the requirements of the definition of an offence should be satisfied, and that the punishment should be fully punitive, retributive and deterrent. That is a condition which is present today, and my concern is to argue that while it may fully meet the demands of a foreign ruler, the outlook is not sufficiently broad or beneficial in an independent community.

What I mean is this. Every case before a court is founded on a disturbance in the harmony of the communal life, through action of a nature which failed to take into account the rights and responsibilities as well of the actor as of the person affected adversely by the action. This is true equally of those matters which are civil wrongs and of those which are counted as crimes. It is of course possible that the degree of violence attending a particular crime in a community may be so great that the full strength of the community may not be able to cope with it, and the support of the State or of some larger unit in the society would be needed to contain the violence of the explosion and to set the matter once again to rights. It is possible also that a civil dispute may involve interests or questions altogether too large or too intricate for a local court to cope with. But if you take it from the communal point of view, the main business is to set things to rights so that life within the community can go on peacefully and harmoniously as before. It is in this sense that one understands the frequent punishment of outlawry which primitive communities used to impose upon incorrigible persons. They were placed outside the pale of the law, for incurable non-conformity. Short of this, the idea was always to retain the offender within the community after suitable correction. The communal Court would incline to regard essentials and ignore technicalities, in ascertaining the fault. Restoration of local peace, reformation of the delinquent's character, and relief to the injured party would be the paramount considerations by which their decision in the case would be determined. If they acted soberly and justly, they would avoid exaggerating the matter.

IV

A case of which I read in a recent issue of the *London Times* furnishes a good example of the extent to which the pursuit of legal formalism can draw a law court away from essentials which would be obvious to a communal court of the kind I have been discussing. The case is of a matrimonial nature, and as you know, such matters have been assigned recently in Pakistan to communal courts under the Family Laws Ordinance. This particular case was before the English Divorce Court. It started in 1957, when the wife sued for divorce on the ground of cruelty, and the husband cross-petitioned for divorce on the ground that she had been cruel to him. Cruelty is a matrimonial offence justifying dissolution, but it is narrowly defined, and so it resulted that in the 1957 cases the Courts held that neither party had established cruelty, and both failed. That is to say, they stayed married, though the fact was that the wife had driven the husband out of the matrimonial home, and there was no prospect of reconciliation. The situation was plainly impossible. Another effort to get free was inevitable. In 1961 the husband sued again for divorce on the ground of desertion namely, that his wife had turned him out of the matrimonial home. Thereupon the wife counter-petitioned for divorce on the ground that *he had deserted her*, pleading that her own conduct was justified by his prior misconduct. In the English law, that amounts to constructive desertion, and you can easily see as what a wide field is thereby opened out for the aggressive spouse to manipulate the weaker partner into a matrimonial offence. It is merely a matter of evidence. The case reported in *Times* was however on a very highly technical point, namely, whether in attempting to establish constructive desertion, the wife could rely on acts of cruelty which had taken place before she filed her suit in 1957. The Judge decided the point by applying the well-known principle of constructive *res judicata*, holding that because she could have pleaded the particular acts in the previous case, and had not done so, she was estopped or prevented from pleading them in the later case. The main case has yet to be decided. The costs to the parties of this *interim* order would be several hundred of pounds, and as it is appealable, further income to the lawyers, and the court is in prospect.

Now, anyone would say that the institution of marriage which is basic to community life is one to be safeguarded to the utmost extent of reason. But when the fact is established that the spouses *cannot* live together as husband and wife, the solution lies in allowing a separation under conditions which are consistent with the general interest of the community. Care should be taken that there is the minimum damage to the personal character of the spouses, that the children are looked after and that the finances of the couple should not be depleted in the process. The question of the impossibility of their living together as spouses is capable of being resolved without any great expenditure. The Scriptures indicate the minimum requirements fairly clearly. English jurisdiction in the case I have cited does not appear to take any of these considerations into account. It was clear enough that the spouses could not possibly hit it off as a married couple. If the matter were before a communal court, I feel no doubt that that conclusion would have been reached at an early stage and dissolution would have been awarded without the great outpouring of money into the pockets of lawyers and on court-fees and other expenses, that has been clearly incurred in the case. Justice has been exercised in such a way that the real purposes, namely, the welfare of the community, the good of the family, and other considerations such as I have mentioned all go by the board. A detached judge and disinterested lawyers are operating a technical and elaborate system which exposes the matrimonial vagaries of the couple to the maximum extent, and reduces the matrimonial store rapidly to the point of exhaustion. Only the courts and the lawyers flourish as a result.

V

Under the personal law prevalent in Pakistan and the new Family Laws Statute, an abuse of this kind is probably not possible. But family laws are only a small part of the laws under which we live. The greater part of these laws is operated by the ordinary courts of British creation. I should like to trace for you quite briefly the methods by which the function of justice was taken away from the people after the advent of British rule, and was transferred to the rulers. In India also at the time when the British came, there was the same diversity among the indigenous courts as to the laws they applied. There were communal courts in the villages which had full powers, and it appears that these extended even to cases of a capital nature, except that in such cases, the sentence had to be referred to the ruler for confirmation. The Hindu rulers are said to have maintained a gradation of courts, though as in Britain in pre-Norman times, there was no regular system of appeals. Under the Mughals also, there were graded courts of the same kind, and they had also a landowner's jurisdiction similar to that of the Lords' Court in Britain. Under this system, the Zamindar of a locality would have certain criminal and civil jurisdiction over his territory, subject to confirmation of the higher punishments by the suzerain. When the company acquired the Zamindari of a certain number of villages around the first settlement at Howrah, their English factors undertook the judicial duties of the Zamindari with one difference namely, that capital cases were referred to the Governor-in-Council at the main settlement for their confirmation, and not to the Nawabs at Murshidabad. Over their own people of course they exercised exclusive jurisdiction, that is to say, to the exclusion of the native courts, and as their power increased, and their employees who were also administrators spread over the country, conditions developed in which while the English subject could sue a native in any local court, no English person could be sued except at the cost of great delay, inconvenience and expense, at Calcutta. In the course of time some of these inequalities were erased, and notable efforts were made, in Madras, and Bombay, in particular, to create borough courts after the pattern then in vogue in England. At first, a few Indians were appointed to these courts, and were described as "black Justices", but later, all appointments were reserved for Europeans and as the power of the East India Company spread over the country, a thorough-going judicial administration was evolved. By a Parliamentary Act of 1761, all posts of Assistant Magistrate, District Magistrate and District and Sessions Judge were reserved for the Indian Civil Service, which was exclusively British. It should be said to the credit of these officers that many of them did not hesitate to record their view that this reservation was unsatisfactory, as they themselves understood very little of the needs, customs and laws of the Indians, and on the other hand there were plenty of nationals who were capable of performing this work. It was not until half a century had passed that Indians began to be employed in fairly large number to deal with the least important civil and criminal cases. As we all know, it was only in the last 25 years of British rule that there was any considerable change in the condition that the principal Magistrate and the principal Judge of a district were always British and in the High Courts, the Indian Judges were always in a minority. I point this out in order to show the importance that was attached by the new rulers from the very commencement of their rule to gaining direct control over the judicial system, and to making laws which would result in the withdrawal of all jurisdiction from the local communal courts.

That is not to say that the communal courts were at all well-organised when the British came. They probably worked in highly irregular fashion and with no great conception of the laws which they administered. It was indeed a major work of great value which the British undertook when they codified the various laws of the country. There were in fact four Law Commissions appointed, with purely British personnel between 1834 and 1879. The bulk of the statute book is made up of laws carefully formulated by these successive Commissions. Nor is it possible to minimise the value of the work done by the Magistrates and Judges of the British period, who worked in compliance with the law. They did great work in establishing a complete system of courts and judiciary, and furnishing an example to the people, over about 200 years of how such a system can be run.

VI

But the other aspect remained, namely, that they were operating a system of justice which was imposed upon the people and did not derive from the life of the people themselves. To lend point to this aspect, I refer to the recent increase of interest in one of the indigenous systems of justice, namely, the Jirga system. I would like to read to you a short passage from Sir Olaf Caroe's book entitled *The Pathans* on the subject of trial by Jirga under the Frontier Crimes Regulation, which was enacted by the British in 1872. The intention was, as Sir Olaf Caroe says, to introduce customary methods into the settlement of "quarrels arising out of the blood-feud, of disputes about women, and questions generally affecting Pathan honour". A group of elders acceptable to both parties was designated by the executive Magistrate, as the *Jirga* and this group was charged with the duty of giving a finding as to the guilt or innocence of the accused in a criminal case, or on the points at issue in a civil dispute. The Jirga was not bound by the strict law of evidence. It was expected to visit the scene of the crime or dispute and by its own methods of enquiry to ascertain the facts and to furnish a solution. Professional lawyers were excluded. This system was used, in its best days, for cases which the executive authorities thought to be such that if the technicalities of the ordinary law of evidence and procedure were applied, it was unlikely that the facts of the case would be properly ascertained. Sir Olaf Caroe was of the view that in trials by Jirga the chance of a person who is innocent being convicted was "so rare as to be negligible". He was obliged to admit that later the reference to Jirga began to be used as "merely an easy means of punishing crime as from the State, without being a recognition of the Pathan idea". This was in the old North-West Frontier Province, and I might say that the strength of the opposition which one sees to the introduction of this system lies mainly in this abuse, which appears to be practised with little or no attempt at concealment. Sir Olaf Caroe points out that the same complaint is not found in Baluchistan, where the Frontier Crimes Regulation is employed as the sole procedural code and not to procure convictions where the evidence is weak, and the ordinary Courts would be bound to acquit. Sir Olaf Caroe concludes his consideration of the Jirga system with the following observation:

> The point to realise is this. Pathan custom requires the satisfaction of the aggrieved rather than the punishment of the aggressor. The law as we understand it concentrates against the aggressor, and compensation for the aggrieved hardly enters the picture. The Panthan in fact treats crime as a kind of tort.
>
> How and when, and in what degree, it may become desirable to shift the emphasis in a Pathan society from law to custom, or from custom to law, is a matter more likely to be resolved by Pakistan than it ever was by ourselves. It is an obvious principle that the law should in some sense grow out of the society; it should be a projection of the common personality. The law of one civilization cannot be applied to a society with utterly different standards without the most dire results.

Sir Olaf Caroe touches in this passage upon a matter of fundamental nature affecting the dispensation of justice among communities at different stages of civilization. A passage from a book by A. T. Carter on the History of the English Courts furnishes a close analysis of the problem and comes to a conclusion which is surprisingly similar to that of Sir Olaf Caroe even in point of language.

Mr. Carter says:

One of the first problems that meet a political society in its early days is how to persuade the plaintiff—for it cannot compel him—to come into Court and deny himself the pleasure of private revenge. The next task is to put pressure on the defendant to come in... It is possible that the offer of trial by battle was another way of inducing the plaintiff to come in. The defendant was forced in by distraint on his property and outlawry. The second stage is that the plaintiff must come and get the judgment of the Court; he is then allowed to go and execute the judgment with his own hands. The Central Government is not yet sufficiently organised to execute its judgment itself. The third and last stage is when the State is strong enough not only to hear the complaint, and give judgment, but to insist on executing its judgment. When this happens, then over a considerable field, the conception of Crime and Punishment supersedes that of Tort and Compensation.

A crime, you should know, is an offence against the State, and punishment is imposed by the State. A tort is a private wrong, and the relief is by way of compensation.

The essence of the problem is very clearly put in the last sentence. To a community, a wrong by one of its members of a nature which disturbs its peace would always appear in a limited light, namely, in those lights which derive from considerations of the common welfare of the community. They would not be inclined to exaggerate the offence, but always to minimise it and keep it at a proper level. Thus for instance, any breach of the peace can be regarded either as a breach of the local peace or breach of the king's peace. The community would tend to keep it at the former level, but the laws are devised so that the State steps in to deal with all except the most trivial breaches, and the matter assumes an extra-communal aspect by the intervention of Police and Magistrates in many cases where such intervention might have been avoided.

I remember myself in my own days as a Magistrate being greatly surprised when a British Deputy Commissioner under whom I was serving as a Sub-Divisional Magistrate took strong exception to my having sanctioned a compromise between a complainant and an accused person in a case where an arm had been broken with a single *lathi* blow. I had questioned the parties and was satisfied that they wished to live at peace for the future, so without referring the matter to the Police, I sanctioned the compromise and acquitted the accused person. But a grievous hurt being a cognizable offence, attracted the direct interest of the Police, and I presume that they thought that the case rated as one of breach of the king's peace, and felt they had been ignored. That case furnishes an index of the general attitude which in the centuries of British rule had been developed by the administration towards the people. I would myself be inclined to allow a local Court to deal with a case of that kind. It usually takes about six hearings before a Magistrate in the district town, causing a great deal of disturbance to the life of the people, and much expense. A village Court would dispose of it in a day, at no expense at all. If they were men of good and strong character, following in the way of religious precept and tradition, they would devise a solution which would not be purely punitive or deterrent. It would provide for compensation, and it would be designed to restore the pre-existing peace. The need for imprisonment would arise only in cases of a serious nature, or where the miscreant was a public danger.

VII

The Martial Law regime took a first step towards this end, by conferring judicial functions upon the Basic Democracies. Its importance does not lie only in the effect upon individual cases, such as I have been discussing. There is a much larger aspect of the matter, on which I have just touched, namely, the discovery and the encouragement of good and strong character among the people, sufficient to render them capable of being judges in the community over all matters within their proper compass. It is not a mere chance that the total seizure of judicial power is the first aim of a foreign conqueror. Apart from the direct control which it provides over the lives of the subject people, it has also a most weakening influence upon the character of the people generally, and in particular, that of their leaders. Their position, as integrating factors within their respective communities, is reduced to that of quislings, with consequent loss of confidence on both sides, and increasing dependence for everything, including the simple function of maintaining the peace among themselves, upon their rulers.

It is interesting to study the historical progress of the conquered peoples, from the loss of their political independence to the restoration of political responsibility to them. As you are aware, the present century's most remarkable feature is the rapidity with which conquered territories are being delivered over, by the conquerors, to the people, to become independent international units. There is a pathology of the subject countries as well as a pathology of the conquering countries, and the labours and anxieties of the political doctors who make it their business to attend to the teething troubles of infant States, just restored to independence, are wonderful to see. Taking first the case of Britain, which lost its independence to the Normans in 1066, we find the conquerors gaining complete control over the judicial system by 1200 A. D., after just about a century and a half. The first Parliament of England, was not summoned until 1265, just two centuries after the conquest, and thereafter, the rule of England passed into the hands of an indigenous dynasty, the Norman conquerors having become absorbed in the nation. By this time, also, the process by which judicial responsibility was partly restored to the people by the general application of the Jury system, was well under way. The jury are representative of the people, and to them is entrusted the duty of deciding on facts. That system is still in operation in England, but at the same time, justice has not become a responsibility of the people, for it has become heavily encrusted with the minutiae of law. It is firmly under the control on the legal side of professional lawyers from among whom all the Magistrates and Judges are chosen.

VIII

In India, loss of political responsibility commenced in 1765 and continued by stages until by 1850 the whole country had been brought under the rule of the East India Company, which was assumed by the Crown shortly after. Side by side, the new rulers took over complete judicial responsibility, not by stages as in England, but immediately. It was not until the Reforms of 1919 that the first really representative Parliaments were summoned under British rule, just about a century and a half after its true commencement, and it took another 28 years before complete political responsibility was restored to the people. But the jury system was never whole-heartedly attempted in India, and such trial as it received, under unfavourable conditions, only resulted in its discredit. The result is that in Pakistan today, the agencies of justice are wholly in the hands of lawyers and official Judges and Magistrates. The people are as yet not associated with the administration of justice, except to the extent recently introduced under the system of Basic Democracies.

The subject will probably be studied in due course, in relation to the large category of newly-liberated countries, as an aspect of political reconstruction. For everywhere, the discovery is being made that independence, even under the safeguards of mutual security among the nations, cannot be sustained by a mere paper Constitution. The machinery of popular representation, the technique of law-making, all the familiar activities of politicians have come to be understood as mere motions in a foreign mode. The more vigorously they are pursued, the nearer the infant State is brought to the point of dissolution. There is a need for intensely careful examination of the causes of this disease. One of its features is that it appears most strongly among vigorous peoples who have a strong faith in their own traditional institutions. Their natural tendency to exploit every freedom to the maximum imposes an immediate strain upon the system by which their lives are governed.

IX

It is also among such a people that you will find the strongest demand for restoration of their original institutions. There is nothing superficial about this desire. It is nothing more or less than a groping for the true roots of their being, as individuals and as a nation. Their years of subjection are but a small part of their history. Foreign rule may have brought in new mechanisms. But the attempt to cut the people away from their roots has been proved through many centuries of conquest—now happily ended, one may hope—to be vain. Alien controls, exercised by foreign hands, and the usual incidents of foreign rule, which derives its strength from the growing weakness of the people, saps the national character, but where that is strong, it can never be wholly destroyed, or even radically changed. It is in this sense that the demand often heard in Pakistan, for restoration of traditional Islamic institutions should be understood. It is the natural cry of a strong organism to be connected once again with its original and proper roots. The matter lies in the field of political therapeutics.

The restoration of a people to their original roots is no light task. In the circumstances we have been considering, it is made no easier by its falling, always with some degree of suddenness, upon national leaders whose position the foreign rulers have done their best to undermine. The people are usually divided among themselves, uncertain which lights to follow, an easy prey to false guidance from within and without. But these very difficulties eventually point the way to the true solution. They must be rebuilt on a basis which, as a part of their being, they accept as the true foundation of their existence as a nation. The point is put very clearly by a notable French woman writer, Simone Weil, in a book entitled *The Need for Roots*, written during the years 1940-45 when France lay under German occupation. The theme of the book is the re-integration of the French people, with the object of offering united resistance to the conquerors. This is what she has to say:

Seeing that we have, in fact, recently experienced a break in historical continuity, constitutional legality can no longer be regarded as having an historical basis; it must be made to derive from the eternal source of all legality. The men who offer their service to the country to govern it will have to publicly recognise certain obligations corresponding to essential aspirations of the people eternally inscribed in the depths of popular feeling; the people must have confidence in the word and in the capacity of these men, and be provided with means of expressing the fact; they must also be made to feel that, in accepting these men, they give an undertaking to obey them.

The overtones in this passage are outside the subject of this talk. My purpose is to point out that a primary task for a newly-established independent National Government is that of repairing the damage done to the national character in the years of subjection. A first requisite for this purpose is a search for the true roots of the nation's being, and following immediately after, there must be restoration of local liberties and powers, as nearly as possible on traditional lines, so that the national character may be rebuilt, in an atmosphere of freedom, under the age-old incentives and controls.

X

The most important of these powers, in my opinion, is the judicial power. A community which is capable of exercising judicial responsibility within its compass, is a community of persons, who have trust and confidence in their own Judges, and these Judges are men with understanding and honesty, deeply imbued with the thought of community welfare, who have the strength of mind and character to reach and pronounce decisions on points of dispute, however unpalatable they may be to a section of the community or even to themselves. There you have all the ingredients of integration of the community, at local level. It is necessary only to re-devise for them the basic principles and procedures of the laws they administer. This is a matter of fundamental importance. Not all the maxims upon which British legal concepts are based are universally true. A good many are opposed to basic concepts in vogue for twenty centuries and more in the countries of the Middle East, to which we in this country are, by religion and culture, most closely allied. To ensure that the maximum good to the national character is produced, it is necessary to pay full attention to "the eternal source of all legality", so that in a real sense "the law may grow out of the society."

It is my belief that the process of restoring judicial responsibility to the people should follow immediately upon their acquisition of full political responsibility, as a first step towards rebuilding of the national character which is, in the last analysis, the true foundation of a nation's strength and independence. Considerations of difficulties in making the change, or of the people being used to certain foreign techniques which have proved successful elsewhere are merely symptomatic of the inertia which afflicts human affairs. Being myself a creature of the judicial system set up by the late rulers, I nevertheless feel that, while upholding the standard of justice as a principle, it is right that I too should attempt to see our system of justice in the light of the true necessities of the nation. For the concept of justice, and of its due processes, is an essential part of the concept of independence, both individual as well as national. It is a vast and profound concept, and to rise to the full vigour of independence, a people must have a true comprehension to the point of actual assimilation, of what is the length, the breadth, the height and the depth of the divine principle of justice which pervades the Universe, and which animates as well as regulates their individual and collective lives. Mere acquaintance with its processes leads to unscrupulous exploitation by the parties, and super-exploitation by the professionals. That must always happen where a system is a thing of mere intellectual apprehension, and not of integral comprehension and assimilation. Seen in a real light, the practice of justice is the true road by which a people may attain that fullness of nobility which was designed by the Creator for human beings and for human society.

Appendix 11

LEADERSHIP AND CHURCHILL: THE POWER OF LANGUAGE

[Cornelius' focus on exemplars of leadership and virtue was both on Muslim and non-Muslim personages. (See text, p. 59) These were passing references—at most a few paragraphs in speeches of ten or more pages. There were two exceptions. The first was a short speech on Iqbal given at the University of the Punjab 21 April 1964. (That speech is not reprinted here because it is a distillation of points of view expressed in the other selections). The second is a perceptive address on leadership which he devotes almost entirely to an analysis of Winston Churchill, whom he greatly admired, and the power of speech. This is an address he made to the Rotary Club of Hyderabad, 13 February 1965. Churchill's power to hold Britain together during World War II was due not only to his remarkable courage but also to his oratorical skill in making manifest the essence of Britain's culture, heritage, and destiny as the saviour of western civilization: As with many of his addresses, Cornelius adds an obiter dictum, *urging the use of Arabic in expounding Pakistan s Fundamental Rights. Only then, he holds, can they be properly related to Qur'anic teaching. (See text pp. 60, 61, notes 94, 95)]*

I

Please believe me when I say that I appreciate your invitation to be present here on this important occasion in the history of the Rotary Club of Hyderabad very greatly. A quarter of a century is no great period of time and yet it cannot be denied that within the last 25 years, as over the whole country very considerable changes have come over your great city as well. As you have said, the passage through the stresses of the Partition did not leave your Club unaffected, and it gives me great pleasure to note, as a one-time honorary Rotarian, that throughout the Club has been functioning in the fullest sense possible within the true traditions of Rotary.

I will not seek to remind you of the mottos that Rotary holds. I have always regarded Rotary as representing a discharge, by those who have gained privileged positions in life, of the responsibility of that position always to remember the struggle of their less privileged brethren. It is an obligation of common humanity to relieve distress among one's fellow beings to the extent of one's power and help them to find a way for advancement for themselves. This is one of the most pleasing exercises in the practice of leadership in a community life in a country like ours where the impact of the general urbanization of civilization is now apparent. It is therefore entirely appropriate that in a rapidly developing city such as Hyderabad, there should be such avenues as are provided by Rotary for the better-endowed members of the urban community to work for the general betterment.

It is axiomatic that leadership lies at the basis of community life. It marches with the commencement and through all stages of the development of the community. The community is of course a thing of natural growth, whose expansion and improvement and organisation are dependent upon the marshalling of all human forces for good that are available among its members. The need for discipline and guidance becomes apparent, and is requisite also for the control of natural human tendencies towards evil courses and consequent demoralization and dissolution. Only discipline at all levels in every branch of the community's activity can halt such a process of deterioration. The role of Rotary may be thought to be cast in the mould of service by the provision of essential leadership to the community in the most benevolent aspect, largely at the individual level.

From community we proceed to the rise of societies, which are appreciated as being not merely biological, but the consequence of the introduction of rational and intellectual routines and attitudes. Beyond societies we then advance to the concept of a nation composed of large numbers of communities and societies and at once the requisites of leadership become enormously magnified. A nation is a dynamic concept. The sound health of a nation requires that there should be a national plan to secure by the aid of organized discipline and prudent direction, the development of a great purpose out of the many smaller purposes that engage the attention of the included communities and societies. How intricate and fascinating such a process of formulation can be! Vague at first and only acquiring outlines in the march of time and by passage through great vicissitudes, it develops finally into the "mystique" of a great nation. How fortunate are we to be living in a period where we can see this process in actual operation in our own country! Very recently there has been carried out a remarkably successful exercise, by a wholly new technique, for the choice of a national leader to carry all the responsibilities of the country. The immediate success of the technique on the first occasion when it was applied is a matter of universal admiration. I will say no more on this subject, being aware that there is considerable difference of opinion as to the scope within which a judge may profess to estimate such matters. The difference of opinion being so great itself possesses a political quality and, in the political field, the right of opinion is perhaps rightly disavowed by judges.

II

But that is no reason why I should go entirely off the fascinating subject of true leadership at a national level. It is a matter which I feel sure is of deep interest to many of you. With your permission, I will dwell for just a little while upon certain aspects of leadership displayed by a very great leader of another country, who went to his last rest very recently, full of years and honour, in the midst of a massive chorus of laudation. Probably all of you have read a variety of appreciations of the qualities of Mr. Winston Churchill in the capacity of a leader and I am sure all of you have views of your own on that subject. I hope I shall not be regarded as presumptuous if I say that I have also asked myself what was the essential foundation of the leadership that Mr. Churchill exercised over the Anglo-Saxon race and the English-speaking world for the brief period of five years, from 1940 to 1945, during which he carried the enormous responsibilities of a war leader with such great success. In a new country like ours, which is advancing rapidly towards its destiny, the study of the true basis of leadership, wherever in the world and at whatever age it manifested itself, is of immense importance to all alike. It is equally important to those who aspire to leadership as to those on whom falls in a humbler capacity the duty of selecting a leader from among themselves.

The first quality of Mr. Churchill that strikes me as being of commanding importance is his devotion to and his understanding of the Word, that is of Scripture of the written Word that among all Asiatic communities following established religions, is believed to have come in the first instance from Divine sources. The phrase "In the beginning was the Word", has more than a theological significance. It connects the nativity of civilization with the birth of an idea, followed by the presentation of that idea in an audible and then in a visible form. It denotes further the propagation, by audiovisual methods, of that idea and its elaborations. It conveys the development of the simple concept through differentiation in application, pragmatically at first and then through intellectual effort, guided always by practical considerations of communications and expression. It predicates finally the ramification of that idea through the organized lives of the entire community, society, and nation. The development of the idea through the differentiated Word represents in itself, a history of the life of that community. The idea is elaborated and its expression through language is modified by stages to show how it passed through periods of want and periods of plenty, through peace and through war, through disease and distress and the not-less pressing dangers that attend a prolonged peace. The Word and its variations expand with the procedures, but not chaotically.

The entire expansion is determined by the earliest form of the idea and its expression so that each new development carries with it the connotations of its first beginnings. All of us I am sure have been impressed by the way in which a familiar Word used in a new context seems suddenly invested with the brilliance which accompanied its first attachment to the thought it conveys. There was, so it appears, a fusion when the idea met its match in the Word, and the incandescence of that moment is still capable of being revived.

III

Many have said that Mr. Churchill was master of the spoken and written Word in the English language, but many others have reached an equal degree of mastery, without being able to evoke, as he did, in each one of many millions of hearers, a call to individual, communal even national destiny. I believe that the reason for his immense success was his developed capacity to use the common Words, which in every-day conversation carry none but immediate implications, to use them when he spoke in moments of stress, anxiety and mounting despair, as notes picked out of the ancient music of men's minds, as if he spoke against a background of prophetic utterances, a background of majestic poetry and impassioned history, of the whole vast literature of phrase and fable, of dangers long past and the concurrent heroism which enabled the men of the time to overcome them. He spoke to the sound of drums, to the tramp of millions of marching feet through centuries of wars, the clamor of the conflicts and victories of the Anglo-Saxon nation down its long and chequered history. Through extensive reading, having become imbued with the grandest and most profound writings in the English language, he gained command over its keynotes. It is as if a master musician should have before him an instrumental keyboard with a million keys, forming the topmost layer of a descending pyramid, each successive layer representing a stage in the development and elaboration of its music, from the first note that sounded in a silent world. The performer should strike unerringly, so as to match to the moment those notes before him which would call up among an integrated people with a long history of culture and civilization the surge of human power. It would reach down through the instrument to the earliest and deepest of the emotions built into their being. In his five years of battle against the awful threat of fascism, Mr. Churchill relied greatly upon that power. He used it with awe-inspiring effect and the total success of his effort saved his people and the civilization for which they stood, from a very near threat of total effacement.

So, one major feature of this remarkable man was that to a people of the Word, a people of Scripture, of recorded history and traditions he spoke unfailingly the Words that united them in emotion and endeavor for their self preservation. He did this to a degree which had not been known since the time when the community was small and in its incipient stages, its protective instincts were at their height. In one aspect, he may be regarded as having triumphed by the exercise of this faculty, over the divisive forces of secularism, over the influence of highly differentiated and widely spread forms of human activity in the field of material things. He revived the ancient spirit, the very essence of the community's being, which came, like all things in the beginning, from the Almighty.

IV

The second main feature of his character that has been widely noted is his courage. Here again, we are involved with the Word written and spoken, for Mr. Churchill's major activities were in the political field. Within the body politic the scope of operation is confined to the concrete aspects of affairs, in the rational order of humanity, covering every type of human endeavor and activity, individual as well as collective, and the high purpose of politics is that all these things should be set in the direction of the public good. For a leader to travel as a guide through the political organisation of a great imperial nation with its multifarious purposes and activities, the first essential was communication, and the second, efficient organisation. Both require, in their several ways superior ability in the use of words. Not merely in the manner of commands at drill, but to ensure persuasion on the basis of inner conviction, inspiring words that are in a true line of pedigree from the birth of the idea through its successive adaptations to cover each fresh phase of human activity. Mastery in this respect alone is not enough—a political commentator or a party whip may have the necessary competence. But for leadership in the direction of public good, there is needed also the capacity to form an individual opinion as to what is best to be done in given circumstances to produce the right results, as to what should therefore be tried out, bravely and tenaciously, and there is merit in the trial, even if it not be immediately or even finally successful. The whole of Mr. Churchill's career shows his intense devotion to the study of public affairs on the largest scale, down the long course of his people's history. He possessed both aptitude for and determination in the formation of opinions, and concurrently and inevitably, the corresponding degree of ambition to gain a position in which he could give effect to those opinions by trying them out in practice. Again as concomitant to the strength of his opinions, honestly held and completely believed in, because they were based on profound study of the past and complete assimilation of the national conscience, he possessed the high degree of courage which went with his strong convictions. Much has been said about the vicissitudes of his political career, but such changes as there were, were changes in the political climate, while he, regardless of the falling away of his friends, regardless of massive opposition by his opponents, remained firm in his belief and his convictions. He appeared finally to embody the spirit of tenacity and infinite endurance, which is believed to distinguish the Anglo-Saxon character. His career given the impression that he set himself deliberately to typify that character.

There was a prolonged period before his rise to supreme power in the United Kingdom when he was isolated and disregarded. Nevertheless, he remained prominent in the political scene, always active and never silent, continuously projecting himself and his views for the advancement of his country's welfare. This pre-occupation was so intense, that the lack of power to give effect to his opinions seemed only to add to the power of the language which he used to express them. All of us have heard the phrase "a voice crying in the wilderness" and many must have felt the power it has to connect the idea of a "wilderness" with the idea of a human voice, breaking the dreadful silence of a savage void. It is a deep and ancient human sentiment. Stranger, however, it is to discover that a cry can itself create a wilderness in the public conscience in the sense of pointing to the existence of an area of darkness within the public mind, where all else is light, a dark area lying unsuspected by those who will not or cannot see. By compulsion of nature we are far more sensitive to light than we are to darkness. And in the darkness lies danger to man, such as calls forth the cry of the prophet and seer, to make man aware of the wilderness in their midst, a miasma of evil forces which might swell so as to engulf the whole scene, if men are not vigilant.

Such a situation did indeed arise in Europe in the years preceding the Second World War. The lone cry in that wilderness was that of Mr. Churchill. He made it resound, without succeeding in getting it heard. The darkness swiftly overcame Europe and there descended a cloud of pre-historic savagery, that gave rise to a vast crop of evils. Soon enough the whole world was involved in a vast conflict of arms. The move darkness into light was a protracted and painful process, requiring the highest form of leadership for the preservation of what was best in human civilization. The call to assume the leadership came to Mr. Churchill as the occasion for which his lifetime of devotion to the pristine Word, of intense attachment to the study of human affairs and his firm adherence to his individually and honestly formed opinions regarding the proper conduct of those affairs, and prepared him. He undertook the task with alacrity. How he carried it out is now a matter of history.

Many other aspects of greatness in Mr. Churchill can be traced through his many-sided career. I do not propose to go beyond those which I have mentioned. I am aware that even so much as I have said may give offence to certain opinion which holds that any extension of approbation to any person or thing outside Pakistan, its people, its culture, its basic philosophy, is a form of near disloyalty. I am aware that Mr. Churchill has been widely criticized for his marked tendency towards authoritarianism. That excess of character was inevitable in a man whose Word had been unquestioningly obeyed by a great number of very able and distinguished men working under his command. I am conscious that with reference to the liberation of the Indian people, his approach was undemocratic and that, too, was inevitable in a person whose attitudes were determined by the rhythms of history, and not entirely by the currents of the day. But in treating of high leadership in a national context we are in an absolute field. The study is for all men, just as to a soldier the study of great battles is important, even though neither he nor his people were either involved or affected by them. The magic point about Mr. Churchill to which I thought I might draw attention is that he is an example of conscious development of a character of great force and range, through cultivation of certain qualities of mind and heart, and of this character matching the moment when only by rising to its full height could the dreadful occasion which faced the nation have been overcome. I feel very strongly that there is guidance in this phenomenon for persons in our country as well.

V

I feel that if there is one feature that stands out in the Constitution that was given to Pakistan by Field Marshal Muhammad Ayub Khan in 1962, it is the provision of opportunities for the development and display of qualities of leadership, throughout the new political structure, from the Basic Democracies upwards. I say that at a slight risk, for a Judge moves with caution in the periphery of matters falling within the sharp-toothed machinery of politics. But if you will bear with me in assuming for the moment that there is provision for the evocation of leadership built into our present Constitution, I am sure that those of you who are familiar with the basic principles, as apart from the machinery aspects of our Constitution, will be unable to deny that here too, we are in need of men, who will take pains to master the spoken and the written word, and thus to call forth from the people their deepest and truest emotions, and so to unite them for their advancement towards the great goal of the nation. What is that goal? In a word, it is the formation of a strong and united nation, organized in the manner of a democracy based upon ideas of social justice. And not merely any ideas of social justice, but social justice according to the dictates of Islam, that is such as are directly based upon divine ordinances, which have been handed down to us from the earliest times.

There is, of course, need for men to interest themselves in public affairs with the utmost keenness, who will acquaint themselves with the principles and the techniques that have been followed elsewhere in the world in the period of a century since democratic institutions first began to make inroads into the then prevalent rule of absolute power. There is a great need that such persons should engage in the pragmatic exercise of adopted political techniques, since adaptation in detail is a condition for success. And there is need for such persons to acquire mastery of the spoken and the written Word for the purpose of establishing communication with the public they serve, and to set up the requisite organizational structure. All this is in what I may describe as the purely secular sphere. But over and above all this, such persons must remember that the guidance they give must be inspired by eternal principles. Theirs is to be no short term tradition going back to the philosophers of the late eighteenth century. Those men were secular thinkers, and in the circumstances, since the ecclesiastical power was then entirely on the side of the royalists and absolutists, it was essential that they should deny the force of religion, if they were to secure conviction for their views among the groaning common people. They did that to the full, but today in Pakistan, a century and a half later, we present to the world a reversal from that enforced position. The Constitution calls for social justice as dictated by Islam, and I can see in that requirement the importance of the development of those modes of expression of which Mr. Churchill was such a master. There is a need under our Constitution for persons who can speak with a voice out of history, when ideas were clear and men's minds were not confused, as they are today, by the welter of material things, in which the ancient norms are apt to be buried out of sight by pre-occupation with immediate material requirements. Some may say that Mr. Churchill's special quality of evoking the ancient spirit of the Anglo-Saxon people, through his sensitive command of words, was only necessary on some occasion of terrible danger, to save the nation. That is, of course, true, but the suggestion I have to make is that under our present Constitution, that quality is called for whether the period through which the nation is passing is one of peace or war, whether there is total safety or total danger. The Constitution itself calls for it, and its principles cannot be denied.

VI

What is more, the Constitution lays down in the Fundamental Rights, the path which leadership is to follow, the overriding principles that are to govern thought and behavior and policy. It is a misfortune in my personal opinion that these are expressed in terms derived from another Constitution, which has been in existence for perhaps half a century. It may be convenient for purposes of judicial interpretation that the expression should be in the English language, but from the point of view of making these amendments a matter of conscience, would there not be in

Pakistan enormous advantage to be gained from setting them out in a Scriptural language, that is in the Arabic language? I conceive that each one of the Fundamental Rights can be shown to derive from the dictates contained in the Holy Scriptures of Islam. If expressed in Arabic, in suitable terms, would they not then be invested with overtones of undeniable obligation? Would not their assimilation into the public conscience be vastly enhanced thereby? I submit that that task, one of no great difficulty, which still awaits a master pen, should attract appropriate attention. The need for men like Mr. Churchill may not arise again in the English speaking world for many centuries, but in the way that I look at the Constitution of Pakistan, there is at present and there will always be in Pakistan, by virtue of its Constitution, the need for men of similarly cultivated mind and mould who will expound and at the same time, give practical effect to the *ethos* of the Constitution, the central idea around which it is built. It is, I submit, leadership with that quality which the Constitution, as it is worded, calls the nation to develop, for the due and full attainment of its great purpose.

Appendix 12

THE LEGAL SYSTEM AS A TRANSNATIONAL, UNIFYING FORCE

[In his plea for a return to indigenous cultural roots as a basis for a judicial system, Cornelius was confronted with the problem of adjusting firmly planted concepts of British law to indigenous Islamic law. He treated this subject in other addresses and opinions. In this speech to the Pakistan Institute of International Affairs in Karachi, 4 June 1964, he approaches the problem somewhat differently. Under British rule, the legal norms of undivided India and, later, Pakistan were clearly subordinate to British norms, symbolized by the ultimate authority of the Privy Council sitting in London. The linkage between British law and the legal system of Pakistan is eroding. It is being replaced by new institutional arrangements uniting Asian countries—all sharing the colonial experience and efforts to reassert their cultural identity. Even more significant is the new linkage forged by Muslim states through such entities as the Organization of the Islamic Conference. Again, he refers to the Mujallah (Majelle) *of Turkey. The spirit of British law, he maintains, still dominates Pakistani jurisprudence. It should be replaced by a code—Shari'a—as comprehensive in scope as the Turkish Mujallah. (See text, pp. xxiv, 34, 59, n. 95)]*

I

It is true that in the absence of any supra-national authority, the concepts and the sanctions of international law are a matter of settlement by discussion and agreement among the nations themselves, and a link is thus provided. That is a large subject in itself, but what I propose to present to this distinguished gathering this evening is the manner in which the domestic law within each nation may be, and has been brought into contact with similar law in other nations for mutual benefit. You are familiar with the fact that international gatherings of lawyers are regularly held and serve a very useful purpose. A more recent development is that of international meetings of judges. I will presently give you an account of one such meeting held in the Philippines which was attended by me. Earlier, there was a meeting between the Superior Judges of the United Kingdom and of the United States at which matters of common interest were discussed, and information regarding procedures was exchanged. In the judicial field, of course, the working of law in each country is treated as strictly a domestic matter, except that by statute and practice in each country, qualified validity is allowed to final judgments of foreign countries delivered in relation to disputes coming before the municipal courts of the country. This, however, has no effect upon contact between countries in the field of law in the larger sense.

II

Taking the matter historically, our country, when it was a part of India, was linked with the law of Great Britain by virtue of its having been conquered. In a short time, the organized processes of justice in force in England began to be introduced into India, first among the settlements of the East India Company and later by the British Government. This innovation was of the greatest value to the country, where justice had been practised largely in the field of community and tribe before the arrival of the British. The effects began to appear very quickly in the shape of codified laws which were applied by the judges and magistrates who, at the outset, were all British. Uniformity in the laws and in the application of the laws was quick to develop, and by the introduction of the system of open trial and open argument on the legal issues as well as the appraisal of evidence, it was brought about that justice became an exercise in the application of reason in a regulated and impartial way by means of the ascertainment and settlement of disputes. In addition, the British brought with them the system of recording of all proceedings in a case concluded with a written judgment dealing with all questions of fact and law. To these processes, we owe the tremendous advance that has been made in the codification of laws and the application thereto of the judicial faculty of interpretation recorded from case to case. It is probably true to say that the security so established in matters of a contentious nature arising among the people in their multifarious activities, both personal as well as institutional, has also been a most powerful aid to the development of initiative among the people themselves. It is not until a person is able to make a fair estimate of the result which may follow and the resolution of difficulties which he may encounter, that he will undertake the enterprise involving the use of capital and the services of others with the consequential risks attached. The steady development of settled law in each field of human activity has greatly assisted in giving to these men of vigor and enterprise that assurance which they needed. There has in consequence been seen over the years, when the British ruled in the country, a general growth of domestic industry and commerce as well as of other fields of human activity, without which the nations which now inhabit the old Indian subcontinent, would not have possessed the ability needed to undertake the huge tasks of development which face them today.

But the link which developed between the law of England and the law of India remained throughout one of subordination. A great number of statutes which were in force in England were introduced into the Indian statute books to deal with expanding fields of activity which were new to the Indians. In almost all the laws which were made for the country, you will find some assimilation of matters borrowed from the British statutes. That was by no means a disadvantage. The British also took pains to codify customs which became ascertained law for the people following those customs. They undertook also the task of making collections from the scriptures and writings of ancient jurists, of laws in the personal field governing the various religious communities in the subcontinent. Thereby, they rendered a great service to the country which its own nationals were at that time unprepared to supply. Due to experience in their own country, extending over some six centuries they were aware that no administration is worth the name, unless it is established and operated under and in accordance with laws at different levels, through an organized system of justice. It is, I believe, the contribution of British practice to the whole world that they developed a three-tier system of graded tribunals where questions of fact were, in the first instance, elucidated by the reception and appraisal of evidence, and upon this was superimposed a first appeal where the facts were finally settled and the law was again examined in its application to these facts. Realizing the intricacies involved in the application of written laws in accordance with established concepts, a further appeal on a point of law was in course of time provided. This system is now in operation in every civilized country. In India too, this system was provided, but a further jurisdiction was superimposed, namely, that of the Sovereign through the medium of the Judicial Committee of the Privy Council. That jurisdiction had long since been abolished in England, where the last Court of appeal was the Judicial Committee of the House of Lords having no direct connection with the exercise of the Sovereign authority. In relation to the dominions and colonies and other dependencies, that jurisdiction was maintained. It was converted into a purely judicial function by the appointment of judges who exercised the jurisdiction on the part of the Sovereign. The Sovereign was obliged by an act of Parliament to accept and implement the advice tendered by the judges.

Thus, it was established that all judicial jurisdictions in the Indian subcontinent were maintained and controlled from a distant land under a link of subordination. That link was not exercised in an arbitrary manner. The judges who sat in the Privy Council were men of the highest judicial distinction. They were assisted in their deliberations, which were restricted to the most intricate and important case coming up from the Indian high courts, by an extremely able body of lawyers. An examination of the reports of cases decided by the Privy Council reveals that the arguments and the judgments exhibit mastery of the entire complex. They expose not only the multifarious facts and circumstances arising in a wholly foreign setting, but also the development of the legal concepts from the earliest times based upon precepts of jurists who wrote thousands of years ago. It is sometimes difficult to believe that the entire exercise was carried out by a group of persons none of whom had any direct knowledge of India, and may never had met an Indian. Each case is proof of the power of written law and a continuous record of cases decided, as a channel of communication between trained minds.

It was of the utmost advantage to the jurisdictions which were operating in the subcontinent to have the benefit of the studies, deliberations and effort which went into the final decisions of each case before the Privy Council, but nevertheless, the Privy Council did not sit as an Indian court. It sat as the court of a foreign Sovereign, and the situation of the Indian courts was inferior in that link of subordination. It is true that, in a few instances, distinguished Indian judges were appointed to the membership of the Judicial Committee, but they sat there as members of a foreign court. Notwithstanding that the Privy Council was the final Court for the subcontinent for nearly a century, and for an appreciable time even after the Partition, there was no attempt on the part of the judges who formed the Judicial Committee to sit even at a conference table with their counterparts in these two countries, at a level of equality. So far as I am aware, it has only been within the last two or three years that steps have been taken towards this end. I refer to the visit paid to England two or three years ago by the Chief Justice of India under the auspices of the British Council, where he was received and treated with the highest dignity. Last year, I was similarly invited in the capacity of Chief Justice of the Supreme Court of Pakistan, and I may acknowledge here that I was received in the highest judicial quarters in England with great kindness and respect. Previously, the most that was done was to allow visiting judges from the countries of the Empire to sit as privileged spectators in one or other of the highest courts in

England. Following upon the visit by the Chief Justice of India and myself, there was a return visit in the last winter by the Master of the Rolls, Lord Denning. That I believe was the first occasion in which a high judicial dignity from the United Kingdom came to our country and made direct contact with our superior judges on a level of equality.

III

But last year also another link was forged in another direction and this time it was uncoloured by any connection of subordination either past or present. This was a conference which was called at the instance of the distinguished Chief Justice of the Philippines. Chief Justices of about 12 countries of the Far East extending from Pakistan to Japan were invited. As a result, there was a getting together of the Chief Justices of Nationalist China, Thailand, India, Malaysia, Pakistan and the Philippines which was attended by associate justices of the Supreme Courts of Japan and South Vietnam substituting for their own Chief Justices who were unable to attend. This was a remarkable conference in many ways. It was firstly marked by being totally independent of governmental influence from any quarter. It happened that the Chief Justice of the Philippines had sufficient amounts available to him in a discretionary fund to cover the expenses of the visiting Chief Justices, and he thus had no need to obtain funds from his Government. One result was that each participating chief justice was enabled to symbolize the justice of his country quite apart from his position in the administrative complex of his country. Since it was a first meeting of its kind, the deliberations were of a purely informatory nature. The subject which had been proposed for discussion was the Development of Oriental Jurisprudence, but that was not touched. Each Chief Justice described his country's legal and judicial system with reference to its constitutional history, and general discussion followed, enabling each of them to understand the historical development of the judicial systems of all the countries and of the techniques which they followed in the dispensation of justice. It would take too long to tell you even in brief regarding all the matters which came under notice at this conference. But I may say that I was greatly struck by the fact that in each of those countries, the three-tier system was in vogue and very well established.

Some of the main impressions of the conference that I brought away with me may be briefly mentioned. It was clear that in each country the judicial system enjoyed the full support of the people, both in sentiment as well as practical employment. Judiciary spoke to Judiciary at this conference through its acknowledged symbols, and the realization was borne in all of us that each judiciary was of ancient and honorable lineage. The complete reliance of the judiciary upon the body of lawyers in each country was also brought out very plainly. The personnel of the judiciary in each country was in a line of pedigree not only of learning, but also of discipleship from the date when each member entered the field of law. That the judiciary in each country had a prime hold on the esteem and affection of its people was thus only natural, for in the East the people have an inherent and unshakable respect for persons and institutions whose existence is founded on long and true tradition. This was particularly significant in a period when in the field of administration, under political modes of government, the ancient ideas have been swept away and the techniques of democracy have placed in positions of directive authority, persons who might not have the background which our ancient peoples are accustomed to expect. All of us appreciated that the kind of justice which we were required to administer was that which is the constant companion of the natural law and which exists for the purpose of enforcing basic human rights in a manner consonant with the positive law. We found, too, great cause for satisfaction in the fact that real importance was given in all countries to the development of legal education. At this conference, it was decided that these meetings should be repeated every two years and this was of course necessary if we are to go on from the preliminary effort to the commencement of a study of the development of Oriental Jurisprudence which is the main objective. At present the intention is that the next conference should be held in Tokyo and it is hoped that it will be attended by many more than the number at the last meeting.

Thus, you will see that, at the initiative of the Chief Justice of the Philippines, a link has been forged between our country and the countries to the East of us which follow essentially similar laws and judicial procedures. One may confidently hope that in the course of years this link will become stronger and provide to each of the countries in the area a source of legal enlightenment and progress. It is remarkable that the initiative should have come from a country so far removed from ourselves, which follows a system of law and justice much closer to the pattern in the United States than to the British mode. Already, by indirect means such as reference to text books and authorities, the forms and concepts of laws which have been brought to a high degree of development in the United States with the aid of learned academicians as well as judges and lawyers, have had their effect upon our jurisprudence. One reason is that we have a written Constitution which embodies a chapter on Fundamental Rights. The courts and the lawyers find but little assistance in the judgments of the English courts. The British Constitution is unwritten, and it is their pride that the Fundamental Rights are assured to their people through the medium of a Common Law operating equally upon the minds of the legislators and their draftsmen, as it does through the arguments of lawyers and the decisions by the Court. The British Common Law also provided one of the ground-norms of our own law in the period of British rule, and to a considerable extent, its precepts and maxims are built into our statute books as well as into the thinking of our lawyers and judges.

IV

From this consideration, there seems to me to arise a basic necessity for our country which, in my submission, can, with comparatively little effort, be made by forging a further link through law between Pakistan and the countries lying to the immediate West. I refer to the requirement of our Constitution that the laws of our country should be made in accordance with the Holy Qur'an and the Sunnah. The Constitution requires that Islamic ideas of social justice shall be enforced. The processes of the law and of justice constitute the most powerful agency towards the end that the country and its various organs can command. From Morocco up to Afghanistan, in country after country the law of the *Shariah* has been applied throughout the centuries since the establishment of Muslim rule over those areas. The judicial structure is not at the same level in each of these countries, but the largest number have a three-tier system closely resembling our own, and in the field of general law their courts follow our own system of open trial and open debate by lawyers in court. They are a long way in advance of the system of *fatwas* and *juris consults* which were at one time the only mode of decision of disputes. I emphasize this point, namely the existence of courts in all these countries, particularly those which have passed through a period of greater or less control by one or other European country, which deal with cases precisely in the manner of our own courts and maintain permanent records of their proceedings including their judgments. I entertain no doubt whatsoever that in each of these countries the ground-norms from which all legal concepts relating to particular subjects and matters are drawn is the law of the *Shariah*. I would have you know that there is nothing medieval about the idea of *Shariah* being such a ground-norm. That is a very common misconception, which has stood awkwardly in the way of introduction of fundamental concepts of Muslim law into our thinking and practice. It is common to regard attempts to bring the *Shariah* into our political thought and practice as a retrograde step. This is largely based upon what I might describe as the secularization of British law and justice, over three centuries. In the year 1653 a judge in England did not hesitate to pronounce that:

> There is no law in England, but is as really and truly the law of God as any Scripture phrase, that is by consequence from the very texts of Scripture: for there are very many consequences reasoned out of the texts of Scripture; so is the law of England the very consequence of the very Decalogue itself: and whatsoever is not Consonant to Scripture in the law of England is not the law of England ... be it Acts of Parliament, customs, or any judicial acts of the Court, it is not the law of England...

That was said at a stage when the courts of England being dissatisfied with the legislation of the time, were searching for grounds on which they could declare the legislative dictates as invalid. The absolute power of statute was a long time in establishing itself. Indeed, for a great number of years, British judges, while they inclined less and less to rely directly on the "law of God," held up the Common Law as the norm by which the validity of legislation was to be judged. They did not hesitate to say that "when an Act of Parliament is against common right and reason, or repugnant, or impossible to be performed, the Common Law will control it and adjudge such Act to be void." The process continued for a considerable period and it required a great deal of effort in the proper quarters, as well as a total reversal of thinking among the lawyers and judges, to reach the position that the power of the Common Law to control statute was no more. In 1871, we find a judge saying:

> It was once said that if an Act of Parliament were to create a man judge in his own cause, the Court might disregard it. That dictum, however, stands as a warning, rather than an authority to be followed. We sit here as servants of the Queen and the legislature. Are we to act as regents over what is done by parliament with the consent of the Queen, lords, and commons? I deny that any such authority exists.

Some may feel surprised to learn of the assumed servitude of the judiciary to the chief executive and to the legislature. Some others may regard the submission as of the essence of the State. It depends upon the belief of the particular critic as to where sovereignty in a State resides. In our own State, I hope, there will be none to deny that sovereignty lies in the law and the Constitution, and while administration is for the Executive, and law-making for the legislature, yet what is constitutional and legal, and what is not, should be declared in independence, bearing in mind only the high interests of the State, by the Courts alone.

It is here then that the question arises-how in our present condition, being already supplied with a complex structure of statutes, a legislature designed on lines imitated from the advanced countries of the West, and an administrative machinery which has been left behind by the British rulers-how in these circumstance, can all those who are responsible to implement the dictate of the Constitution, best proceed to inject into the country, the Islamic ideas of equality, of social justice and all of those things which go to make up the life of the State?

V

The answer, in my humble opinion, may be found in the establishment of a further link through law with our neighbor Muslim countries to the West, and in particular with those which as I have said here gone through a period of development of their jurisprudence through processes of justice similar to our own. I feel assured that the lawyers, the judges and the administrators of these countries of the Middle East and Northern Africa will be found to have been implementing, through their thoughts and actions, the basic principles of *Shariah* in which they have been born and by which they have lived their lives. For, throughout the centuries of Muslim history, the Prophetically revealed law of Islam based upon Holy Scriptures has been a bond which has united all Muslims throughout the world. The *Shariah* has been described as the rock of Islam, and each of the great political philosophers of Muslim history has unquestioningly accepted the duty of all administrators to act in accordance with the *Shariah*. I quote from three of the principal thinkers whose names are well known to all of us. In the early 14th century, Ibn Khaldoon, speaking of Government, while observing that all kings whether Muslim or non-Muslim should first establish their rule by force and superior power, and then attend to the general welfare of the subjects, remarked that the difference between the two kinds of kings was—

> that the Muslim kings act in accordance with the requirements of the Islamic *Shariah* as far as they can. Hence their laws are composed of statutes of the *Shariah*, relations of right conduct, regulations which are natural for political association and necessary things concerning powers...

Ibn Sina, whose analysis of the philosophy of Plato is of the highest importance, and who did not hesitate to give the Platonic concepts their due, nevertheless declared that prophecy and the *Shariah* are indispensable for the life and preservation of mankind, as they are for the dispensation in the hereafter. In his view, an expert knowledge of the *Shariah* was a requisite for the philosopher-ruler. And Ibn Rushd was most emphatic in his declaration of the supremacy of the *Shariah* in the ideal state. It is remarkable that of these great thinkers, the two latter had absorbed to the full all that was of meaning and excellence in Platonic philosophy, on which indeed our modern concepts of democracy are based, but nevertheless they adhered to the view that the integrity of the Muslim state is bound up with adherence to *Shariah*.

These are common place for most of my listeners and I only mention them in order to emphasize what I said a little earlier, namely, that the men in these Muslim countries who have through the centuries made and administered and interpreted the laws there in force, through the judicial process, are persons into whose body and brain the fundamental principles of the

Shariah have been assimilated through countless generations. What is more, their outlook was never sullied, much less blinded as perhaps was that of a great may intellectuals in the old subcontinent, through the depression of their true sources of law by the presence of foreign rule, and the continuous pressure upon their minds of the ideas and techniques which the rulers imported into and firmly established in the great land they had conquered. When therefore we attempt to discover ways and means of carrying one of the basic requirement of our Constitution that the State of Pakistan should be a true Islamic state, no better guidance shall we find for the infusion of the great principles of Muslim law, or the *Shariah* into our own legal system, than the exposition of that law which appears in the judicial records of these countries, which were established as Muslim states and have ever since continued as such. The common impression that a number of these countries are at a low level of legal and judicial development is totally false and I entertain no doubt that just a few occasions of contact between our judges and lawyers and those of these countries will quickly serve to dispel that belief, where it exists.

VI

I will give you an instance from the legal history of the Empire of the Turkish Sultans. About the middle of the 19th century, the Sultan constituted a great body of Muslim jurists to draw up a code of the general law of the Empire on the lines of the Napoleonic Code of France. These jurists were aided by European advisers in regard to matters of codification and after a great effort, they produced a document which is known as the *Mujallah*. This collection of laws is prefaced by a hundred maxims basic to the substantive and procedural requirements of all laws. It includes chapters on practically all the different branches of law which were in need at that time, for the administration and dispensation of justice throughout the Turkish Empire. From the subject of agency to the subject of trusts, codes were laid down and you will find that there do exist, to this day, commentaries on these books, which, for the rest of the life of the Turkish Empire were prescribed in the Turkish universities. What is more, the learned commentators were at pains to establish that each maxim that was included, and each principle of law appearing in the codes was derived directly from the basic law of the *Shariah*. That indeed was the charge entrusted to those jurists who sat to compile the *Mujallah*, namely, to lay down principles in every field of law which they were required to cover, such as were consistent with the true meaning and the fundamental law of the *Shariah*, as expounded through the centuries since the foundation of Islam. Today, the *Mujallah* as a piece of positive law is no longer in force. Under the stresses of the first World War which led to the dissolution of the Turkish Empire, various parts came under the influence of different European countries, and each of the mandatory powers introduced its own practices in regard to laws and procedures. Though the textual validity of the *Mujallah* is no more, its principles have been worked into, and embodied in the codified laws which are now in force in those countries, all of which today are practically free of European control. Even where the *Mujallah* never was in force, we may feel assured that the laws laid down there are within the spirit of the *Shariah* to an extent which in our country is unknown, for the simple reason that the spirit that has been built into our laws is that of the British Common Law. I apprehend that the task of replacing this by the true spirit of the *Shariah* and thus bringing to a reality the dictate of the Constitution to which I have already referred is not one of such great volume as it might appear at first sight. It is a task which, in my humble opinion, will appear to be comparatively easy, once a link in the field of law is established between our country and those Muslim countries to which I have referred, where the judicial system is essentially parallel with our own. I feel no doubt that approaches towards this end would be happily received and that enlightenment would follow and thus the way of appreciation and adoption of the basic norms which are the requisite of our Constitution will be cleared and made to appear easy. The judicial process that we follow is such that assimilation of these legal concepts, once they are mentally accepted, into the working of our legal system would be almost automatic. The barrier of language would, at the end of the task, appear to be a mere incident in a labour or devotion, and therefore of love. A great many Arabic legal expressions are already common in the language we speak, and to explain and define their meaning in a legal sense would not be an insurmountable problem.

So here is a further field where the link through law appears for Pakistan to be not merely of value but a positive necessity. We in this country live under a thorough-going system of laws, and for a country so constituted there is no question but that the law provides a medium of communication and understanding which is more basic than mere treaties or compacts or common membership of international bodies. Where that law has grown out of the religious consciousness of the peoples, a tie would emerge which no one could possibly break.

Appendix 13

CRIME AND THE PUNISHMENT OF CRIME

[This address attracted more attention outside Pakistan than any other speech by Cornelius. It was given at the Third Commonwealth and Empire Law Conference in Sydney, Australia 27 August 1965. It is a lucid description, crafted for a foreign audience, of Pakistan's criminal justice system. There are two extraordinary features of the address: His description of the Northwest Frontier Crimes Regulation included a vigorous defense of the jirga *system used in certain tribal areas which allowed for adjudication by a council of tribal elders using tribal standards with no recourse to English law or lawyers. He thus reiterated the praise of tribal criminal justice made seven years earlier in the* Dosso *case. But the feature which attained international notoriety for the speech was its advocacy of a modern variation of punishment by body mutilation for certain crimes. This controversial recommendation was included at the end of the speech and appears to be almost an afterthought—an* obiter dictum*—but Cornelius intended it to be the most significant comment in the address. This is the part which he read to me in advance of his trip to Sydney when he foretold that it was likely to have a dramatic impact. (See text, pp. 35, 36, notes 52, 53)]*

I

A major concern of present day thinkers on criminal law appears to be the safety of the criminal or rather the accused person, through the processes of justice. Attention is focused on the development of new and recondite defences, such as that of automatism. A survey of the results of criminal proceedings in Pakistan leaves the impression that any further attention paid to such matters in my country would place accused persons at an advantage which, in the public interest, would be unconscionable and even somewhat dangerous. The figures that I have been able to collect are scarcely up to date, but they are sufficient to illustrate my point. You should know that my country is divided into two parts lying on the two sides of the mainland of India. In 2East Pakistan, in the year 1960, the total number of cases dealt with at the initial stages by the police, on report, and by magistrates on complaint, was 221,773. Preliminary investigation established that some 80 percent of these cases were *prima facie* true cases and were accordingly brought to trial. Out of these over 90 percent were tried by magistrates and the percentage of conviction is no more than 28.5. More serious cases, tried at sessions, with the aid of assessors, after a magisterial proceeding for commitment numbered 1,456 and resulted in 85 percent of convictions. Only 12 death sentences were imposed, in addition to 277 sentences of transportation for life, which can mean as little as 12 years imprisonment, if all remissions are earned. Seven hundred and fifty cases of corruption by public servants tried by special judges resulted in only 22 percent of convictions. Appeals from convictions go before district magistrates from the subordinate magistracy, before sessions judges where the sentences are up to four years imprisonment and in other cases before the High Court. Appeals before district magistrates numbered 315 of which 20 percent resulted in acquittal. Those before the sessions courts numbered about 5,000 and the success here was 42 percent. This was out of 28.5 percent convictions by magistrates and as it is probably true to say that in almost every case where imprisonment is awarded as punishment, there is an appeal, the resulting figure of convictions maintained through appeal is reduced to less than 20 percent of the cases tried. Appeals in the High Court numbered 748 of which 17 percent resulted in acquittal; an equal percentage resulted in modification of the sentences.

The most recent figures available for West Pakistan relate to the year 1957, when the number of cases at the initial level for disposal reached 724,386 of which 90 percent were found after investigation by the police and by magistrates to be "true" in the sense that there was a *prima facie* case. The largest proportion of these cases was of minor offences under special and local laws.

The cases of serious crimes punishable under the Penal Code, numbered 116,000. Of about 200,000 persons brought to trial in these cases, no more than 22 percent were convicted. The results of further appeal were that 26 percent of those who appealed to District Magistrates, 20.3 percent of those who appealed to the Sessions Courts and 21.5 percent of those whose appeals were heard in the High Court were acquitted.

These statistics speak for themselves. A person in Pakistan, against whom a true case is found at preliminary investigation can hardly complain that the dice are loaded against him in the subsequent judicial proceedings. Certain figures relating to murder cases which are available only for West Pakistan are of great interest. Including cases of homicide and attempted homicide, altogether 2,910 cases were brought to trial in 1957 involving 9,094 persons of whom only 2,454 were convicted, there being 563 death sentences imposed. Of these only 279 were confirmed by the High Court in appeal, that is to say, less than half, and even of these 27 death sentences were commuted by the higher executive authorities under the prerogative of mercy. I feel safe in saying on the basis of these figures that in Pakistan the danger of the guilty receiving more than his deserts is of no great significance. On the other hand, the question gains importance whether the agencies of law and justice are functioning with the degree of efficiency necessary for the protection of society.

All these cases were tried under the Criminal Procedure Code, which in its main features is parallel to similar codes operating in countries that have received their system of criminal administration from British sources. The Criminal Procedure Code prescribes the courts which are competent to try each offence specified in the Penal Code. Speaking generally, for offences carrying punishments of seven years' imprisonment of more, commitment by an enquiring magistrate is prescribed, followed by trial at sessions, that is by a sessions judge sitting with assessors. In this respect, there is a difference recently introduced between the law in West Pakistan from what it still is in East Pakistan, namely, that in West Pakistan, sessions judges no longer sit with assessors. The advantage of having assessors sitting with the trial judge lay in the fact that the entire proceedings had to be presented in a manner within the comprehension of moderately well-educated and well-informed citizens belonging to the administrative district to which the case related. The number of assessors varied between 3 and 5. For the benefit of the assessors, the case had to be explained at the outset by the prosecution in the vernacular, and again at the close of the trial, counsel for the two sides summed up their respective cases for the assessors, again in the vernacular, following which the trial judge also summed up the case before obtaining the view of the assessors on the crucial points in the case. The whole case as it proceeds is thus brought fully within the comprehension of the accused as well as of the public attending the trial. It is in truth a public trial of which the principal features are fully understood by a great many persons other than those principally involved in the presentation and elucidation of the case. This system still holds good in East Pakistan, where also with the exception of a single district, all cases prescribed by the Criminal Procedure Code are tried at sessions.

In West Pakistan where the crime figures, as will have been observed are much higher, in order to relieve the strain involved in commitment proceedings upon the police and the magistrates, there is also in force a system by which experienced magistrates are empowered to try all offences not punishable with death, and to award sentences up to seven years' imprisonment. As a consequence a great many of the offences which the Criminal Procedure Code prescribes for trial at sessions are tried before magistrates, sitting singly, the rest being tried by sessions judges, also sitting singly. The law has been amended in the belief that the presence of assessors at the trial has not proved by experience to be of material benefit, while on the other hand, it adds to the expense and has also led to the suspicion that the assessors, whose opinions, though not binding, nevertheless carry some little weight with the trial judge, and before appellate courts, were susceptible of approach by interested parties. A feature of a trial at sessions before the judge sitting singly which needs to be mentioned is that as the records are kept in the English language (the evidence also being recorded in the vernacular) and as the judgment is delivered in English, the exposition of the case at the stage of arguments tends to be of little advantage to the accused person or to the public attending the trial, who mostly are ignorant of that language. The innovation being so recent will perhaps be regarded as in the nature of an experiment whose advantages and disadvantages yet remain to be assessed.

II

In West Pakistan also, in certain areas, that is to say in the extreme West, where the organization of society is mainly on tribal lines, there was in force from the very commencement of British administration, a mode of trial of offences which goes by the description of the *Jirga* system. This system derives from tribal practice and consists in the submission of cases by the police, under the orders of the executive head of the administrative district, for trial to a group of headmen belonging to the tribe. In certain parts of the tribal areas, no other system of justice was applied, the *Jirga* system being best adapted to the conditions of a scattered population living under primitive pastoral and agricultural conditions, who responded best to the disciplines imposed by their own tribal chieftains and headmen. In more settled districts, the choice whether a case should go to the ordinary courts or be tried by *Jirga* was within the discretion of the district head, who would send a case for *Jirga* trial if he thought that it was inexpedient that it should be tried before the ordinary courts. In the year 1957, about 2,500 offences were referred to *Jirgas* involving some 5,700 persons of whom no more than 17 percent were convicted. A principal ground for reference of cases to *Jirgas* was that it was difficult to obtain evidence of the offence by the use of the methods prescribed by the Criminal Procedure Code, and within the requirements of the law of evidence, which in Pakistan is based largely on the rules of the English law. Therefore, a high percentage of convictions is not to be expected at the hands of *Jirgas*. I shall have something more to say regarding this system of communal justice towards the end of this paper. Its utility in the special conditions of society prevailing in West Pakistan has been recognized by the legislature to the extent that a similar law has now been applied to the entire province. The provisions of this law are of some interest and will be noticed later.

I have mentioned the Penal Code. This has been in force in the subcontinent of India from as early as 1860 and can be truly described as a comprehensive work of monumental proportions. It contains very detailed and extremely carefully worded propositions on all relevant points of criminal liability in respect of a great variety of offences falling in the category of general crime, as well as some of a special nature, such as weights and measures. The provisions relating to such matters as the right of private defence and of abetment are in admirably specific terms, such that there has been the minimum of difficulty in applying them to an infinite variety of cases arising during the past 100 years. The law relating to corruption by public servants, to false evidence and other offences against public justice, to matters of public health, decency and morals has been analyzed and set out with detail in different chapters. The treatment of the subject of homicide is particularly noteworthy. It is dealt with in some 20 different sections. The distinction between murder in the first degree and culpable homicide not amounting to murder is drawn with a high degree of precision in some five sections, the application of which has greatly facilitated the development of the criminal law on this subject in the subcontinent. I mention this particularly owing to the great interest that has been aroused by a recent case, involving what may be described as "intentional murder". The Penal Code of Pakistan makes it homicide to do an act with intention to cause death, by whatever agency, or with intention to cause bodily injury likely to cause death, or with the knowledge that the act is likely to cause death. Where reliance is placed on the third limb of the definition, and direct intention to cause death or fatal bodily injury cannot be postulated, the requisite for the act to fall within the first degree is that it should be "imminently dangerous" to life and should have been committed "without any excuse for incurring the risk of causing death". The formula is one which is capable of application to an infinite variety of conditions, for it leaves the human elements involved to be judged within a narrow compass. There is no case in the *corpus juris* of Pakistan of which I am aware which approximates to that of a fugitive from justice shaking off a policeman who is hanging on to his car, in the way of oncoming traffic, but in the vast volume of reported cases, in the subcontinent, a number can be found in which the questions of "imminent danger" and of the absence of "excuse for running the risk" were decided on their peculiar facts.

In recent years, the question of diminished responsibility has been the subject of intensive consideration by courts and writers, and is now dealt with by statute in certain countries. In Pakistan, the matter is still dealt with at the level of insanity, that is of unsoundness of mind rendering a person incapable of knowing the nature of his act or that what he is doing is either wrong or contrary to law. The rule applied in cases of intoxication is also of respectable antiquity, namely, that it should be such as to amount to unsoundness of mind, and should be caused by administration of intoxicants without the knowledge or the will of the agent. Unsoundness of mind such as renders the accused person incapable of making his defence is dealt with in the usual way, that is, by not proceeding with the trial and taking precautions to see that the accused is kept in proper custody and is made available for trial, if and when he regains sanity. Where at trial it is found that he was of unsound mind at the time when he committed his offence, the law requires that he should be detained in custody until the further orders of the provincial government, so that if and when it becomes safe to release him, an order to that effect may be made after proper enquiry. The prescribed modes are applied only to a condition of absolute unsoundness of mind and there are no provisions in the law to meet a case of irresistible impulse or of temporary insanity. The matter is taken care of in cases of murder by the simple provision of two sentences, namely, the death sentence and the sentence of transportation for life. The courts in Pakistan have not hesitated to apply the milder sentence, where they are left, in doubt as to whether the act was performed in an aberration of mind which appears from the evidence to be likely to have supervened. A case which is seen from time to time is that of religious frenzy. There are persons who suffer from manic depression, often induced by excessive application to religious exercises, and who without motive whatsoever, rise and kill one of their relatives when in a state of mental exaltation, following a period of depression, and in such cases, the courts on obtaining proof of such a disease, have invariably applied the lesser sentence. A remarkable case of this kind which came before the Supreme Court in East Pakistan deserves special mention. A Hindu devotee of the goddess Kali, who is thought to be appeased by human sacrifices, without provocation or preliminaries, whatsoever struck off the head of a young Muslim boy with a single blow of a sword in a street and carried the bleeding head triumphantly to the nearby temple of the goddess. The sentence imposed by the High Court was of transportation for life, and when the provincial government sought leave to appeal against the sentence on the ground that for a cruel and senseless act of killing, devoid of provocation, the appropriate sentence was death, the Supreme Court appreciated that there was a degree of irresponsibility produced by momentary exaltation under religious influences, and accordingly refused to interfere. An interesting case of a psychopathic nature was that of young man who was the black sheep of a very respectable family in modest circumstances. On a visit to the house of a relative, he was allowed at his request, to take an incessantly crying infant for an outing by way of help to the mother, who was busy at the time. The infant was pacified and the accused was seen sitting with it in his lap under a tree near the house. Shortly after, he disappeared and the child was later found strangled to death, in the room he occupied at a little distance. In the High Court, it was appreciated that there was no motive whatsoever for the crime, and that it was probably due to irresistible impulse growing out of the guilt complex which the accused had developed over a course of years, through continuous failure to live up to the standards of his family. Accordingly, the lesser sentence was imposed. These are instances of the utility of an alternative to the capital sentence as a means of adjusting the punishment to the true nature of the crime viewed in the light of the mentality of the agent as it appears from the evidence. The courts in Pakistan see no merit in shortening the term of imprisonment of an admittedly unbalanced person with criminal tendencies. So far, there is no provision for psychiatric treatment for such person in prisons.

III

It will have been evident from the figures I have given showing how small is the proportion of death sentences imposed which are eventually carried into execution, that the courts are applying this penalty with great restraint and circumspection. At the same time, the large number of murder cases, particularly in West Pakistan, is a sufficient justification for the retention of this penalty as a deterrent as well as for its retributive effect. There is no move for its abolition. The law requires a court which finds an offence punishable with death to have been committed, to give reasons why that penalty is not imposed, but in Pakistan, the courts are not found hesitant to ascertain and state such reasons in the majority of cases. A few instances will illustrate. In West Pakistan over a large part of which the organization of village life is on tribal lines, crimes of honor are very frequent, and the courts have never hesitated to give effect to the intensity of the sentiment prevailing, particularly among the rural landed proprietors, that an insult to honor must be avenged. An interesting case of this kind was that of a group of men who went out in search of one of their young girls who had been kidnapped by the opposite-party. Hoping to recover the girl without resort to violence, they dressed themselves as policeman and at dead of night demanded entry, for the purpose of search, into a house where they thought the girl was being kept. While they were carrying on the pretence, one of the inmates recognized a person in the raiding party and called out his name, whereupon that person immediately fired a shot and killed him. At the last stage, in the Supreme Court, the view was taken that there was never any intention to recover the girl by the use of force, and that on the other hand, an effort of this kind to recover the girl was exactly in accordance with the strongest sentiments of the offended party, and since the shooting had been on the instant, in the embarrassment caused by the discovery, the death sentence was not necessarily called for. Another instance of recognition of the people's way of life is afforded by the case of an old man who was enraged with a younger person, when the latter checked him as he was driving away some noisy small children from his front door. Following an equal exchange of abuses, the old man struck the younger one a blow or two with a stick as a result of which he died. It was held that although in the circumstances the provocation, being confined to words, was not sufficient to reduce the offence to culpable homicide not amounting to murder, yet the actions of the young man were in violation of the conventional acceptance of the authority which goes with great seniority in respect of age, and consequently, the senior had received provocation sufficient to justify the lesser sentence. The influence of an elder is frequently recognized in cases where two persons of different ages join in the commission of a crime, particularly where they are related to each other. The courts habitually grant to the younger person the benefit of having acted under the influence of his elders, when settling the question of sentence. An unusual case of this kind was of two brothers charged with a joint act of murder of an enemy. In appeal, the benefit of certain doubts arising out of the evidence was given to the elder who was acquitted. The younger appealed to the

Supreme Court against his conviction and sentence of death. The conviction was upheld, but on the point of sentence it was held that the younger person was equally entitled to the benefit of the doubt as to whether his brother was with him or not, to support the possibility that he acted under the direct influence of his elder, and his sentence was accordingly reduced to transportation for life.

The two latter cases may serve as an indication of the extent to which the law supports the indigenous disciplines operating in our society, through the authority of elders, and that may be one reason why the problem of juvenile delinquency in Pakistan has not attained serious proportions. The strength of the family bond remains unimpaired in Pakistan and by reason of the discipline of their elders, the young have so far been prevented from indulging to any appreciable extent in the excesses which have gained some notoriety in western countries. Concern is however being felt among the general public as to the possible effect upon young persons, particularly of the educated classes, of the increasing prevalence of imported cinema-films, depicting carefully planned acts of violence, as well as of the spread among such children of unhealthy comics also imported from abroad. Crime by juveniles is mostly of a casual nature, and the courts either grant probation orders (for which purpose probation officers are appointed in certain areas) or where the crime is serious, generally being committed in association with older persons, detention in a reformatory prison is ordered.

In the matter of sexual morals as well, the country is largely free of those developments, which have received notice in western countries through commissions of enquiry and with increasing frequency, through the courts. According to the oriental ethic, there are restraints imposed upon the freedom of behavior of women which are effective to lessen the need for law to intervene for the purpose of checking excesses by both sexes. A recent case before the Supreme Court was that of a father, who finding his daughter absent from her bed in the very early hours of the morning and suspecting that she was out with the neighbor's son, went out in search and found the two together in a tall field close to the house, in what is usually described as a compromising position. He was carrying a hatchet and instantly used it to kill the girl. In the High Court, the view had been taken that in thus coming out to look for this daughter, the accused had himself sought the provocation, which he pleaded in mitigation. The Supreme Court held that the time had not yet come when it could be said that in acting so as to prevent acts of immorality by his womenfolk, a man could be thought to be exceeding the authority vested in him as the head of the family and consequently his offence was found to be one of culpable homicide not amounting to murder. Adultery is a criminal offence, and in some parts of the country, it is an offence for which the police may arrest an offender without a warrant. The enticing away of married women is also an offence, for which the husband may prosecute. Abduction of women is visited with severe punishment, when the object is illicit intercourse. The procurement of minors for the purpose of prostitution is also punished with severity. Homosexuality, in the widest sense, does not come within the mischief of the law. What is punishable, and with great severity, is carnal intercourse against the order of nature.

As in most countries, prostitution is to be found in Pakistan in the main cities, practised as a profession, and usually confined to particular localities. There is no complaint whatsoever of street walking or open soliciting by prostitutes, and consequently there has never been any need for either the law or the courts to control that type of nuisance. Lately, the social conscience has been greatly aroused in respect of prostitution as a whole, it being contrary to the religious beliefs and sentiments of the Muslim majority in Pakistan, and steps are being taken under law to abolish these colonies and to ban prostitution. Steps are being taken at the same time, and with some success to rehabilitate the prostitutes by finding other means of livelihood for them. Public drunkenness is almost unknown in Pakistan, and even in such a matter as motor driving offences, in regard to which drunkenness is a subject of acute consideration in several Western countries, there is little evidence to connect such offences with intoxication.

Speaking generally, the more refined forms of defence to criminal actions, such as irresistible impulse, automatism and diminished responsibility have not yet been introduced into the criminal jurisprudence of Pakistan. This may be due in part to the fact that such mental aberrations are not of frequent occurrence. By and large, all crimes in Pakistan can be traced to normal motivations. Also, the general practice in criminal trials is to present a defence of innocence and false implication and the effort most frequently is to break down the evidence for the prosecution on grounds of falsity through interest, and by establishing discrepancies between the evidence of different witnesses. Matters going to the psychological condition of the accused person are most frequently raised by the courts themselves. In the few cases in which lunacy is pleaded, it is more often than not found to be feigned. The cases of accused persons being found unfit to plead fall in a different category.

IV

On the subject of sentences imposed, the claim can be made with confidence that in Pakistan a high degree of uniformity is maintained. Under certain provisions of law, sentences are specified, including minimum sentences of imprisonment in a few cases. But quite apart from this, probably as a result of the High Courts and the other appellate courts maintaining over a long period a uniform standard of sentencing for the various offences, within the maximum provided in the Penal Code, the subordinate courts have before them a standard to follow. Cases in which ludicrously low or exaggeratedly severe sentences are imposed, are generally explained by the immaturity of the magistrate or judge, but occasionally the explanation may be less innocent. It is rare for the superior courts to have to interfere with sentences for the purpose of ensuring that no one of several persons convicted for the same offence is left with a sense of grievance by reason of unequal punishment. As in most other countries, there is provision for persons under the age of 18 years to undergo their imprisonment in reformatories or in borstals. As a rule care is taken to avoid the imposition of short sentences, it having been long recognized that this results in over-crowding of prisons, and in converting them into academies of crime, from which the inmates never emerge with the same degree of innocence which they possessed when they entered. Adult prisoners who have shown good behavior in prison may be sent to designated farms, to serve out their sentences as agricultural laborers, under conditions of comparative freedom, suitable to their own nature and upbringing. There is also power given to the authorities to release prisoners on parole, not only for temporary occasions, but also for such purposes as employment under selected masters.

From what I have said earlier, it will have appeared that steps have been taken in West Pakistan for the restoration of communal justice through trials otherwise than by the elaborate processes of the Criminal Procedure Code, and unhampered by the not less elaborate law of evidence. I have said that the system of trial by *Jirga* has been in force in the western parts of West Pakistan for a very considerable time, and I should have mentioned that in the parts further west, that is to say, in the Middle East, such a mode of trial is universal, as being suited to scattered populations where the main crimes are of murder, for honor or in a blood feud, and of robbery, kidnapping and cattle-lifting. Cattle-lifting, in particular, among peoples with a pastoral background of history is not merely a major criminal activity, often very well organized, but it may also be described as one of the agencies by which the local "big men" are able to maintain their influence. Owing to the great spaces and distances involved, to the people living in isolated hamlets, as well as to the powerful influences working behind the scenes, the investigating police are faced with insuperable difficulties in their attempt to secure evidence of a reported crime, that a regular court could accept. Yet the organization of these rural communities is such that nearly in every case, local information regarding the identity of the culprits is both complete and accurate. The figures which I gave at the commencement of this paper show how small is the proportion of success achieved in the control of crime through the courts by the method of conviction, compared with the very large number of cases which are shown at investigation to the *prima facie* true cases. In these circumstances, those concerned with the maintenance of law and order are in duty bound to examine whether the very elaboration of the laws at their disposal is not working in aid of the criminal and to the detriment of the public peace. In these circumstances, it is natural that they should turn to the indigenous systems of justice, for a possible solution. The problem is a large one calculated to cause concern to those interested in the instrumentality of law as an effective mode of social discipline. I had occasion to make some observations on the subject in a speech which I delivered in July 1962, from which I propose to quote here a few passages which sufficiently express my own line of thought. Dealing with the criticism often heard in Pakistan by persons who oppose the reform of law, that the laws left behind by the British rulers have been adapted to requirements over a great many years and again that the British system of justice is applauded all over the world, so why should there be a change, I said that the mere fact that cases are decided under this system does not necessarily mean that it is fully adapted to the understanding and sentiment of the people, I went on to observe:

> We all know of civil cases where after getting a decision from the final court, the parties have to go home and make a compromise as to produce a practical result more in consonance with what they know to be the natural justice of the matter. As for criminal cases it is probably correct to say that under the present system every decision has the quality of breeding more cases of the same kind. The courts now rely upon evidence given in open court under an oath whose value is precisely nil, and they follow a strict technique of exclusion of evidence, some of which would be most valuable for the ascertainment of the truth. The result is that cases in which guilty

persons are acquitted probably form the majority. On the other hand there are a number of cases in which innocent persons are convicted on the basis of oral evidence and even suffer death. In both these eventualities, the seeds of revenge have been well sown.

Referring to the rule of British law that the "benefit of all presumptions should go to an accused person and the whole burden of proof by evidence which is received under highly technical rules is upon the prosecution, I said:

Cases are common enough where 10 or 15 persons have jointly slaughtered 3 or 4 of their enemies, and carried their heads in triumph aloft on spears through the village. One supposes that when they are acquitted, as they often are, the village lives in a state of terror from these persons when they return and the whole balance of life is upset once again, as it was when the murder took place and during the ensuing police investigation. By the inscrutable workings of the judicial system, a situation has been created, to which under the necessities of life the people have to adapt themselves and, at the cost of a part of their true character, they do so. Unfortunately, what is damaged in this process is that part of their character, which is the distinguishing feature of the strong and noble human being. Belief in truth diminishes. Denial of the strength of evil becomes impossible. So also when an innocent person has been hanged on the basis of evidence which the village knows to be false, I imagine that the relatives accept it as a stroke of fate and the rest of the village, as an incident of the judicial system from which at least one party has gained some advantage. But in this case as well, there is definitely a diminution in the public character in those respects which make for strength and stability.

One is tempted to ask—would not such results be avoided, if the function of doing justice were placed in the hands of the people themselves? How far can justice be allowed to travel away from the truth? Can such a state of affairs be allowed to continue indefinitely, without basically endangering the body politic? How does it happen that this condition has been developed in so many countries? It derives from the system and cannot be attributed solely to the character of the people. For there are no men on earth, who if involved in a court case, would not use all means in their power to manipulate it to their advantage.

I set out the beneficial aspects of a scheme under which all crime, except such as are detrimental to the direct interest of the State might, be dealt with locally, in the following passage:

Every case before a court is founded on a disturbance in the harmony of the communal life, through action of a nature which failed to take into account the rights and responsibilities as well of the actor as of the person affected adversely by the action. This is true equally of those matters which are civil wrongs and of those which are counted as crimes. It is of course possible that the degree of violence attending a particular crime in a community may be so great that the full strength of the community may not be able to cope with it, and the support of the State or of some larger unit in the society would be needed to contain the violence of the explosion and to set the matter once again to rights. It is possible also that a civil dispute may involve interests or questions altogether too large or too intricate for a local court to cope with. But if you take it from the communal point of view, the main business is to set things to rights so that life within the community can go on peacefully and harmoniously as before. It is in this sense that one understands the frequent punishment of outlawry which primitive communities used to impose upon incorrigible persons. They were placed outside the pale of the law, for incurable nonconformity. Short of this, the idea was always to retain the offender within the community after suitable correction. The communal court would incline to regard essentials and ignore technicalities in ascertaining the fault. Restoration of local peace, reformation of the delinquent's character, and relief to the injured party would be the paramount considerations by which their decision in the case would be determined. If they acted soberly and justly, they would avoid exaggerating the matter.

And with special reference to the *Jirga* system I quoted extracts from a book entitled *The Pathans* by Sir Olaf Caroe, a member of the Indian Civil Service, who had spent his whole service among the Pathans in the administration of the North-West Frontier Province, eventually as Governor of that Province. The Pathans, you must know are the people living on the west bank of the Indus up to the border with Afghanistan on the west, and down to the borders with Baluchistan on the south. Sir Olaf Caroe was intimately acquainted with their way of life and their customs. He spoke of the *Jirga* system as being designed for the settlement of "quarrels arising out of the blood-feud, of disputes about women, and questions generally affecting Pathan honor." In his experience the change of a person who was innocent being convicted by *Jirga* was "so rare as to be negligible". He made certain points concerning the *Jirga* system in the following passage which I quote *verbatim*:—

> The point to realize is this. Pathan custom requires the satisfaction of the aggrieved rather than the punishment of the aggressor. The law as we understand it concentrates against the aggressor, and compensation for the aggrieved hardly enters the picture. The Pathan in fact treats crime as a kind of tort.
>
> How and when, and in what degree, it may become desirable to shift the emphasis in a Pathan society from law to custom, or from custom to law, is a matter more likely to be resolved by Pathans than it ever was by ourselves. It is an obvious principle that the law should in some sense grow out of the society; it should be a projection of the common personality. The law of one civilization cannot be applied to a society with utterly different standards without the most dire results.

The conclusion which I drew in my speech was that the notion of the King's peace may have been carried to excess by bringing within the jurisdiction of the established courts offences of all kinds, many of them being such that their impact would never go outside a small locality. The community would treat such a crime as a tort to be met with compensation and possibly with some punishment, viewing it in a limited light, that is, from considerations of the common welfare of the community. A communal court or Jirga would not be inclined to exaggerate the offence, but always to minimize it and to keep it at a proper level. On the other hand, under the law as it exists, the agencies of the state step in to deal with all breaches of law except the most trivial. A great many matters thus assume an extra-communal aspect, through the intervention of police and magistrate, in which such intervention might well have been avoided and the whole affair could have been settled locally to the general satisfaction. It is well-known that all over the Semitic world and even in most of the Muslim countries outside the Middle East, disturbances of the communal peace, resulting from blood feuds which are universal, are often settled by one family giving their daughters in marriage in exchange for girls belonging to the opposing family, and although this may not operate as a final end to the feud in most cases, yet it indicates that these communities, living in a traditional manner according to their religious ideas, attach the highest importance to the restoration of harmony, among the opposing factions so that life, as they live it, should go on.

V

It is in that light that I am inclined to consider the provisions of a new Act passed in 1963 by the West Pakistan Legislature, which extends to the whole province. Briefly, this law extends the *Jirga* system to certain specified offences, which experience shows to be the most difficult to investigate in a manner appropriate for effective presentation before the courts working under the regular laws. The prescribed offences include homicide, and attempts to murder, but with the use of fire arms only, the latter being cases in which evidence to fix the identity of the person who fired the shot from a distance is most difficult to procure and when procured is scarcely ever believed. Other scheduled offences are those of kidnapping and robbery and of arson, which mostly take place at night and are extremely difficult to prove by evidence. Cases of theft, robberies, receiving stolen property and house breaking, are also scheduled, but only when cattle-theft is involved. Lastly, offences of corruption by public servants, which are notoriously difficult to prove in the regular way, have been included. Trial is to take place before a *Jirga* or tribunal of five persons of whom the chairman is to be an experienced magistrate, and the other four persons are selected by the head of the district from a panel of names of respectable persons belonging to the district. The accused is entitled to object to the selection of any one of the later persons. The *Jirga* is not bound by the ordinary laws of evidence except by the provisions relating to privilege, but the trial is held in the presence of the accused, evidence is called and recorded, the aid of lawyers is permitted, and the tribunal is required to record reasons for its findings. Sentencing is by the head of the district, and there is no appeal, but the commissioner of the division (which includes a number of districts) has power in revision, either *suo motu* or upon application, to interfere with the sentence imposed by the district head. The maximum sentence of imprisonment which may be imposed for any offence is 14 years' imprisonment. A provision in this Act which again is exactly in line with traditional and religious sentiments is that enabling composition of offences of homicide and attempted murder. This may be effected by the next of kin of the murdered person, or otherwise by the person injured but requires the permission of the Provincial Government. The law does not provide for any punishment to be undergone in addition in such cases, although some might think that there being an element of offence against the State also involved in the more serious crimes, the satisfaction of the injured person or his heirs is not in all cases the only or final consideration.

This then is a bold experiment in the way of restoration of communal justice. In its present shape, it is confined to a number of offences of a serious character which experience has shown to be difficult to prove in the regular way. Certain considerations which I canvassed in the passages from my speech quoted above might however be thought to operate in favor of extending the range of communal justice to cover also the lesser forms of crime which have only a local impact.

VI

I may appropriately end this paper by stating my doubts regarding the utility of imprisonment in all cases as a mode of punishment for a crime. At a time when the common person all over the world is finding it increasingly difficult to provide subsistence for himself, there is something of absurdity involved in the consideration that he can procure such subsistence and a good many amenities and facilities besides (such as medical care) by simply committing a crime. The possibility is known to be exploited by individuals, in every country. Although it would be too much to say that conviction and imprisonment have totally lost their deterrent effect, except perhaps in relation to political offences, yet the ever-increasing burden of maintaining prisons and highly paid staff to provide accommodation, care, proper food and other amenities for persons of proved anti-social quality is one from which an intelligent citizenry may justifiably seek to be relieved if alternative methods, cheaper and not less effective, can be found to create the desired effects of punishment, retribution and reformation. I may mention here and I hope it will create no great shock among my readers—that no one from Pakistan who visits Saudi Arabia for the pilgrimage ever returns without a strong impression of the very high degree of security of property which prevails in that country. One and all put it down to the fact that the punishment for theft is the cutting off of hands, which punishment is very promptly and publicly administered, and has proved to be an extremely effective deterrent against that form of crime, although it is applied only in a very small number of cases. The thought is excited that perhaps there is something in the ancient doctrine that "whatever moved to do the deed is dead and forfeited". There are many crimes of a violently anti-social nature which could be thought of in similar terms. Dacoity, meaning robbery with violence, committed by a gang of five or more persons, mostly, at night, from peacefully sleeping citizens in isolated localities, is made possible by the abuse of the faculty of mobility. It is very often accompanied by murder. A habitual burglar or house-breaker uses his limbs and power of movement for a purpose most gravely disturbing to peaceful society. A cattle lifter falls in the same category, finding it easy to make away with property which is itself mobile, with the aid of his own mobility. Is there anything gravely shocking to the public conscience in the thought that such persons should be deprived of their mobility, either permanently or temporarily as the true and just punishment for their criminal acts and tendencies? It is not necessary in this scientific age to suppose that this can only be done by amputation of the legs. Medical science having advanced so greatly, it should be possible to deprive a criminal of the use of a hand or a whole limb, by a small piece of surgery. I conceive that it may even be possible to produce this effect without surgery, and the further possibility appears of setting an approximate term to the deprivation. Even if surgery be resorted to, experience gained in the rehabilitation of persons disabled in war, might provide a means of restoring the use of the limb, on proof of true reformation. In any case, the sufferer would not be totally deprived of the capacity to make his livelihood through being rendered lame or palsied in one arm for his criminal deeds. Even if the disability imposed be extensive, it would certainly be better than mere detention in prison, if the disabled criminal were to be sent to a rehabilitation centre, to earn a livelihood along with others suffering from a similar disability, but for more innocent reasons. The public conscience has been long accustomed to the imposition of death as a punishment in appropriate cases. It would scarcely suffer a shock if, for its protection, so just and appropriate a punishment as disablement were applied, with proper qualifications, for the control of crime of certain kinds.

Apart from the possibility of using temporary or permanent disablement, in appropriate cases, as a just punishment, should not more attention be paid to the question whether an obligation to compensate for the wrong done through crime which was the rule in ancient times, should not be more commonly imposed? It would be, in effect, an economic control which in these modern times is of no less efficacy than the merely punitive processes of whipping, imprisonment and the rest. A criminal would feel a keener and more continuous remorse for his crime if he knew that the fruit of his labor over an extended period was going to the benefit of his victim whom he had unjustly wronged. This might be ensured, even in imprisonment, if he were required to undertake gainful occupation, the gain from which was to go to his victim, as compensation. I am aware that the subject of punishment for crime is receiving intensive examination in many quarters and in the light of the results achieved, the suggestions I have made might be merely superficial. But I do believe that the universal practice of imprisonment for crime is by no means the most intelligent or effective means for its prevention, or for the protection of the interests of society generally.

It must be recognized that crime is a biological fact of society, whether ancient or modern. It grows out of social condition and is not to be contained without the most careful examination of its aetiology. Plainly the controls applied through the prevailing modes of investigation, trial and punishment are not effective to check the growth of this disease, whose manifestations are constantly on the increase. The need for fresh thinking on all aspects of these controls cannot be denied. In that process, it would be well not to reject, out of hand as being out-dated, the principles and techniques laid down and applied by the ancients, for dealing with the problem in their times. They may have their uses, and certainly in Eastern countries, they still possess validity.

Appendix 14

PARAMOUNTCY OF ISLAMIC LAW : THE EXAMPLE OF THE
MAJELLE (MUJALLAH) OF TURKEY

*[In this address, given at the Karachi High Court Bar Association
Dinner, 15 February 1968, Cornelius reiterates a theme he developed
in greater detail in 1965. He was impressed by a compendium of Islamic
jurisprudence in use in Turkey. In earlier speeches, he transliterates
this as* Mujallah; *here he refers to it as* Majelle. *This address shows
his consistency in emphasizing endogeneity, that is, the importance of
relating jurisprudence to indigenous values. Elsewhere in 1965, he
advocated the learning of Arabic by Pakistani lawyers so that they
could understand the spirit of* Shar'ia *(See Appendix 10). In this
address, he notes that knowledge of English has steadily declined in
Pakistan. Hence, it is essential that native languages be increasingly
used in the operation of the legal system. (See text, pp. 33-34, notes 44,
45)]*

I

I have been privileged to address the Karachi High Court Bar
Association on three previous occasions, and I have spoken on
matters of mutual interest, such as administrative tribunals, the
fundamental freedoms, academic training in law, the
establishment of legal journals. I have spoken too of the positive
duty which rests upon all those concerned with the law in
Pakistan to infuse into our existing system, the substantive
principles of the *Sharia* of Islam. The Sharia is not to be
understood in any static sense. The great Muslim political
thinker, Ibn Khaldun, in the early 14th century, had said of
Muslim kings that they should "act in accordance with the
requirements of the Islamic Sharia," and therefore their laws
were to be "composed of statutes of the *Sharia*, relation of right
conduct, regulations which are natural for political association
and other necessary things concerning power". These views were

endorsed by Ibn Sina and by Ibn Rushd and indicate beyond question that in the views of these great political philosophers, the integrity of the Muslim state is bound up with adherence to the *Sharia*.

The Sharia is not to be understood in any limited sense. In fact, its meaning is almost synonymous with the expression *Fikah* as appears clearly from the following quotations taken from the Preface to the *Majelle*. The *Majelle* is the work of a learned commission appointed by the Sultan of Turkey in the last quarter of the 19th century to draw up a civil code of contemporaneous character. In the preface, the members of the commission spoke of His Imperial Majesty having "entrusted to His humble servants the important work, the production from the practical part of the *Sharia* (*Fikah*) of the beneficial work so that it shall be sufficient for application to the transactions of people which happen every day, according to the wants of the time". In submitting their report to the Sultan, the committee stated that they had collected the opinions of the *Hanafi* and also "cases from the practical part of the *Sharia* about transaction". They had submitted their work to the Sheikh ul-Islam and two other persons who had "sufficient knowledge of the matter and were skilled in the science of the practical *Sharia* (*Fikah*)," and the suggestions which these learned persons had made have been incorporated in their work.

II

I have taken the liberty to mention this in detail, because, with the courtesy of Hon'ble the Chief Justice of Iraq, there has been published in Pakistan by those admirable publishers who describe themselves as All-Pakistan Legal Decisions, a reprint of an English translation of the *Majelle* prepared in the year 1901. It is a book which I would like to recommend to you Mr. President and to every member of the High Court Bar Association for study and use on every possible occasion. I would describe it as an invaluable intermediate course in Muslim law. The 1,851 articles which it contains in addition to the 100 maxims which appear at the commencement are expressly stated by the compiler to have been drawn up in accordance with recognized principles of *Fikah* and of the practical part of the *Sharia*, and moreover, these articles and maxims have been verified by other learned men of the time and have received appreciation for being in conformity with those principles.

Though in our country we have statutes covering to a very every field of human relationships and transactions on the secular side, we have not paid enough attention to this aspect of legal development. It may be said that if the legislators, the courts and the lawyers did not care to examine the question whether the laws which are being made and implemented in Pakistan are or are not consistent with the tenets of Islam, then their negligence would give birth to tendencies which would not be consistent with the dictates of our Constitution and would be injurious to the full, development of Pakistan as a just society in the way of Islam. I have not advocated any upheaval of the present system either of legislation or of the courts. I simply suggest that there should be injected into the system, through the decisions of the courts, the spirit and the letter of the principles of the *Sharia*. These are dynamic principles, based upon the dictates of Holy Scripture, drawn in accordance with the correct rules of jurisprudence and adapted to meet the changing requirements of the time, in particular the circumstances of each case coming before the courts. Under our system, the law declared by the superior courts has a binding effect on all subordinate courts. Inevitably if the superior courts care to make use of Islamic jurisprudence, the law they declare will become incorporated in the judicial system of the country.

Any one of you who desires to look into the *Majelle* will find instances of approachs to legal matters significantly different from that to which we are accustomed. As an example, there is a law of pre-emption which is dealt with in the *Majelle* in some 37 articles. Under Article 1029 a demand for pre-emption has to be made immediately and the action to pre-empt must be brought within a month. The right to pre-empt can be destroyed if the pre-emptor delays in making his formal demand. The comparatively lengthy periods of limitation which we observe form no part of this law. And the very short period provided for bringing a suit is another indication that the intention is that the pre-emptor should not take any steps to his own detriment that could later be raised as a bar. In other branches of secular law too, there are similar differences of a significant nature, which seem to me to operate to minimize litigation, and in particular the abuse of the legal process.

I would most sincerely advise the members of your Association and all the lawyers in Pakistan to make a study of the *Majelle*. All human activity can, in my submission, be likened to the function of cultivating a garden. In that garden, those plants and trees are most appropriate and therefore most beautiful which grow naturally out of the soil. The duty is to preserve the good and the useful, allowing them to grow to their full size and height, while at the same time discouraging everything in the nature of weeds and other obnoxious growth. We who serve the law and justice also have our garden and it is a great garden indeed. The present condition could perhaps be described somewhat as follows. Instead of maturing and developing the plants and trees of value which are natural to the soil we are engaged in maintaining a garden which is composed almost exclusively of plants and trees which are of exotic growth. We labor incessantly to promote the growth of these foreign forms of vegetation. Many of us find our greatest satisfaction in having created this artificial garden and we require the whole population to take the judicial fruit from these foreign plants and trees and to be satisfied with it. Our own natural growth are allowed to become matters of dusty record in foreign countries, to be buried in libraries and museums, while we diligently and with enormous labor apply ourselves to cultivate and promote the foreign vegetation with which we are seeking to populate our garden. That is why we fail to produce the finest fruit of which our soil and our labor is capable. The fruit that we produce is a low-level product, compared to that of the gardens where such growth are natural, and it necessarily fails to satisfy the basic sentiments and requirements of our people. Our own plants and trees are relegated to the position of weeds and rough undergrowth in this process. When the master gardeners and their employers were all of foreign origin this was unavoidable. But today we cannot be content with the thought that our laws and our own principles of justice are relegated to a subordinate and indeed an almost irrelevant position as if they have no place in the garden which we are engaged daily in nourishing. These principles are of the highest validity. The practices of justice based on *Sharia* and *Fikah* need not give way to any corresponding rules that we found suitable in other countries. Therefore, legislators, judges and lawyers alike should cultivate this garden with the finest trees and plants which belong to our own history and culture. Then only can the fruit have the true quality of justice that our people demand.

III

There is need for bringing all the processes of justice into the common languages of the people. That indeed is a part of the argument I have just been presenting, for it would be strange indeed if we were to become convinced that unless we use a foreign language, the propagation of our own laws and beliefs as to justice would not be successful. So far it is difficult to see any sign of departure from the course which we have been following, i.e., working for the development of law through the medium of English language. But as time goes on, it is becoming apparent that the substratum necessary to continue that state of affairs is beginning to fail. Interest in the study of, and more so, the mastery of the English language is steadily declining. It no longer approaches the degree of command necessary for the due appreciation and expression of the finer development of the law. Already judgments are appearing from the subordinate courts whose faulty English clearly indicates that the entire thinking has been in the writers' language and that he would have been greatly assisted in making his meaning clear if he had allowed himself to use that language. That is an unmistakable sign of a change that is inevitable. It may not come in our time but it is certain to come.

IV

It is well known that the whole operation of law is a continuous and endless stream in which all of us are merged. Our thoughts and deeds that have gone into the arguments and the judgments that have been written have become an integral part of that stream. We ourselves are not originators. We have sat at the feet of learned teachers and seniors who in turn have received instruction at the hands of their elders. The whole body of law is a long record whose principles stretch back to the distant past when human beings first became aware of their duty as moral agents in the way of God. The earliest learned writings in law are based on these scriptures. We have used those writings and reports continuously in our work to maintain the steady flow of that great stream. The opportunities of correction within that stream of law are so numerous that the maintenance of its purity is indeed guaranteed. Although active engagement in the process of justice is not open to a judge after he retires, he has a great satisfaction in knowing that in his time he has been a part of that living and moving stream and perhaps has been fortunate enough to leave a mark here and there which could serve as landmarks of justice. Though not in the main-stream, he may yet assist from the outside by contributions in writing to the better understanding of the laws. Speaking for myself I do not feel that I can ever become a stranger to this stream. I owe and hereby tender my very sincere thanks to my learned colleagues who have sat with me, and to the many lawyers whose labors have assisted in the accomplishment of any work that has passed though my hands.

Appendix 15

ISLAM AND HUMAN RIGHTS

[The conflict between the alleged universality of human rights and varying cultural interpretations of the specificity of those rights is one of the most significant issues in international politics. It is especially pertinent to Muslim states because of views on the role of religion, family values, reproduction rights, the sanctity of the Qur'an and the relative importance of community as against individual rights. In this address, delivered at the Pakistan Academy for Rural Development, Peshawar, 8 November 1977, Cornelius deals with this conflict. The consistency of his views on this matter is suggested by his quotations from a speech on the same subject given sixteen years earlier. The 1977 speech is, in my view, the clearest and most erudite analysis of human rights and Islam that has come to my attention. See text, pp. 68-72, notes 106-10)]

I

Looking back on the earlier years of what has now become a long life, I am somewhat surprised that although I had been in Government service on the law-and-order side for over twenty years, it was not till about the years 1948 that awareness of the concept of human rights first entered my mind. By that time I had completed about 16 years of judicial service at district and high court level, and had a fair conception of the rights of parties in criminal and civil law within the domestic field. The writ jurisdiction was unknown then, and against orders of public authorities, the only remedy was by suit after notice, proceedings in which followed the usual leisurely tempo, and were mostly without urgency or acrimony. There had been, of course, in the last years of British rule, much political agitation with its crop of detention and arrests, followed by petitions under the Criminal Procedure Code, in the nature of *habeas corpus*. In nearly all cases, the question was reduced to whether or not there had been compliance with a statute, meaning a rule or regulation generally under the Defence of India Act. The power of the legislature to make that act, or of the Government to make the particular rule or regulation was never questioned. There were no norms or ground-norms or abstract principles that the laws had to satisfy. If the rules passed an unconscionable law, it was binding on people and courts alike, until it was repealed, as was the infamous Rowlatt Act of 1917. Things changed with the grant of Independence, on the terms that the two new countries which replaced the British Indian Empire were to be organized and should continue to be governed as democracies under the Government of India Act, 1935. Not long thereafter, the expression *Fundamental Rights* became current, with the inclusion in the Constitution of a chapter of such rights, based on pre-existing models in the American and other constitutions.

There is a radical difference between *fundamental rights* and *human rights*, though over a considerable area, the subject-matter might appear to be the same. The fundamental rights are those which a state through its constitution confers on its citizens, for the fulfillment of which provision by way of judicial or other machinery must be provided by the state itself. The sanction for human rights is supranational. For instance, there is in Europe, by compact among the nations, a European Commission of Human Rights, to which not only Governments, but even individuals may complain of denial of one or more of the human rights, as a result of governmental action, and the Commission has powers of enquiry and redress. This is working very successfully, despite the seeming relinquishment of sovereignty. Some similar organizations in the Americas, where the necessary degree of amenability is not equally found in many of the affiliated countries, have a less notable record. The more common recourse is to international bodies, of which a considerable number have been set up by the United Nations, and, usually concurrently, to the international communications media. The matter is thrown, if important enough, into the maelstrom of international politics, giving added and sometimes irresistible strength to dissident elements in the country concerned, which is already sufficiently harassed by the divisive forces inherent in the democratic process.

II

Human rights were first set down, in authoritative form, in the Universal Declarations of Human Rights, by the General Assembly of the United Nations, in 1948. It is amongst the newcomers in the world, a little newer than the atom bomb, but a couple of decades older than the neutron bomb, whose contribution to human effort is that it spares the products and only destroys human and other forms of life. A considerable number of the articles in the Charter, as it is commonly called, are undoubtedly beneficent and not usable for the creation of discord, within and among nations; but there are some with explosive potentialities. For instance, it recognizes the rights of liberty and personal security, of equality before the law, and somewhat gratuitously, in Article 8, gives everyone the right to effective protection, through national tribunals, "for acts violating the fundamental rights granted him by the Constitution or by Law." Similarly, it seems unnecessary to mention matters such as arbitrary arrest and detention, proper judicial trials, the presumption of innocence, crimes and punishments not to be created with retrospective effect, safeguard of privacy and honor, marriage or property-holding, since in all organized states, these are secured under law, and constitution. Perhaps some of these were intended for states that verged on barbarism whom some powerful group intended to add to its number in the Assembly, as hints on qualification. Certainly, a strong lead was given in Article 21. This begins with the mention of participation, directly or indirectly, in the government of one's country, and of equal entry into public service, and then goes on to define, in precise terms, the essence of democracy—

The will of the people shall be the basis of the authority of government; this will shall be expressed in periodic and general elections which shall be by universal and equal suffrage and shall be held by secret vote or by equivalent free voting procedures.

A great many people would question the validity of this proposition as a "human right". There have been, and within living memory, other modes of government under which the people have been not less happy and well governed than under present-day democratic systems, in which the divisive elements easily gain mastery over factors of integration.

Freedom of "thought, conscience and religion" are lumped together in Article 18. By themselves, thought and conscience do not always appear in action; conscience is sometimes put forward as a ground for violation or disobedience of the law, and thought becomes tangible through expression. The Charter cannot condone breaches of national law, and as for expression, it receives the most sympathetic protection in Article 19, giving the right to "freedom of opinion and expression" which is elaborated to include "freedom to hold opinions without interference and to seek, receive and impart information and ideas through any media and regardless of frontiers". As we see today, the acute conflict between the major political and economic ideologies are providing a fertile, profitable and happy hunting-ground for those dissidents in each country who have the power of expression sufficiently to make use of this freedom. A constant stream has developed in certain countries composed of persons of seditious tendencies who can make enough trouble to attract the attention of the law-and-order authorities. Prosecutions follow, and demands to be allowed to leave the country, under Article 13, which says in simple terms, "everyone has the right to leave his country". The next Article to be invoked is, conveniently, Article 14, guaranteeing the "right to seek and to enjoy in other countries asylum from persecution", which is only denied "in the case of prosecutions genuinely arising from non-political crimes and acts contrary to the purposes and principles of the United Nations". The acts committed by dissidents are never non-political and if committed to acquire the benefits of Articles 13 and 14, would be well within the aforesaid "purposes and principle". For benefits there certainly are. In the welcoming arms of a sufficiently powerful country with a contrary ideological base, their right of freedom of expression and opinion is exercisable to the full, in praise of their rescuers, dispraise of the community which gave them nurture, and with profit to the point of affluence to themselves.

The framers of this Charter seem to have been averse to the concept of commitment and loyalty to one's country of birth, for all they have to say on that subject is that "everyone has duties to the community in which alone the full and free development of his personality is possible", a formula which seems to specialize the kind of community to which duties are owed, and so to leave the matter to personal choice and decision. The very basis of citizen loyalty is here denied, or so it seems to me. I refer here to Article 29, which goes on to say that the only limitations upon the exercise of the rights and freedoms defined in the Charter are those "determined by law solely for the purpose of securing due recognition and respect for the rights and freedoms of others, and of meeting the just requirements of morality, public order and the general welfare in a democratic society". Due respect for the right and freedom of a nation to choose its own form of government, its own political and economic ideologies, that nation into which one is born and grown to adulthood, nowhere appears in the picture. The limitations also ignore the primary need of the integrity and security of the nation, of its need for defence of its rights to sacrifice by the people of their personal interests in the national cause, and the great variety of bonds that, prior to this formulation, were thought to be of the very essence of nationality. The individual citizen and his fellow-citizens, again regarded as individuals, occupy the centre of the stage, while the nation to which they belong loses definition altogether, except as having frontiers which the individual citizen has the right to cross at will, in his person, and, more importantly, through his views such as are disliked at home, but are gladly accepted by other, mostly unfriendly countries.

III

The view I am putting forward may seem ungenerous, for it is more common to regard the Charter as a monument of beneficence to humanity. I find that aside from a number of confirmations of rights already enjoyed in their own country, assuming it is organized in a civilized manner, the new and additional matter shows a quality of over-stress on the freedom of the individual citizen in default and despite his obligations to the nation and State to which he is attached for the time being. It is assumed that this attachment is not permanent, and has value only for providing the citizen with a recognized nationality—this is assured by Article 15, in the words "Every one has the right to a nationality"—one of the main advantages of which is the right to be given travel documents. I have the impression that the shadow of the Second World War and its aftermath in the Western European countries has lain heavily upon the formulation of these particular rights in the Charter. There had been vast dislocation and destruction further East as well, but the sympathies of those in control were primarily attracted to the peoples of the West. Ideas of motherland and homeland, of national pride were thought to have been swept into oblivion in the general holocaust. The people were like lost sheep; they had to be saved, to exercise their acknowledged talents under optimum conditions, in a land of promise. Escape from the scene of carnage and ruin must be made easy for them. The refugee, *qua* refugee, became the focus for conferment of rights.

At the recent Helsinki Conference, decisions were taken confirming, in particular, the "free circulation of persons and free exchange of information", and we have seen how quickly advantage has been taken of this re-declaration by dissidents in a number of countries, and how widely their views and the treatment they are receiving in their countries have been publicized. No importance is given to the consideration that where the very basis of a state is on defined political and economic opinions, which the Government is obliged to promote and defend, contrary opinions must be discouraged and prevented from gaining currency. It is natural too that a State should take note of attempts by its nationals, with the aid of the communications media, to bring the State into international disrepute, while enjoying all the general rights of citizens. We have seen too how promptly interested States, with irresistible power behind them, have seized the opportunity to issue public criticisms, and even to issue sympathetic commendation, from the highest quarter, to winning dissidents. Throughout history it has been familiar practice for states to attempt to weaken neighboring states by clandestine support provided to claimants to the throne, or to groups of disaffected courtiers or nobles. This was indeed one of the principal functions of ambassadors. In the present day and age such states do not have to use their legates for this purposes; the Charter is sufficient for attacking an ill-wished state at its very foundation, its roots of political and economic ideology, without which no democratically organized state can exist. The Charter has seen to that, by declaring that 'the will of the people shall be the basis of the authority of government', and that will can only be determined through the dissemination and propagation of ideas, political and economic, by political parties, in open conflict with each other. When one party gains the majority, its manifesto becomes the will of the people, and its ideas are the life-blood of the sovereignty of the State. When the attack upon these ideas, within the state, is given open support by other ill-disposed states, what becomes of the accepted rule that all states should respect the sovereignty of each state?

IV

The expression *human rights* sounds homely and comforting, but its formulation has ensured that it becomes a powerful and ready instrument in the dangerous game of international politics. Equally, the formulation of *fundamental rights*, now found in the constitutions of most states has an important political element of domestic impact. The necessity of these formulated rights is also traceable to the coming of democracy. These formulations do not derive from Magna Carta or the Bill of Rights of 1688 in England. Those instruments were executed between the then kings and the privileged minority of nobles and status-holding citizens, for the imposition of limitations on royal powers, which earlier had been founded on divine right. They had the effect of inducing the monarchs from that time onwards, to moderate their demands on the exchequer and their interference in the affairs of the government and the people. This has been so successful that in the United Kingdom no need has been felt for a formal constitution or for any statement of fundamental rights to this day. The rights of the people are safeguarded in that country more jealously and accurately than, perhaps, in any other country. That can be said too, of periods well in the past, for do we not see that in the American colonies, which remained under British rule until 1776, more than a hundred years, after the 1688 Bill of Rights in England, the demand for guaranteed rights for the newly independent people was never raised earlier? The reason is to be found in the fact that henceforth the people were to live under majority rule. The demand was put before the farmers of the American constitution of 1776. It was met by the following reply—

Bills of Rights are, in their origin, stipulations between Kings and their subjects, abridgement of prerogatives in favor of privilege, reservation of rights not surrendered to the prince. It is evident, therefore, that according to their primitive signification they have no application to the constitutions professedly founded upon the power of the people and executed by their immediate representatives and servants. Here, in strictness, the people surrender nothing; and as they retain everything, they have no need of particular reservations.

These brave words won the day, but not for very long. In time, there were added to that constitution, comprehensive expressions of the rights which we now call fundamental, by the 5th and several later amendments, notable among them being the fourteenth. As has been said in an American judgment, the very purpose of these Bills of Rights "was to place certain subjects beyond the reach of majorities and officials, and to establish them as legal principles to be applied by the Courts". In another case, it was said, with reference to the limitations imposed by the formulation of such rights—

> The enforcement of these limitations by judicial power is the device of self-governing communities to protect the rights of individuals and minorities, as well the power of numbers, as against the violence of public agents.

Our famous jurist, Mr. A. K. Brohi, in his monumental work *The Fundamental Law of Pakistan*, has observed:

> In those written constitutions where fundamental rights are guaranteed, the underlying assumption is that majority rule is likely to interfere seriously with the rights of the people. The people are, 'by and large distrustful of legislative supremacy, and have faith in the Judges to uphold the rights of individuals against executive and legislative assaults'. In this, the people are surely wise, for they have before them the example of the United Kingdom, where human rights of all kinds have been safely preserved and dispensed through the self-restraint of Parliament on the one hand, and the firmness and good sense of judges on the other. The laws there are made after prolonged consideration and public discussion and debate, so that in the process the areas of acute conflict between the Government party and the opposition are minimized, and the implementation by the public officials under the supervision of the political ministers is maintained in a generous and impartial spirit, so that recourse to the courts against the actions of government is infrequent, and where it is made, the people have confidence that they will get the full relief that the law allows, and with that they are content.

V

There is no doubt that the existence of a law is by itself conducive to actions thereunder, in the sense that, although it might have been possible to bring such an action under another law or the general law, the thought is excited more strongly and immediately at sight of the new law, specifically enabling such an action. In our country, and in neighboring countries which, like us, have the fundamental rights and the writ jurisdiction, we have seen the spectacle of new laws being made by ordinance, without notice, of laws being rushed through the legislative houses with the minimum of debate, these most often being laws designed to secure a particular, mostly political, object. The sequel is also thoroughly familiar, namely batches of writ petitions challenging action under these laws, charging that they are void for violation of one or more fundamental rights and often adding the further ground of partial and unjust application of the new law. This phenomenon of massive recourse to the courts in assertion of the fundamental rights cannot be said to be due only to the presence of those rights in the Constitution. It is rather to be regarded as proof of the necessity of such legal controls on law-making by the majority in the legislatures, and on the implementation of those laws through public servants, under the aegis of that same majority, whose selected representatives occupy the seats of authority in the political government. The remedies are necessary for dealing with evils that follow on each other, all stemming from the same source, namely, popular democracy. This is not the kind of political society which Aristotle said exists for the sake of "noble actions". Benevolence and beneficence in a general way are far to seek. The good of one is sought regardless of the injury to many others, so long so these others are in the opposite political camp. Vision is narrowed, so that the Aristotelian maxim that 'the State must aim at the highest good' seems fanciful. The equation of the social contract between the surrender by the citizen of part of his natural liberty to his community in order to gain greater freedom and through participation in a form of representative government, seeming to obey none but himself has proved illusory. The price of democracy is partisan politics, and the citizen must needs develop immunity to that insidious poison.

This picture, you might think, is too darkly painted. There are advantages in the acceptance of the democratic mode of government, as the standard form, not only by the generality of states, but also by the major international body, the United Nations. Clear expressions of fundamental rights for citizens of states, and of the rights of the human being as a citizen of the world have at least the effect that with the aid of compulsive processes, such rights are being allowed more uniformly than before. Yet the thought with which I opened this talk comes back to mind—in the period of foreign rule in India in which I lived and served for some 24 years before it came to an end, was there general denial of human rights in any respect, any general misery or general complaint that the citizen, as an individual, was being denied "the economic, social and cultural rights indispensable for his dignity and the free development of his personality"? Certainly, under foreign rule, his civil and political rights were at a lower level than they are today, owing to reservations of powers in favor of the British Government. To the extent that they were independent, the foreign officers in the administration, from the Governor-General down, acted for the most part with due regard for the general good and the requirement of justice, both generally as well as in individual cases. It cannot be said that the laws were unequally or partially applied, either by the executive or by the judiciary. The laws were made with circumspection after due study of the previous state of laws and due examination of relevant conditions, after inviting public comment and proper debate in the legislatures. Under stress of the World War which was continued and intensified by the struggle for independence, peremptory ordinances and defence rules did become the order of the day, in the closing stages, to cloud the aspect of benevolence that had earlier prevailed. Something of the technique by which full human rights are secured to all residents in the United Kingdom, without the need of a constitution or any formulation of such rights, was in operation.

VI

I mention that time for the particular reason that the scheme of things then prevailing was somewhat closer to the principles of the theoretical Islamic state than are the conditions of today.

The foundation of the Islamic state was laid concurrently with the establishment of the religion itself, in full detail, through direct inspiration from Allah to the Holy Prophet (Peace be upon him) to whom such clarity of vision, depth of understanding and strength of mind was vouchsafed that, in the very short period of ten years, through Qur'anic revelation and the Holy Prophet's practice, all the principles of governmental organization, of jurisprudence, of the conduct of foreign affairs, indeed of the full apparatus of an empire that covered the whole of Arabia, had been laid down. These principles were carried by the soldiers of Islam under distinguished leaders to the numerous territories which were brought within the rule of Islam in less than four decades after the death of the Holy Prophet. These stretched from Iran in the East to Egypt on the West, and the smoothness and swiftness of the absorption can be explained in no other way than that the offer of allegiance to the one true Diety, coupled with promise of rule under genial and amenable principles to which the people of those territories had long been strangers. And the evident personality and quality of the leaders and their soldiers, gained ready and peaceful acceptance. No great battles, much less wars, had to be fought for the acquisition of these territories. They have never, since that day, shown any tendency to diverge from Islam, though they have undergone vicissitudes of the most stringent nature, in particular, the devastating attack by the Mongols at the end of the 13th century when the heartland of Islam was practically demolished.

In the truest and most literal sense, Muslim rule in that age was the rule of Islam itself, based on obedience to the directions of Allah contained in the Holy Qur'an and the pursuit of righteousness according to the practice of the Holy Prophet (Peace be upon him). The essentials of that rule appear most clearly from a detailed letter of instructions sent by the Caliph Hazrat Ali to one Malik Ashtar, whom he had appointed to be governor of the newly absorbed territory of Egypt less than 40 years after the death of the Holy Prophet (PBUH). It has been preserved in full and furnishes a blue-print of the aims and purposes of the Islamic system of government then, and since then.

The major guide-line is given in the following words "the real satisfaction of administrators lies in establishing justice, and cultivating relations of love with the people, for their love is the basis of the safety and security of administrators". The governor must endeavor by his actions to prove to be a blessing to the people. To ensure just rule, his actions should be inspired by respect for the rights of Allah and the rights of man, as set out in the Holy Qur'an and the *Sunnah*. The consent of the people as a whole should be sought for his major actions, by direct contact with the common people; he must not be guided by the views of the privileged few. Harshness, cruelty and the shedding of blood without cause must be avoided: "blood willfully shed shortens the life of the State". The classes of people to be dealt with were enumerated and it was emphasized that 'these classes are interdependent, their relationships are governed by a system of rights and duties laid down in the Holy Qur'an and the *Sunnah*, and the governor must strive to enforce that system with an eye to the good of all and to do this, he must take personal interest and seek help from Allah. Attention to the needs of the poor was enjoined in the strongest terms. "Beware, fear Allah when dealing with the poor, do not let any preoccupations cause you to forget them, for no excuse whatsoever for the disregard of their rights will be acceptable to Allah" are the words of Hazrat Ali (RA), who added further authority by saying "I have heard the Prophet of Allah saying that no nation or society will prosper in which the strong do not discharge their duty to the weak". The governor was enjoined to practise purity in his private life and not to neglect the prescribed devotions. Concluding the instructions, Hazrat Ali (RA) invited the governor "to pray with me for grace so that both of us may surrender our wills to the will of Allah, that we may acquit ourselves well in His sight, and before all His creation, and that our work may survive, and men may cherish our memory".

The emphasis is on good government, which has been said to be no substitute for self-government. Within our own experience, many would say that, equally, self-government *per se* is no substitute for good government. What is more, under self-government, it is far more difficult to ensure good government than it is under autocratic rule. And, in this talk I have been concerned to show that that particular difficulty is accentuated, rather than eased, by precise definition of the rights of the individual citizen, regardless of his duties to the community and the state of which he is a member.

In the Islamic way of thinking, as I understand it, importance is primarily given to human communities, their integrity, security, welfare and progress. The rights of individual members and of sections of the community to other sections are detailed in the scriptures. In his letter to Malik Ashtar, Hazrat Ali (RA) laid stress on the duty to respect these rights. All such rights are consonant with the maintenance of cohesion, healthy activity and proper progress of the community; the individualistic color is absent. Tendencies towards abandoning the community into which one is born and in which one has been brought to maturity, and the encouragement of such persons to seek asylum in hostile communities would certainly not be countenanced by any right thinking person who appreciates that, by the dispensation of the Almighty, men are organized as members of families, of groups and of the larger community. All humanity is composed of such communities, and the welfare of humanity is bound up with the development and progress of these communities. Without minimizing the importance of each community paying attention to the welfare of individual members, the obligations of those members to the community must surely rank higher. The encouragement of individualistic tendencies on a world scale presupposes that faith in the vitality and essentiality of existing communities has been lost—that all, or some of them are either in, or are approaching, a state of dissolution. The truth is otherwise.

The factor which makes clear the superiority of the Islamic attitude towards human rights is that it places their formulation and fulfillment entirely and squarely within the religious obligation, the duty to obey the dictates of Holy Scripture and the practice of the Holy Prophet (PBUH) and the responsibility to answer for all actions at the last Judgment. An instrument such as the Universal Declaration takes account only of secular obligations, in disparate fields, so that fragmentation of responsibilities results in partial satisfactions and even contradictions. The religious obligation is all embracing.

VII

In a speech delivered in 1961 at a symposium in Karachi on the 13th anniversary of the Universal Declaration, I spoke on this aspect at some length. I trust the present audience will permit me to read to them some passage from that speech.

I said I was struck by the small place which the Declaration gives to the subject of religions which is mentioned only in Article 2, as the fifth in order among human factors of differentiation that must not be allowed to affect entitlement to all rights and freedoms and in Article 18, which gives precedence to thought and conscience over religion at his own choice and may manifest his religion by practice and other visible actions. I proceeded to remark that:

a person unfamiliar with religion, say a visitor from some other planet where religion is unknown, might easily gain the impression that religion is but a small thing of limited scope, interest and influence. Religion is mentioned as if it were treated on a par with a private hobby, as if it might be photography, and provision were made that everyone pursuing this hobby should be entitled to a dark room where he could practise it to his heart's content, that he would be entitled to change his cameras at his own sweet-will, or change from black-and-white to color photography without let or hindrance by any other power in the family or State.

I said far greater importance is given throughout the Declaration to matters which lie in the field of social obligation, or economic obligation, or that most highly surcharged field of human activity, the field of political obligation. Pointing out that with all its numerous organs and agencies in the field of human rights, the only sanction available seems to be that of mounting upon the delinquent the pressure of world opinion I gave the instance of South Africa, a member of the United Nations, upon which such pressure had recently been exercised, describing it as a country where glaring inequalities in the social, economic and political fields are found, which are enforced with the aid of that power and influence which has enabled the white section of the population to dominate the colored human beings in the territory. There was clear violation of Article 1, which says that all human beings are born free and equal in dignity and right, and of Article 21 requiring that the will of the people, expressed through universal and equal suffrage, shall be the basis of the authority of the Government. There were violations of other articles as well, which the Government of South Africa probably justified on social, economic or political grounds which today exert the most compulsive influence upon the actions of Government. I went on to say:

> The salvation (of the colored peoples) can only be achieved if the highest obligation of all, which embraces every obligation of a secular character, namely, the religious obligation, were duly brought home to the enforcers of inequality among human beings under the domestic control. For no religion worth the name, and particularly, no religion founded on Divine revelation, can fail to inculcate in every follower, a sense of total obligation to observe its principles and follow its dictates. The religion which the ruling class in South Africa professes is no local mumbo-jumbo or composite of fairy tales

with which to frighten or amuse children. It is one of the major religions which enjoins equality of human beings before God. But, being a secular state religious injunction is thrust into the background, as if it might not exist, and action is based exclusively upon weighing the situation in its social, political and economic aspects, which must always result in favor of those who hold the scales.

The conclusion that I reached was stated as follows:

Organized and established religion, such as we are familiar with, still remains the most powerful safeguard against man's inhumanity to man. It is a question which I find of profound interest, whether, if South Africa were to become a religious state, there would not be that shift of opinion among the ruling class, who all profess Christianity, in favor of free and equal treatment to the underprivileged persons in their midst, which the recently reported resolution of the General Assembly seems scarcely capable of accomplishing.

I ended the speech with the following words:

I submit that this Universal Declaration is founded too exclusively on the concept of the secular state. It is in consequence supported by nothing better than the social conscience, which cannot be other than condescending, or by the economic conscience which hardly consists with the idea of equality, or by the political conscience which is only too often visibly cynical. I suggest that the sounder and safer sanction is that of the religious conscience, and that the future calls for a great deal of consideration whether this Declaration would not be more effective over large parts of the earth's surface, if it gave a real place to religion in its formulation.

These distinct and fragmented consciences, often at odds with each other, furnish no confident recipe for peaceful co-existence among the peoples, whether within a state or among the states. Islam recognizes a single all-pervading and all-controlling conscience based on faith and fear of Allah and the Last Day. From the inception of Islam, its leaders and rulers have had before them the clear injunction to show respect for the rights of Allah and the rights of man in all their actions. They were to seek guidance from the Holy Qur'an and the *Ijtihad* of the Holy Prophet, namely the *Sunnah,* for implementation of the system of rights and duties there laid down. As we have seen, the Caliph Hazrat Ali, in his letter of instructions to a governor, repeatedly warned him that he was answerable for his actions before Allah, and called upon him to join in a prayer "for grace, so that both of us may surrender our wills to the will of Allah". The function of justice, of doing right to all manner of men could be more safely entrusted to human agency.

VIII

Today, in the constitutions of most modern Muslim states, there are chapters guaranteeing human rights, whose wording follows the earlier western examples, for the most part. Each declares that Islam is the state religion, which in the case of Iran is defined as the orthodox Jafari doctrine, but even there as elsewhere, submission is made to the general principles of Islam, and the practice of the Holy Prophet. It is typical of the basic tolerance in Islam that so many sects, with varying views flourish in all Muslim states. Non-Muslim communities have existed in Muslim countries from the very beginning. Indeed, the charge that forcible conversion on a large scale was the rule in such states is thoroughly negated by the admitted fact that, having large populations, mostly non-Muslims, to cater for, under the handful of Muslims the early conquerors forbade such action for the good financial reason that they needed the income from the *jizya* or poll-tax laid on all non-Muslims as the price of exemption from military service and other official responsibilities. When states became prosperous, even this was excused, and non-Muslim communities are known from history to have been granted virtual autonomy, making their own personal laws, appointing their own judges and administrators under a leader chosen by themselves, who was given treatment as head of State. A Jewish writer, Max Dimont, in his book entitled *Jews, God and History* has spoken of a "Golden Age" enjoyed by the Jewish community from about 800 A.D. to about 1300 A.D. under the rule of the Caliphs of Baghdad, until the destruction of that city by the Mongols. The case was similar in Spain, for some 500 years, until in the 16th century, the Jews were expelled from that country along with the Muslims. In the Holy Qur'an itself, there is severe condemnation of the Jewish people as enemies of the Muslims, which makes it all the more remarkable that such treatment should have been accorded to them by the Muslims, when they were at the height of their power. In recent times, since that fateful year, 1948, opposition between the followers of Islam and Judaism has, for reasons of lost territory, become acute, but my listeners will be both surprised and pleased to be told that, as recently as 1925, in the Constitution of the then Kingdom of Iraq, there was provision for spiritual councils for the Jews and the Christians, with powers and jurisdictions conferred by law. The Constitution declared that these councils were competent to deal with matters relating to marriage, dowry, divorce, separation, alimony, attestation of wills, and any other matters of personal status if the parties so agree. When so much attention and regard was paid to the preservation of rights of whole communities, which had never throughout history, been particularly friendly to Muslims, and had often been violently and bitterly opposed to them, one need not enquire into the extent of guarantee of rights to their own Muslim peoples by these governments, for has it not been said by Sa'adi:

Dostan ra Kuja Kuni Mehroom.
Tu ke ba-dushmanan khabar dari.

Appendix 16

THE CONCEPT OF ISLAMIC JUSTICE

[Of all fifty-seven speeches known to be extant, this speech is the most explicit in its exposition of Islamic law and the most detailed in its reliance on the text of the Qur'an. The exact date and place of delivery are not known. It was probably given in 1977 or 1978. Cornelius emphasizes the elements of mercy as a mitigating factor in the imposition of penalties for certain crimes. This is a quality to which he referred repeatedly in judicial decisions as well as public addresses. He reiterates the superiority of Islamic justice. But in this speech, he does not do so by comparing it to British law as he did in other addresses. Now, for the first time, he makes his point by exclusive reference to Qur'anic chapter and verse.

It is not known what source Cornelius used in this speech for his translated quotations from the Qu'ran. His English versions are different from such translations as those of Abdullah Yusuf Ali, M. M. Pickthall, and T. B. Irving. Nor are they derived from the official Saudi Arabian revision of the Yusuf Ali translation. I was sorely tempted to convert the Cornelius renditions to the revised Yusuf Ali translation not only because of its better style but also because it is now regarded as an authorized translation. But this would have compromised the quotations based on the translations he used.

This is the only Cornelius speech which has been edited. The typescript he gave me was probably a rough draft. It was repetitious and many references to the Qur'an did not match the quotations. The references have been corrected. Some repetitious quotations have been deleted and the sentence order has been slightly changed. Except in one instance (Surah 23:96) his quotations from the Qur'an have not been altered. The references are shown by Surah (chapter) number separated by a colon from the ayat (verse) number. (See text pp. 47-51, notes 79-87)]

Justice, as an abstract quality, is difficult to define. To say that it enables distinction to be made between right and wrong does not simplify the matter because opinion on rights and wrongs vary widely. To say that every human being is equipped with a sense of justice is of little help, since the thought of each individual is limited by the conscious knowledge he possesses. It is clearly a quality attaching to actions, and therefore to living things that are capable of action. The effect of an action could be narrow and particular in a certain aspect or, on a large scale, as between human beings. Despite the scope of the judicial function within a community being ever on the increase, it yet does not, in my opinion, represent the widest stretch of the meaning of the word "justice". That, perhaps, is to be found in the relationships of all living things to everything in their natural environment. With the exception of man, all other things have limitations upon the extent of their activity, which are designed to operate for promotion of a balanced life for all, so that the will of the Almighty should be fulfilled by the continual betterment of His creation. The agency of man, to whom has been entrusted control of everything else in nature, is an element of the greatest importance in that fulfillment. If in exercising that control, he is to carry out the Divine purpose, he must have appreciation of the exactness of the adjustments that nature, in its justice, has provided for the governance of relations between living beings and inanimate things in creation. Lately, evidence has been gathered which shows the enormous damage done to the environment by the naked pursuit of advantage and profit to themselves, by groups of human beings, notably in western countries. They had interfered with the economy of nature, without understanding the linkages between and the justice operating through all its creatures, animate and inanimate, until the detriment to themselves stared them in the face. They had done injustice to their environment and punishment had followed.

A definition of the quality of justice has been attempted in the great work of Shah Waliullah, entitled *Hujjat Allah al-Baligha*. *Adalat* is there specified as one of four faculties, by the fostering and development of which, perfection in human happiness may be attained. *Adalat* is that quality in a member of a society which enables him, without effort and with perfect naturalness to act always so as to strengthen the bonds of union in the society. The ideal is that of a healthy body made of perfectly correlated parts operating in unison, free from internal obstruction. The just man has the special capacity, by his actions in everyday life, to assist towards the end that all the members of the society live together in their separate walks as a single corporate, integrated body. Such a person furthers the intention of Allah, in respect of all human communities, that their affairs should be conducted in the best possible way, to ensure continuous improvement. They should be imbued with a feeling of total involvement in the activities of the people. An analogy is that of a head of family being sensitive to innermost feelings of its members and thoughts, cognizant of their settled technique in the implementation of their desires, competent to guide their energies into beneficial channels. Possessing the basic virtue of gentleness in thought and action, and free from harshness and hatred, his adaptation to the human environment is such that all his actions are in just proportion to the occasion. Such a person with this special quality is, in Shah Waliullah's opinion, well suited to control the affairs of state. Among those affairs, not the least in importance is the function of the judiciary, for the dispensation of justice in the wide area of conflict of interest between citizens, and between citizens and the ruling authorities.

Among the many distinctions to which the religion of Islam can lay claim, one that in the context of human affairs can claim the highest importance is that its acceptance and establishment proceeded concurrently with the establishment of the Islamic State. This occurred under the inspired leadership of the Apostle of Allah, the Holy Prophet Muhammad (Peace be upon him). In the first thirteen years after he received the call to Prophethood, he received the bulk of the revelations vouchsafed to him by the Almighty. He was tested and tempered through a fierce fire of determined and seemingly invincible opposition by his own people in the holy city of Mecca. Under Divine guidance, he then moved to the city of Medina, and immediately the number of his followers multiplied to the extent that it fell to him to lay down the constitution of his state, and to provide it with the full apparatus of a government. That he did so in the light bestowed upon him by Allah is apparent from the fact that a great proportion of the divine injunctions relating to human affairs is to be found in the four *Surahs 2-5*, which were revealed at Medina. Under direct guidance from the Almighty, the Holy Prophet conducted all the central affairs of the new State, laid down principles of government and organization, established institutions, directed foreign affairs, conducted negotiations and concluded treaties, sent out embassies, and carried the war with his Meccan opponents to a successful conclusion. He was, at the same time, in direct touch with all his followers, accessible at all times to each of them, and the judged every case himself. The record of the revelations he received is contained in the Holy Qur'an; the record of his actions as reported by his personal companions or other reliable persons who had received it from the companions is in the *Sunnah*. It is from these two scriptures that the governing principles of justice in Islam are derived. Over and above the detailed and particular principles, there is to be read the direction of Allah, contained in *Surah 4:105*: "We have revealed the Book comprising the Truth, so that you may judge men in the light of Allah", and it is made plain that the dispensation of justice is to proceed on regulated lines in the injunction to King David, in *Surah 38:22*: "and judge between men on right principle and not follow your own inclinations, for they will cause you to stray from the path of Allah".

Decisions were not to be based on whim or caprice, but on proper canons of justice and equity. A model was thus set up for the Holy Prophet and his successors to follow, and indeed they followed it. Equity, which may be described as mitigation of the harsher aspects of justice according to the circumstances, is a basic rule of Islamic justice.

The Holy Qur'an is replete with injunctions that are relevant to justice. In *Surah 4:135* it is said 'Believers: bear aloft the standard of justice', and *Surah 5:8* proclaims that justice has a quality that brings it near to piety and the fear of Allah. *Surah 5:8* and *Surah 6:152* warn against allowing ill-will or affection to color a judgment. In the matter of private retributive justice, there are several directions for the observation of equality and proportion, and each is supplemented by a recommendation to mitigation or forgiveness. For instance, *Surah 2:178*, says that for murder, the retaliation must be equal, freeman for freeman, slave for slave, woman for woman, but immediately thereafter comes the mitigation in His mercy. Allah ordains that the next-of-kin has the option to refrain from retaliation on receiving material compensation, which should be agreed in proper manner, and received graciously, that is, retaining no rancor. *Surah 42:40* says—"Believers, if you must take revenge, do it in proportion to the injury suffered" and immediately after "but if you suffer patiently, that is better for the sufferers". Self-defence is approved in *Surah 42:39*. *Surah 23:96* takes the matter even further, when it says—"Repel evil by that which is best".

The jurisprudence of a particular system of justice is founded on maxims, rules, principles and precedents. These are not to be expected in such precise form, as Qur'anic Scripture, but there is a great deal to be found which is of directory effect to the spread of justice within the community of Islam, as well as to the dispensation of justice. The entire field is placed under the religious obligation, surrender of the will to Allah and answerability on the Last Day. But there are rules of conduct laid down in many matters out of which resort to law most frequently arises, which may be recounted briefly.

Thus provocation, which is a common cause of conflict, is frowned upon in *Surah 4:148-150*, where the faithful are enjoined against the spreading of evil by public speech. It warns against shouting evil words. In *Surah 17:53*, it is said—that we should speak well to safeguard against dissension. Aggressiveness in behavior is condemned in *Surah 16:90* in the words: "Allah forbids evil and rebellion". *Surah 49:9* requires that the aggressor in a fight be humbled. Oath-taking in order to deceive is expressly forbidden in *Surah 2:224.* Scandal-mongering receives special treatment at many places. Thus, *Surah 104:1* declares "Woe to all back-biters and slanderers", and a biting condemnation is contained in *Surah 49:12,* in the words—"Avoid back-biting: would you wish to eat the flesh of a dead brother?" The spreading of rumors not based on knowledge is declared a grave fault in of *Surah 24:10-25* in which it is said that calumniators cannot injure good people. Indecency in behavior, both open and hidden, is forbidden by Allah in *Surah 4:15-18,* and a painful punishment in both lives is declared for those who spread immorality. Privacy of homes is safe-guarded by injunctions in *Surah 24:27-29,* where entry only with permission and after greeting the inmates is enjoined. Careless behavior in this regard could be a source of grave trouble. *Surah 24:30-32* prescribes correct and respectful behavior between the sexes: men are to lower their gaze on meeting women, and women must do likewise when meeting men, and at the same time, should cover themselves up.

Extravagance being contrary to just behavior, and a bad example to others, is specially mentioned in *Surah 2:188,* where it is said—"Eat not up your property in vanity" and in *Surah 17:27,* spendthrifts are characterized as "brothers of the devils". Drink and gambling are condemned in *Surah 5:90-91,* as "Satan's handiwork out of which enmity and hatred grow and such as make you forget prayer". *Surah 2:219* confirms these vices as great sins.

For the dispensation of justice, one indispensable requirement is oral as well as documentary evidence. It is important that evidence should be forthcoming, and *Surah 2:283,* gives the direction "Do not conceal testimony: to do so is sinful". *Surah 5:8* cautions, "stand out firmly to fair dealing" and in *Surah 2:282-283* it is said giving false evidence is forbidden. Those who stand by their testimony are, in *Surah 70:33* to be saved from hell. To give evidence for the sake of Allah without fear or favor, is enjoined in *Surah 4:135,* where it is said "Bear testimony even against yourself, your parents and your kinsfolk". Documents

have value for avoidance of falsity and fraud and the Holy
Qur'an prescribes the writing of deeds in, at least, five cases,
viz., loans, sales, wills, divorces and the freeing of slaves. *Surah
2:282* prescribes that a debt should be put into writing; the scribe
should not refuse to record it; the contents should be dictated by
the debtor, and there should be at least two witnesses; persons
asked to witness should not refuse. The same verse requires that
sales should also be put into writing and witnessed in the same
way, and the scribe and the witnesses should be held free of
harm. *Surah 65:2* directs that when a woman is given release
from her marriage, a deed should be inscribed, attested by two
witnesses. Special provision in *Surah 5:107* is made for wills to
be in writing, attested by two witnesses from among the
relations, and the testator may put these witnesses to the oath
that they will, when the occasion arises , support the will, and
not back out for money or for fear of offending other heirs. It is
even laid down that if the attesting witnesses back out, others
may be produced who should be put to the oath that their
testimony is true. One sees the great care taken to ensure that
truth and justice should prevail. By *Surah 24:33*, it is required
that a slave should be given a written release if he asks for it. In
certain cases, e.g. the attesting of wills, a standard of competency
for being a witness is laid down : they must be 'just men'. Certain
persons, e.g. those found guilty of preferring a false charge of
unchastity against honorable women, are debarred for life from
giving evidence (*Surah 24:4-10*). To keep the judiciary free from
corruption, the faithful are warned by *Surah 2:188* not to use
their money to gain the favor of judges, and so to devour the
property of others.

To ensure the orderly devolution of estates, bequests are
recommended, by *Surah 2:180,* to be made to parents and near
relatives, as a "safeguard against sin", and those are commended
who advise the testator on making a fair distribution. Blood
relations are to be preferred above other believers and the
refugees, but even to a friend, a bequest may be made. *Surah
2:240* dictates that a person approaching death should make

special provision for his wife, leaving enough for a year's maintenance, while living in his house. These precautionary admonitions are clearly designed to secure justice to all entitled persons in the distribution of the estate of a deceased relative, out of which great and lengthy disputes are apt to arise.

To the same purpose, there have been provided clear rules of succession to such estates in *Surah 4:7, 12, 13,* and *176.* These are too well known to require mention by me. They are still in force throughout the Muslim world. The scheme is elaborate and, what is more, unique among known systems of succession. It is so close to the ideal both from the viewpoint of the beneficiaries as well as the health and wellbeing of the economy that, in India, Hindu judges of High Courts have applied it to the distribution of estates in regard to which the personal law of the parties was not clear, at the same time observing that the system was both just and beneficial.

Similar comprehensive rules are laid down in the Holy Qur'an in regard to the regulation of matrimonial affairs, out of which troubles are apt to arise in all societies. These too are very well known, and I need only touch upon them briefly. Women were not to be forced into marriage against their will. The practice of widows being forced to marry a kinsman of the deceased husband, as a matter of inheritance, was forbidden in *Surah 4:19.* The consent of the relatives of a slave-girl was made requisite, by *Surah 4:25,* for her marriage to her owner. In another verse, the man was required to give a portion at marriage to the wife, even if she were a slave, and taking back of what was given was forbidden by *Surah 4:20,* unless the woman were guilty of fragrant lewdness. In case of disagreements between the spouses, recourse was first to be had to reconciliation (*Surah 4:129*) but when a total breach was feared, their case was to be referred to two *hakma* (judges or arbitrators) one from each side (*Surah 4:35*). The care of the Almighty for the good of the parties was indicated by the words in the same verse—"if they are inclined to peace, Allah will bring them to agreement. But if they are bent on separation, *Surah 4:130* gives the assurance that "Allah will fulfill the needs of both". Elaborate rules to govern divorce are contained in *Surah 2*. Two golden threads run through the entire code of divorce, namely (1) kindness and consideration for the woman (2) avoidance of haste in divorcing. A period of waiting was imposed upon the divorced wife before she could marry again, for the obvious purpose of keeping the lines of pedigree pure. Such women were not to be prevented from marrying again.

Rules are also laid down in the Holy Qur'an in regard to such matters as trusts, and business relationships. *Surah 2:282* and *Surah 4:58* enjoin the fulfillment of trusts and *Surah 70:32* imports the religious obligation when it says that paradise is assured to those who are faithful to their trusts and covenants. Honesty in trade is enjoined by the injunction "Weigh and measure full and fair" contained in *Surah 17:35*. *Surah 83:1-4* condemns traders who demand full measure from others but give less themselves. Observance of contracts is made obligatory in *Surah 2:283*. There are severe injunctions against usury, by which money is doubled and quadrupled; some practice it under the cover of trade; it is a thing of the Devil and Allah puts a blight on it. (*Surah 2:275* and *Surah 3:130*).

Orphans, being easy victims of their guardians, the Holy Qur'an makes special provision in several places to ensure proper treatment for them and proper care of their property during their minority. The Holy Prophet was himself an orphan brought up first by his nurse then by his grandfather and later by his uncle, Abu Talib. He received loving care from all these guardians. *Surah 93:6* refers to the Prophet as an orphan and in verse 9 of the same *Surah* all are admonished to "treat not the orphan with harshness". *Surah 2:220* prescribes that the welfare of the orphans should come first and that they should be treated as brothers. *Surah 4:2-10* prescribes that the property of orphans be kept intact, that it not be co-mingled with the guardian's property and that the property be released to them when they are of marriageable age. This is reiterated in *Surah 6:152* with the additional admonition that orphan's property can be touched only to improve its value. This principle is stated again in *Surah 17:34* with the additional warning of divine retribution for those who do not observe it.

There is much more in the Holy Qur'an that is relevant to law and justice, but for the present purpose, this account of the directions on certain subjects is sufficient to establish that a comprehensive jurisprudence was given to the faithful of Islam. Both *Surah 4:59* and verse 127 of the same *Surah* clearly establish the paramountcy of the Holy Qur'an and the Prophet as its interpreter. Verse 59 is an overall injunction which states that in any disagreement the final determination must be made by referral to Allah and His Messenger. In verse 127 concerning women, orphans, and children we are reminded that the final authority is the Holy Qur'an as it has been "rehearsed unto" the Prophet.

I have not dealt with the matters of crime and punishment that are detailed in the Holy Qur'an as there are very well known. The best known matters seem to be the *hadd* (plural: *hudood*), i.e. maximum punishments. This has throughout been interpreted to mean that the line of decision is to be sought in the Holy Qur'an, and the word of the Holy Prophet (Peace be upon him) spoken in his lifetime and as recorded in the *Sunnah* after his death. What is much less known is that the principle of mitigation in relation to the circumstances has been applied from the very first days of Islam. In *Surah 2:178*, which I have mentioned earlier, where blood-money was declared to be an acceptable alternative to equal retaliation, the words were added "this mitigation is provided through the mercy of your Lord". Shah Waliullah, in the *Hujjat Allah Al-Baligha* points out that the *hadd* punishment was applied to offences of three kinds—(1) those subversive of public order and disturbing to the community (2) those, if not prevented early, could be repeated so as to become habitual and (3) such that the victim could not get redress for himself. For treason and sedition, the most severe punishment was prescribed and mitigation was inadmissible. For theft, the punishment was prescribed in the Holy Qur'an, namely, hand-cutting, the offence being one easy to commit, and therefore apt to become both habitual and widespread. The Holy Prophet (Peace be upon him) as a lawgiver is reported to have imposed this punishment only where the value of the stolen property was more than a quarter of a *dirham*. He also laid down the principle that for applying this punishment, the taking must be from actual safe-custody, or under protection, besides being of the requisite value. So, for plucking fruit from a tree or taking animals that were straying in the hills, lesser punishments were given, including a fine of double the value of the thing taken. Cases of crimes which cannot be requited by the victim are ravaging the modesty of respectable women, highway robbery, false imputation of unchastity, and for these the *hadd* punishment was appropriate. Mitigation was also laid down for slaves, who did not possess full freedom of will; for them, punishments were halved. The Holy Prophet (Peace be upon him) said—"if a female slave commits an offence, beat her; if a male slave commits theft, sell him". Another tradition is to the effect that when a complaint was made against a slave by his owner, that he had committed theft, the Holy Prophet said "both belong to you; one is merged in the other". There are traditions also with reference to the *hadd* punishment for adultery that qualified mitigation was applied, according to the facts. With regard to intoxication through drink, the Holy Prophet strengthened the Qur'anic injunctions by declaring it to be *haram*. He ordered the punishment of 40 lashes for drunkenness. Here too, the offence is one easily committed, and apt to become habitual so that full severity in punishment was justified. Later, it was increased to 80 lashes. A very impressive instance of the Holy Prophet's inclination towards mercy is to be found in the tradition that when a man brought before him as an offender who had incurred a punishment of 100 lashes, proved to be sick and a cripple, he said "take a branch with a hundred twigs and give him one blow with it".

The concept of compassionate forgiveness is so pervasive in the Qur'an that it is found as a mitigant even in the most heinous crime of treason against the state or Allah. *Surah 5:33-4* prescribes execution, amputation or exile as punishment. But if the criminal repents "before they fall into your Power, know that Allah is oft-forgiving, most merciful". An exception is the crime of fornication for which *Surah 24:2-3* prescribes 100 lashes publicly administered but "do not let compassion move you".

During the period when the Holy Prophet (Peace be upon him) was the sole Judge of his people, he enlarged the jurisprudence of Islam in several directions. The record of his decisions and *dicta* is contained in the *Ahidith*. It was he who laid down the rule that in a trial of suits, the onus of producing evidence to support his claim is on the plaintiff, the defendant must take an oath that his case is true. The reason given was that if relief were always given to plaintiffs on evidence alone, unjust results could follow. Another rule that he laid down is that in cases of doubt, the antecedents of witnesses should be checked. Supplementing the rule of the Qur'an that one who is proved to have made a false imputation of unchastity against an honorable woman is forever disqualified as a witness in judicial proceedings, the Holy Prophet disqualified also persons who have committed breach of trust or adultery, as well as those who were enemies of the accused. Rules were laid down as to the taking of oaths—the formula of words, the time and the place. The words should bring to mind the total power and the total knowledge of Allah; the time should be after the '*Asar* prayer; in Mecca, the place was within the precincts of the *Kaaba*, and in Medina, at the mosque of *Tayyaba*. The Holy Prophet greatly disapproved of litigious persons saying that in the view of Allah these were the most troublesome, but those who avoided contention were praised as magnanimous. False evidence and false cases were regarded with a very severe eye; they show disrespect to Allah, they disturb the harmony of society and so attract the wrath of Allah, who loves not the trouble-maker and desires that social order should be maintained. The Holy Prophet said—"he who makes a false case to get another's property is not of my people; he should find his place in Hell". A judgment does not make that lawful which is itself unlawful, and the Holy

Prophet added great emphasis by saying: "Remember that I am like one of you. If a clever litigant, by artful words convinces me so that I decide a case in his favor, because he is a brother Muslim, such a litigant will go to Hell".

In his decisions, the Holy Prophet always upheld the principle of public good. Thus in a case of damage to a garden by a stray camel, he laid down that if it happened in the daytime when the garden-owner should have guarded his property, there was no blame to the camel owner, but if it happened at night, when the camel-owner should have kept his animal secure, the camel-owner was liable. The maxim *al-khiraj biz-zaman*, meaning that the profit from a thing belongs to him who is responsible for its existence, from which is derived the corollary *al-uzm bil-ghuman* meaning he who pays for a thing is entitled to the benefit from it comes from the Holy Prophet himself. In his time was laid down the salutary principle that all transactions that pre-dated the advent of the Islamic state were to be left as they were, untouched by the new order of things. The rule favoring the person in possession, where the ownership of property is involved, and the evidence is either doubtful or equal on the two sides was applied by the Holy Prophet in a case he decided. With regard to property of which no owner could be found, he laid down that its disposal should be governed by the element of benefit to all Muslims as well as to the thing itself, and secondly, by the element of prior possession; failing these, by the casting of lots. He held that contracts should be enforced to the letter, unless anything agreed makes that *halal* (lawful) which religion declares to be *haram* (unlawful). Where the parties are not agreed as to the terms of a contract, it should be declared void, and in a particular case, the Holy Prophet said—"When seller and buyer are not agreed, and the word of neither can be accepted, if the thing allegedly sold be there, the word of the seller should be accepted, but if the buyer does not agree, the contract should be declared void". Many cases are recorded in which the Holy Prophet (Peace be upon him) laid down canons of justice of general application. In one case the paternity of the child of a slave-girl was contested. One party claimed that his brother, when dying had said the child was his and should be looked after in his family. The other declared it was the child of his father's slave, and was born in his father's house. The Holy Prophet pronounced judgment as follows: "the child belongs to the owner of the house in which it was born; for the adulterer there is stoning". He decided that in a built-up area, where trouble had arisen through the paths being encroached upon by builders, the minimum width of the path should be seven cubits; so a public nuisance was removed. In a case where a person had cultivated land belonging to a tribe other than his own, without authority, the Holy Prophet decided that the man had no right to the produce, but could ask for payment of his expenses of cultivation. He laid down the principle in a pre-exemption case, that the "right or pre-exemption exists only so long as partition has not been effected, so that rights remain joint; when every field has been demarcated, and each owner has his separate way, no right of pre-exemption remains".

I found these few examples in Shah Waliullah's book, to which I have referred to earlier but I have no doubt that many other precedents are recorded in the main books of *Ahadith*. What I have said so far is sufficient to show that by the time that it became necessary for the Holy Prophet (Peace be upon him) to send *Qazis* (judges) to the new provinces which had acknowledged Islam and the rule of the Prophet, there was already established in the Holy Qur'an and the record of decided cases, a sufficient volume of maxims, rules, principles and precedents to constitute the corpus of Islamic jurisprudence. The procedure of trial of cases through presentation by the parties, supported by evidence in the face of the Court, was well established. A code classifying offences and the *hadd* punishments therefore, as well as the grounds of mitigation, had already been settled. It is recorded that the Holy Prophet interviewed a person who was to go as *Qazi* to the new Province of the Yemen. Part of the dialogue was as follows:

Q.On what will you base your legal decision?

A. The Qur'an.

Q. But if that contains nothing for the purpose?

A. Then upon your tradition and practice.

Q. But if that also fails you?

A. Then I will follow my own opinion.

The Holy Prophet approved these answers. In common with many persons who have read that little dialogue, I had the impression that the Holy Prophet was only testing the man's faith and allegiance to the Holy Qur'an, and to himself. Its true significance was brought home to me, in the course of the study that has gone into the present paper. The Holy Prophet (Peace be upon him) was making sure that the man realized that he was being sent to operate and propagate the new jurisprudence of Islam, according to right principles and that he knew where those principles were to be found. He was not to dispense justice in the manner of the pre-Islamic period, the *Jahaliyat*, or in the indigenous way of the people who had been recently brought within the authority of Islam. The fact was recognized also that the code, being new, was not complete so as to provide, in detail, for every kind of case, and so the appointee was permitted to use in such cases, his own judgment. The compilation of the *Ahadith* went on for almost a hundred years, and we may be sure that copies were sent to all the administrators and judges, far and near. Work on the formulation of the *Sharia*, the comprehensive code for the guidance of Muslims, continued for the next three hundred years, when it was completed separately, with variations by the four great Imams. It was settled that the laws of the Muslims were to be derived from, firstly the Qur'an, secondly the, *Sunnah* of the Holy Prophet, thirdly by assemblies of the learned, known as *Ijmaa*, and lastly, by *Ijtihad*, meaning ratiocination by individuals. Three of these sources were in operation from the outset, with the approval of the Holy Prophet himself, as we have seen. The fourth, the making of laws by assemblies failed of its purpose, since the assemblies were to be confined to scholars of individual schools, and the results produced lacked universality. But one thing is clear, namely, that from the very inception of Islam, the dispensation of justice has proceeded on regulated lines, on principles formulated in writing and with the aid of precedents, in the form of judicial decisions that go back to the Holy Prophet (PBUH) himself. The people of Islam can take just pride in the thought that their judicial system was placed from the beginning on lines that in substance are no different from those of the best systems of today. Compared with the other prevalent systems, it was distinguished by a higher degree of humanity towards criminals, even towards prisoners taken in religious wars, and a deeper understanding of the basic needs of human beings living in settled communities. In my belief, that remains the condition even today.

The progressive elements among the recognized sources of law in Islam are those of *ijtihad*, the advancement of law through ratiocinative processes, and *ijmaa*, which means codification and modernization of laws through deliberative assemblies. Our poet-philosopher, Iqbal, relates *ijtihad* to the original thinking of exceptionally gifted persons. This is a very acceptable view, but it is possible to see that at the level of our superior courts, the process of *ijtihad* is applied in every case where under minute examination, the judges are expected to apply the law to new and unanticipated situations, and even in some cases, to fill gaps in the law. As for *ijmaa*, under modern conditions and in the enlarging fields of human affairs that are outside the strict teaching of the four main schools, it is possible to regard the legislative assemblies of today as being competent to discharge that function in this aspect of modernization. The task of codification has been frequently attempted by Muslim rulers of the past. Such an attempt was made by the Mogul Emperor, Aurangzeb Alamgir, and the result was the *Fatawa Alamgiri*, which retains importance even today despite its character of a compilation of judicial *dicta*, often related to particular facts, whose application to new cases gives rise to difficulty. That collection was made some 275 years ago, but another attempt at codification of Islamic laws, that was made by the Sultan of

Turkey, entitled *Mejelle el-Ahkam-i-Adliya* is much more recent, having been completed and promulgated as the law of the vast territories of the Turkish Empire a mere hundred years ago. It was replaced by a new Code in 1926.

An English translation of this valuable source book of Islamic law has been published in Pakistan, by All Pakistan Legal Decisions of Lahore, and is readily available. When published originally, it was described as "a complete code of Islamic civil law", though it excludes the important subject of marriage (*munakiahat*) and is confined to "dealings between people and their relations with and conduct towards each other" that are included within the comprehensive description of *mu'amelat*. The book is prefaced by a collection of a hundred maxims, followed by 1851 Articles, adapted for application by the *Nizam* courts, as distinguished from the *Sharia* Courts. Although the propositions of law are not set out or worded in the manner of statutes in the English mode, and the translation is cumbrous because it is too literal, yet the book has the merit of being arranged in chapters, subject-wise from contracts of sale and lease, surety and pledge, to torts, pre-exemption, judicial guardianship, partition and partnership, limitation, etc. and so is of practical use as a reference. It contains elaborate provisions for implementation of Holy Prophet's injunction "proof is for the plaintiff; oath for the defendant, besides rules of evidence". The Holy Prophet's direction to examine the credibility of witnesses is carried out in a set of rules on the subject.

This compilation was the work of a Commission of Jurists appointed by the Sultan for "the production from the practical part of the *Sharia* (*Fiqh*) of a beneficial work, so that it shall be sufficient for application to the transactions of people, which happen everyday "in the words of the compilers, who purported to follow those opinions of *Hanafi* doctors which are most in harmony with the exigencies of modern life and business" (from the Foreword by Mr. Justice S. A. Rahman of the Supreme Court of Pakistan). The duty of adherence to *Sharia* law in the *Hanafi* school was borne in mind by the compilers, and there is thus assurance of such conformity for those who seek guidance in the paths of Islamic jurisprudence from this book. For that purpose, I think it can safely be recommended for study by the great number of persons in Pakistan, who have been encouraged by recent events to hope for the establishment of a genuine *Nizam-e-Mustafa* in Pakistan.

I have come to the end of my discourse. I am conscious that it had dealt largely with the subject of Islamic jurisprudence, and that the concept of justice has received little mention. Justice in the abstract is a subject for philosophers and metaphysicians, and in the field of law, perhaps for meta-lawyers and meta-jurists, an extremely rare species. I have preferred to keep my feet on the ground, and to place before you as much as I could ascertain of the institution of justice, operating among the men and the affairs of Islam. And it has given me great pleasure to demonstrate to you that the edifice of justice in Islam was founded and built up to a substantial degree by no other than the Apostle of Allah, Muhammad Mustafa (Peace be upon him). There can be no greater proof of its excellence and its right to be accepted with total confidence, for in the words of *Sa'adi* the poet of *Shiraz*:

Cheh gham deewar-e-ummat ra ke darad choon tu pushteban
Cheh bak as mauj-e-bahr an ra ke darad Nooh kishteban

Appendix 17

MORALS: THE ISLAMIC APPROACH

[This essay was written in late 1983 or early 1984, some fifteen years after Cornelius retired and about four years before he was bedridden and unable to write. Submitted in response to a request from the President of the Hamdard Foundation in Karachi, it was subsequently published (Hakim Mohammed Said, ed., Voice of Morality, *(Karachi, Hamdard Foundation Press, 1985, 148-167.) A redacted version of the essay without publishers' attribution appeared in* Islamic Horizons, *September/October 1997; 38-42.*

The Hamdard publication is a compilation of responses from ninety-four contributors from twenty-six countries to the editor's request for opinions on the "moral bankruptcy" of nations and on the impact of such "moral lapses" on peace and social order. Few challenges would have had greater appeal to Cornelius than this. His 20-page response was the longest and most erudite of all 94. The length of most contributions was two or three pages (a few were half a page). Only one other contribution, that of Walter Frank of Germany, was of comparable length (17 pages). The Cornelius essay is a serious, carefully reasoned analysis enriched by Qur'anic references and citations to British and American sources. It is typical of his approach to intellectual challenges of this kind.

He spells out in detail and with uncommon candour the Muslim position on such controversial moral issues as adultery, pornography, abortion, homosexuality and the causes of crime. He finds western attitudes towards these behaviours abhorrent and unequivocally affirms the superiority of the Islamic perception of morality.

This affinity for the moral canon of Islam may have been smoothed by its similarity (except for the doctrine of original sin) with Roman Catholic teaching. If Cornelius compared the two doctrines he would have no cause for concern but he compares Islamic doctrine with western (Christian) behaviour. He makes no mention of deviant behaviour in Muslim societies which, while perhaps not as pervasive, is nevertheless prevalent.

This essay is probably his last serious written work. While not absolutely certain of this, my research has not uncovered anything written later. His views in this essay, written when he was about eighty years old, certainly support the characterization made by Justice Shahabuddin fully twenty-five years earlier that he was more Muslim than the Muslims. It also corroborates the view of his son, Michael, that towards the end of his life he became more and more attached to Islam both as a religion and a culture. There is no evidence to warrant an assumption that he considered conversion but there is every reason to suggest that he certainly followed the moral compass of Islam. We cannot know whether or not he embraced its theology but short of proclaiming the essential Shahadah *he accepted the spirit of Islam with admiration and the word of Islam with respect. (See text pp. 61-66; notes 103-6)]*

The Western approach to the subject of morals has undergone a vast change in recent years. With the recession in the influence of religion, the scriptural injunctions in their scriptures have been pushed into the background, as being out of consonance with the ways of life that Western peoples have developed for themselves, under ever increasing secular influences. Morals are no longer a matter of right and wrong, of good and evil as understood and universally preached, not only from pulpits, down to the Victorian and Edwardian ages. The art of justification of deviations in human behavior is now in an advanced stage of refinement, partly through the open violations of truth and correct action by the States that exercise the predominant power in world affairs, violations which the communications media of each of these States have no difficulty in presenting to the utmost advantage or disadvantage, to carry the public with them, and partly the universal resort to the techniques of psychology, psychiatry and even some measure of mysticism, in the evaluation of individual misdeeds. The effect on the morals of peoples subjected to the falsification of facts and motives so regularly practised by the communications media, at the highest level, and under the highest authority, and the evaluation of such effect, are large questions outside the scope of this paper. But few can have failed to notice that in the Western world, hardly any offence of any significance, particularly by a white person, that is reported is not accompanied by a word of apologetics, as if the offender was incapable of such an action, and had it not been for some psychological disturbance, or a twist in his mind brought about by some experience in his past, even some severe beating justly given to him by his mother in his childhood, that a psychiatrist has been able to ferret out, the offence would never have been committed. There is even a tendency to draw mystical influences into the evaluation of the incident. In our country, there is no such development, for here there is no theory of redemption from original sin. And there is little danger that our judgments might be influenced in the same way, if we suffer an increase in the number of expert psychologists and psychiatrists. The Islamic view in these matters places the full responsibility upon the doer, in the light of the facts and circumstances of the incident, and will not accept any recondite and speculative internal condition of his mind as an apology for his doings. It is simple and straightforward in its outlook in all human affairs, in accordance with the dictates of Islam, which cover every aspect of the lives of Muslims, and are themselves of the most direct nature. Has it not been said in the Qur'an—'Allah has laid on you no impediment in your religion' (*Surah, 22:78*). So the exposition is clear. There are no stumbling-blocks; no 'ifs' and 'buts', no 'notwithstanding', no complexities to be handy instruments for the analytical experts to build liberal theories on, for their apologetic purposes.

The key appears in the very first *Surah* of the Qur'an, the *Surah Fateha*, than which it is difficult to find a more comprehensive prayer for man, in the increasingly intricate situation in which he is placed in the affairs of life. Man lifts his eyes up to the Almighty, Lord of all Worlds, and then, turning his eyes on himself, declares that he, himself, is an object of the generosity and mercy of Allah, reminding himself that he is answerable for his doings on the Day of Judgement, of which Allah is the Lord and Master. He then makes his confession of faith—'Thee alone we serve and on Thy aid alone we rely'. Then follows the payer—'Guide us to the Way of Righteousness, the Way of Thy blessed ones', and, by way of contrast, to remind himself that human beings are apt to follow other paths, he adds—'not the way of those who have incurred Thy wrath or of those who have gone astray'. The Arabic words— *Sirat-al-Mustaqeem* are generally rendered, by English translators, as 'straight path', but many roads which are straight lead in the wrong direction, and indeed, the easiest courses are generally the short way to perdition. I may be permitted to refer to a later passage in the Quran where mere straightness will not render the full meaning of the Arabic word *mustaqeem*. It will be found in *Surah 81:27-29*, where it is said that the message of Islam is a message to all the worlds in case there be one among you who wishes for *an yastaqeem*; but none of you will wish for it, unless Allah, Lord of the Worlds, Himself wishes it for you'. The words *an yastaqeem* must be given a fuller meaning here than merely 'straight path'; they must cover the whole message of Islam, which is a command to righteousness. The purpose of the prayer in the *Surah Fateha*, to be guided to the way of righteousness is made plain by these later verses; the devotee must first ask for this guidance, thus proving that the Almighty has desired that he should seek it, and then it will be vouchsafed to him.

The devotee, having asked for guidance to the 'Way of Righteousness' in all the problems of his life, is provided with a comprehensive set of rules, in the Qur'an, for the general conduct of his affairs. Some of the major rules are collected in a verse or set of verses. The first such verse is in *Surah 2:177*, containing the following catalogue: (1) Belief in Allah and the Last Day, in the angels, the Scriptures and the Prophets. (2) Giving of one's wealth to kinsfolk, to orphans and the needy, and to the wayfarer, for love of Allah. (3) Setting slaves free. (4) Observing proper worship. (5) Paying the poor-due (*Zakat*). (6) Being faithful to one's contracts, and to one's oaths. (7) Being patient in tribulation and adversity.

Another list appears in *Surah 6:151-152*, as follows: (1) Accept no partners for Allah. (2) Be good to your parents. (3) Do not kill your children, out of fear of poverty. (4) Avoid lewdness. (5) Slay not life, except in the case of justice. (6) Do not take the property of orphans. (7) Give full measure and full weight, in justice. (8) Be as good as your word. (9) Fulfil your covenant with Allah.

The following verse, v. 153, expressly declares—'This is the *Sirat-e-Mustaqeem*, indicating with clarity, that the rules of behaviour in the moral sense were a part of Holy Religion, the Way of Righteousness.'

Next, in *Surah 17:23-37*, the list is repeated, with some additions, as below: (1) In giving, be not niggardly, nor yet too generous so as to make yourself destitute. (2) Avoid adultery; it is a shameful deed, opening the road to other evils. (3) Do not follow that of which you have no knowledge. (4) Do not tread the earth exultantly.

The list is added to in *Surah 23:1-11*, as follows: (1) Humble yourself in your prayers, and be mindful of them. (2) Avoid vain talk. (3) Be active in deeds of charity. (4) Men should have intercourse only with their spouses, and (within limits) with the female slaves they possess. (5) Be faithful to your trusts and covenants.

Then, in *Surah 33:35*, there is given a list of the good qualities that are possessed by the Blessed. They are: (1) Resigned to the Will of Allah, (2) they believe, (3) are obedient, (4) are truthful, (5) are steadfast, (6) are humble, (7) are charitable, (8) keep the prescribed fasts, (9) are chaste and (10) keep Allah constantly in their thoughts.

In *Surah 42:37-43*, Allah promises to those who believe in and put their full trust in Him, that they will have a better and more lasting reward from Him, if they (1) have faith, (2) avoid grievous sins and open indecency, (3) are ready to forgive though angry, (4) obey Allah, (5) say their prayers, (6) decide all affairs by mutual consultation, (7) spend out of their means, (8) defend themselves against aggression, (9) avoid aggression and arrogance, themselves and (10) show patience and readiness to forgive the aggressor.

A further list of actions which will earn for worshippers a place in the gardens of the Blessed is given in *Surah 70:23-35*, of which only one is an addition to the qualities already mentioned, namely, that they stand by their testimony given as witnesses.

Besides these sets of virtues presented in the Qur'an as the major features of the quality of righteousness, there are a great many to be found all over the Holy Book that deal with particular matters, of which I select a few for mention below. Taking first the subject of conflicts, both domestic and external, *Surah 49:10*, enjoins Muslims to resist any aggressor, but also to make peace between the fighting parties. An external aggressor who fights Muslims for their faith, or to drive them out of their homes is entitled to no mercy. But otherwise, they are to be resisted, until they incline to peace, whereupon they are to be dealt with justly and kindly, for it may be that Allah will cause love to spring between Muslims and those who are their present enemies (*Surah 60:7, 8*). Treaties are to be observed, even with Pagans; *Surah 9:4*.

Disaffection towards the administration and rebellion are frowned upon in the comprehensive instruction in *Surah 4:59*— 'Obey Allah, the Apostle and those charged with authority among you'. The practice of bribery is condemned in *Surah 2:188*, where it is said—'Do not seek by use of your property to gain the ear of judges, so as to devour other people's property wrongfully'. Perjury is forbidden, by reason of the numerous injunctions to Muslims to be faithful to their oaths, and to stand by their testimony given as witnesses. Disapproval of scandal mongering, slander and libel is expressed in a number of verses, the most exhaustive exposition being in *Surah 24:10-20*, and in *Surah 33:58*, where it is said—'Those who malign believing men and believing women without justification, bear the guilt of slander and manifest sin'. And *Surah 24:19* makes clear the penalty—'Those who love that slander should be spread concerning the believers, theirs will be a painful punishment in the world and in the Hereafter'. It is not necessary to find authority for disapproval of offences against private property such as theft, larceny and robbery. The principle runs through the Holy Book, as does the condemnation of false pretenses. Embezzlement is forbidden by the dictate in *Surah 4:58* in the following words—'Allah commandeth you that ye restore deposits to their owners'. These are some of the deviations from right conduct which, in the Western practice are classed as crimes, but that is a purely secular attitude. In Islam, avoidance of such deviation is a matter of religious obligation.

It is in the field of morals pertaining to sex that the vast difference, indeed amounting to contradiction, between the purely secular approach now universal in Western communities and the Islamic injunctions, appears most clearly. Obscenity and indecency are forbidden in Islam by the word of Allah. The crux of this offence lies in the public exposure of the private parts, and as to this the command is put in the clearest words in *Surah 7:26-28*, from which I quote:

> Children of Adam! We have provided for you raiment to cover your shameful parts...but the raiment of restraint from evil is best...Let no Satan tempt you as he brought your parents out of the Garden, stripping them of their garments to show them their shameful parts... Those who commit an indecency say 'We found our fathers practising it, and the Almighty has commanded it.' Say, in reply 'Allah does not command indecency; why do you say concerning Allah such things as you know not?'

These injunctions are literally obeyed in Muslim countries. So far from exposing their "shameful parts", men and women alike go covered from head to foot, and even nakedness by children is frowned upon. What do we find in Western countries?

Children are being educated from a very young age, from illustrated books, in the facts and practices of sex. For adults there are more advanced books as well as articles in the popular press on the open and less-open facts of sexual activity. In addition, there are purely pornographic books and publications, frankly published for no purpose connected with the betterment of morals, and there are pornographic cinema shows of three-dimensional pictures, larger than life. In America, the New York Telephone Company has reserved a dozen lines, to which calls may be made at two rates, one cheaper than the other. The cheap calls produce for the caller a gushing female voice, prerecorded, which tells the caller exactly what kind of sexplay the girl would provide for him if he were there. At the higher rate, live females answer the call, with similarly fantasised sexual acts, of all kinds, duly personalised. Many of the callers are children from long distances, and parents are complaining, not only of the expense. A commission is looking into the complaints, and has allowed 90 days for public comment. In the meantime, big money is being made; some 3 million dollars a year out of the 'prerecorded fantasies' and some 6 million dollars a year by the Telephone Company. (*Newsweek*, 26th Sept. '83).

Readers will be interested to know that these developments, and also the spread of public nudity in Western countries were envisaged and strongly advised by no less influential a writer than Bertrand Russell, in a book entitled *Marriage and Morals*, published in 1929, which has gone through more than eighteen printings. Quoting freely from the Christian scriptures, but generally to negate the views there expressed, after closely reasoned argument, he comes to the following conclusions: (1) publications which are frankly pornographic would do very little harm if sex education were rational; (2) there ought to be no law whatsoever on the subject of obscene publications; (3) the only way to avoid indecency is to avoid mystery, and therefore children should be permitted to see each other and their parents naked; the taboo against nakedness is an obstacle to a decent attitude on the subject of sex; (4) public nudity is to be supported as a health incentive in sunny weather 'out-of-doors and in the sunshine and in the water'; standards of health and even of beauty would improve.

These views have obviously been adopted generally in Western countries, and are being widely acted upon. People take pride in going nude at popular resorts and the seaside, and in being photographed nude for publication in magazines. Not long ago, it was reported from England that a husband and wife, who were heads of a well-known school, had been dismissed because their nude pictures had been published in a magazine. And in a comment on certain legal changes in Greece, the prestigious *Sunday Telegraph* (21st Aug. 1983) observed that holiday-makers would be relieved to learn that the proposed legislation takes a more lenient view of sunbathing, and there would be no penalties unless some member of the public specifically objected to nudists.

These practices are thoroughly obnoxious to Muslims all over the world, and we may be certain that they will not be allowed to develop in Pakistan. They seem to be based on a complete under-estimate of the power of the sex-urge in human beings, and of the very important part that restraint in the practice and exposure of this urge has, throughout the history of humanity, played in the development of human character, particularly in the field of self-discipline. Now that laxity has reached the utmost limits in the highly populated Western countries, the results on the people's character in general will be awaited with interest. For ourselves, we may be grateful that no such experiments are likely ever to be tried here.

The same wide difference is noticeable between the views held in regard to chastity and adultery, in the Western countries and by the Muslim peoples. In Islam, the guiding lines are laid down in the Qur'an. In *Surah 51:49*, it is declared by Allah that 'of everything We have created pairs', and *Surah 30:21* says—'Allah created for you spouses, that you might find repose in them, and placed between the twain, love and sympathy'. The injunction to chastity for the unmarried is clearly put in *Surah 24:33*—'let those who find not the means to marry be abstinent, till Allah enriches them of His bounty'. Men are enjoined to marry single women or virtuous slave-girls by v. 32 of the same *Surah*. And *Surah 70:26-30* says that those who believe in the Day of Judgement and fear the final doom 'preserve their chastity save with their wives and their slavegirls...but whoever looks for more than that is among the transgresors'. It is otherwise now in the West, with the universal use of contraceptives. In the concluding chapter of Bertrand Russell's book cited above, we find the following passage:

> As for the pre-Christian elements in sexual ethics, these have been modified by one factor, and are in process of being modified by yet another. The first of these factors is contraceptives, which are making it increasingly possible to prevent sexual intercourse from leading to pregnancy, and are therefore enabling women, if unmarried, to avoid children altogether, and, if married, to have children only by their husbands, without in either case, finding it necessary to be chaste...A second factor, however, in the change which is coming over sexual morals, is liable to have more far-reaching effects. This is the increasing participation of the State in the maintenance and education of children....

The argument proceeds to envisage the 'substitution of the State for the father, and if institutions for the care of children from infancy onwards come to be provided in sufficient number, of the substitution of the State for the mother as well. It is argued that though at first these changes will affect the wage-earning classes only, they 'will ultimately extend to the whole population'. (p. 152).

Treating of the subject of prostitution, Russell says (p. 79)—

> the young man who would formerly have been driven to occasional visits to prostitutes, is now able to enter upon relations with girls of his own kind, relations which are on both sides free, which have a psychological element quite as important as the purely physical, and which involve often a considerable degree of passionate love on both sides. From the point of view of any genuine morality, this is an immense advance upon the older system... The new freedom between young people is, to my mind, wholly a matter for rejoicing...

One can readily understand it, if this view gains common acceptance, and it is possible to find items in almost any daily newspaper from the West, to prove that indeed common acceptance has been gained, in those countries. Chastity and adultery, in the Islamic sense, have no meaning now in Western countries. Again, a strong instrument of personal discipline, for the development of human character has been thrown overboard, on theoretical grounds, and it remains to see what the ultimate result will be.

Russell might have added another factor, to the two which he was put forward in support of his argument, and that is the availability of abortion. This is a subject of excited interest in the Western world at present. In some countries, abortion is available, through the state free of charge or at a charge, upon request. England is one such state. In Ireland, abortion was illegal, but yet abortions freely take place, and an English newspaper recently carried the report that the Greek record for the number of abortions undergone by a single woman was now 44, indicating intensive activity, probably of an irregular nature. In Islam, abortion would amount to killing of a child. It is enjoined in *Surah 6:151*, and again in *Surah 17:31*—'Do not kill children for fear of becoming poor'. The kind of abortions freely practised in the West surely derive from economic motives, or at the best socio-economic motives, and both are forbidden in Islam. And, in Islam, there is no question that the child in the womb is a life, a human life, from the moment of conception. For it is said, in *Surah 39:6*—'Allah created you in the womb of your mother, creation following creation, under threefold darknesses'. The continuity of the process of creation within the mother's womb is made clear by these words, and it is a living thing which is being created, from the conception thought the period of gestation. The question what is the earliest stage at which a child extruded from its mothers's womb can survive is not relevant, when it is a living being from the moment of conception onwards. The Western outlook is totally different from the Islamic, in this as well as in the ethical and moral sense.

No discussion of sexual morals can be complete without treating of the subject of homosexuality. Islam is content to regard this practice as totally unacceptable and forbidden by Holy Religion, on the strength of the references to the Prophet Lut, of which one may be quoted, viz. *Surah 7:80-84*:

And Lot, when he said to his people "what! Do you commit such indecency as never any being in all the world committed before you? You approach men lustfully instead of women; you as a people go to excess". And the only answer of the people was "Expel them from your city; these folk keep themselves pure". So We delivered him and his family, except his wife, who tarried. And we rained down upon them a rain; so behold what was the end of those sinners.

In *Surah 11:25-49*, where the story is retold the rain is said to be of stones. A more detailed version of the destruction of Sodom and Gomorrah which the Prophet Lut (Lot in the Bible) endeavoured to save is contained in the Old Testament, and is well known by Christians. What now is the condition in relation to homosexuality in the Christian West? Russell has favoured it in sharp terms, in the book cited above, from which I quote:

> Homosexuality between men, though not between women, is illegal in England, and it would be difficult to present any argument for a change in the law in this respect which would not itself be illegal on the ground of obscenity. Yet every person who has taken the trouble to study the subject knows that this law is the effect of a barbarous and ignorant superstition, in favour of which no rational argument of any sort or kind can be advanced.

It seems probable that other writers have propagated the same views, for in recent years homosexuality has been made legal in England, between consenting adults. The result in the media has been quite remarkable. Homosexuality is mentioned with the same frequency as say, drink, and with equal absence of hesitation. It seems that a great number of European men who attained sufficient distinction in other activities to have their biographies published, were homosexuals, in a big way, but the then general feeling of shame connected with the practice stood in the way of making the fact public. Now that sense seems to have disappeared altogether. For instance, in the *Sunday Telegraph*, a highly regarded weekly from London, it was stated, in bland fashion, in the issue of the 21st August 1983, that "Marcel Proust was a notorious homosexual". In the Weekly

Guardian, a prestigious English paper, of the 18th September, 1983, there is a review of a book on Colin Macinnes, a book writer who died in 1976. It says that the writer of the book named Gould—"has probed into Macinnes's sexual life and concludes that he began to practice love-making with other men (following in his father's footsteps) while he was in the Army, ferreting out Nazis, in a manner which his wartime comrade, Robert Waller thought 'unnecessarily sadistic'". According to Gould, Waller remembers that while they were together in North Germany, Colin Macinnes boasted of having slept with the entire police force in one place: "He was always interested in policemen."

The same book was reviewed in the *Sunday Telegraph* of the 11th September 1983, with equal candour regarding this abominable propensity. The review says:

(Macinnes) was also a homosexual nomad whose London address was never fixed. In Australia, he had been attracted to aborigines; in England, he was turned on by Blacks. He associated West Indians with spontaneity and licentiousness and expected them to rejuvenate a tired nation. Later, he became lyrical about teenagers.

Most people will agree that some ten years ago, such explicit mention of homosexuality and its accompanying acts could *never* have appeared in any newspaper in England. It seems evident that the practice is accepted in the most respectable circles, as a subject for polite conversation, not merely scientific or philosophical discussion. Homosexuality has already given rise to its own disease, going by the genial (and new) name of AIDS. Attempts are being made to establish preparatory schools for young boys to meet the needs of older men, under the Greek name 'Paedophilia', a composite word, carrying the derivative meaning of 'love for children/boys', particularly the latter, as appears from the word 'paederasty', which plainly refers to 'commerce with boys'. An article in the *London Times* of the 2nd September 1983 mentions a 'Paedophile Information Service' set up in England, which, however, is attracting the reprehensive attention of the Home Secretary, and parents have been warned to keep an eye on their children, particularly in the evening. In the United States, where the pursuit of money by any means is taken to the limit, there has been established in Boston, some 4 years ago, an institution 'by the name of NAMBLA. The full name, following the American practice of setting out everything for the understanding of all, from the Sunday School child, to the highest in the land, is 'North American Man-Boy-Love Relationship', and one of its purposes is to procure repeal of the law fixing the age of consent for homosexual relationships, thus to ensure its commercial success.

In West Germany and France, such activity is prohibited, but in France there is a Society compaigning for children to be free to take up sexual activity at any age.

As is well known, in some major cities in the United States, there are sections exclusively occupied by homosexuals and the practice is spreading, so that in time, this detail might be put into biodata and identity cards, for the convenience of authorities such as airline ticket-issuers, or hotels etc. since with the total elimination of the element of shame, there is no need for secrecy now in those countries. A distinguishing expression for a man who takes up with another, in a passive capacity, remains to be coined, like the term 'Mrs'. applied to married woman. Laws to regulate property and other rights, *inter se*, will probably follow. Attempts are already being made to overcome the Christian religious bias against the practice. In the *London Times* of the 23rd August 1983, it was reported that a Catholic priest held a solemn High Mass in Stockholm Cathedral in Sweden, for homosexuals exclusively.

It has been thought necessary to deal with this unpleasant subject at some length, to emphasise what enormous dangers, not only to morals but also to the very structure of human society, are being released in countries where the voice and actions of the Almighty have been rejected by secular Governments, as 'barbarous and ignorant superstitions'. So long as the moral code of Islam stands firmly on the *Sirat-al-Mustaqeem* we, in Pakistan, and all those in Muslim countries are safely protected against these perils. As is said in the Qur'an, *Surah 6:70*—'Leave to themselves those who take their religion for a sport or diversion, and are deluded by the life of the world, and counsel them, so that none may be trapped in his own doings, for he will have no helper but Allah, nor will he find any intercessor.'

It remains to present outlines of the ethic of Islam in regard to the treatment of women by men. *Surah 4:34*, describes men as being in charge of women, having been made to excel them, and because they are required to support women out of their means. For this reason women are obedient; some force may be used against them if they are not. For settlement of breaches, arbiters are suggested. Yet, as declared in *Surah 2:228*, women have rights in relation to their men similar to those which their men have in relation to women, according to custom, though men are a degree above them. The initiative in a divorce comes from the man by 'forswearing' his wife, i.e. stay away from the marriage bed, *Surah 2:226*, but it is made clear that reconciliation is better. Thereafter, that is, after waiting four months, the man may pronounce the first divorce and then another, and then a final divorce, so that there is ample opportunity for coming together again. After pronouncement of the first two divorces, the woman is not to be turned out of the house, and she may be taken back in kindness or allowed to go in kindness (*Surah 65:1, 2*). Even after the final divorce, the wife is to be allowed to go 'in kindness', being allowed her dues, and no obstacles are to be placed in the way of her marrying again. One about to die should bequeath to his wife a 'provision for a year' in his house, and may also make a provision for a divorced wife 'in kindness' (*Surah 2:240-241*). Throughout, the emphasis is on the man showing kindness and consideration.

In ordinary life, men are required to keep their eyes down when they meet a woman, and women are required to cover up modestly, and not make a display of their persons (*Surah 24:30-31*). These rules are for persons outside the prohibited degrees, but even as among relations and in the privacy of homes, they apply to an extent, and are in fact observed by most Muslims. The family, among Muslim people, being close-knit, and tribal bonds being still strong, all marriages of children are arranged by their elders, often many years in advance. The consequence is that, to a very great extent, the young people do not, and do not have to, hunt for mates themselves. Discreet parents arrange early marriages for their children, and thus temptations to enter upon relations with other young people are voided.

Under such auspices, marriages in Islam brought about by parents on both sides, have a greater prospect of success than a love-marriage, however passionate the love may be at the start. It cannot be denied that the marital family system of this kind provides far greater assurance of maintenance and furtherance of moral standards in the society than marriages based on nothing more than mutual attraction between the couple, as is the universal practice in the West. Even as regards divorce, the Muslim system in practice, which does not require resort to Court, is both practical and successful, as experience in all Muslim countries proves. Provided the man is faithful to the Quranic injunctions and acts always with grace and 'kindness', observing the requirements as regards pronouncements, accommodation and allowances for the wife, and bears in mind the possibility of reconciliation, the wife's outlay of love and affection on him and her children can be thought to be requited. She gets her legal rights, as to dower and the like, in any case.

Islamic morals are indeed a major part of the outward and visible proof of the success Muslims have achieved in their prayer to be guided to the *Sirat-al-Mustaqeem* the Path of Righteousness. It is part of their effort, in the line of religious duty, to earn the right to the name they carry, for the word 'Muslim' means 'one who has submitted', that is, to the Will of Allah. The Qur'an says that the name Muslim was first given to them by the Patriarch Ibrahim, and this was done with the purpose that there should arise a Prophet who would bear witness to them, and they themselves should bear witness to the whole world of men. So they will, one may hope, for in many respects, men of other faiths are forsaking the path of righteousness, described as 'barbarous and ignorant', for pleasurable paths of their own devising. In many respects, the contrast stands out clearly in favour of Muslims. Assuredly, the same result will appear in all other respects, in the affairs of life, if all Muslims were to raise the prayer, before every action—'Guide us to the path of righteousness!'.

APPENDICES

THE CORNELIUS MEMORIAL LECTURES

Appendix 18

**FIRST CORNELIUS MEMORIAL LECTURE
24 DECEMBER 1993**

SUPREMACY OF THE CONSTITUTION: RECENT
DEVELOPMENTS
Nasim Hasan Shah
Chief Justice of Pakistan (Retired)

[Biographical information on Chief Justice Nasim Hasan Shah can be found in the Preface to this volume, pp. vv-xvi]
This lecture by Dr. Nasim who worked closely with Chief Justice Cornelius, is the only memorial lecture which deals explicitly and exhaustively with Cornelius' decisions and subsequent judgments influenced by them. Emphasis is given to the Maulvi Tamizuddin Khan and the Maulana Maudoodi cases. These cases clearly established judicial review and independence, and the right of the legislative to make law without the assent of the executive. Later opinions by Chief Justice Nasim affirmed the right of political parties to organize, and for

free elections to be held. He views his judgment in Mian Muhammad Nawaz Sharif v. President of Pakistan and others, (PLD 1993 SC 473) *as probably the first time in history that an overthrown government was restored to power by a judicial opinion. This he regards as the triumph of constitutionalism in Pakistan.]*

I feel greatly honoured to be given the privilege of delivering the First Cornelius Memorial Lecture. The subject of my lecture is, as you all know already, the "Supremacy of the Constitution: Recent Developments".

Before I embark upon the subject itself, may I, on a personal note, mention that I had the good fortune to work with the late Justice A. R. Cornelius quite closely. I was editor of the *Pakistan Supreme Court Reports* in which he took great personal interest and was also before him very frequently as a counsel in his Court. As a matter of fact, a special bond developed between the late Chief Justice and myself, a bond not dissimilar to the one which exists between a loving master with his devoted pupil. Hence I am very happy to deliver this lecture in his memory.

You may recall that in my tribute to the late Mr. Justice A. R. Cornelius, on his passing away, I ventured to say "the Supreme Court of Pakistan under the able stewardship of Mr. Justice A. R. Cornelius was like a mighty citadel from which, however, grave the night and, however, heavy the gloom, the bright light of law always shone forth ushering and sustaining the rule of law". Therefore, before I dwell upon the recent instances wherein the Courts have asserted the supremacy of the Constitution, a short reference on this point to the work of Justice Cornelius will not be inappropriate.

The journey of constitutional rule in Pakistan has indeed been a stormy one. Soon after the establishment of the State of Pakistan, the country was beset by one constitutional crisis after another. The news that a proclamation of emergency had been declared on the ground that the constitutional machinery in a province had broken down necessitating the enforcement of the Governor's Rule became, unfortunately, a common phenomenon.

Graver constitutional crisis followed. The body charged with the framing of the Constitution—The Constituent Assembly—was itself dissolved by the Head of the State leading to a battle royal in the Superior Courts.

Mr. Justice A. R. Cornelius was one of the members of the bench which heard the appeal of the Government in Maulvi Tamizuddin's case (*Federation of Pakistan and another v. Maulvi Tamizuddin Khan PLD 1955 FC 240*). Mr. Justice Cornelius was unable to agree with the majority view. He was, therefore, constrained to deliver a dissenting judgment. His dissent was prefaced as follows:

> The resolution of a question affecting the interpretation of important provisions of the interim Constitution of Pakistan in relation to the very high matters which are involved, entails a responsibility going directly to the oath of office which the Constitution requires of a Judge, namely, to bear true faith and allegiance to the Constitution of Pakistan as by law established and faithfully to perform the duties of the office to the best of the incumbent's ability, knowledge and judgment.

The dissent he went on to deliver has brought him everlasting honour.

A few years later, on 7th October, 1958, the country was confronted with an even more grave crisis. It was placed under Martial Law, the Constitution of 1956 was abrogated and the country was to be governed henceforth under the Laws (Continuance in Force) Order, 1958. The question arose before the Supreme Court some months later whether the words of Article 2(1) of the Order, namely, that Pakistan "shall be governed as nearly as may be in accordance with the late Constitution" had the effect of rendering the fundamental rights guaranteed in the 1956 Constitution as no longer enforceable or whether they could be held to have survived the revolution, as such rights. Justice Cornelius was of the opinion that the citizens of Pakistan could still avail of the said rights provided their enforcement would not come in opposition to the operation of the Martial Law itself. Expression to this opinion was given in a very original way, as follows in the case of *Province of East Pakistan v. Muhammad Mehdi Ali Khan Panni* (*PLD 1959 SC 387*). He said:

During the past nine months, it has clearly appeared that the provisions of the late Constitution are indeed being observed, not as a mere matter of courtesy or of merely general guidance, but that in actual practice, where the provisions of the late Constitution are applicable in their terms to matters arising for governmental action, they are being applied, according to their terms. Equally, as a matter of practice where in the circumstances a variation is desired it is supported by the authority of a Presidential Order or a Regulation of the Chief Administrator of Martial Law as the case may be. Where, on the other hand, the case is one of application of the provisions in the altered conditions, it seems that discretion is exercised by the executive authorities in making the necessary adaptation to suit the changed circumstances.

This degree of adherence to the provisions of the late Constitution at all levels induces me to make the observation that perhaps the words 'shall be governed as nearly as may be in accordance with the late Constitution' have been somewhat undervalued on the last occasion when they were brought up before this Court for examination. The full power and purpose of these words may not have been appreciated at that early date. They may indeed be an indication that the Martial Law under which the country was placed by the Presidential Proclamation of the 7th October, 1958 is different in essential respects from the ordinary conception of Martial Law. The words 'shall be governed' are mandatory in expression as well as in effect and by saying that the provisions in question shall be operative subject to specified written instruments issued by the highest authorities of the new regime, the value and force of the words in which these provisions are embodied in the late Constitution is certainly raised, in a legal sense much beyond that of words in a mere book of reference.

After the lifting of Martial Law on 8th June, 1962 and the promulgation of the 1962-Constitution, two very important cases raising issues of grave constitutional import came before the Supreme Court namely the case of *Mr. Fazlul Quader Chowdhury and others v. Mr. Muhammad Abdul Haque (PLD 1963 SC 486)* and the case of Maulana Abul Ala Maududi *(PLD 1964 SC 673)*.

In the first case, the question was whether the members elected to the National Assembly, who had accepted office of ministers had lost their seats in the Assembly on account of the provisions of Article 104 of the Constitution 1962. This article provided, *inter alia*, that should a member of an Assembly be elected or be appointed a minister or to any other office of profit, he shall forthwith cease to be member of the Assembly on the day on which he enters upon such office. This disability, which was sought to be removed under the Removal of Difficulties (Appointment of Ministers) Order (34 of 1962) had been questioned as being *ultra vires* of the Constitution of 1962. While dealing with this matter, Justice Cornelius observed that the judges of the Supreme Court and the High Courts are required to swear an oath that they will "preserve, protect and defend the Constitution" when they enter upon their office. He went on to add that accordingly the said two courts are bound by their oath and duty to act so as to keep the provisions of the Constitution fully alive and operative and to preserve them in all respects. The order was declared *ultra vires* of the Constitution and the supremacy of the Constitution was given effect to and fully preserved.

In Maulana Madoodi's case certain provisions of Criminal Law (Amendment) Act, 1908 fell for interpretation and the important question was whether the "opinion" formed by the executive authorities was subject to judicial review or not? Justice Cornelius held:

> ...it is a duty of Provincial Government to take into consideration all relevant facts and circumstances. That imports the exercise of an honest judgment as to the existence of conditions in which alone the opinion may be formed, consequent upon which the opinion must be formed honestly, that the restriction is necessary. In this process, the only element which I find to possess a subjective quality as against objective determination, is the final formation of opinion that the action proposed is necessary. Even this is determined, for the

most part, by the existence of circumstances compelling the conclusion. The scope for exercise of personal discretion is extremely limited... As I have pointed out, if the section be construed in a comprehensive manner, the requirement of an honest opinion based upon the ascertainment of certain matters which are entirely within the grasp and appreciation of the governmental agency is clearly a prerequisite to the exercise of the power. In the period of foreign rule, such an argument, i.e. that the opinion of the person exercising authority is absolute may have at times prevailed, but under autonomous rule, where those who exercise power in the State are themselves citizens of the same State, it can hardly be tolerated.

Justice Cornelius demonstrated the dominance of the Constitution again, in the case of *Malik Ghulam Jilani v. The Government of West Pakistan and another (PLD 1967 SC 373)* wherein the question arose whether the assertion made by the detaining authorities that it was "satisfied" in terms of Rule 32 of the Defence of Pakistan Rules was subject to judicial review. According to Justice Cornelius the word "satisfaction" must be a state of mind which has been induced by the existence of reasonable grounds for such satisfaction. He, accordingly, held that "the power of an authority acting under Rule 32 is, therefore, no more immune to judicial review". This indeed was a significant breakthrough, as by so holding Justice Cornelius was making a clear departure from the view earlier expressed by the House of Lords in Liversidge's case *(L.R. 1942 A.C. 206)* and the Privy Council in Sibnath Banerji's case *(L. R. 72 I.A. 241)* and followed by Courts in India and Pakistan. It is to the everlasting credit of Justice Cornelius, that his views were soon adopted both by the British and Indian Courts in subsequent cases and they followed the rule laid down in Malik Ghulam Jilani's case, in preference to their earlier judgments.

Mr. Justice A. R. Cornelius retired from the Supreme Court shortly after delivering this historic judgment on March 1, 1968, and has since been a legend in his country—Pakistan.

Since the subject of this lecture is concerned with the recent developments in relation to the supremacy of the Constitution, I will not weary you any further with all the details of Pakistan's difficult and painful constitutional history after 1968 but will proceed to discuss the role played by the Judiciary in establishing the supremacy of the Constitution in recent years.

After a long and extremely difficult "rope-a-dope" with the Martial Law regime of Gen. Zia-ul-Haq and after restoration of the Constitution in the year 1985 superior judiciary of Pakistan did not wait for long for re-assessing the supremacy of the Constitution, for steering the country away from totalitarianism and to put it back on the rails of constitutional democracy. The major breakthrough in this respect was achieved between the months of June and November, 1988 when the Supreme Court of Pakistan decided in quick succession some very important constitutional cases which paved the way for political party-based general elections in the country, put fetters on the presidential discretion of dissolving the National Assembly, diluted the apparently complete immunity enjoyed by the legislative and administrative steps taken by the Martial Law authorities, resolved the economical explosive issue of drawing from the Federal and Provincial Consolidated Funds and also ensured the holding of fair elections in the country through insistence upon production of the National Identity Card by every voter desiring to cast his vote.

The first of those cases was *Ms. Benazir Bhutto v. Federation of Pakistan and another (PLD 1988 SC 416)* which was decided on 20-6-1988. In that case the petitioner Miss Benazir Bhutto, Co-Chairperson of the Pakistan Peoples Party, had, by invoking the original constitutional jurisdiction of the Supreme Court of Pakistan, challenged certain amendments made in the Political Parties Act, 1962, including those relating to compulsory registration of the political parties before they could participate in any general election in the country, as violative of Articles 17 and 25 of the Constitution, the *vires* of the Freedom of Association Order, 1978 as being unconstitutional and the constitutionality of Article 270-A purportedly providing blanket immunity to all legislative measures taken during the period of Zia-ul-Haq's Martial Law. That petition was ultimately accepted, the offending provisions of the Political Parties Act, 1962 were struck down, the Fundamental Right guaranteed by Article 17 of the Constitution was given its full effect and a major obstacle in the way of restoration of Constitutional democracy in our country was removed. I too recorded my separate note in that case in support of the leading judgment delivered by the then Chief Justice Muhammad Haleem and I concluded my observations in the following words:

> Persons elected to the legislatures in their personal capacities have hardly any importance. They just toss around on the political scene, rudderless and without a destination. It is only when they band themselves into a group, as a party, that they become a force exercising some influence by their activities. It is only as members of a political party and not as individual members of the legislatures; can they achieve their objectives....
>
> Indeed, our very State of Pakistan itself could never have come into existence if a political party (the Muslim League) was not allowed to function as a party, without let or hindrance. As early as in 1942 in a speech made by the Quaid-i-Azam at a reception in Delhi on the occasion of his birthday on 25th December, he said: "The position of Muslim India during the last 200 years has been that of a ship without a rudder and without a captain, floating on the high seas full of rocks. For 200 years it remained floating, damaged, disorganised, demoralised, still floating. In 1936 with the cooperation of many others we salvaged the ship. Today the ship has a wonderful rudder and a captain who is willing to serve and always to serve. Its engines are in perfect working order, and it has got its loyal crew and officers. In the course of the last five years it has turned into a battleship'."
>
> If members of the Muslim League were allowed to contest elections only in their individual capacities and not as a "loyal crew" i.e. as members of the Muslim League Party, there would have been no battle, no victory, no Pakistan.
>
> Thus, the provisions of Section 3-B of the Political Parties Act, 1962 which require compulsory registration for a political party cannot be sustained. The conditions laid down in the said section are not warranted by Article 17 of the Constitution....
>
> In view of the guarantee of freedom of association including the right to form a political party, conferred by the Constitution in Article 17, such a restriction cannot be sustained.

The second of those cases was *Ms. Benazir Bhutto and another v. Federation of Pakistan and another (PLD 1989 SC 66)* which was decided on 2-10-1988. In that case the petitioner Ms. Benazir Bhutto, Co-Chairperson of the Pakistan Peoples Party, had, by invoking the original constitutional jurisdiction of the Supreme Court of Pakistan again, challenged certain amendments made in the Representation of the People Act, 1976 and prayed for removing the clogs in the way of allocation of an election symbol to a political party contesting a general election as a party. That petition was also ultimately accepted, the offending provision of the Representation of the People Act, 1976 was struck down, the Fundamental Right guaranteed by Article 17 of the Constitution was given its fuller effect and another obstacle in the way of restoration of constitutional democracy in our country was removed. In my separate note in that case in support of the leading judgment delivered by Mr. Justice Shafiur Rahman and I concluded my observations in the following words:

> The term 'election' is a comprehensive term and includes all the stages of the election commencing from the calling of the electorate to vote until the declaration and notification of the final result. Obviously casting of votes for the candidates is the most important stage in the process of elections. Now while Rule 9 of the Rules permits a political party to obtain a common symbol to facilitate the voter to identify his party candidate, section 21 of the Act omits to recognize this right. But this Court has found that elections may be held on party basis in every constituency by virtue of the Fundamental Right conferred on the citizens of this country by Article 17(2) of the Constitution. Thus, an inconsistency exists between section 21 of the Act and the Fundamental Right aforesaid. Section 21, as it now stands, is neither cognizant of the existence of political parties nor accords any recognition to them. Indeed the failure therein to make any provision for allocation of any symbol to a political party, which alone can enable it to effectively participate in the process of elections, renders nugatory the right to form a political party and accomplish its objectives, namely, to organise and fight an election with a view to capture political power. Accordingly, I agree with my learned brother Shafiur Rahman J., that section 21 is violative of the Fundamental Right contained in Article 17(2) and is void to the extent indicated by him. The petition, accordingly, must succeed.

The third of those cases was *Federation of Pakistan and others v. Haji Muhammad Saifullah Khan and others (PLD 1989 SC 166)* which was decided on 5-10-1988. In that case Haji Muhammad Saifullah Khan and others had, through writ petitions filed before the Lahore High Court, Lahore, challenged the dissolution of the National Assembly of Pakistan ordered by General Zia-ul-Haq on May 29, 1988 exercising the President's power under Article 58(2)(b) of the Constitution. The High Court had declared the dissolution of the National Assembly to be unconstitutional but had refused the relief of restoration of the National Assembly. The matter then came to the Supreme Court of Pakistan where the judgment of the High Court was ultimately upheld. Through an interpretative approach the Supreme Court declared the discretionary power of the President to dissolve the National Assembly to be justiciable and then found the exercise of that discretion by the President to be unconstitutional as the same had no sufficient nexus with the grounds upon which the Constitution permitted a dissolution. I had the privilege of writing the main judgment in that case and I had observed therein that:

> True enough, it is within the discretion of the President to determine whether these conditions are met or not but this discretion has to be exercised in terms of the words and spirit of the Constitutional provision....
>
> The discretion conferred by Article 58(2)(b) of the Constitution on the President cannot, therefore, be regarded to be an absolute one, but is deemed to be a qualified one, in the sense that it is circumscribed by the object of the law that confers it....
>
> The circumstance that the impugned action has political overtones cannot prevent the Court from interfering therewith, if it is shown that the action taken is violative of the Constitution. The superior Courts have an inherent duty, together with the appurtenant power in any case coming before them, to ascertain and enforce the provisions of the Constitution and as this duty is derivable from the express provisions of the Constitution itself the Court will not be deterred from performing its Constitutional duty, merely because the action impugned has political implications.

Just a week after the decision of Haji Saifullah's case the Supreme Court of Pakistan, on 12-10-1988, decided the case of *Federation of Pakistan and another v. Malik Ghulam Mustafa Khar (PLD 1989 SC 26)* which significantly diluted the immunity granted by Article 270-A of the Constitution to the convictions recorded by the Military Courts during the days of Zia-ul-Haq's Martial Law. Speaking for the Court Mr. Justice Saad Saood Jan observed that:

> Acts, actions or proceedings which could not be treated as relatable or having nexus with the 'previous operation' of the Martial Law Orders and Regulations would hardly fall within the protection offered by this paragraph. As observed by Kaikaus, J., in *Abdur Rauf v. Abdul Hamid Khan (PLD 1965 SC 671)* no Legislature when it grants power to take action or pass an order contemplates a mala fide exercise of power; a mala fide order is a fraud on the statute. Apart from that, in view of the assurance given to the citizens by Article 4 of the Constitution, such acts, actions or proceedings which suffered from lack or excess of jurisdiction or were mala fide or were coram non judice could not conceivably be regarded as done, taken or held in connection with the previous operation of a Martial Law Regulation or Martial Law Order.

Within a fortnight of the decision in Malik Ghulam Mustafa Khar's case the Supreme Court of Pakistan, on 24-10-1988, decided the *President's Reference No. 1 of 1988 (PLD 1989 SC 75)* regarding drawing of money from the Federal and Provincial Consolidated Funds and, thus, forestalled the impending financial deadlock in the country through the means of Constitutional interpretation.

Within the next three weeks of rendering of the opinion in the said President's Reference No. 1 of 1988 the Supreme Court of Pakistan, on 12-11-1988, granted special leave to appeal in *Federation of Pakistan v. Aitzaz Ahsan and another (PLD 1989 SC 61)* regarding the requirement of production of a national identity card by every voter for the purposes of casting his vote and also suspended the order of the Lahore High Court, Lahore which had done away with the said requirement. This order of the Supreme Court went a long way in ensuring fair holding of many elections that followed.

Some people called those months a period of judicial statesmanship when the Supreme Court of Pakistan was acting vigorously in all directions. I would rather term that period as one of the supremacy, not of the Supreme Court, but of the Constitution. In other words that was the time when the rule of law was the name of the game and the Constitution, being the supreme law, reigned supreme. Even since, the courts in Pakistan have never looked back in their march toward supremacy of the Constitution and establishment of constitutionalism as a way of life in our society.

In the field of enforcement of the Fundamental Rights guaranteed by the Constitution the record of the superior courts in Pakistan in the recent past is indeed enviable, to say the least. According to Article 8 of the Constitution any law, or any custom or usage having the force of law, in so far as it is inconsistent with the Fundamental Rights conferred by the Constitution shall, to the extent of such inconsistency, be void. A number of important cases have recently been decided by our superior courts wherein different laws have been struck down as they were found to be inconsistent with those Fundamental Rights.

In the case of *Ms. Benazir Bhutto v. Federation of Pakistan and another* (PLD 1988 SC 416) the offending provisions of the Political Parties Act, 1962 were struck down, the Fundamental Right guaranteed by Article 17 of the Constitution was given its full effect and, thus, supremacy of the Constitution was ensured.

In the case of *Ms. Benazir Bhutto and another v. Federation of Pakistan and another (PLD 1989 SC 66)* the offending provision of the Representation of the People Act, 1976 was struck down, the Fundamental Right guaranteed by Article 17 of the Constitution was given its fuller effect and the supremacy of the Constitutional rights over ordinary legislation was asserted.

In the case of *Federation of Pakistan and another v. Malik Ghulam Mustafa Khar (PLD 1989 SC 26)* the citizen's constitutionally guaranteed 'inalienable right' to be treated in accordance with the law was recognized over and above the purported immunity granted to the actions of the Martial law authorities under Article 270-A of the Constitution itself.

In the case of *Shirin Munir and others v. Government of Punjab and another (PLD 1990 SC 295)* the Fundamental Right guaranteed by Article 25 of the Constitution was given full effect and the discrimination in admission to medical colleges on the basis of sex alone was struck down.

A few years ago in the matter of proposed public hangings of criminals sentenced to death for commission of heinous offenses the Supreme Court of Pakistan took notice of the same upon a telegram received from the Amnesty International and stayed such public hangings by finding them prima facie to be violative of the Fundamental Right of human dignity guaranteed by Article 14 of the Constitution. Subsequently the said proposal was shelved by the Government.

The case of *Ghulam Ali and others v. Mst. Ghulam Sarwar Naqvi (PLD 1990 SC 1)* is a landmark in respect of protection which the Courts in Pakistan are ready to afford to the illiterate and deprived female population of the country qua their rights over property and inheritance.

The case of *Dershan Masih alias Rehmatay and others v. The State (PLD 1990 SC 513)* opened new vistas of public interest litigation and human rights cases in Pakistan and, ever since the superior Courts, utilising Constitutional provisions, have taken significant strides in the fields of human rights, environment protection and public interest litigation.

Islam and Islamic way of life being the cornerstones of our Constitution, the constitutional mandate in that field has been carried into effect in letter and spirit by the superior courts of Pakistan. Islamisation of laws and striking down of un-Islamic provisions contained therein by the Federal Shariat Court and the Shariat Appellate Bench of the Supreme Court of Pakistan have been a regular feature in the recent past. The list of such cases is so long that it cannot conveniently be reproduced here. Effective fulfillment of this constitutional mandate has not only accomplished one of the main objectives of the creation of

Pakistan but has also conclusively established the supremacy of the Constitution in this regard.

The introduction of Article 2-A into the Constitution made the principles and provisions set out in the Objectives Resolution passed by the First Constituent Assembly of Pakistan in the year 1949 substantive part of the Constitution and required that effect shall be given to the same accordingly. Initially Article 2-A, posed some difficulties and created a lot of confusion and uncertainty in various Courts of Pakistan regarding its true import and applicability. So much so that in one case the Lahore High Court, Lahore denuded Article 45 of the Constitution of its effect by holding that the same came in conflict with the said Article 2-A. Ultimately, in the case of *Hakim Khan and others v. Government of Pakistan and others (PLD 1992 SC 595)* the Supreme Court of Pakistan had to clarify the true position regarding Article 2-A and in that judgment I made the following remarks:

> The role of the Objectives Resolution, accordingly in my humble view, notwithstanding the insertion of Article 2-A in the Constitution (whereby the said Objectives Resolution has been made a substantive part thereof) has not been fundamentally transformed from the role envisaged for it at the outset; namely that it should serve as beacon light for the Constitution-makers and guide them to formulate such provisions for the Constitution which reflect the ideals and objectives set forth therein. Thus, whereas after the adoption of the Objectives Resolution on 12th March, 1949, the Constitution-makers were expected to draft such provisions for the Constitution which were to conform to its directives and the ideals enunciated by them in the Objectives Resolution and in case of any deviation from these directives, while drafting the proposed provisions for the Constitution the Constituent Assembly, before whom these draft provisions were to be placed, would take the necessary remedial steps itself to ensure compliance with the principles laid down in the Objectives Resolution. However, when a Constitution already stands framed (in 1973) by the National Assembly of Pakistan exercising plenary powers in this behalf wherein detailed provisions in respect of all matters referred to in the Objectives Resolution have already been made and Article 2-A was made a mandatory part thereof much later i.e. after 1985 accordingly now when a question arises whether any of the provisions of the 1973-Constitution exceeds in any

particular respect, the limits prescribed by Allah Almighty (within which His people alone can act) and some inconsistency is shown to exist between the existing provision of the Constitution and the limits to which the man-made law can extend; this inconsistency will be resolved in the same manner as was originally envisaged by the authors and movers of the Objectives Resolution namely the National Assembly itself. In pratical terms, this implies in the changed context, that the impugned provision of the Constitution shall be corrected by suitably amending it through the amendment process laid down in the Constitution itself.

In that case Mr. Justice Shafiur Rahman had also observed that:

The provisions of Article 2-A were never intended at any stage to be self-executory or to be adopted as a test of repugnancy or of contrariety. It was beyond the power of the Court to have applied the test of repugnancy by invoking Article 2-A of the Constitution for striking down any other provision of the Constitution (Article 45).

That case set the whole controversy over Article 2-A of the Constitution at rest and conclusively established the supremacy of the Constitution in that respect.

The high water-mark in this march towards supremacy of the Constitution came in the recent case of *Mian Muhammad Nawaz Sharif v. President of Pakistan and others (PLD 1993 SC 473)* when the dissolution of the National Assembly ordered on April 18, 1993 by President Ghulam Ishaq Khan was set aside as un-Constitutional and the National Assembly as well as the Government and the Cabinet of Mian Muhammad Nawaz Sharif was restored by the Supreme Court of Pakistan. Regarding maintainability of that petition before the Supreme Court on the basis of violation of the Fundamental Right guaranteed by Article 17 of the Constitution I had observed in my judgment as follows:

Fundamental Rights in essence are restrains on the arbitrary exercise of power by the State in relation to any activity that an individual can engage. Although Constitutional guarantees are often couched in permissive terminology, in essence they impose limitations on the power of the State to restrict such activities. Moreover, Basic or

Fundamental Rights of individuals which presently stand formally incorporated in the modern Constitutional documents derive their lineage from and are traceable to the ancient Natural Law. With the passage of time and the evolution of civil society great changes occur in the political, social and economic conditions of society. There is, therefore, the corresponding need to re-evaluate the essence and soul of the fundamental rights as originally provided in the Constitution. They require to be construed in consonance with the changed conditions of the society and must be viewed and interpreted with a vision to the future....

Thus, in the scheme of our Constitution, the guarantee 'to form a political party' must be deemed to comprise also the right by that political party to form the Government, wherever the said political party possesses the requisite majority in the Assembly....

Accordingly, the basic right "to form or be a member of a political party" conferred by Article 17(2) comprises the right of that political party not only to form a political party, contest elections under its banner but also, after successfully contesting the elections, the right to form the Government if its members, elected to that body, are in possession of the requisite majority. The Government of the political party so formed must implement the programme of the political party which the electorate has mandated it to carry into effect. Any unlawful order which results in frustrating this activity, by removing it from office before the completion of its normal tenure would, therefore, constitute an infringement of this Fundamental Right.

Convinced by the fact that the law is mightier than the king of kings I went on to hold that:

Unfortunately, this belief that he [the President] enjoys some inherent or implied powers besides these specifically conferred on him under Articles 46, 48(6), 101, 242(1-A) and 243(2)(c) is a mistaken one. In a Constitution contained in a written document wherein the powers and duties of the various agencies established by it are formulated with precision, it is the wording of the Constitution itself that is enforced and applied and this wording can never be overridden or supplemented by extraneous principles or non-specified enabling powers not explicitly incorporated in the Constitution itself. In view of the express provisions of our written Constitution detailing with fullness, the powers and duties of the various agencies of the Government that it holds in balance there is no room of any residual or enabling powers inhering in any authority established by it besides those conferred upon it by specific words.

After carefully analyzing the grounds of dissolution given by the President the same were found by the Supreme Court to be falling short of the requirements of Article 58(20)(b) of the Constitution. I had concluded my judgment in that case in the following words:

> The people of Pakistan have willed to establish an order wherein the State shall exercise its powers and authority through the chosen *representatives of the people*; wherein the principles of democracy, freedom, equality, tolerance and social justice, as enunciated by Islam, shall be fully observed (Article 2-A).
>
> No one man howhighsoever can, therefore, destroy an organ consisting of the chosen representatives of the people unless cogent, proper and sufficient cause exists for taking such a grave action. Article 58(2)(b), no doubt, empowers the President to take this action but only where it is shown that 'a situation has arisen in which the Government of the Federation cannot be carried on in accordance with the provisions of the Constitution'....
>
> In these circumstances, the dismissal of the Prime Minister along with his Cabinet and the dissolution of the National Assembly under the purported exercise of powers conferred on the President under Article 58(2)(b) cannot be upheld. The action taken did not fall within the ambit of this provision. This unlawful action moreover was also violative of Fundamental Right 17. As this Court is duty bound to enforce Fundamental Rights and will not hesitate to enforce them whenever it is established that they have been violated, the necessity for taking action under article 184(3) of the Constitution arose in this case.

Thus, through our judicial verdict, a discretionary order of the highest functionary of the State, i.e. the President of Pakistan, was set aside and the action taken thereunder was rolled back. This, probably, was the first time in the known history of democratic and civilized world that an overthrown government and Assembly were put back in power through a judicial verdict having no coercive force other than commitment to constitutionalism. The acclaim received nationally as well as internationally by that judgment of the Supreme Court of Pakistan has not only acknowledged the undaunted independence of our judiciary but has also demonstrated it as a fact that, having achieved the cherished goal of supremacy of the Constitution and adopted constitutionalism as a way of life, Pakistani society has come of age.

Appendix 19

THE SECOND CORNELIUS MEMORIAL LECTURE
27 December 1994

THE SIGNIFICANCE OF THE CORNELIUS DISSENTS
Supreme Court Justice (Retired) Abdul Shakurul Salam

[Justice Salam was appointed to the High Court of Lahore in 1974 and served as its Chief Justice in 1988-89. He was later appointed to the Supreme Court from which he retired in 1993. Born in Hansi, East Punjab in 1928, he studied at the Law College of Aligarh University. He has written many notable decisions in the Cornelius tradition. He was the first judge to uphold the right of women for admission to medical colleges on the same basis as men (Mussarat Uzma Usmani v. Government of the Punjab, PLD 1987 Lahore 178). *As Chief Justice of the Lahore High Court he invalidated the martial law order dissolving the National Assembly* (Kh. Mohammad Sharif v. Federation of Pakistan, PLD 1992 LHR 46). *Later, on the Supreme Court, he wrote a dissent similarly objecting to the power of the executive to dissolve the legislature* (Kh. Ahmad Tariq Rahim v. Federation of Pakistan, PLD 1992 SC 46). *He holds LL.M. degrees from London and Yale Universities. He is currently serving as Federal Ombudsman in the government of Pakistan.*

This lecture emphasizes the importance of the 53-page Cornelius dissents in the Maulvi Tamizuddin Khan case (PLD 1955 FC 240) *which later influenced the opinion in the* Usif Patel case (PLD 1955 FC 387). *Justice Salam lauds the restrictions which the Cornelius dissents placed on arbitrary, unchecked power by the executive branch thus calling attention to the ultimate rectifying power of dissent.]*

Honorable President, Mr. Afzal H. Mufti, Hamid Khan, Jawwad S. Khawaja, Ladies and Gentlemen.

I am embarrassed to open my mouth. It is the norm of civilized behavior in this part of the world not to speak in the presence of elders. Here I have my elder brother Mr. Justice Ghulam Mujadid Mirza, who has always been kind and whose footsteps I have followed. I feel very small in his presence. His presidency makes me feel that he permits me to speak so as to judge how his younger brother performs. It is a pleasure and great privilege to speak about a gentleman whom I have admired since my student days as an outstandingly eminent judge and whom I found to be a decent human being when I appeared in his court. His was a beacon light throughout my career both as a lawyer and a judge. In retirement I now enjoy his writings in my leisure time.

While I was studying for my LL.M. degree at University College, London, the Federal Court of Pakistan issued momentous decisions which diverted the normal course of our constitutional development. One of the judgments was the Maulvi Tamizuddin Khan case of April 1955. Until then, the constitutional position, as many of you would know, under the Indian Independence At of 1947 passed by the British Parliament and the Government of India Act 1935 as adapted by Pakistan was that the Constituent Assembly, entrusted with the task of framing a constitution for Pakistan, would pass drafts of a constitution or amendments to the Indian Independence Act.

When it acted as a federal legislature its bills would be placed before the Governor-General for assent. The Constituent Assembly passed numerous constitutional amendments. One such constitutional amendment dated July 16, 1954 empowered the superior courts in Pakistan to issue writs. Three months later Governor-General Ghulam Muhammad, dismissed the Constituent Assembly. The speaker of the Assembly, Maulvi Tamizuddin Khan, challenged the dismissal before the Chief Court of Sind. A Full Bench of five judges heard the case. Government pleaded that the constitutional amendment by which power had been conferred on the courts was not valid as it had not been assented to by the Governor-General. The reply on behalf of the Speaker was that constitution-making or amending power was entrusted to the Constituent Assembly and when it functioned as such no assent of the Governor General was required. Since the time of the Quaid-i-Azam, no Governor General had claimed such power. The Court accepted the plea and issued the writs. Government filed an appeal. The Federal Court held that the assent of the Governor-General was necessary in all circumstances. The result was that a host of laws concerning Constitution-making became invalid. Justice A. R. Cornelius in a famous 53-page opinion dissented. The Governor General promulgated an ordinance to validate these laws. It was held that, the following the ruling in the Usif Patel case (*PLD 1955 FC 387*) he could not do so. The Governor General made a reference to the Federal Court in its advisory jurisdiction as to whether the Constituent Assembly was legally dissolved by the Governor General. The Federal Court said, yes. Justice Cornelius pointing out in his dissent that the hazard of granting power to an individual leads to the destruction of a democratic polity, said:

> These affairs belong to a period when, and to territories where, the power of the King was, in fact, supreme and undisputed. The records of these affairs are hardly the kind of scripture which one could possibly expect to be quoted in a proceeding which is essentially one in the enforcement and maintenance of representative institutions. For they can bring but cold comfort to any protagonist of the autocratic principle against the now universal rule that the will of the people is sovereign. In the case of North America, the territory was lost eventually to the British Crown through the maintenance of just such reactionary opinions, as those which senior counsel for the Federation of Pakistan has been pleased to advance for acceptance by the Court. And in the English case, the fate of the King, and the judges who delivered the opinion favoring absolute power in the King, stands for all time as a warning against absolutism, and as a land mark in the struggle for the freedom and eventual sovereignty of the people. (*Reference by His Excellency, the Governor-General PLD 1955 FC 515-16*)

But who learns from history? After these decisions, the Constitution of the Islamic Republic of Pakistan was passed in 1956. Two years later, it was abrogated by President Iskander Mirza who appointed the Commander-in-Chief, General Muhammad Ayub Khan, as the Chief Martial Law Administrator.

Two sovereigns cannot sit together. The General whisked away the President and assumed the office himself. The latter promulgated the Constitution of 1962 and when he could govern no more, he asked his Commander-in-Chief, General Muhammad Yahya Khan, to perform his constitutional duty. The latter did so by abrogating the Constitution, imposing Martial Law and becoming both President and Chief Martial Law Administrator. He lost half of the country in 1971 and handed over power to the leader of the National Assembly left behind, Mr. Zulfikar Ali Bhutto. The latter got the Constitution of 1973 passed with the consensus of all the leading political parties.

In view of this past experience, no power was vested in the President as head of State to dismiss the assemblies. But he did not realize that governance of a State is a delicate affair dealing with human beings of all levels with diverse aspirations and ambitions, susceptible to motivations and manipulations for good or bad. On a mountain one may move in any direction for miles but on a precipice a wrong step can be fatal. The instrument of governance, the Constitution, may be perfect but it cannot shield the gaping holes in governance against organized, determined and powerful onslaughts. Mr. Bhutto had appointed a general out of turn, not that he was the most meritorious but on the belief that, as the Chief of Army Staff, he would be loyal to him. When the circumstances ripened, the Chief of the Army Staff Gen. Muhammad Zia ul-Haq in 1977 moved to take over the government, dismissed the provincial assemblies, imposed Martial Law and appointed himself as the Chief Martial Law Administrator and subsequently President. He did not lift Martial Law until 1985 when he was given the power to dismiss the National Assembly. Individual power was resurrected. He exercised the same in 1988 over his own elected Assembly. His successor exercised the same and dismissed the second Assembly in 1990. This was upheld by the Supreme Court although I dissented holding that the power had lapsed with the person on whom it was conferred. When the Assembly was dismissed for the third time in 1993 the Supreme Court held that it could not be done. It was not done again fearing that the order might be set aside again. To complete the narration of events it may be stated that subsequently the leader of the National Assembly the Prime Minister advised the dissolution of the National Assembly in accordance with a parliamentary form of Government.

This series of incidents are all relevant to the Tamizuddin case and its famous Cornelius dissent. They all deal with the fundamentals of the basic law of the State; the Constitution. If the Cornelius dissents had been adopted and acted upon we need not have suffered these pitfalls in our constitutional development and lost prestige in the comity of nations for the last forty years. But as the saying goes: do not take one as lost if he returns by evening. Let us hope that the latest judgment of the Supreme Court finally accepts the principle that the will of the people is sovereign and is to be exercised by its representatives and not by an autocratic individual, lest he face the fate of the English monarch and of those judges who upheld his power. That the dissenting opinion of Justice Cornelius holds the field after forty years, is not unusual in the annals of constitutional history. The dissent of Justice John Marshall Harlan that separate schools for white and black were against the equality provision of the Constitution of United States became the unanimous judgment of the Supreme Court in 1954 in the famous case of Brown vs. Board of Education—58 years later. Incidentally, the grandson of the first Justice Harlan sat on the Court.

I must say in conclusion that the age-old dictum of Lord Acton must never be forgotten: power tends to corrupt and absolute power corrupts absolutely. This applies not only to those who wield power but to society as a whole. It is a *jin* to be kept securely in a bottle. Its service can be commanded by Suleiman (peace be upon him) but only once. This monster has the tendency to devour its own master and destroy whosoever comes its way. It must be kept bottled up and, when released, supervised with great care.

Ladies and gentleman, I do not wish to take more or your time and keep you away from a hot cup of tea which has been promised us. I only wish and pray that the soul of Mr. Justice A. R. Cornelius rests in peace and we follow his footsteps in public and private life.

I thank you most sincerely, ladies and gentleman, for your patient hearing. I beg your leave.

Appendix 20

THIRD CORNELIUS MEMORIAL LECTURE
23 December 1995

THE INDEPENDENCE OF THE JUDICIARY
Supreme Court Justice (Retired) Dorab F. Patel

[Biographical information on Justice Patel can be found in the Analysis chapter of this volume, pp. 13-14.

The choice of Dorab Patel as the Third Memorial Lecturer is fitting for several reasons. He, like Cornelius, belonged to a minority community (Parsis). He also showed the courage of his convictions by resigning from the Supreme Court in protest against incursions on its independence.

In this lecture Patel describes in detail the principles for appointment of judges. This was a burning issue at the time of the lecture and Patel reflected the deep concern of the legal community that the existing appointment process eroded judicial independence. This lecture is noteworthy because it is the most detailed and carefully reasoned analysis of judicial appointments ever made by a Pakistani jurist. The Patel lecture differs from the First and Second Memorial Lectures in that it makes no attempt to trace the lineage of Cornelius' decisions. Indeed there is only one mention of Cornelius in the lecture and that is incidental rather than substantive. It's main theme, however, is an issue which Cornelius dealt with in many decisions which laid the basis for judicial independence]

An independent judiciary is a judiciary which is able to resist the pressures not only of the government but also of public opinion and of popular prejudices. In the third world, an independent judiciary has also to resist the pressures or provincialism and of ethnicity. And in the long run, a judiciary will not remain independent if it is not able to fight the enemy within. Every person has his biases, and as a judge is a human being, he must always guard against his judgments being influenced unconsciously by his biases, especially in cases with political overtones. The late Justice William Douglas of the American Supreme Court has written in his autobiography that his Chief Justice, Justice Charles E. Hughes, told him one day, "Mr. Justice Douglas, you must remember one thing: at the constitutional level where we work, ninety percent of any decision is emotional. The rational part of us supplies the reasons for supporting our predilections". And a judge can overcome his emotions only if he is aware of them.

The qualities required of a judge are a sound knowledge of law, capacity for hard work, honesty, both financial and intellectual, and moral courage. And a good judge will also have patience, compassion for the poor and the determination to fight injustice and oppression. The qualities required of a good judge are therefore so many that it is difficult to find them in a single person.

Let me turn to the rules for the appointment of judges. The subject is very wide so I will only examine the constitutional provisions for the appointment of judges to High Courts and to the Supreme Court.

A person cannot be appointed a judge of a High Court unless he is 40 years old and, as in all common law countries, he can be elevated from the Bar or from the judicial services. To ensure that only persons with a sound knowledge of law are elevated, Article 193 provided that an advocate can be elevated only if he has been an advocate of a High Court for 10 years. Similarly, a member of the judicial services can be appointed only if he has held a judicial office for 10 years. In my opinion, this period of 10 years is not sufficient to enable a person to acquire the knowledge and understanding of the law which is expected of High Court judges, and as a matter of fact, most of the advocates appointed to High Courts have been elevated after a practice of about 15 years. Similarly, judges from the services are generally elevated after a service of about 15 years. This is as it should be.

I now turn to clause 2(b) of Article 193. Provided a person has served for 10 years in a prescribed administrative service, he can be elevated to a High Court if he has served as a district judge for 3 years. This provision is absurd, because a person appointed under it need not have studied law. It discriminates against judges appointed from the Bar and the judicial services. Secondly, one of the traditions of the judiciary was its rigid aloofness from the executive. But a civil servant is a part of the executive, and he cannot in 3 years alter his habits and become rigidly aloof from the executive.

Unfortunately as this clause 2(b) is a part of the Constitution, it cannot be challenged as a violation of the equality clause in Article 25. Therefore, it is essential for the Bar to advocate the repeal of Clause 2(b) of Article 193, and I may point out that as this clause had been for the benefit of ICS officers in British days, you will find it even in the Government of India Act of 1911. It is a relic of colonialism and India deleted it from its Constitution in 1950. It is time for us to do so also.

However, most judges have been appointed first as additional judges of High Courts under Article 191 of the Constitution and then confirmed as permanent judges of High Courts under Article 193. The difference between a judge and an additional judge is that the judge cannot practice as an advocate in the court of which he was a judge, while an additional judge can. The convention of many decades was that an additional judge was appointed for 2 years, and at the end of this term, he was free to go back to the Bar if he was an advocate. Similarly if an additional judge was not up to the mark, the Chief Justice of the High Court did not put up his name to the Government for confirmation as a judge under Article 193.

An additional judge is a judge on probation, but there is nothing derogatory in being on probation as a judge of a High Court, because the appointment alters a person's life and habits. To give a couple of examples, a very successful advocate might discover, after his elevation, that he lacked the objectivity to be a good Judge, or that the secluded life of a Judge did not suit him.

I personally knew two judges who could not tolerate the secluded life of a Judge. One of them resigned even before completing his term of two years, and went back to his very lucrative practice at the Bar. The other Judge had been confirmed, and therefore he could not resume practice as an advocate. He remained a disgruntled judge until he became sixty-two and retired. This practice of first appointing a judge as an additional judge is in the interests of the Bar and also in the public interest, because if the person appointed is not up to the mark, it is better that he should cease to be a judge at the end of his term of two years.

The unfortunate consequence of our second and third Martial Law regime was that the Government departed from the convention of confirming or dropping an additional judge after two years. During the last Martial Law, the terms of additional judges were extended at the whim of the Government, sometimes to 2-1/2 years, sometimes to 3 years and sometimes to more than 3 years. This damaged the image of the judiciary, as the popular perception is that a judge will be independent only if he has security of tenure until he reaches the age of retirement. That perception is often wrong, but justice must not only be done but must also be seen to be done.

We should therefore go back to the convention inherited from the British that the appointment of an additional judge should only be for 2 years. And as an independent Bar cannot survive without an independent judiciary, it is necessary to revive the convention that additional judges should be appointed for 2 years and that at the end of their term, they should either be dropped or confirmed on the advice of the Chief Justice of the High Court.

The provisions for the appointment of Judges under Article 193 and 197 are naturally identical, and cause (1) of Article 193 reads:

> 193.(1) A Judge of a High Court shall be appointed by the President after consultation – (a) With the Chief Justice of Pakistan; (b) With the Governor concerned; and, (c) except where the appointment is that of Chief Justice, with the Chief Justice of the High Court.

The President has to exercise his powers under Article 193 on the advice of the Prime Minister, and he is under an obligation to make the appointments of judges of High Courts after consulting the Chief Justice of the Supreme Court and of the High Court concerned. An appointment made without consulting the chief justices would therefore be illegal, even if the persons appointed have been duly recommended by the governor concerned. Secondly, if the two chief justices are not in agreement about an appointment the President has to decide whom he will appoint. After the retirement of Justice Munir, Justice Cornelius often did not agree with the recommendation of the Chief Justice of the West Pakistan High Court. According to Justice Moulvi Mushtaq Hussain, President Ayub sent for him when he was the law secretary and told him that he did not want to interfere with the appointment of judges to High Courts and that the differences of opinion between the chief justices placed him in a dilemma. So Justice Moulvi Mushtaq Hussain advised him to call the candidates for an interview and make the appointment on the basis of his own intuition. Thus began the practice of candidates for the Bench appearing before the President for an interview. This practice was detrimental to the image of the judiciary, but it went on until the second Martial Law. In 1969 General Yahya Khan was the chief guest at the annual dinner of the Karachi High Court Bar Association. Justice A. S. Faruqui gave the vote of thanks to General Yahya and told him in his speech that this practice of the President interviewing candidates for the Bench was improper. It is to the credit of General Yahya that he accepted this advice and discontinued the practice of interviewing candidates for appointments to High Court.

Generally, however, the Chief Justice of Pakistan and the chief justices of High Courts recommend the same persons for appointment to High Courts. In such cases, is their advice binding on the President? Article 193 only imposes an obligation on the President to consult the chief justices. But Articles 217 of the Indian Constitution is almost identical to Article 193 of our Constitution, and reversing its earlier view, the Indian Supreme

Court has recently held that the concurrent advice of the chief justices about an appointment of a judge of High Court is binding on the Indian President. I regret my inability to agree with this view. The appointment of judges of High Courts is too serious a matter to be left to the judiciary alone.

Judges are part of the society in which they live, and family pressures can influence even chief justices. For the first time in Indian history, there was a move last year to impeach a judge of the Supreme Court. The resolution to impeach him was defeated in the Lok Sabha. Many years earlier, this judge had been an advocate of a High Court, and it was alleged in an Indian journal that he had been appointed a judge of that High Court, not because he was a well known advocate, but because he was a close relation of the chief justice of that High Court. Unfortunately nepotism is a hazard in appointments to the judiciary in South Asia, and this state of affairs will continue as long as the press and the Bar associations are weak. In any case, the view that the people through their elected representatives should not have any voice in appointments to the Superior Courts is, in my opinion, contrary to democratic norms. The view of the Indian judges must have been influenced by the fear that the President would use his power to appoint to High Courts judges who had been the sycophants of the ruling party. That is a danger, but our courts and the Indian courts have taken the view that the power vested in any authority by the constitution cannot be exercised arbitrarily, and they have struck down the arbitrary exercise of power by the President. Therefore the question is of principles or conventions which have to be followed by the President in appointing judges of the Superior Courts.

The President can reject the advice of the chief justice or the chief justices only if their recommendations are inconsistent with the object of the Constitution. Ours is a democratic constitution. Democracies cannot survive without an independent judiciary. If the President, for example, appoints a judge in order to advance the interests of the ruling party, the appointment will be arbitrary and should be struck down by the courts. But the President can and should reject a recommendation if it is of a person who lacks integrity or sufficient knowledge of the law. A chief justice is in a far better position than the President to assess the ability of advocates and of district judges, but as he is not likely to know much about their private lives, he may, in good faith, recommend for appointment to the High Court an advocate who lacks integrity, who has resorted to sharp practices and got away with it. Or he may be influenced to recommend an inexperienced advocate for appointment. A more difficult case would be if a chief justice does not recommend a deserving person for appointment because of some personal or parochial prejudice. Society in this subcontinent is riddled with such prejudices, and chief justices are part of the society in which they live. That is why I said that the appointment of judges to the superior courts is too serious a matter to be left only to judges. The makers of the Constitution have therefore made the President the arbiter of appointments to the higher judiciary.

In making the President the appointing authority, we have merely followed the provisions of the Government of India Act 1935 and of the Indian Constitution. The method of appointment laid down in the Government of India Act worked satisfactorily, because British governors-general, who were the appointing authority under that Act, followed the convention of respecting the recommendations of the chief justices, except when their recommendations were palpably wrong. There are frequent complaints that the conventions bequeathed to us by the British have eroded in the last quarter of a century. Perhaps it is time to find a better way for appointing judges, but before doing so, I will briefly discuss the provisions for the appointment of the chief justice of the Supreme Court (who is always referred to as the Chief Justice of Pakistan) and of chief justices of High Courts, and of acting chief justices both of the Supreme Court and of the High Court.

Article 177 of the Constitution reads: "The Chief Justice of Pakistan shall be appointed by the President." The Constitution does not require the President to consult anyone when he appoints the Chief Justice of Pakistan. But as the Chief Justice of Pakistan may not be able to perform his duties on account of his illness or absence, clause (b) of Article 180 authorizes the President to appoint the senior-most Judge of the Supreme Court as the acting Chief Justice of Pakistan. Clause (b) of Article 196 empowers the President in similar situations to appoint an Acting Chief Justice of a High Court, but the acting Chief Justice of a High Court can be any other judge of that High Court or even a judge of the Supreme Court and there is no ambiguity about these provisions. Appointments under clause (b) of Articles 180 and 196 are for the period during which the Chief Justice is unable to perform his duties. Normally such appointments are for short periods. But clause (a) both of Article 180 and Article 196 empower the President to appoint an acting chief justice when the office of the Chief Justice of Pakistan or of the High Court is vacant. But chief justices (by which I mean permanent chief justices) are also appointed when the office of the chief justice is vacant under Article 177 and 193 of the Constitution. Therefore, the question is when would the President be justified in appointing an acting chief justice for the Supreme Court or for a High Court?

The provision that there should be an acting chief justice when the office of the chief justice is vacant goes back more than two hundred years to the Supreme Court of Calcutta which was set up in 1774. The Supreme Courts of Madras and Bombay were set up at the beginning of the 19th century, and the judges of these three Supreme Courts were always barristers sent out from England. The expectation of life was much lower in the nineteenth century than it is today, and judges of the Supreme Court had died in office. I would like to recall the name of one of the judges of the Supreme Court of Calcutta, Sir William Jones, who died 201 years ago in his late forties. He was a scholar of Persian, Arabic and Sanskrit, and he took under his supervision the translation of the Shar'ia and of the Hindu scriptures for the assistance of the English judges of East India Company. He also translated Hafiz into English and French and Kalidasa's *Shakuntala* into English. I enjoyed reading his English translations of Hafiz and of Kalidasa and as a judge, I had felt proud of the traditions of scholarship we had inherited from our predecessors. Now as death in office was an imminent possibility for judges in those days, the regulations governing the Supreme Courts contained provisions for the appointment of chief justices and of acting chief justices. The provision for an acting chief justice was necessary because a chief justice could die in office and the appointment of a successor could take many months. An acting chief justice became necessary for the proper running of the Supreme Courts. But such appointments were temporary, lasting for the period required for the new Chief Justice to take over his duties. This was also the rule of the Presidency High Courts of Bombay, Calcutta and Madras, which were the successors of the Supreme Courts. These provisions for the appointments of chief justices and acting chief justices were followed in the High Courts set up after 1861. And we had followed this practice from 1947 until 1981.

These provisions for the appointment of chief justices and of acting chief justices when the office of the chief justices became vacant through retirement or through premature death were re-enacted in the Government of India Act, 1935. And as the provisions for the appointments of chief justices and of acting chief justices for the Federal Court and for the High Courts were identical, I would quote sub-section 1 of section 202 of the Government of India Act. Sub Section 202 reads:

202(1). If the office of Chief Justice of India becomes vacant, or if the Chief Justice is, by reason of absence or for any other reason, unable to perform the duties of his office, those duties shall, until some person permanently appointed to the vacant office has entered on the duties thereof, or until the Chief Justice has resumed his duties, as the case may be, be performed by such one of the other Judges of the Court as the Governor-General may appoint as acting Chief Justice.

The Chief Justice of the Federal Court of India was called the Chief Justice of India. The first Chief Justice of India was Sir Maurice Gwyer. Some months before his retirement, Lord Wavell, the Governor-General of India, took up the question of Sir Maurice Gwyer's successor with the Secretary of State for India. The relevant correspondence is contained in *The Transfer of Power Documents, 1942 to 1947*, published by the British Government. Lord Wavell wrote in his letter to the Secretary of State that the senior judge of the Federal Court was a Hindu of great integrity and ability, but he did not consider it appropriate to recommend a Hindu as Chief Justice of India, because it would aggravate the Hindu-Muslim conflict. Therefore, he advised the Secretary of State that the second Chief Justice should also be an English barrister. The Secretary of State accepted Lord Wavell's advice and the second Chief Justice of India, Sir Patrick Spens, took over from Sir Maurice Gwyer as soon as he retired.

This practice was followed after we became independent until 1981. None of our chief justices has died in office, except the late Justice Tufail Ali Rahman of the Sindh High Court. And steps were always taken to appoint a new chief justice before the retirement of the old chief justice. So, for example, even though it was Martial Law, Justice Cornelius took over as Chief Justice of Pakistan as soon as Justice Munir retired.

The provision for the appointment of an acting chief justice, when the office of the chief justice is vacant, is meant only for the situation when the office of the chief justice becomes vacant through the sudden death or resignation of the chief justice. And so I come to 1981.

The Provisional Constitutional Order came into force on the 25th of March, 1981 as soon as 7 of the 9 judges of the Supreme Court took oath to uphold this order. The Chief Justice, Justice Anwarul Haque, and I refused to take this oath, so we ceased to be Judges. This was a sudden crisis which took the President by surprise, and Article 180 of the Constitution imposed on him an obligation to appoint the senior-most Judge of the Supreme Court as the acting Chief Justice. He did so immediately, but this did not relieve him of his obligation to appoint a permanent Chief Justice within a reasonable period, which cannot possibly mean more than a few weeks. But he appointed the Acting Chief Justice as the Chief Justice of Pakistan after nearly 3 years. This scandalous delay in appointing the Chief Justice of Pakistan was a flagrant violation of Article 177 of the Constitution. But no one challenged General Zia ul-Haq's action, because it was Martial Law and because he could, under the Provisional Constitution Order, alter or repeal any Article of the Constitution.

General Zia ul-Haq extended this practice of appointing acting chief justices to high courts also. As the chief justices of high courts retired, their successors were appointed for long periods, generally more than a year, as acting chief justices, but almost all of them were appointed chief justices a few weeks before their retirement. The popular perception of these appointments was that the military authorities thought that they would be able to influence the judiciary by having acting appointments. Whether this perception was right or wrong was immaterial, but it did untold damage to the judiciary. Therefore, the practice of acting appointments of chief justices should have been discontinued as soon as Martial Law was lifted. Unfortunately this practice still continues.

I have discussed the question of acting appointments at length because there are three types of judges in the Supreme Court: permanent judges appointed under Article 177, acting judges appointed under Article 181, and *ad hoc* judges appointed under Article 182. All these appointments are made by the President after consulting the Chief Justice, and the common qualification for all the appointments is that the judge elevated to the Supreme Court should have been a High Court judge for five years. But an advocate who has been a High Court advocate for fifteen years can be directly appointed to the Supreme Court under Article 177. No advocate has ever been appointed directly to the Supreme Court. Mistakes can also be made in the appointment of judges. But an appointment under Article 177 is a permanent appointment. A judge appointed under this article cannot practice as an advocate in any court, and if an advocate appointed under this article is not up to the mark or does not like being on the Bench, he is in a very difficult position. I am therefore of the view that the appointments of judges to the Supreme Court should only be from judges of High Courts.

The President can appoint an acting judge to the Supreme Court when the office of a judge is vacant or when a judge of the court is temporarily unable to perform his duties. The first part of this article overlaps with an appointment made under Article 177. The difference is that an appointment under Article 177 is of a permanent judge. But appointments to the highest court of the country should always be of permanent judges, the more so as the Supreme Court has to decide cases of a politically sensitive nature, and if temporary Judges hear such cases, their judgments do not command confidence. That is why the practice of High Courts for generations was that additional judges who were also temporary judges were not put on benches hearing politically sensitive cases. But additional judges had a guaranteed term of two years before the 2nd Martial Law. The appointment of an acting judge of the Supreme Court can be terminated by the President the day he does not like the look of a judge. The abrupt termination of the appointment of an acting judge in 1990 came as a shock to me, and was a humiliation for the judiciary. Further, as according to clause (7) of Article 260, an acting judge of the Supreme Court is a judge of the Supreme Court, a High Court judge who has acted as a Supreme Court judge is debarred from practicing as an advocate in any court after his retirement. The President's power to terminate the appointment of an acting judge is thus a harsh and arbitrary power and constitutes a threat to the independence of the judiciary. The exercise of arbitrary power can of course be challenged, but it will be a sad day for the courts if a judge of the Supreme Court has to file a writ in the courts to secure his rights.

I must point out here that until the last Martial Law, High Court judges were appointed acting judges of the Supreme Court for very short periods, when a judge of the Supreme Court was temporarily not available. But during our third Martial Law, a judge who had been a judge of the High Court for more than ten years was appointed an acting judge in April 1978. He was one of the majority judges who had confirmed the sentence of death against Mr. Bhutto and dismissed his appeal. Nearly three months after this judgment, he was made a permanent judge of the Supreme Court. As the Constitution was then in force, this appointment of acting judge for such a long period was based on an erroneous interpretation of Article 181. Secondly, whilst I had no doubt that the judge would have dismissed Mr. Bhutto's appeal even if he had been appointed a permanent judge long before the hearing of this appeal, the perception of large sections of the public was that he might have been pressured into dismissing the appeal because he was an acting judge. This perception was wrong, but it shows how acting appointments of judges are bad for the judiciary. And after 1979 acting judges have been appointed for long periods to the Supreme Court. One judge was an acting judge from March 1982 until his retirement quite a few years later.

The Indian Constitution does not have any provision for the appointment of acting judges to the Supreme Court. The Supreme Court of the United States does not have acting judges, nor does the House of Lords have them. I am aware that it may be necessary to appoint judges temporarily to the Supreme Court. But as Article 182 permits the appointment of *ad hoc* judges to the Supreme Court, a provision for the appointment of acting judges is unnecessary. I am of the view that Article 181 should be repealed and meanwhile there should be no further appointments of acting judges.

Ad hoc judges are appointed under Article 182, and, as in India, a retired Judge of the Supreme Court can be appointed an *ad hoc* judge provided he is not over sixty-eight years. The President can also appoint a person who has been a High Court judge for five years as an ad hoc judge. *Ad hoc* judges can be appointed either "for want of quorum of judges of the Supreme Court" to hear a case, or when for any other reason it is necessary to increase temporarily the number of judges of the Supreme Court. In the quarter century after the Federal Court took over the jurisdiction of the Privy Council, the appointment of ad hoc judges to the Supreme Court was very unusual, as in India, but it became the practice from 1976. In 1976, the Supreme Court had an ad hoc judge in March for three months and again in November for seven weeks, but in January 1977, Chief Justice Yaqub Ali, told me that he was asking Mr. Bhutto for the appointment of 2 *ad hoc* judges. He felt that if these two judges sat with us for a year, the arrears of the Court would be cleared. The two *ad hoc* judges continued for two years, but the arrears were not cleared. One reason for the Court's inability to clear the arrears was the hearing of Mr. Bhutto's murder appeal, which took more than six months. But all proceedings in this appeal were over by the end of March 1979. After the conclusion of these proceedings, one of the *ad hoc* judges was made a permanent judge in June 1979. In 1979-80, the Chief Justice had asked for and obtained the appointment of two *ad hoc* judges for a period of one year. These judges had served for more than eight years as High Court judges, but as the arrears in the Court had not been cleared, Justice Anwarul Haque told me that he would again ask the President to renew the two *ad hoc* appointments for another year, I protested. We had not been able to clear the arrears in the Court although we had had *ad hoc* judges for more than four years. Litigation had increased and was increasing and, therefore, we needed more permanent judges.

But reverting to my conversation with Chief Justice Yacub Ali, I told him that if judges who worked in High Courts for many years were appointed as *ad hoc* judges, the public would think that the *ad hoc* judges were not fit to be judges of the country's highest Court. The Chief Justice did not agree with me. My impression of the public reaction to *ad hoc* appointments to the Supreme Court has been confirmed by my enquiries after I ceased to be a judge. It distressed me to be told by people in all walks of life that temporary judges were likely to succumb to the pressures of the Government. This popular perception is based on the assumption that every temporary judge, without any exception, pursues his ambition at the cost of his duty. I do not think this assumption is correct, but the Martial Law policy of appointing of acting and ad hoc judges to the Supreme Court for long periods was bad for the judiciary. It should have gone with Martial Law. It is a tragedy that this policy is still being followed. Therefore, it is time to think of better ways for all appointments to the Supreme Court also.

I would now make a few suggestions for the appointment of Judges. The people must have a voice in those appointments, but at the same time, as far as is possible, judges should not be beholden to any political party for their appointments. High Court judges should be appointed by a Commission consisting of the Chief Justice of Pakistan, the Chief Justice and the Senior Judge of the High Court, and the provincial Chief Minister and the Leader of the Opposition. But for obvious reasons such a Commission should sit without any judge of the High Court when it has to appoint its Chief Justice.

The appointment of all Judges to the Supreme Court should be made by a Commission of five members: the Chief Justice of Pakistan, the two senior-most Judges of the Supreme Court, the Prime Minister and the Leader of the Opposition. Such a commission would not be appropriate for the appointment of the Chief Justice, because senior judges of the Court would be eligible for this appointment: In my opinion, the appointment of the Chief Justice of the country has to be left to the President, as is the practice in most democratic countries. This should not cause any anxiety, because the Chief Justice of a Court is only the first among equals in his Court. Even if the President makes a bad appointment, the traditions of a Court should be sufficient to prevent damage through one bad appointment. And the character of a Chief Justice, like that of all persons, is unpredictable. I will illustrate this by an example.

General Eisenhower was elected President on the Republican ticket and it would be an understatement to say that the

Republican party of the U.S.A. is a conservative party. In 1953 President Eisenhower appointed Earl Warren the Chief Justice of the Supreme Court. Earl Warren had completed two terms as the Republican Governor of California, so the President felt that Earl Warren would be a safe, conservative Chief Justice, but in his long term of sixteen years, Earl Warren proved to be one of the most liberal Judges of the U.S.A. Long after his retirement, General Eisenhower was asked what was his biggest mistake as President. He said it was his appointment of Earl Warren as Chief Justice.

Finally, security of tenure is considered to be necessary for safeguarding the independence of judiciary, and according to Article 209 of our Constitution, judges of High Court and of the Supreme Court can only be removed from office by the Supreme Judicial Council on a reference moved by the President. The members of this Council are the senior-most judges of the country. A judge can be removed on the ground that he has become incapable of performing his duties on account of physical or mental incapacity or on the ground that he has committed misconduct. The provision that judges of the superior Courts can only be removed by their peers, namely the senior-most judges of the country, was a departure from the common law practice that judges can only be removed if they are impeached by Parliament. I think that our system is better, but I would make two suggestions. It is unwise to give the President the monopoly of moving a reference against a judge. Perhaps members of Parliament or a fixed percentage of members of parliament can also be given the power to move a reference against a judge. It would also be consistent with democratic norms if the Prime Minister and the Leader of the Opposition were made ex-officio members of the Supreme Judicial Council when it sits to hear a reference against a judge.

I have made a few suggestions for amendments in the Constitution, which would, in my opinion, protect the independence of judiciary. But it is the character of judges which, in the long run, preserves the independence of a country's judiciary, as the example of Earl Warren shows. Character is unpredictable, but the character of all persons working in any institution is influenced by the traditions of that institution, and so I would turn to the traditions of our judiciary.

I belong to the generation of common law judges. My generation has passed out, but we had inherited from the long line of judges, British and Indian, who preceded us traditions of service, of learning and scholarship, of integrity, financial and intellectual, and of social aloofness. These traditions had been built through sacrifices. As Sindh was a part of Bombay Presidency for more than 75 years, I will give an example of the Supreme Court of Bombay. In some civil litigation, the bailiff of the Supreme Court went to the Governor's House to serve a summons of the Court on a member of the Governor's staff. He was ordered to get out. After a few days, he again went to serve the summons. This time he was threatened. The Chief Justice sent for the Commissioner of Police and told him to send a senior police officer to accompany the bailiff to serve the summons. The bailiff went with a senior police officer to the Governor's House to serve the summons, but they were both threatened and had to return. The Chief Justice locked the Supreme Court, returned to England and lodged a complaint against the Governor with the Board of Directors of the East India Company. As the Directors did not take action against the Governor, the Chief Justice resigned. But his resignation was not in vain. Never again did the Bombay Government treat the Court with contempt. But the most valuable legacy of this clash with the Governor was that the judges of Bombay developed a tradition of rigid aloofness of the judiciary from the executive. In my opinion a judiciary cannot remain independent without this tradition. When I became a judge of the West Pakistan High Court, the Chief Justice of West Pakistan, Justice Wahid-ud-din Ahmed, had told me in this city that I had to change my life and habits because I had become a judge. He told me that it was my duty to lead a secluded life and to avoid meeting prime ministers, chief ministers and politicians. I had tried to follow his advice.

I hope I did, because we were the trustees of the traditions we had inherited from the judges before us.

However the winds of change caused by the break-up of the country in 1971 has led to a prejudice against what was good and of value in western ideas, but strangely enough not against what is bad in western ideas, like consumerism. I also think the practice of High Court judges working as law secretaries had helped to undermine the tradition of the aloofness of the judiciary from the executive, and the last Martial Law has almost destroyed this tradition. On the morning of the 5th of July, 1977 General Zia had, to his great relief, obtained the consent of the chief justices of High Courts to act as governors of the provinces. And as these chief justices acted as governors for a long time, it led to social intercourse between the higher judiciary and the executive to an extent which would have shocked the judges of an earlier generation. Now because of the restoration of Fundamental Rights, judges have to decide cases of a political nature frequently, therefore, the Bombay tradition of the rigid aloofness of the judiciary from the executive is essential for the independence of the judiciary. The practice of appointing Chief Justices of High Courts as Governors should be discontinued, the more so as it is inconsistent with the mandate in the Constitution for the separation of the judiciary from the executive.

Finally, I would be failing in my duty if I do not refer to threats against judges and lawyers by extremists. I was disturbed three or four years ago by reliable reports that Muslim advocates were being warned by extremists not to take up the case of Ahmadis in Faisalabad courts. We did not protest against these attempts to interfere with the administration of justice, because we thought this was a local and passing problem. We were wrong. Intolerance spreads if it is not challenged, and when the Supreme Court admitted a review against the majority judgment upholding the validity of the Ahmadi Ordinance, there was a demonstration outside the Supreme Court to intimidate the judges. Nor was this the only demonstration of its kind. When the bell tolls for judges, it also tolls for advocates, but no Bar association protested about this demonstration. The intimidation of lawyers increased and Lahore High Court advocates received assassination threats, which were reported in most English language newspapers. Bar associations, political leaders and the majority of intellectuals remained silent, while the police took no action. So as night follows day, the extremists were emboldened to make a murderous attempt on the life of Mrs Asma Jehangir, Hina Jilani and members of their family.

It is meaningless to talk of the independence of the judiciary if judges and lawyers are threatened for the performance of their duties. These threats are the consequence of the wave of religious intolerance which is sweeping through many parts of the world and especially the countries of South Asia, and until the tide turns, this intolerance will continue to affect the independence of the judiciary. The struggle for the independence of the judiciary has therefore become a part of the struggle for re-building tolerant societies in South Asia, societies which respect human rights and especially the individual's right of dissent. In the long run, an independent judiciary can survive only in a free society. We have a long and difficult struggle before us. I hope we will have the courage and the perseverance to carry on this struggle.

ABOUT THE AUTHOR

Ralph Braibanti, Ph.D., L.H.D. is James B. Duke Professor Emeritus of Political Science at Duke University where he has been a member of the faculty since 1953. He was the first American to study the Pakistani judiciary. As chief advisor to the Civil Service Academy 1960–62, he was in a uniquely advantageous position to observe and, in some instances, participate in the events discussed in this volume. He is founding president of the American Institute of Pakistan Studies. In 1990, the American-Arab Affairs Council (now the Middle East Policy Council) appointed him the King Faisal Distinguished International Lecturer. The cabinet secretariat of the government of Pakistan reprinted several of his studies in 1987 in a single volume edited by Jameelur Rahman Khan under the title *Evolution of Pakistan's Administrative System: The Collected Papers of Ralph Braibanti*. In 1995, Duke University Library established the Ralph Braibanti Endowment in Islamic Studies to which Jordan, Saudi Arabia, and Pakistan contributed. In announcing its contribution to the Endowment, Pakistan stated that 'Dr Braibanti's works are considered indispensable to the study of the political process in Pakistan'. His latest publications include *The Nature and Structure of the Islamic World* (1995) and *Islam and the West: Common Cause or Clash?* (1999). Other publications include *Research on the Bureaucracy of Pakistan* (1966). He is co-editor and co-author of *Tradition, Values and Socio-Economic Development* (1960); *Administration and Economic Development in India* (1963); *Pakistan: The Long View* (1976). He is co-author and editor of *Asian Bureaucratic Systems Emergent from the British Imperial Tradition* (1966); *Political and Administrative Development* (1969).

INDEX

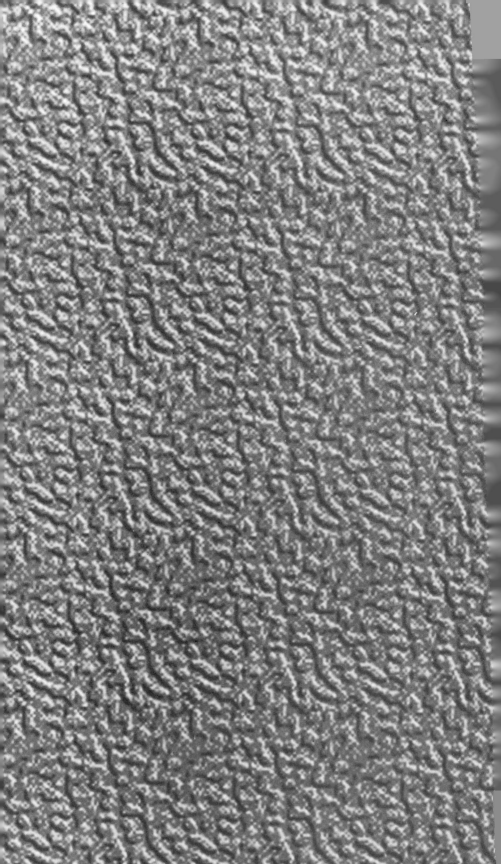